C. L. R. JAMES

The Black Jacobins

C. L. R. James (1901–1989) was a Trinidadian-born historian, literary critic, and philosopher, and a leader of the Pan African movement. A prodigious and eclectic intellectual, he debated Marcus Garvey in England, confronted Trotsky in Mexico, and influenced leaders of African revolutions, including Kwame Nkrumah of Ghana. He is perhaps best remembered for his 1938 masterwork, *The Black Jacobins*, the first major analysis of the Haitian Revolution in the context of the French Revolution. In addition to his many works of history and his political activism, he was known as well for occasional playwriting and fiction; his novel *Minty Alley*, written in 1927, was the first by a black West Indian to be published in Britain. James was also known as an avid sportsman; he was the cricket writer for *The Manchester Guardian* beginning in the 1930s, and his 1963 book, *Beyond a Boundary*, which he described as "neither cricket reminiscences nor autobiography," has been hailed as the best single book on cricket ever written.

BOOKS BY C. L. R. JAMES

Letters from London

Minty Alley

*Toussaint Louverture, The Story of the Only Successful
Slave Revolt in History; A Play in Three Acts*

*World Revolution 1917–1936:
The Rise and Fall of the Communist International*

A History of Pan-African Revolt

The Black Jacobins

Beyond a Boundary

The Black Jacobins

The Black Jacobins

TOUSSAINT L'OUVERTURE AND THE SAN DOMINGO REVOLUTION

***

C. L. R. JAMES

Introduction by David Scott

VINTAGE BOOKS
A Division of Penguin Random House LLC
New York

VINTAGE BOOKS EDITION 1963, 2023

Copyright © 1963 by Random House, a division of Penguin Random House LLC, copyright renewed 1991 by Robert A. Hill. Introduction copyright © 2023 by David Scott

Cataloging-in-Publication Data is available at the Library of Congress.

Vintage Books Trade Paperback ISBN: 978-0-679-72467-4
eBook ISBN: 978-0-593-68733-8

vintagebooks.com

Printed in the United States of America
1st Printing

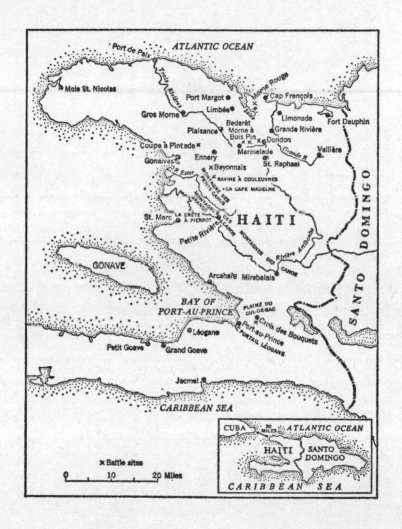

ATLANTIC OCEAN

Port de Paix

Môle St. Nicolas

Gros Morne
Port Margot
Limbées
Morne Rouge
Cap François
Limonade
Fort Dauphin
Plaisance
Bedarèt
Morne à
Bois Pin
Grande Rivière
Dondon
Vallières
Coupe à Pintade ×
Marmelade
Grande R.
St. Raphaël
Ennery
Gonaïves
× Bayonnais
RAVINE À COULEUVRES
R Ester
MONTAGNE DES
PETITS CAHOS
× LA CAPE MADELNE
St. Marc
LA CRÊTE
À PIERROT
MONTAGNES DES CAHOS
HAITI
Petite Rivière
MONTAGNES DES CAHOS
Rivière Artibonite
GONAVE
Arcahaïe Mirebalais
CAHOS
BAY OF
PORT-AU-PRINCE
PLAINE DU
CUL-DE-SAC
Croix des Bouquets
Port-au-Prince
PORTAIL LÉOGANE
Léogane
Petit Goave   Grand Goave
Jacmel
CARIBBEAN SEA

× Battle sites

0   10   20 Miles

CUBA   50 MILES   ATLANTIC OCEAN
HAITI   SANTO
DOMINGO
SANTO DOMINGO
CARIBBEAN   SEA

To My Good Friends
Harry and Elizabeth Spencer
of Nelson, Lancashire, England

CONTENTS

PREFACE TO THE FIRST EDITION (1938)

IN 1789 the French West Indian colony of San Domingo supplied two-thirds of the overseas trade of France and was the greatest individual market for the European slave-trade. It was an integral part of the economic life of the age, the greatest colony in the world, the pride of France, and the envy of every other imperialist nation. The whole structure rested on the labour of half-a-million slaves.

In August 1791, after two years of the French Revolution and its repercussions in San Domingo, the slaves revolted. The struggle lasted for 12 years. The slaves defeated in turn the local whites and the soldiers of the French monarchy, a Spanish invasion, a British expedition of some 60,000 men, and a French expedition of similar size under Bonaparte's brother-in-law. The defeat of Bonaparte's expedition in 1803 resulted in the establishment of the Negro state of Haiti which has lasted to this day.

The revolt is the only successful slave revolt in history, and the odds it had to overcome is evidence of the magnitude of the interests that were involved. The transformation of slaves, trembling in hundreds before a single white man, into a people able to organise themselves and defeat the most powerful European nations of their day, is one of the great epics of revolutionary struggle and achievement. Why and how this happened is the theme of this book.

By a phenomenon often observed, the individual leadership responsible for this unique achievement was almost entirely the work of a single man—Toussaint L'Ouverture. Beauchamp in the *Biographie Universelle* calls

Toussaint L'Ouverture one of the most remarkable men of
a period rich in remarkable men. He dominated from his
entry until circumstances removed him from the scene.
The history of the San Domingo revolution will therefore
largely be a record of his achievements and his political
personality. The writer believes, and is confident the narrative will prove, that between 1789 and 1815, with the
single exception of Bonaparte himself, no single figure
appeared on the historical stage more greatly gifted than
this Negro, a slave till he was 45. Yet Toussaint did not
make the revolution. It was the revolution that made
Toussaint. And even that is not the whole truth.

The writing of history becomes ever more difficult. The
power of God or the weakness of man, Christianity or the
divine right of kings to govern wrong, can easily be made
responsible for the downfall of states and the birth of new
societies. Such elementary conceptions lend themselves
willingly to narrative treatment and from Tacitus to Ma-
caulay, from Thucydides to Green, the traditionally famous
historians have been more artist than scientist: they wrote
so well because they saw so little. To-day by a natural reaction we tend to a personification of the social forces,
great men being merely or nearly instruments in the hands
of economic destiny. As so often the truth does not lie in
between. Great men make history, but only such history
as it is possible for them to make. Their freedom of achievement is limited by the necessities of their environment. To
portray the limits of those necessities and the realisation,
complete or partial, of all possibilities, that is the true business of the historian.

In a revolution, when the ceaseless slow accumulation
of centuries bursts into volcanic eruption, the meteoric flares
and flights above are a meaningless chaos and lend themselves to infinite caprice and romanticism unless the observer sees them always as projections of the sub-soil from
which they came. The writer has sought not only to analyse,
but to demonstrate in their movement, the economic forces
of the age; their moulding of society and politics, of men
in the mass and individual men; the powerful reaction of

these on their environment at one of those rare moments when society is at boiling point and therefore fluid.

The analysis is the science and the demonstration the art which is history. The violent conflicts of our age enable our practised vision to see into the very bones of previous revolutions more easily than heretofore. Yet for that very reason it is impossible to recollect historical emotions in that tranquillity which a great English writer, too narrowly, associated with poetry alone.

Tranquillity to-day is either innate (the philistine) or to be acquired only by a deliberate doping of the personality. It was in the stillness of a seaside suburb that could be heard most clearly and insistently the booming of Franco's heavy artillery, the rattle of Stalin's firing squads and the fierce shrill turmoil of the revolutionary movement striving for clarity and influence. Such is our age and this book is of it, with something of the fever and the fret. Nor does the writer regret it. The book is the history of a revolution and written under different circumstances it would have been a different but not necessarily a better book.

C. L. R. JAMES

PREFACE TO THE VINTAGE EDITION (1962)

THIS book was written in 1938. Today, I have little to add to or subtract from the fundamental ideas which governed its conception. They are far more common property now than they were twenty-five years ago. Where they fly in the face of historical events I have omitted or altered them, never more than to the extent of a few lines.

I have retained the concluding pages which envisage and were intended to stimulate the coming emancipation of Africa. They are a part of the history of our time. In 1938 only the writer and a handful of close associates thought, wrote and spoke as if the African events of the last quarter of a century were imminent.

The Appendix, "From Toussaint L'Ouverture to Fidel Castro," attempts for the future of the West Indies, all of them, what was done for Africa in 1938. Writers on the West Indies always relate them to their approximation to Britain, France, Spain and America, that is to say, to Western civilization, never in relation to their own history. This is here attempted for the first time.

C. L. R. JAMES

JANUARY 4, 1962

INTRODUCTION: THE RADICAL NOVELTY
OF TOUSSAINT LOUVERTURE (2023)

1.

C. L. R. James's *The Black Jacobins* was first published in London in the summer of 1938 by Secker and Warburg (later that year it would appear from Dial in New York). James (b. 1901) had moved from colonial Trinidad to metropolitan Britain only six years before, in March 1932.[1] Initially a self-consciously literary man oriented vaguely toward Bloomsbury modernist realism, and with no more than an incipient sense of anticolonial, let alone socialist, politics, within these six years he had more or less abandoned his commitment to writing fiction and established himself at the center of both the Marxist debate about the Soviet Union and the prospect of a new International Left, and the anticolonial debate about national and Black self-determination. These would form interlocking axes shaping the analytical and political framework of *The Black Jacobins*.

Specifically, the anticolonial question in the British West Indies was centrally a question about the rise and fall and social and economic effects of plantation slavery. In 1933–34, shortly after James's arrival in Britain, there were centennial celebrations of the passage of the parliamentary act abolishing slavery throughout the British empire (the act received royal assent on 28 August 1833, and took effect on 1 August 1834), and in particular, of the role of William Wilberforce and his humanitarian allies in overcoming the prevailing West India slaving interests. Thereafter, the widely accepted story of slavery abolition in British historiography was motivated and animated by the idea (one may as well say, the racist conceit)

[1] For details of James's life, including the circumstances around the writing of *The Black Jacobins*, see John L. Williams, *C. L. R. James: A Life Beyond the Boundaries* (London: Constable, 2022).

that abolition was largely a benevolent act of English charity toward a benighted people good for little more than service and brute labor. It was a story, therefore, that occluded, or disavowed, both the fact of the unjust enrichment of Britons and British society out of the plunder and violation of Black people for more than two hundred years, and the fact that the enslaved were not mere passively grateful objects of rule, abjectly accommodating themselves to their condition, but actively involved in their own emancipation. In *The Black Jacobins*, James addresses himself to both these strands of racial prejudice in British historiography. But between them, his principal focus is the latter, namely, the role of the enslaved in liberating themselves from their bondage. And clearly the most dramatic historical instance of the self-emancipation of the enslaved was the Saint-Domingue insurrection that led to the Haitian Revolution.[2] For James in *The Black Jacobins*, the story of the Haitian Revolution, told as a revolutionary account of a revolutionary history (learned in part from Jules Michelet's *History of the French Revolution* and Leon Trotsky's *History of the Russian Revolution*) is the story of Black anticolonial self-determination embodied in the vindicating singularity of Toussaint Louverture.

Above all, it is Toussaint that fascinates James, almost to the point, perhaps, of identification. Indeed, James was already thinking about Toussaint and what he represented as a heroic Black figure before he left Trinidad for Britain. And throughout *The Black Jacobins* he struggles with how best to render his protagonist satisfactorily as a distinctive historical actor—the circumstances of his condition as a relatively privileged enslaved man (James apparently did not know that Toussaint was already a free and slave-owning Black at the time of the insurrection), the noteworthy qualities of his personality, the ideas and forces that moved him, and so on. For James, Toussaint is exceptional, unprecedented, novel. He is not only a Caribbean Creole and therefore neither African nor Euro-

[2] James uses the English "San Domingo," but I will follow the contemporary convention and use the French "Saint-Domingue." Similarly, I shall follow the current usage of "Toussaint Louverture" rather than James's "Toussaint L'Ouverture."

pean; he is entirely *modern*, a subjugated product of the shaping social and economic technologies of the proto-factory sugar plantation. But this is not all. Toussaint is not only modern (in a sense *all* the enslaved were obliged to be—or become—modern); he is the embodiment of that quintessentially modern subject, the *intellectual*. The intellectual is not merely someone who thinks creatively, but someone whose very form of life is mediated and activated through the temporal fold of reflexive being. In this respect, for James, Toussaint is wholly unlike most of his Black contemporaries, unlike Makandal (an earlier rebel leader), for example, and unlike Jean-Jacques Dessalines (Toussaint's general and successor), both men of remarkable intelligence, courage, and will—but *not* intellectuals. And part of what intrigues James about this quality is that it is at once a gift and a curse: it is what enables Toussaint to see, in a visionary way, what others around him cannot see; and it is also what, from a certain point in his career of leadership, blinds him to what lies under his nose and clouds the clarity and decisiveness of his actions. Across the arc of *The Black Jacobins*, James endlessly troubles over the form of life of an intellectual and political leader who is struggling to do what has never been done before.

It is a central dimension of Toussaint's singularity, of the sheer novelty of his subjectivity and his undertaking that he did not know with certainty where he was going or how he would get there. *This* is crucial to James's point about Toussaint: he could *not* have known. He had no blueprint to guide him. And so, he could not have foreseen what the horizon or endgame of the insurrection he was leading should be. He could not know, for example, as those after him would claim to know, that he should have been heading toward nation-state sovereignty all along. We who read *The Black Jacobins* in our time, with a ready-made anticolonialism that Toussaint could not have had, follow him, sometimes with frustration, as he stumbles around his given world without a map, trying to find his way. He knows that his is a fight for freedom from slavery, but even with so (to us) elementary a project he has to work out through experience and reflection the idea that the relevant freedom cannot be for himself and a few select officers alone, but must be for all the enslaved. Nor is it transparently clear that he should become governor of the colonial territory, let alone its sovereign. This idea of independence is a hard-earned notion of political order that Toussaint's educated and well-traveled contemporaries in the newly minted United States are only then beginning to work out. How and by what process he comes to the conclusions he arrives at are questions that intrigue James.

Again, in trying to work out the mode of labor that should accompany liberation from slavery Toussaint angers some of his most trusted comrades (his nephew, Moïse, among them), when he returns the enslaved to the plantations and, to add insult to injury, sometimes even to their former enslavers. But for James, this is not, surely, because Toussaint is cynically indifferent to the brutality of plantation labor or ignorant of what it symbolizes to the enslaved, but rather because he can dimly, inchoately, recognize that Saint-Domingue is integrated into a wider system and he thus believes that the sugar plantation is a necessary part of the survival of his fledgling state. In the postcolonial world this belief is now a familiar one. After all, from the vantage point of decolonization, it is easy to see that de-linking from colonial capitalism might have been at least as catastrophic to Toussaint as neocolonial political leaders have imagined (or feared) in the contemporary Caribbean.

Similarly, James was well aware that he would have to meet the question of Toussaint's supposed enchantment with Europe. Was Toussaint merely a supine Europhile, a mimic-man? Was Europe simply the hegemonic condition of his formation (as a man, an intellectual, and a political leader), or was it also, and more deeply, the motivating impetus of his moral aspirations? Given the formation of the Caribbean (the destruction of the native population, and the fragmenting cultural processes involved in the enslavement of Africans) these were unavoidable questions. And they would have had a special resonance for James as a Caribbean colonial intellectual and political activist himself grappling with the presence of Europe in his own orientations, attitudes, desires, and so on, and searching for an idiom in which to express his own distinctive individuality. Undoubtedly, for James, Toussaint was not merely superficially formed by European civilization as a normative structure of dominant language, ideas, values, technologies, and expectations. He was also a man of the radical Enlightenment (this is the point of his seeming acquaintance with the Abbé Raynal's famous book *A Philosophical and Political History of the Settlements and Trade of the Europeans in the East and West Indies*), and therefore, as James puts it, revolutionary France constituted more than the "framework of his mind"; it was the fertile ground for the new mode of social existence—based on the idea of natural liberty—that was now justifiably open to him. And yet, notably, James is also careful to say that while Toussaint held European civilization in the highest esteem, he was not seduced by it, he conferred upon it no moral superiority. He remained undeceived by the criminality and duplicity and racism of European imperialism.

2.

Throughout his life, James kept returning to *The Black Jacobins* in a revisionary attitude, as though it kept generating new questions for him—especially new questions about Toussaint Louverture. In the preface to the first edition, James had located the writing he had carried out in the context of certain world-historical circumstances (Stalin's purges, the Spanish Civil War, the emergence of an International Left around Trotsky), and indicated that had it been written under other circumstances it would have been a different (if not a better) book. For James, then, circumstances mattered. When in the early 1960s he returned to the text, the context was substantially different from the one in which he had originally written it in the 1930s: in particular, there was the new dawn of African and Caribbean independence, with its hopes and disappointments; and there was the Cuban Revolution offering an example of political sovereignty more radical than any prevailing in the Caribbean.[3] The second and revised edition of *The Black Jacobins* was published in New York by Vintage in 1963, and it brought the text to the attention of a whole new generation of

3 See Rachel Douglas, *Making "The Black Jacobins": C. L. R. James and the Drama of History* (Durham: Duke University Press, 2019).

readers ready for a story of revolutionary change in the Caribbean. In the new edition, James introduced two principal revisions that, in some respects, gave the book a slightly different
feel than the original edition.

The first of these revisions consists of the six dense paragraphs added to the beginning of the final chapter, "The War
of Independence," the great climax to the story of slave revolution. These paragraphs explicitly introduce the theme of the
tragic in understanding the rise and fall of Toussaint Louverture. James had been thinking systematically about tragedy as
a principle of historical poetics since the 1950s, especially in
the context of the work that informed *Mariners, Renegades,
and Castaways* (published in 1953). Why did Toussaint make
the errors that, from a certain point in his leadership, drove
him inexorably toward disaster? Characteristically refusing the
psychological description of Toussaint as a divided personality,
the idea of the tragic gave James a way of situating Toussaint's
dilemma in terms of an actor at a historical crossroads caught
in a paradoxical moment of incommensurable alternatives
between which it was, nevertheless, necessary to decide—
either a return to slavery (as he knew Napoleon was planning),
on the one hand, or a Saint-Domingue without France, on
the other. Given who he was, a former slave and a man of the
Enlightenment, neither was possible for him to imagine. And
so, from being a leader of decisive action, Toussaint became
the paralyzed embodiment of a vacillation that was eventually
to ruin him. Insisting as always on Toussaint's human com-
plexity and integrity, James urges us to see in him a man with
unblemished intentions derailed neither by cowardice nor
complicity but by circumstances that were at once constitutive
of his predicament and beyond his personal control.[4]

The second major revision in the 1963 edition consists
of the inclusion of a now-famous appendix, "From Toussaint L'Ouverture to Fidel Castro." What connects Toussaint
Louverture and Fidel Castro, James memorably argued, is not
the obvious fact that they were leaders of successful revolu-

4 See David Scott, *Conscripts of Modernity: The Tragedy of Colonial Enlightenment* (Durham: Duke University Press, 2004).

tions. Rather, what links them is that they are exemplars of a Caribbean sensibility, and the processes that they set in motion were derived from a distinctly Caribbean historical predicament, perhaps even a distinctive Caribbean *civilization*. The history of the Caribbean, James said, was governed by two principal factors, the sugar plantation and Black slavery, and these together had imposed a process of social structure and a pattern of social identity across the Caribbean that differentiated it from Europe and Africa, as well as continental America. In one of the most insightful passages in the appendix, James says that the sugar plantation was simultaneously a *demoralizing* and *civilizing* institution; it introduced powers that both destroyed old moral and cultural forms of life and conscripted the enslaved into a new, and entirely *modern*, social existence. By this James means to point to the modern proto-factory character of the plantation as a labor regime, and to its insertion into a modernizing capitalist world system. Consequently, from the outset, as James puts it, the enslaved lived an essentially and inescapably modern life.

Less than a decade later, in 1971, James returned once more to the text of *The Black Jacobins* in another revisionary attitude—and once again with implications for our understanding of Toussaint Louverture. The occasion was a series of lectures at the Institute of the Black World, Atlanta, a remarkable institution that (between 1969 and 1983) served as a forum for radical Black discussions, not least between Caribbean and American intellectuals. James gave three lectures: "How I wrote *The Black Jacobins*," "*The Black Jacobins* and *Black Reconstruction*: A Comparative Analysis," and "How I would Rewrite *The Black Jacobins*."[5] Each of the lectures is a tour de force of originality, erudition, and lucidity, not least James's deeply appreciative reflections on W. E. B. Du Bois's 1935 account of post-slavery America. Perhaps, though, of most significance here is the third of the lectures, James's reflections on what he might do differently were he to be writing the book

5 These were published as C. L. R. James's "Lectures on *The Black Jacobins*" in *Small Axe* no. 8 (September 2000): 65–112, with a preface by Robert A. Hill (61–64) and an afterword by Anthony Bogues (113–17).

then, in the early 1970s. Again, the context matters. This was the era of Black Power in the United States and there was a deeper sense (certainly keener than was the case in the 1930s or even in the early 1960s) that Black history should be written, not from the perspective of elites, but from the point of view of the folk, of the ordinary and largely unremembered men and women who make history *from below*. James, who had been teaching at Federal City College in Washington, DC, as a visiting professor, was clearly attuned to this critique of the historiographical mode of heroic agency. In his lecture, he tells his audience that were he writing *The Black Jacobins* then, he would not write it from the perspective of Toussaint and the other well-known leaders, but from that of the nameless slave rebels who actually made the revolution what it was.

Writing history, for James, was an endless, recursive process of revision, of recontextualization, of asking again and again what the present circumstances enabled him to see or urged him to emphasize of the past he was recounting.

3.

The Black Jacobins is undoubtedly a classic of historical literature. But what makes it so? And why should we think of it as a classic not only of Caribbean history specifically, or Black history, but rather of *world* history? A classic, evidently, is a book one feels compelled to return to again and again, a book read by generation after generation, not because it offers us invaluable information or irrefutable facts, but because it tells a story that reflects back to us recognizable dimensions of a human spirit struggling against vicious odds to affirm, enhance, and expand, the given boundaries of our common humanity. This is what *The Black Jacobins* offers us in a luminous, unforgettable narrative whose attentive rhythms and dramatic contours point toward the sustaining exigencies of a common human value.

Pivotal to this sense of *The Black Jacobins* as an irrepressible classic, I believe, is precisely its evocation of the radical novelty and radical universality of Toussaint Louverture. As James says of him in the closing poignant sentence of the 1963 appendix, Toussaint was "the first and greatest of West Indians." By this he means that Toussaint was literally unprecedented, unparalleled, not simply in the sense that he had no equal, but in the strict sense that he was original, singular, a hitherto inconceivable form of human life. As everyone who reads the book will immediately recognize, James's Toussaint was not simply an ordinary figure of remote and provincial local knowledge; he was the larger-than-life figure of a heroic world-historical universality. He was a man who, while completely shaped by the constraining particularities of his degraded, enslaved circumstances, was nevertheless not reducible to them. His life and his project have a meaning, in other words, that transcends the specific framework of his time and place—or rather, in Toussaint, that specificity of time and place are lived in the dimension of universality. His vision, not given to him all at once but emerging stage by stage through the gradual assimilation and transformation of the experience of the White supremacist normativity of a slave empire, forged an inaugural idea of human freedom—namely, a freedom born of slave emancipation. In striving to define and redefine the terms of this emancipation, it is true, Toussaint falters and, in the end, he fails perhaps, but the gift of his example has already been received, even by his mortal enemies, and that seeming failure is itself, paradoxically, the exemplary mark of his tragic humanity. This is what James so unwaveringly admires in his hero (even when he disappoints him): the audacity with which, to the very end, he claims his moral and political right to the self-determination violently denied him and his fellow liberators, and his willingness to sacrifice what Abraham Lincoln famously called the "last full measure of devotion" in the vindication of that claim. And for giving us this vivid picture of one of the exemplifications of virtue and excellence, we remain indebted to C. L. R. James.

DAVID SCOTT
February 2023

David Scott teaches in the department of anthropology at Columbia University. He is the author of a number of books,

including *Refashioning Futures: Criticism after Postcoloniality,
Conscripts of Modernity: The Tragedy of Colonial Enlightenment, Stuart Hall's Voice: Intimations of an Ethics of Receptive Generosity*, and *Irreparable Evil: An Essay in Moral and
Reparatory History*. He is currently at work on a biography
of Stuart Hall. Scott is the founder and editor of the journal
Small Axe and director of the Small Axe Project.

The Black Jacobins

PROLOGUE

CHRISTOPHER COLUMBUS landed first in the New World at the island of San Salvador, and after praising God enquired urgently for gold. The natives, Red Indians, were peaceable and friendly and directed him to Haiti, a large island (nearly as large as Ireland), rich, they said, in the yellow metal. He sailed to Haiti. One of his ships being wrecked, the Haitian Indians helped him so willingly that very little was lost and of the articles which they brought on shore not one was stolen.

The Spaniards, the most advanced Europeans of their

day, annexed the island, called it Hispaniola, and took the backward natives under their protection. They introduced Christianity, forced labour in mines, murder, rape, blood-hounds, strange diseases, and artificial famine (by the destruction of cultivation to starve the rebellious). These and other requirements of the higher civilisation reduced the native population from an estimated half-a-million, perhaps a million, to 60,000 in 15 years.

Las Casas, a Dominican priest with a conscience, travelled to Spain to plead for the abolition of native slavery. But without coercion of the natives how could the colony exist? All the natives received as wages was Christianity and they could be good Christians without working in the mines.

The Spanish Government compromised. It abolished the *repartimientos*, or forced labour, in law while its agents in the colony maintained it in fact. Las Casas, haunted at the prospect of seeing before his eyes the total destruction of a population within one generation, hit on the expedient of importing the more robust Negroes from a populous Africa; in 1517, Charles V. authorised the export of 15,000 slaves to San Domingo, and thus priest and King launched on the world the American slave-trade and slavery.

The Spanish settlement founded by Columbus was on the south-east of the island. In 1629 some wandering Frenchmen sought a home in the little island of Tortuga, six miles off the north coast of San Domingo, to be followed by Englishmen, and Dutchmen from Santa Cruz. Tortuga was healthy and in the forests of western San Domingo roamed millions of wild cattle which could be hunted for food and hides. To Tortuga came fugitives from justice, escaped galley-slaves, debtors unable to pay their bills, adventurers seeking adventure or quick fortunes, men of all crimes and all nationalities. French, British and Spaniards slaughtered one another for nearly 30 years, and the British were actually in possession of Tortuga at one time, but by 1659 the French buccaneers prevailed. They sought the suzerainty of France and demanded a chief and some women. From Tortuga they laid a firm basis in San Do-

mingo and moved there. To drive away these persistent
intruders the Spaniards organised a great hunt and killed
all the bulls they could find in order to ruin the cattle business. The French retaliated by the cultivation of cocoa;
then indigo and cotton. Already they knew the sugar-cane.
Lacking capital they raided the English island of Jamaica
and stole money and 2,000 Negroes. French, British and
Spaniards raided and counter-raided and burnt to the
ground, but in 1695 the Treaty of Ryswick between France
and Spain gave the French a legal right to the western part
of the island. In 1734 the colonists began to cultivate coffee.
The land was fertile, France offered a good market. But
they wanted labour. In addition to Negroes, they brought
whites, the *engagés*, who would be freed after a period of
years. So little did they bring the Negroes because these
were barbarous or black, that the early laws prescribed
similar regulations for both black slaves and white *engagés*.
But under the regimen of those days the whites could not
stand the climate. So the slavers brought more and more
Negroes, in numbers that leapt by thousands every year,
until the drain from Africa ran into millions.

I

The Property

THE SLAVERS scoured the coasts of Guinea. As they devastated an area they moved westward and then south, decade after decade, past the Niger, down the Congo coast, past Loango and Angola, round the Cape of Good Hope, and, by 1789. even as far as Mozambique on the eastern side of Africa. Guinea remained their chief hunting ground. From the coast they organised expeditions far into the interior. They set the simple tribesmen fighting against each other with modern weapons over thousands of square miles. The propagandists of the time claimed that however cruel was the slave traffic, the African slave in America was happier than in his own African civilisation. Ours, too, is an age of propaganda. We excel our ancestors only in system and organisation: they lied as fluently and as brazenly. In the sixteenth century, Central Africa was a territory of peace and happy civilisation.[1] Traders travelled thousands of miles from one side of the continent to another without molestation. The tribal wars from which the European pirates claimed to deliver the people were mere sham-fights; it was a great battle when half-a-dozen men were killed. It was on a peasantry in many respects superior to the serfs in large areas of Europe, that the slave-trade fell. Tribal life was broken up and millions of detribalised Africans were let loose upon each other. The unceasing destruction of crops led to cannibalism; the captive women became concubines and degraded the status of the wife. Tribes had to supply slaves or be sold as slaves themselves. Violence and ferocity became the necessities for survival, and violence and ferocity survived.[2] The stockades of grinning skulls, the human sacrifices, the selling of their own children as slaves, these horrors were the product of an intolerable pressure on the African peoples, which became fiercer through the centuries as the demands of industry increased and the methods of coercion were perfected.

The slaves were collected in the interior, fastened one to the other in columns, loaded with heavy stones of 40 or 50 pounds in weight to prevent attempts at escape, and then marched the long journey to the sea, sometimes hundreds of miles, the weakly and sick dropping to die in the African jungle. Some were brought to the coast by canoe, lying in the bottom of boats for days on end, their hands bound, their faces exposed to the tropical sun and the tropical rain, their backs in the water which was never bailed out. At the slave ports they were penned into "trunks" for the inspection of the buyers. Night and day

[1] See the works of Professor Emil Torday, one of the greatest African scholars of his time, particularly a lecture delivered at Geneva in 1931 to a society for the Protection of Children in Africa.
[2] See Professor Torday's lecture mentioned above.

thousands of human beings were packed in these "dens of putrefaction" so that no European could stay in them for longer than a quarter of an hour without fainting. The Africans fainted and recovered or fainted and died, the mortality in the "trunks" being over 20 per cent. Outside in the harbour, waiting to empty the "trunks" as they filled, was the captain of the slave-ship, with so clear a conscience that one of them, in the intervals of waiting to enrich British capitalism with the profits of another valuable cargo, enriched British religion by composing the hymn "How Sweet the Name of Jesus sounds!"

On the ships the slaves were packed in the hold on galleries one above the other. Each was given only four or five feet in length and two or three feet in height, so that they could neither lie at full length nor sit upright. Contrary to the lies that have been spread so pertinaciously about Negro docility, the revolts at the port of embarkation and on board were incessant, so that the slaves had to be chained, right hand to right leg, left hand to left leg, and attached in rows to long iron bars. In this position they lived for the voyage, coming up once a day for exercise and to allow the sailors to "clean the pails." But when the cargo was rebellious or the weather bad, then they stayed below for weeks at a time. The close proximity of so many naked human beings, their bruised and festering flesh, the foetid air, the prevailing dysentery, the accumulation of filth, turned these holds into a hell. During the storms the hatches were battened down, and in the close and loathsome darkness they were hurled from one side to another by the heaving vessel, held in position by the chains on their bleeding flesh. No place on earth, observed one writer of the time, concentrated so much misery as the hold of a slave-ship.

Twice a day, at nine and at four, they received their food. To the slave-traders they were articles of trade and no more. A captain held up by calms or adverse winds was known to have poisoned his cargo.[3] Another killed some of

<hr/>

[3] See Pierre de Vaissière, *Saint-Domingue* (1629-1789). Paris, 1909. This contains an admirable summary.

his slaves to feed the others with the flesh. They died not only from the régime but from grief and rage and despair. They undertook vast hunger strikes; undid their chains and hurled themselves on the crew in futile attempts at insurrection. What could these inland tribesmen do on the open sea, in a complicated sailing vessel? To brighten their spirits it became the custom to have them up on the deck once a day and force them to dance. Some took the opportunity to jump overboard, uttering cries of triumph as they cleared the vessel and disappeared below the surface.

Fear of their cargo bred a savage cruelty in the crew. One captain, to strike terror into the rest, killed a slave and dividing heart, liver and entrails into 300 pieces made each of the slaves eat one, threatening those who refused with the same torture.[4] Such incidents were not rare. Given the circumstances such things were (and are) inevitable. Nor did the system spare the slavers. Every year one-fifth of all who took part in the African trade died.

All America and the West Indies took slaves. When the ship reached the harbour, the cargo came up on deck to be bought. The purchasers examined them for defects, looked at the teeth, pinched the skin, sometimes tasted the perspiration to see if the slave's blood was pure and his health as good as his appearance. Some of the women affected a curiosity, the indulgence of which, with a horse, would have caused them to be kicked 20 yards across the deck. But the slave had to stand it. Then in order to restore the dignity which might have been lost by too intimate an examination, the purchaser spat in the face of the slave. Having become the property of his owner, he was branded on both sides of the breast with a hot iron. His duties were explained to him by an interpreter, and a priest instructed him in the first principles of Christianity.[5]

The stranger in San Domingo was awakened by the cracks of the whip, the stifled cries, and the heavy groans

[4] De Vaissière, *Saint-Domingue*, p. 162.
[5] This was the beginning and end of his education.

of the Negroes who saw the sun rise only to curse it for
its renewal of their labours and their pains. Their work
began at day-break: at eight they stopped for a short breakfast and worked again till midday. They began again at
two o'clock and worked until evening, sometimes till ten
or eleven. A Swiss traveller [6] has left a famous description
of a gang of slaves at work. "They were about a hundred
men and women of different ages, all occupied in digging
ditches in a cane-field, the majority of them naked or covered with rags. The sun shone down with full force on their
heads. Sweat rolled from all parts of their bodies. Their
limbs, weighed down by the heat, fatigued with the weight
of their picks and by the resistance of the clayey soil baked
hard enough to break their implements, strained themselves
to overcome every obstacle. A mournful silence reigned.
Exhaustion was stamped on every face, but the hour of
rest had not yet come. The pitiless eye of the Manager
patrolled the gang and several foremen armed with long
whips moved periodically between them, giving stinging
blows to all who, worn out by fatigue, were compelled to
take a rest—men or women, young or old." This was no
isolated picture. The sugar plantations demanded an ex-
acting and ceaseless labour. The tropical earth is baked
hard by the sun. Round every "carry" of land intended for
cane it was necessary to dig a large ditch to ensure circulation of air. Young canes required attention for the first three
or four months and grew to maturity in 14 or 18 months.
Cane could be planted and would grow at any time of the
year, and the reaping of one crop was the signal for the
immediate digging of ditches and the planting of another.
Once cut they had to be rushed to the mill lest the juice
became acid by fermentation. The extraction of the juice
and manufacture of the raw sugar went on for three weeks
a month, 16 or 18 hours a day, for seven or eight months
in the year.

Worked like animals, the slaves were housed like animals, in huts built around a square planted with provisions

[6] Girod-Chantrans, *Voyage d'un Suisse en différentes colonies,*
Neufchâtel, 1785, p. 137.

and fruits. These huts were about 20 to 25 feet long, 12 feet wide and about 15 feet in height, divided by partitions into two or three rooms. They were windowless and light entered only by the door. The floor was beaten earth; the bed was of straw, hides or a rude contrivance of cords tied on posts. On these slept indiscriminately mother, father and children. Defenceless against their masters, they struggled with overwork and its usual complement—underfeeding. The Negro Code, Louis XIV's attempt to ensure them humane treatment, ordered that they should be given, every week, two pots and a half of manioc, three cassavas, two pounds of salt beef or three pounds of salted fish—about food enough to last a healthy man for three days. Instead their masters gave them half-a-dozen pints of coarse flour, rice, or pease, and half-a-dozen herrings. Worn out by their labours all through the day and far into the night, many neglected to cook and ate the food raw. The ration was so small and given to them so irregularly that often the last half of the week found them with nothing.

Even the two hours they were given in the middle of the day, and the holidays on Sundays and feast-days, were not for rest, but in order that they might cultivate a small piece of land to supplement their regular rations. Hardworking slaves cultivated vegetables and raised chickens to sell in the towns to make a little in order to buy rum and tobacco; and here and there a Napoleon of finance, by luck and industry, could make enough to purchase his freedom. Their masters encouraged them in this practice of cultivation, for in years of scarcity the Negroes died in thousands, epidemics broke out, the slaves fled into the woods and plantations were ruined.

The difficulty was that though one could trap them like animals, transport them in pens, work them alongside an ass or a horse and beat both with the same stick, stable them and starve them, they remained, despite their black skins and curly hair, quite invincibly human beings; with the intelligence and resentments of human beings. To cow them into the necessary docility and acceptance necessitated a régime of calculated brutality and terrorism, and it is this that explains the unusual spectacle of property-owners apparently careless of preserving their property: they had first to ensure their own safety.

For the least fault the slaves received the harshest punishment. In 1685 the Negro Code authorised whipping, and in 1702 one colonist, a Marquis, thought any punishment which demanded more than 100 blows of the whip was serious enough to be handed over to the authorities. Later the number was fixed at 39, then raised to 50. But the colonists paid no attention to these regulations and slaves were not unfrequently whipped to death. The whip was not always an ordinary cane or woven cord, as the Code demanded. Sometimes it was replaced by the *rigoise* or thick thong of cow-hide, or by the *lianes*—local growths of reeds, supple and pliant like whalebone. The slaves received the whip with more certainty and regularity than they received their food. It was the incentive to work and the guardian of discipline. But there was no ingenuity that fear or a depraved imagination could devise which was not employed to break their spirit and satisfy the lusts and resentment of their owners and guardians—irons on the hands and feet, blocks of wood that the slaves had to drag behind them wherever they went, the tin-plate mask designed to prevent the slaves eating the sugar-cane, the iron collar. Whipping was interrupted in order to pass a piece of hot wood on the buttocks of the victim; salt, pepper, citron, cinders, aloes, and hot ashes were poured on the bleeding wounds. Mutilations were common, limbs, ears, and sometimes the private parts, to deprive them of the pleasures which they could indulge in without expense. Their masters poured burning wax on their arms and hands and shoulders, emptied the boiling cane sugar over their heads, burned them alive, roasted them on slow fires, filled them with gunpowder and blew them up with a match; buried them up to the neck and smeared their heads with sugar that the flies might devour them; fastened them near to nests of ants or wasps; made them eat their excrement, drink their urine, and lick the saliva of other slaves. One colonist was known in moments of anger to throw himself on his slaves and stick his teeth into their flesh.[7]

Were these tortures, so well authenticated, habitual or were they merely isolated incidents, the extravagances of a few half-crazed colonists? Impossible as it is to substantiate hundreds of cases, yet all the evidence shows that these bestial practices were normal features of slave life. The torture of the whip, for instance, had "a thousand refinements," but there were regular varieties that had special names, so common were they. When the hands and arms were tied to four posts on the ground, the slave was said to undergo "the four post." If the slave was tied to a ladder it was "the torture of the ladder"; if he was suspended by four limbs it was "the hammock," etc. The pregnant woman was not spared her "four-post." A hole was dug in the earth to accommodate the unborn child. The torture of the collar was specially reserved for women who were suspected of abortion, and the collar never left their necks until they had produced a child. The blowing up of a slave had its own name—"to burn a little powder in the arse of a nigger": obviously this was no freak but a recognised practice.

After an exhaustive examination, the best that de Vaissière can say is that there were good masters and there were bad, and his impression, "but only an impression," is that the former were more numerous than the latter.

There are and always will be some who, ashamed of the behaviour of their ancestors, try to prove that slavery was not so bad after all, that its evils and its cruelty were the exaggerations of propagandists and not the habitual lot of the slaves. Men will say (and accept) anything in order to foster national pride or soothe a troubled conscience. Undoubtedly there were kind masters who did not indulge in these refinements of cruelty and whose slaves

[7] *Saint-Domingue*, p. 153-194. De Vaissière uses chiefly official reports in the French Colonial archives, and other documents of the period, giving specific references in each case.

merely suffered over-work, under-nourishment and the whip. But the slaves in San Domingo could not replenish their number by reproduction. After that dreaded journey across the ocean a woman was usually sterile for two years. The life in San Domingo killed them off fast. The planters deliberately worked them to death rather than wait for children to grow up. But the professional white-washers are assisted by the writings of a few contemporary observers who described scenes of idyllic beauty. One of these is Vaublanc, whom we shall meet again, and whose testimony we will understand better when we know more of him. In his memoirs[8] he shows us a plantation on which there were no prisons, no dungeons, no punishments to speak of. If the slaves were naked the climate was such as not to render this an evil, and those who complained forgot the perfectly disgusting rags that were so often seen in France. The slaves were exempt from unhealthy, fatiguing, dangerous work such as was performed by the workers in Europe. They did not have to descend into the bowels of the earth nor dig deep pits; they did not construct subterranean galleries; they did not work in the factories where French workers breathed a deadly and infected air; they did not mount elevated roofs; they did not carry enormous burdens. The slaves, he concluded, had light work to do and were happy to do it. Vaublanc, in San Domingo so sympathetic to the sorrows of labour in France, had to fly from Paris in August, 1792, to escape the wrath of the French workers.

Malouet, who was an official in the colonies and fellow-reactionary of Vaublanc against all change in the colonies, also sought to give some ideas of the privileges of slavery. The first he notes is that the slave, on attaining his majority, begins to enjoy "the pleasures of love," and his master has no interest in preventing the indulgence of his tastes.[9] To such impertinent follies can the defence of property drive even an intelligent man, supposed in his time to be sympathetic towards the blacks.

[8] Quoted extensively in de Vaissière, pp. 198-202.
[9] De Vaissière, p. 196.

The majority of the slaves accommodated themselves
to this unceasing brutality by a profound fatalism and a
wooden stupidity before their masters. "Why do you ill-
treat your mule in that way?" asked a colonist of a carter.
"But when I do not work, I am beaten, when he does not
work, I beat him—he is my Negro." One old Negro, having lost one of his ears and condemned to lose another,
begged the Governor to spare it, for if that too was cut off
he would have nowhere to put his stump of cigarette. A
slave sent by his master into his neighbour's garden to steal,
is caught and brought back to the man who had only a
few minutes before despatched him on the errand. The
master orders him a punishment of 100 lashes to which the
slave submits without a murmur. When caught in error
they persisted in denial with the same fatalistic stupidity.
A slave is accused of stealing a pigeon. He denies it. The
pigeon is discovered hidden in his shirt. "Well, well, look
at that pigeon. It take my shirt for a nest." Through the
shirt of another, a master can feel the potatoes which he
denies he has stolen. They are not potatoes, he says, they
are stones. He is undressed and the potatoes fall to the
ground. "Eh! master. The devil is wicked. Put stones, and
look, you find potatoes."

On holidays when not working on their private plots,
or dancing, they sat for hours in front of their huts giving
no sign of life. Wives and husbands, children and parents,
were separated at the will of the master, and a father and
son would meet after many years and give no greeting or
any sign of emotion. Many slaves could never be got to
stir at all unless they were whipped.[10] Suicide was a common habit, and such was their disregard for life that they
often killed themselves, not for personal reasons, but in
order to spite their owner. Life was hard and death, they

[10] Incredible as this may sound Baron de Wimpffen gives it as
the evidence of his own eyes. His record of his visit to San
Domingo in 1790 is a standard work. A good selection, with very
full notes, is published, under the title, *Saint-Domingue à la
veille de la Révolution*, by Albert Savine, Paris, 1911.

believed, meant not only release but a return to Africa. Those who wished to believe and to convince the world that the slaves were half-human brutes, fit for nothing else but slavery, could find ample evidence for their faith, and in nothing so much as in this homicidal mania of the slaves.

Poison was their method. A mistress would poison a rival to retain the valuable affections of her inconstant owner. A discarded mistress would poison master, wife, children and slaves. A slave robbed of his wife by one of his masters would poison him, and this was one of the most frequent causes of poisoning.[11] If a planter conceived a passion for a young slave, her mother would poison his wife with the idea of placing her daughter at the head of the household. The slaves would poison the younger children of a master in order to ensure the plantation succeeding to one son. By this means they prevented the plantation being broken up and the gang dispersed. On certain plantations the slaves decimated their number by poison so as to keep the number of slaves small and prevent their masters embarking on larger schemes which would increase the work. For this reason a slave would poison his wife, another would poison his children, and a Negro nurse declared in court that for years she had poisoned every child that she brought into the world. Nurses employed in hospitals poisoned sick soldiers to rid themselves of unpleasant work. The slaves would even poison the property of a master whom they loved. He was going away; they poisoned cows, horses and mules, the plantation was thrown into disorder, and the beloved master was compelled to remain. The most dreadful of all this cold-blooded murder was, however, the jaw-sickness—a disease which attacked children only, in the first few days of their existence. Their jaws were closed to such an extent that it was impossible to open them and to get anything down, with the result that they died of hunger. It was not a natural disease and

[11] See *Kenya* by Dr. Norman Leys, London, 1926, p. 184. "Some rivalry for a native woman is probably the explanation of most crimes of violence committed by Africans against Europeans in Kenya."

never attacked children delivered by white women. The Negro midwives alone could cause it, and it is believed that they performed some simple operation on the newly-born child which resulted in the jaw-sickness. Whatever the method this disease caused the death of nearly one-third of the children born on the plantations.

What was the intellectual level of these slaves? The planters, hating them, called them by every opprobious name. "The Negroes," says a memoir published in 1789, "are unjust, cruel, barbarous, half-human, treacherous, deceitful, thieves, drunkards, proud, lazy, unclean, shameless, jealous to fury, and cowards." It was by sentiments such as these that they strove to justify the abominable cruelties they practised. And they took great pains that the Negro should remain the brute beast they wanted him to be. "The safety of the whites demands that we keep the Negroes in the most profound ignorance. I have reached the stage of believing firmly that one must treat the Negroes as one treats beasts." Such is the opinion of the Governor of Martinique in a letter addressed to the Minister and such was the opinion of all colonists. Except for the Jews, who spared no energy in making Israelites of their slaves, the majority of the colonists religiously kept all instruction, religious or otherwise, away from the slaves.

Naturally there were all types of men among them, ranging from native chieftains, as was the father of Toussaint L'Ouverture, to men who had been slaves in their own country. The creole Negro was more docile than the slave who had been born in Africa. Some said he was more intelligent. Others doubted that there was much difference though the creole slave knew the language and was more familiar with his surroundings and his work. Yet those who took the trouble to observe them away from their masters and in their intercourse with each other did not fail to see that remarkable liveliness of intellect and vivacity of spirit which so distinguish their descendants in the West Indies to-day. Father du Tertre, who knew them well, noted their secret pride and feeling of superiority to their masters, the difference between their behaviour before their masters and when they were by themselves. De Wimpffen, an exceptionally observant and able traveller, was also astonished at this dual personality of the slaves. "One has to hear with what warmth and what volubility, and at the same time with what precision of ideas and accuracy of judgment, this creature, heavy and taciturn all day, now squatting before his fire, tells stories, talks, gesticulates, argues, passes opinions, approves or condemns both his master and everyone who surrounds him." It was this intelligence which refused to be crushed, these latent possibilities, that frightened the colonists, as it frightens the whites in Africa to-day. "No species of men has more intelligence," wrote Hilliard d'Auberteuil, a colonist, in 1784, and had his book banned.

But one does not need education or encouragement to cherish a dream of freedom. At their midnight celebrations of Voodoo, their African cult, they danced and sang, usually this favourite song:

> Eh ! Eh ! Bomba ! Heu ! Heu !
> Canga, bafio té !
> Canga, mouné de lé !
> Canga, do ki la !
> Canga, li !

"We swear to destroy the whites and all that they possess; let us die rather than fail to keep this vow." The colonists knew this song and tried to stamp it out, and the Voodoo cult with which it was linked. In vain. For over two hundred years the slaves sang it at their meetings, as the Jews in Babylon sang of Zion, and the Bantu to-day sing in secret the national anthem of Africa.[12]

---

[12] Such observations, written in 1938, were intended to use the San Domingo revolution as a forecast of the future of colonial Africa.

All the slaves, however, did not undergo this régime. There was a small privileged caste, the foremen of the gangs, coachmen, cooks, butlers, maids, nurses, female companions, and other house-servants. These repaid their kind treatment and comparatively easy life with a strong attachment to their masters, and have thus enabled Tory historians, regius professors and sentimentalists to represent plantation slavery as a patriarchal relation between master and slave. Permeated with the vices of their masters and mistresses, these upper servants gave themselves airs and despised the slaves in the fields. Dressed in cast-off silks and brocades, they gave balls in which, like trained monkeys, they danced minuets and quadrilles, and bowed and curtseyed in the fashion of Versailles. But a few of these used their position to cultivate themselves, to gain a little education, to learn all they could. The leaders of a revolution are usually those who have been able to profit by the cultural advantages of the system they are attacking, and the San Domingo revolution was no exception to this rule.

Christophe, afterwards Emperor of Haiti, was a slave —a waiter in a public hotel at Cap François, where he made use of his opportunities to gain a knowledge of men and of the world. Toussaint L'Ouverture[13] also belonged to this small and privileged caste. His father, son of a petty chieftain in Africa, was captured in war, sold as a slave and made the journey in a slave-ship. He was bought by a colonist of some sensibility, who, recognising that this Negro was an unusual person, allowed him a certain liberty on the plantation and the use of five slaves to cultivate a plot of land. He became a Catholic, married a woman who was both beautiful and good, and Toussaint was the eldest of his eight children. Near to the household lived an old Negro, Pierre Baptiste, remarkable for his integrity of character and a smattering of knowledge. The Negroes spoke a debased French known as creole. But Pierre knew French, also a little Latin and a little geometry, which he had learned from a missionary. Pierre Baptiste became Toussaint's godfather and taught his godson the rudiments

[13] As a slave he was called Toussaint Bréda.

of French; using the services of the Catholic Church he
instructed him also in the rudiments of Latin; Toussaint
learned also to draw. The young slaves had the care of the
flocks and herds, and this was Toussaint's early occupation. But his father, like many other Africans, had some
knowledge of medicinal plants and taught Toussaint what
he knew. The elements of an education, his knowledge of
herbs, his unusual intelligence, singled him out, and he
was made coachman to his master. This brought him further means of comfort and self-education. Ultimately he
was made steward of all the live-stock on the estate—a
responsible post which was usually held by a white man.
If Toussaint's genius came from where genius comes, yet
circumstances conspired to give him exceptional parents
and friends and a kind master.

But the number of slaves who occupied positions with
such opportunities was infinitely small in comparison with
the hundreds of thousands who bore on their bent backs
the whole structure of San Domingo society. All of them
did not submit to it. Those whose boldness of spirit found
slavery intolerable and refused to evade it by committing
suicide, would fly to the woods and mountains and form
bands of free men—maroons. They fortified their fastnesses
with palisades and ditches. Women followed them. They
reproduced themselves. And for a hundred years before
1789 the maroons were a source of danger to the colony.
In 1720, 1,000 slaves fled to the mountains. In 1751 there
were at least 3,000 of them. Usually they formed separate
bands, but periodically they found a chief who was strong
enough to unite the different sections. Many of these rebel
leaders struck terror into the hearts of the colonists by
their raids on the plantations and the strength and determination of the resistance they organised against attempts
to exterminate them. The greatest of these chiefs was
Mackandal.

He conceived the bold design of uniting all the Negroes and driving the whites out of the colony. He was a

Negro from Guinea who had been a slave in the district of
Limbé, later to become one of the great centres of the
revolution. Mackandal was an orator, in the opinion of a
white contemporary equal in eloquence to the European
orators of the day, and different only in his superior strength
and vigour. He was fearless and, though one-handed from
an accident, had a fortitude of spirit which he knew how
to preserve in the midst of the most cruel tortures. He
claimed to predict the future; like Mahomet he had revelations; he persuaded his followers that he was immortal and
exercised such a hold over them that they considered it an
honour to serve him on their knees; the handsomest women
fought for the privilege of being admitted to his bed. Not
only did his band raid and pillage plantations far and wide,
but he himself ranged from plantation to plantation to
make converts, stimulate his followers, and perfect his
great plan for the destruction of white civilisation in San
Domingo. An uninstructed mass, feeling its way to revolution, usually begins by terrorism, and Mackandal aimed at
delivering his people by means of poison. For six years he
built up his organisation, he and his followers poisoning
not only whites but disobedient members of their own
band. Then he arranged that on a particular day the water
of every house in the capital of the province was to be
poisoned, and the general attack made on the whites while
they were in the convulsions and anguish of death. He had
lists of all members of his party in each slave gang; appointed captains, lieutenants and other officers; arranged
for bands of Negroes to leave the town and spread over
the plains to massacre the whites. His temerity was the
cause of his downfall. He went one day to a plantation,
got drunk and was betrayed, and being captured was burnt
alive.

The Mackandal rebellion never reached fruition and
it was the only hint of an organised attempt at revolt during the hundred years preceding the French Revolution.
The slaves seemed eternally resigned, though here and
there a slave was manumitted or purchased his freedom
from his owner. From their masters came no talk of future

emancipation. The San Domingo colonists said that slavery was necessary, and for them that finished the argument. Legislation passed for the protection of the slaves remained on paper in face of the dictum that a man could do as he liked with his own. "All laws, however just and humane they may be, in favour of Negroes will always be a violation of the rights of property if they are not sponsored by the colonists. . . . All laws on property are just only if they are supported by the opinion of those who are interested in them as proprietors." This was still white opinion at the beginning of the French Revolution. Not only planters but officials made it quite clear that whatever the penalties for the illtreatment of slaves, these could never be enforced. The slaves might understand that they had rights, which would be fatal to the peace and well-being of the colony. That was why a colonist never hesitated at the mutilation, the torture or the murder of a slave who had cost him thousands of francs. "The Ivory Coast is a good mother" was a colonial proverb. Slaves could always be bought, and profits were always high.

The Negro Code was enacted in 1685. A century after, in 1788, the Le Jeune case[14] laid bare the realities of slave law and slave justice in San Domingo.

Le Jeune was a coffee planter of Plaisance. Suspecting that the mortality among his Negroes was due to poison, he murdered four of them and attempted to extort confessions from two women by torture. He roasted their feet, legs and elbows, while alternately gagging them thoroughly and then withdrawing the gag. He extorted nothing and threatened all his French-speaking slaves that he would kill them without mercy if they dared to denounce him. But Plaisance, in the thickly-populated North Province, was always a centre of the more advanced slaves, and 14 of them went to Le Cap and charged Le Jeune before the law. The judges could do no less than accept the charges. They appointed a commission which made an investigation

[14] De Vaissière, pp. 186-188.

at Le Jeune's plantation and confirmed the testimony of the
slaves. The commission actually found the two women
barred and chained, with elbows and legs decomposing,
but still alive; one of them had her neck so lacerated by
an iron collar that she could not swallow. Le Jeune insisted that they were guilty of the poisonings which for so
long had ravaged his plantation and gave in evidence a box
taken in the women's possession. This, he said, contained
poison. But when the box was opened it was found to contain nothing more than ordinary tobacco and rat dung.
Defence was impossible, and when the two women died,
Le Jeune disappeared just in time to escape arrest. The
case was clear. At the preliminary hearing the 14 Negroes
repeated their accusations word for word. But seven white
witnesses testified in favour of Le Jeune and two of his
stewards formally absolved him of all guilt. The planters
of Plaisance petitioned the Governor and the Intendant on
behalf of Le Jeune, and demanded that each of his slaves
be given 50 lashes for having denounced him. The Chamber of Agriculture of Le Cap asked that Le Jeune should
merely be banished from the colony. Seventy planters from
the north made a similar petition, and the Philadelphian
Circle, a centre of San Domingo culture, was asked to make
representations on Le Jeune's behalf. Le Jeune's father
asked for a writ of intervention against one of the official
investigators whose evidence he impugned. "To put it
shortly," wrote the Governor and the Intendant to the
Minister, "it seems that the safety of the colony depends
on the acquittal of Le Jeune." It did, if the slaves were to
be kept in their place. The judges, after a thousand delays,
returned a negative verdict, the charges were declared null
and void and the case dismissed. The public prosecutor
demanded an appeal before the Superior Council of Port-
au-Prince, the official capital of the island. All white San
Domingo was up in arms. The Intendant appointed the
oldest member of the Council to be the *rapporteur*, thinking that he could be depended upon to ensure justice. But
on the day of the trial, fearing that he would not be able
to secure a conviction he absented himself, and the Coun-

cil once more acquitted Le Jeune. The Home Government
could pass what laws it liked. White San Domingo would
not tolerate any interference with the methods by which
they kept their slaves in order.[15]

This was the problem to be solved.

Hope from the planters there was none. In France
Liberalism was still an aspiration and "trusteeship," its
fig-leaf, was as yet unknown. But on the tide of humanitarianism rising on the bourgeois revolt against feudalism,
Diderot and the Encyclopaedists had attacked slavery.
"Let the colonies be destroyed rather than be the cause of
so much evil," said the Encyclopaedia in its article on the
slave-trade. But such outbursts neither then nor now have
carried weight. And wordy attacks against slavery drew
sneers from observers which were not altogether unde-
served. The authors were compared to doctors who offered
to a patient nothing more than invectives against the disease which consumed him.

But among these literary opponents of slavery was
one who, nine years before the fall of the Bastille, called
boldly for a slave revolution with a passionate conviction
that it was bound to come some day and relieve Africa and
Africans. He was a priest, the Abbé Raynal, and he
preached his revolutionary doctrine in the *Philosophical
and Political History of the Establishments and Commerce
of the Europeans in the Two Indies.* It was a book famous

[15] The French colonists were not freaks. For murders of two
Kenya natives by the sons of a bishop and a peer respectively
and the absence of any serious punishment, see *Kenya*, by Dr.
Norman Leys, pp. 176-180. In a footnote on p. 180 Dr. Leys
quotes the British Colonial Secretary in 1924: "Cases of this
kind are of rare occurrence in the history of the colony," and
adds, "a far from accurate statement." This does not by any
means imply that all the bestialities of San Domingo are practised in Africa. But the régimes are strictly parallel, otherwise
the conditions noted by Dr. Leys could not exist.

in its time and it came into the hands of the slave most
fitted to make use of it, Toussaint L'Ouverture.

"Natural liberty is the right which nature has given
to every one to dispose of himself according to his
will. . . .

"The slave, an instrument in the hands of wickedness,
is below the dog which the Spaniard let loose against the
American. . . .

"These are memorable and eternal truths—the foundation of all morality, the basis of all government; will they
be contested? Yes! . . ."

And the most famous passage:

"If self-interest alone prevails with nations and their
masters, there is another power. Nature speaks in louder
tones than philosophy or self-interest. Already are there
established two colonies of fugitive negroes, whom treaties
and power protect from assault. These lightnings announce
the thunder. A courageous chief only is wanted. Where is
he, that great man whom Nature owes to her vexed, oppressed and tormented children? Where is he? He will
appear, doubt it not; he will come forth and raise the
sacred standard of liberty. This venerable signal will gather
around him the companions of his misfortune. More impetuous than the torrents, they will everywhere leave the
indelible traces of their just resentment. Everywhere people will bless the name of the hero who shall have rees-
tablished the rights of the human race; everywhere will
they raise trophies in his honour."

Over and over again Toussaint read this passage: "A
courageous chief only is wanted. Where is he?" A courageous chief was wanted. It is the tragedy of mass movements that they need and can only too rarely find adequate
leadership. But much else was wanted.

Men make their own history, and the black Jacobins
of San Domingo were to make history which would alter
the fate of millions of men and shift the economic cur-
rents of three continents. But if they could seize opportunity they could not create it. The slave-trade and slavery

were woven tight into the economics of the eighteenth
century. Three forces, the proprietors of San Domingo, the
French bourgeoisie and the British bourgeoisie, throve on
this devastation of a continent and on the brutal exploitation of millions. As long as these maintained an equilibrium
the infernal traffic would go on, and for that matter would
have gone on until the present day. But nothing, however
profitable, goes on forever. From the very momentum of
their own development, colonial planters, French and British bourgeois, were generating internal stresses and in-
tensifying external rivalries, moving blindly to explosions
and conflicts which would shatter the basis of their dominance and create the possibility of emancipation.

II

The Owners

OF THE THREE, San Domingo planters, British bourgeoisie and French bourgeoisie, the first and most important were the planters of San Domingo.

On such a soil as San Domingo slavery, only a vicious society could flourish. Nor were the incidental circumstances such as to mitigate the demoralisation inherent in such a method of production.

San Domingo is an island of mountain ranges rising in places to 6,000 feet above sea-level. From these flow innumerable streams coalescing into rivers which water

the valleys and not inconsiderable plains lying between
the hills. Its distance from the equator gives an unusual
lusciousness and variety to the natural exuberance of the
tropics, and the artificial vegetation was not inferior to the
natural. Field upon field, the light green sugar-cane, low
and continually rippled in the breeze, enclosed the factory
and the dwelling houses like a sea; a few feet above the
cane-stalks waved the five-foot leaves of the banana-trees;
near the dwelling-houses the branches of the palm, crown-
ing a perfectly rounded and leafless column of 60 or 70
feet, gave forth, like huge feathers, a continuous soothing
murmur; while groups of them in the distance, always
visible in the unclouded tropical air, looked like clusters
of giant umbrellas waiting for the parched and sun-baked
traveller. In the season, mango and orange trees, solitary
or in groves, were a mass of green leaves and red or golden
fruit. Thousands of small, scrupulously tidy coffee-trees rose
on the slopes of the hills, and the abrupt and precipitous
mountain-sides were covered to the summits with the lux-
uriant tropical undergrowth and precious hardwood forests of San Domingo. The traveller from Europe was enchanted at his first glimpse of this paradise, in which the
ordered beauty of agriculture and the prodigality of Nature
competed equally for his surprise and admiration.

But it was monotonous. Year in year out, day after
day, it was the same, a little greener in the wet season, a
little browner in the dry. The wilder scenery was constantly magnificent, but in the colonist who had seen the
same domestic landscape from his earliest hour, it
awakened little response. To the emigrant who was at first
charmed and exhilarated, monotony bred indifference,
which could develop into active dislike, and longing for
the seasons returning with the year.

The climate was harsh, and for the Europeans of the
eighteenth century without modern knowledge of tropical
hygiene almost intolerable. The burning sun and humid
atmosphere took heavy toll of all newcomers, European
and African alike. The African died, but the European ail-
ments were dreaded by the planters whose knowledge and

habits were powerless to combat them. Fever and dysentery in the hot season; cold, rheumatism, nasal catarrhs and diarrhoea in the wet; at all times a disinclination for sustained labour, fostered by the gluttony and lasciviousness bred by abundance and scores of slaves waiting to perform any duty, from pulling off shoes to spending the night.

Indulgence had the white colonial in its grip from childhood. "I want an egg," said a colonial child. "There are none." "Then I want two." This notorious anecdote was characteristic. To the unhealthiness of the climate and the indulgence of every wish were added the open licentiousness and habitual ferocity of his parents, the degradation of human life which surrounded the child on every side.

The ignorance inherent in rural life prior to the industrial revolution was reinforced by the irascibility and the conceit of isolation allied to undisputed domination over hundreds of human beings. The plantations were often miles apart and, in those days of horse-traffic and few or bad roads in a mountainous country, communication with neighbours was difficult and rare. The planters hated the life and sought only to make enough money to retire to France or at least spend a few months in Paris, luxuriating in the amenities of civilisation. With so much to eat and drink, there was a lavish hospitality which has remained a tradition, but the majority of the great houses, contrary to the legend, were poorly furnished, and their owners looked on them as rest-houses in the intervals of trips to Paris. Seeking to overcome their abundant leisure and boredom with food, drink, dice and black women, they had long before 1789 lost the simplicity of life and rude energy of those nameless men who laid the foundation of the colony. A manager and an overseer, and the more intelligent of their slaves were more than sufficient to run their plantations. As soon as they could afford it they left the island, if possible never to return, though they never formed in France so rich and powerful a social and political force as the West Indian interest in England.

The women were subjected to the same evil influences. In the early years of the colony they had been imported like slaves and machinery. Most of the first arrivals were the sweepings of the Paris gutter, bringing to the island "bodies as corrupt as their manners and serving only to infect the colony." [1] Another official, asking for women, begged the authorities not to send the "ugliest they could find in the hospitals." As late as 1743 official San Domingo was complaining that France still sent girls whose "aptitude for generation was for the most part destroyed by too great usage." Projects for some educational system never came to fruition. With increasing wealth the daughters of the richer planters went to Paris where, after a year or two at a finishing-school, they made distinguished matches with the impoverished French nobility. But in the colony they passed their time attiring themselves, singing stupid songs, and listening to the gossip and adulation of their slave attendants. Passion was their chief occupation, stimulated by over-feeding, idleness, and an undying jealousy of the black and Mulatto women who competed so successfully for the favours of their husbands and lovers.

To the men of divers races, classes and types who formed the early population of San Domingo had been added as the years passed a more unified and cohesive element, the offshoots of the French aristocracy. Deprived of political power by Richelieu and converted by Louis XIV into a decorative and administrative appendage of the absolute monarchy, the younger sons of French noblemen found in San Domingo some opportunity to rebuild their shattered fortunes and live the life of the country magnate now denied them in France. They came as officers in the army and officials, and stayed to found fortunes and families. They commanded the militia, administered a rude justice. Arrogant and spendthrift, yet they were a valuable section of white San Domingo society and knit together more firmly a society composed of such diverse and disintegrating elements. But even their education, traditions and pride were not proof against the prevailing corruption, and one could see a "relation of the

[1] De Vaissière, pp. 77-79.

de Vaudreils, a Châteauneuf, or Boucicaut, last descendant
of the famous marshal of France, passing his life between
a bowl of rum and a Negro concubine." [2]

Town life is the nurse of civilisation. But apart from
Port-au-Prince, the capital, and Cap François, the towns
of San Domingo at the height of its prosperity were little
more than villages. In 1789 St Marc had only 150 houses,
Môle St Nicholas, the Gibraltar of the Caribbean Sea, had
only 250; Léogane, one of the most important towns in
the West Province, consisted of between 300 and 400
houses laid out in 15 streets; Jacmel, one of the key towns
in the South, had only 40. Even Cap François, the Paris
of the Antilles, and the entrepôt of the European trade
had a population of only 20,000, of whom half were slaves.
Yet Le Cap, as it was familiarly called, was a town famous
in its time and in its way unique. An incessant activity
reigned there, with its harbour always filled with ships and
its streets with merchandise. But it too bore the imprint of
savagery which seemed inseparable from everything connected with San Domingo. One of the most distinguished
colonial historians, Moreau of Saint-Méry, admits that the
streets were sewers and that people threw all their garbage
into them. The Government begged people in vain not to
commit nuisances in the street, to be careful of the disposition of "faecal matter," not to let sheep, pigs and goats
wander loose. No one paid any attention to these injunc-
tions.

In Port-au-Prince, the official capital of the colony,
the population washed their dirty linen, made indigo and
soaked manioc in the water of the only spring which supplied the town. Despite repeated prohibitions they continued to beat their slaves in the public streets. Nor were
the authorities themselves more careful. If it rained at
night, one could not walk in the town the next day, and
streams of water filled the ditches at the side of the street
in which one could hear the croaking of toads. De

[2] De Vaissière. p. 217.

Wimpffen called Port-au-Prince a Tartar camp, and Moreau de Saint-Méry, himself a colonial, deprecates the sharpness of the expression but admits that it was not entirely inapplicable.

Such culture as there was centred in these towns. In Le Cap there were various masonic and other societies, the most famous of which was the Philadelphia Circle, a body devoting itself to politics, philosophy and literature. But the chief reading of the population consisted of lascivious novels. For amusement there were theatres, not only in Le Cap and Port-au-Prince, but in such small towns as Léogane and St Marc, where the melodramas and the thrillers of the day were played to packed houses. In 1787 there were three companies in Port-au-Prince alone.

What the towns lacked in intellectual fare they made up for in opportunities of debauchery—gambling-dens (for everyone in San Domingo played and great fortunes were won and lost in a few days), dance-halls, and private brothels whereby the Mulatto women lived in such comfort and luxury that in 1789, of 7,000 Mulatto women in San Domingo, 5,000 were either prostitutes or the kept mistresses of white men.

The regular clergy of San Domingo instead of being a moderating influence were notorious for their irreverence and degeneracy. In the early years they consisted chiefly of unfrocked monks. Later came a better class of priests, but in that turgid, overheated society few were able to withstand the temptations of easy money, easy living, and easy women; many of them lived openly with their concubines. Their greed for money led them to exploit the Negroes with the same ruthlessness as the rest of white San Domingo. About the middle of the eighteenth century one of them used to baptise the same Negroes seven or eight times, for the ceremony amused the slaves and they were willing to pay a small sum for each baptism. As late as 1790 another was competing with the Negro obeah-men for the coppers of the slaves, by selling charms against illness and talismans to insure the success of their petty ventures.

In the towns the great merchants and the wealthy agents of the maritime bourgeoisie were included with the planters as big whites. On the plantations the managers and the stewards were either agents of the absentee owner, or were under the eye of the planter himself and, therefore, subordinate to him. These in the country, and in the towns the small lawyers, the notaries, the clerks, the artisans, the grocers, were known as the small whites.[3] Included among the small whites was a crowd of city vagabonds, fugitives from justice, escaped galley slaves, debtors unable to pay their bills, adventurers seeking adventure or quick fortunes, men of all crimes and all nationalities. From the underworld of two continents they came, Frenchmen and Spaniards, Maltese, Italians, Portuguese and Americans. For whatever a man's origin, record or character, here his white skin made him a person of quality and rejected or failures in their own country flocked to San Domingo, where consideration was achieved at so cheap a price, money flowed and opportunities of debauchery abounded.

No small white was a servant, no white man did any work that he could get a Negro to do for him. A barber summoned to attend to a customer appeared in silk attire, hat under his arm, sword at his side, cane under his elbow, followed by four Negroes. One of them combed the hair, another dressed it, a third curled it and the fourth finished. While they worked the employer presided over the various operations. At the slightest slackness, at the slightest mistake, he boxed the cheek of the unfortunate slave so hard that often he knocked him over. The slave picked himself up without any sign of resentment, and resumed. The same hand which had knocked over the slave closed on an enormous fee, and the barber took his exit with the same insolence and elegance as before.

[3] These should not be confused with the modern "poor whites" in America or South Africa. Some of these, especially in America, live at a standard almost as low as that of the Negroes in their community.

This was the type for whom race prejudice was more important than even the possession of slaves, of which they held few. The distinction between a white man and a man of colour was for them fundamental. It was their all. In defence of it they would bring down the whole of their world.

Big whites and small whites did not exhaust the white population of San Domingo. Over them both was the bureaucracy, composed almost entirely of Frenchmen from France, who governed the island. The heads of the bureaucracy were the Governor and the Intendant. The Governor was the official representative of the King, with all that this implies even to this day in the administration of distant colonies. His official salary might be as much as 100,000 livres[4] a year, besides the profits common to such posts in the twentieth as well as in the eighteenth century: the granting of concessions, the acting on the quiet as agent for European merchandise in the colonies and for colonial merchandise in Europe. A French nobleman was as greedy for a governorship of San Domingo as his British counterpart for a viceroyalty of India. In 1787 the Governor was a brother to the French Ambassador in London, and he left the post of Governor to become Minister of Marine.

Next to the Governor was the Intendant, who was responsible for justice, finance and general administration, and sometimes drew a salary of 80,000 livres a year. The Governor was a soldier and aristocrat, the Intendant was a bureaucrat, and the military and the civil were constantly at variance. But against the local whites they and their staff, the commandants in the districts and the senior officials, represented the King's authority and the commercial privileges of the French bourgeoisie. They could arrest without warrant, they could refuse to carry out the instructions of the Minister, they could force the members of the local advisory councils to resign, could grant favours, pronounce confiscations, increase taxes, in fact their

4 About ⅔ of a franc.

arbitrariness had no legal bounds. "God was too high and the King too far."

The colonists hated them. In addition to their absolute power they were wasteful and extravagant, their malversations were constant and enormous, and they treated the local whites with an arrogance and superciliousness that galled these little potentates with their two or three hundred slaves. There were good and bad Governors, good and bad Intendants, as there were good and bad slaveowners. But this was a matter of pure chance. It was the system that was bad.

There was some pretence at local self-government. Both at Le Cap and at Port-au-Prince there were local councils which registered the royal edicts and the decisions of the local government. Shortly before the revolution there was also appointed a council of the richest and most powerful of the whites who were supposed to represent local opinion. But the Intendant, like the Governor in the British Legislative Councils of to-day, could accept or reject their advice as he pleased.

The bureaucracy, with the source of its power so many thousands of miles away, could not depend only on the two French regiments in the colony. In 1789 the functionaries in San Domingo, where the white population was about 30,000, numbered only 513. Without some mass support government would have been impossible. Bringing with them from France the traditional hostility of the absolute monarchy to the political power of the feudal nobility, the bureaucrats sought a counterweight to the power of the planters in the small whites of town and country. The chief complaint of the small whites was against the militia which policed the districts and frequently encroached on the Intendant's administration of justice and finance. To these complaints the Intendant was always sympathetic. In 1760 one Intendant went so far as to dissolve the militia altogether and appointed syndics to carry on the local government. The colony was thrown into disorder, the Home Government had to re-establish the militia and restore its former powers to the military. Straight-

way an insurrection broke out in the island, led by the
local justices of the peace, lawyers, notaries and prosecu-
tors. The planters complained that the supporters of this
rebellion were the lowest sections of the population, in
one district three Portuguese Jews, a notary, a steward, a
tailor, a shoemaker, a butcher's assistant and a former soldier of the ranks. The scorn of the planters is overwhelming
for "these rascals who have occasioned these troubles and
of whom we can say with justice that they are the vilest
canaille, whose fathers and mothers have been lackeys or
domestic servants, or even of an origin still lower." [5] It
was not their low origin which justified the attack of the
planters upon the small whites. Tailors, butchers and soldiers from the ranks were to play the decisive part in the
French Revolution—and by their spontaneous efforts save
Paris from the counter-revolution at home and abroad. But
most of the small whites were a rabble and filled no important function in the economy of the colony. If every
single one of them had been deported from the country,
such work as they did could have been done by free Mulattoes, free blacks, or even slaves. They were not an integral part of San Domingo society, either by function,
birth or tradition. But they were white, and as such of use
to the bureaucracy. In 1771 we find the Intendant again
complaining of military tyranny. "Since the militia are re-
established," he complains, "the officers are every day
depriving the ordinary judges of all their prerogatives."

Here then was the first great division, that between
great whites and small whites, with the bureaucracy bal-
ancing between and encouraging the small whites. Nothing
could assuage or solve this conflict. The moment the revolution begins in France these two will spring at each other
and fight to a finish.

There was another class of free men in San Domingo,
the free Mulattoes and free blacks. Neither legislation, nor
the growth of race prejudice, could destroy the attraction

[5] De Vaissière, pp. 145-147.

of the black women for the white men of San Domingo. It was characteristic of all classes; the rabble on the shorefront, the planter or overseer who chose a slave to pass the night with him and drove her from his bed to the lash of the slave-driver next morning; a Governor of the colony, newly arrived from France, who was disturbed at finding himself seized with a passion for the handsomest of his four black maids.

In the early days every Mulatto was free up to the age of 24, not by law, but because white men were so few in comparison with the slaves that the masters sought to bind these intermediates to themselves rather than let them swell the ranks of their enemies. In those early years race prejudice was not strong. The Negro Code in 1685 authorised marriage between the white and the slave who had children by him, the ceremony freeing herself and her children. The Code gave the free Mulattoes and the free Negroes equal rights with the whites. But as the white population grew larger, white San Domingo discarded the convention, and enslaved or sold their numerous children like any king in the African jungle. All efforts to prevent concubinage failed, and the Mulatto children multiplied, to be freed or to remain slaves at the caprice of their fathers. Many were freed, becoming artisans and household servants. They began to amass property, and the whites, while adding unceasingly to the number of Mulattoes, began to restrict and harass them with malicious legislation. The whites threw as much as possible of the burdens of the country upon them. On attaining their majority they were compelled to join the *maréchaussée*, a police organisation for arresting fugitive Negroes, protecting travellers on the high road, capturing dangerous Negroes, fighting against the maroons, all the difficult and dangerous tasks which the local whites might command. After three years' service in the *maréchaussée*, they had to join the local militia, provide their own arms, ammunition and accoutrements, and, without pay or allowance of any kind, serve at the discretion of the white commanding officer. Such duties as the forced upkeep of the roads were made to fall on them with

extra severity. They were excluded from the naval and military departments, from the practice of law, medicine, and
divinity, and all public offices or places of trust. A white
man could trespass on a Mulatto's property, seduce his wife
or daughter, insult him in any way he chose, certain that at
any hint of resentment or revenge all the whites and the
Government would rush out ready to lynch. In legal actions
the decision nearly always went against the Mulattoes, and
to terrorise them into submission a free man of colour who
struck a white man, whatever his station in life, was to
have his right arm cut off.

But by some fortunate chance, the amount of property
that they could hold was not, as in the English islands,
limited. Of fine physique and intelligent, administering
their enterprises themselves without exhausting their fortunes in extravagant trips to Paris, they began to acquire
wealth as master-artisans and then as proprietors. As they
began to establish themselves, the jealousy and envy of the
white colonists were transformed into ferocious hatred and
fear. They divided the offspring of white and black and
intermediate shades into 128 divisions. The true Mulatto
was the child of the pure black and the pure white. The
child of the white and the Mulatto woman was a quarteron
with 96 parts white and 32 parts black. But the quarteron
could be produced by the white and the marabou in the
proportion of 88 to 40, or by the white and the sacatra, in
the proportion of 72 to 56 and so on all through the 128
varieties. But the sang-mêlé with 127 white parts and 1
black part was still a man of colour.

In a slave society the mere possession of personal freedom is a valuable privilege, and the laws of Greece and
Rome testify that severe legislation against slaves and freedmen have nothing to do with the race question. Behind all
this elaborate tom-foolery of quarteron, sacatra and marabou, was the one dominating fact of San Domingo society
—fear of the slaves. The mothers of the Mulattoes were in
the slave-gangs, they had half-brothers there, and however much the Mulatto himself might despise this half of
his origin, he was at home among the slaves and, in addi-

tion to his wealth and education, could have an influence among them which a white man could never have. Furthermore, apart from physical terror, the slaves were to be kept in subjection by associating inferiority and degradation with the most obvious distinguishing mark of the slave— the black skin. Few of the slaves being able to read, the colonists did not hesitate to say openly: "It is essential to maintain a great distance between those who obey and those who command. One of the surest means of doing this is the perpetuation of the imprint that slavery has once given." No Mulatto, therefore, whatever his number of white parts, was allowed to assume the name of his white father.

But despite these restrictions the Mulattoes continued to make progress. By 1755, little more than three generations after the Negro Code, they were beginning to fill the colony, and their growing numbers and riches were causing alarm to the whites.

They lived (ran a report)[6] like their forebears, on the local vegetables, drinking no wine, confining themselves to the local liquors brewed from the sugar cane. Thus their personal consumption contributed nothing to the maintenance of the important trade with France. Their sober ways of living and their small expenditure enabled them to put away most of their income every year, they accumulated immense capital, and grow more arrogant as their wealth increased. They bid for all properties on sale in the various districts, and raised prices to such fantastic heights that the whites who were not wealthy could not buy, or ruined themselves by attempting to keep pace with them. Thus, in some districts, the finest properties were in the possession of the half-castes, and yet they were everywhere the least ready to submit to statute labour and the public dues. Their plantations were the sanctuary and asylum of the freedmen who had neither work nor profession and of numerous fugitive slaves who had run away from their gangs. Being so rich they imitated the style of the whites and sought to drown all traces of their origin. They were

[6] De Vaissière, p. 222.

trying to get high commands in the militia. Those who had ability enough to make them forget the vice of their origin were even seeking places in the judiciary. If this sort of thing went on, they would soon be making marriages with distinguished families, which would bind these families in alliance with the slaves in the gangs, whence the mothers of these upstarts came.

This was no cantankerous croak from a jealous colonist. It was an official memorandum from the bureaucracy to the Minister. Increasing numbers, increasing wealth were giving the Mulattoes greater pride and sharpening their resentment against their humiliations. Some of them were sending their children to France to be educated, and in France, even a hundred years before the revolution, there was little colour prejudice. Up to 1716 every Negro slave who touched French soil was free, and after an interval of fifty years another decree in 1762 reaffirmed this. In 1739 a slave served as trumpeter in the royal regiment of Carabineers; young Mulattoes were received in the military corps reserved to the young nobility and in the offices of the magistracy; they served as pages at court.[7] Yet these men had to go back to San Domingo and submit to the discriminations and brutality of the San Domingo whites. And as the Mulattoes began to press against the barriers, white San Domingo passed a series of laws which for maniacal savagery are unique in the modern world, and (we would have said up to 1933) not likely to be paralleled again in history. The Council of Port-au-Prince, holding up the race question as a screen, wanted to exterminate them. Thus the whites could purge their system of a growing menace, get rid of men from whom they had borrowed money, and seize much fine property. The Council proposed to banish all the half-castes up to the degree of quarteron to the mountains ("which they would bring into cultivation"), to forbid the sale of all property on the plains to half-castes, to deny them the right of acquiring any house-property, to force all those up to the degree of quarteron and all those

[7] Lebeau, *De la Condition des Gens de Couleur Libres sous l'Ancien Régime*, Poitiers, 1903.

whites who had married people of colour to that degree, to
sell all their slaves within a year. "For," said the Council,
"these are dangerous people, more friendly to the slaves, to
whom they are still attached, than to us who oppress them
by the subordination which we demand and the scorn with
which we treat them. In a revolution, in a moment of tension, they would be the first to break the yoke which
weighed on them, the more because they are richer and are
now accustomed to have white debtors, since when they no
longer have sufficient respect for us." But the colonists could
not carry out these sweeping plans. The Mulattoes, unlike
the German Jews, were already too numerous, and the revolution would have begun there and then.

The colonists had to content themselves with throwing
on these rivals every humiliation that ingenuity and malice
could devise. Between 1758 and the revolution the per-
secutions mounted.[9] The Mulattoes were forbidden to wear
swords and sabres and European dress. They were forbidden to buy ammunition except by special permission with
the exact quantity stated. They were forbidden to meet
together "on the pretext" of weddings, feasts or dances,
under penalty of a fine for the first offence, imprisonment
for the next, and worse to follow. They were forbidden to
stay in France. They were forbidden to play European
games. The priests were forbidden to draw up any documents for them. In 1781, eight years before the revolution,
they were forbidden to take the titles of Monsieur and
Madame. Up to 1791, if a white man ate in their house,
they could not sit at table with him. The only privilege the
whites allowed them was the privilege of lending white
men money.

Short of insurrection, there was no way out of this.
And until the Bastille fell the efforts of the Mulattoes to
emancipate themselves assumed strange forms. De Vaissière has unearthed a story, which we can understand better after Hitlerism than we could have done before. In

[8] Lebeau, *De la Condition* . . . ; De Vaissière, Chapter III;
*Saint-Domingue à la veille de la Révolution. Souvenirs du Baron
de Wimpffen*, Edited by Savine, pp. 36-38 etc.

1771 the Sieur Chapuzet had obtained from the Council
of Le Cap a decree which gave him the privileges of a
white man, his obscure career preventing any questions
begin raised about his origin. A little later he attempted to
become an officer in the militia. Four lieutenants in the
militia of the North Plain made minute researches into the
records and presented an exact genealogy of the Chapuzet
family, proving that a maternal ancestor, 150 years back,
was a Negro from St. Kitts. De Chapuzet defended himself, "in law and in fact," in law because the power of deciding on the status of a citizen was the prerogative of the
Government and not of private individuals, in fact because in 1624 there were no Negroes in St Kitts. Colonial
history was now the terrain. With extracts from the historians the whites proved that there were slaves in St Kitts
in 1624. Chapuzet admitted defeat and left for France.

Three years after, he returned, calling himself M.
Chapuzet de Guérin, or familiarly M. le Guérin. Aristocrat
at least in name, by means of a sponsor he again brought
his case for being considered a white man before the courts.
Once more he was defeated. But Chapuzet was a man of
resource. He claimed that this ancestor, "the St Kitts
Negro", was no Negro, but a Carib, a free-born Carib, a
member of "that noble race on whom the French and Spaniards had imposed the law of conquest." Chapuzet triumphed. In 1779 two decrees of the Council declared that
his claims were justified. But he did not get his rank. The
local officials dared not appoint him. Following the publica-
tion of the decrees, the people of colour abandoned themselves to such demonstrations of joy and foolish hopes that
the consequences of Chapuzet's appointment might have
been very dangerous. The doors of Chapuzet's lawyer were
besieged with quarterons and other fair-skinned Mulattoes
seeking to have their remote slave ancestors transformed
into free and noble Caribs.

The advantages of being white were so obvious that
race prejudice against the Negroes permeated the minds of

the Mulattoes who so bitterly resented the same thing from the whites. Black slaves and Mulattoes hated each other. Even while in words and, by their success in life, in many of their actions, Mulattoes demonstrated the falseness of the white claim to inherent superiority, yet the man of colour who was nearly white despised the man of colour who was only half-white, who in turn despised the man of colour who was only quarter white, and so on through all the shades.

The free blacks, comparatively speaking, were not many, and so despised was the black skin that even a Mulatto slave felt himself superior to the free black man. The Mulatto, rather than be slave to a black, would have killed himself.

It all reads like a cross between a nightmare and a bad joke. But these distinctions still exercise their influence in the West Indies to-day.[9] While whites in Britain dislike the half-caste more than the full-blooded Negro, whites in the West Indies favour the half-caste against the blacks. These, however, are matters of social prestige. But the racial discriminations in Africa to-day are, as they were in San Domingo, matters of Government policy, enforced by bullets and bayonets, and we have lived to see the rulers of a European nation make the Aryan grandmother as precious for their fellow-countrymen as the Carib ancestor was to the Mulatto. The cause in each case is the same—the justification of plunder by any obvious differentiation from those holding power. It is as well to remind the reader that a trained observer travelling in the West Indies in 1935 says of the coloured men there, "A few at the top, judges, barristers, doctors, whatever their shade of colour, could hold their own in any circle. A great many more are the intellectual equals or superiors of their own white contemporaries." [10] Many of the Mulattoes and free blacks were backward in comparison to the whites but their capacity was perfectly obvious in San Domingo in the years before

[9] Still true, in 1961.
[10] Macmillan, *Warning from the West Indies*, London, 1936, p. 49.

1789. It took gunpowder and cold steel to convince the San Domingo whites. And if, as we have seen, the most intelligent of them did not delude themselves about the materialist origins of their prejudice against the Mulattoes, we yet will make a great mistake if we think that they were hypocrites when they claimed that a white skin guaranteed to the owner superior abilities and entitled him to a monopoly of the best that the colony afforded.

"Upon the different forms of property, upon the social conditions of existence as foundation, there is built a superstructure of diversified and characteristic sentiments, illusions, habits of thought, and outlooks on life in general. The class as a whole creates and shapes them out of its material foundation, and out of the corresponding social relationships. The individual in whom they arise, through tradition and education, may fancy them to be the true determinants, the real origin of his activities." [11] On this common derivation of prejudice, small whites, big whites and bureaucracy were united against Mulattoes. It had been so for one hundred and fifty years, and therefore it would always be so. But would it? The higher bureaucrats, cultivated Frenchmen, arrived in the island without prejudice; and looking for mass support used to help the Mulattoes a little. And Mulattoes and big whites had a common bond—property. Once the revolution was well under way the big whites would have to choose between their allies of race and their allies of property. They would not hesitate long.

Such was the society of this famous colony. These were the people, and this the life, for whom in part so much blood was shed and so much suffering borne. The best minds of the time had no illusions about it. Baron de Wimpffen, who saw the colony in 1790 at the very summit of its prosperity, one day saw a slave leaning on the handle of his hoe, looking sadly into the sunset. "What are you doing, Nazimbo?" he asked. "What are you looking at?"

[11] Karl Marx, *The Eighteenth Brumaire*.

Nazimbo extended his hand towards the setting sun. "I see my own country," he replied, and tears rolled from his eyes. "I saw my own country there also," said de Wimpffen to himself, "and I have the hope of seeing it again one day, but you, poor Negro, will never see yours again." Educated Liberal and common slave alike detested the place. A few months later de Wimpffen left and put his opinion on record. It is a fitting epitaph of that society which within three years was to be destroyed. "Do you wish to know my final word on this country? It is that the more I get to know the men who inhabit it, the more I congratulate myself on leaving it. . . . When one is what the greater part of the planters are, one is born to own slaves. When one is what the greater part of the slaves are, one is born to be a slave. In this country everybody is in his place."

Prosperity is not a moral question and the justification of San Domingo was its prosperity. Never for centuries had the western world known such economic progress. By 1754, two years before the beginning of the Seven Years' War, there were 599 plantations of sugar and 3,379 of indigo. During the Seven Years' War (1756-1763) the French marine, swept off the sea by the British Navy, could not bring the supplies on which the colony depended, the extensive smuggling trade could not supply the deficiency, thousands of slaves died from starvation and the upward rise of production, though not halted, was diminished. But after the Treaty of Paris in 1763 the colony made a great stride forward. In 1767 it exported 72 million pounds' weight of raw sugar and 51 million pounds of white, a million pounds of indigo and two million pounds of cotton, and quantities of hides, molasses, cocoa and rum. Smuggling, which was winked at by the authorities, raised the official figures by at least 25 per cent. Nor was it only in quantity that San Domingo excelled but in quality. Each coffee tree produced on an average a pound weight, equal sometimes to that of Mocha. Cotton grew naturally, even without care, in stony ground and in the crevices of the rocks. Indigo also grew spontaneously. Tobacco had a larger leaf there than in any other part of the Americas and sometimes equalled in quality the produce of Havana. The kernel of San Domingo cocoa was more acidulated than that of Venezuela and was not inferior in other respects, experience proving that the chocolate made of the two cocoas in combination had a more delicate flavour than that made from the cocoa of Venezuela alone.

If on no earthly spot was so much misery concentrated as on a slave-ship, then on no portion of the globe did its surface in proportion to its dimensions yield so much wealth as the colony of San Domingo.

And yet it was this very prosperity which would lead to the revolution.

From the beginning the colonists were at variance with the French Government and the interests it represented. The French, like every other Government in those days, looked upon colonies as existing exclusively for the profit of the metropolis. Known as the Mercantile system in England, the French called this economic tyranny by a more honest name, the Exclusive. Whatever manufactured goods the colonists needed they were compelled to buy from France. They could sell their produce only to France. The goods were to be transported only in French ships. Even the raw sugar produced in the colonies was to be refined in the mother-country, and the French imposed heavy duties on refined sugar of colonial origin. "The colonies," said Colbert, "are founded by and for the metropolis." This was not true. The colonists had founded San Domingo themselves, and the falsehood of the claim made the exploitation all the harder to bear.

In 1664 the French Government, in accordance with the custom of those days, handed over the rights of trade with San Domingo to a private company. But the monopolists either could not or would not send out all the goods that the colonists wanted, and charged them nearly twice as much as they were accustomed to pay. The colonists revolted and the Governor was compelled to ease the restrictions. In 1722 the same thing happened. Agents received from the company the exclusive grant of the African trade, in return for supplying San Domingo with 2,000 Negroes every year. But by 1720 the colonists were needing 8,000 slaves a year, and they knew that in addition to supplying them with only one-quarter of their needs, the company would raise the price. There was another insurrection. The colonists arrested the Governor and put him in prison, and the Government had to modify the privileges of the company. The colonists saw themselves held in check by the Exclusive for the benefit of the metropolis, and as their prosperity grew they found the restrictions more and more intolerable. Political dependence on the mother-country was now retarding the economic growth of San Domingo. The colonists wished to shake off these shackles as Britain's American colonies were to shake off theirs. Thus if big whites and small whites were in permanent conflict with each other, they were united against the Mulattoes on the one hand and against the French bourgeoisie on the other. They could persecute the Mulattoes, but against the French bourgeoisie they could do nothing but rage. Long before 1789 the French bourgeoisie was the most powerful economic force in France, and the slave-trade and the colonies were the basis of its wealth and power.

The slave-trade and slavery were the economic basis of the French Revolution. "Sad irony of human history," comments Jaurès. "The fortunes created at Bordeaux, at Nantes, by the slave-trade, gave to the bourgeoisie that pride which needed liberty and contributed to human emancipation." Nantes was the centre of the slave-trade. As early as 1666, 108 ships went to the coast of Guinea and took on board 37,430 slaves,[12] to a total value of more than 37 millions, giving the Nantes bourgeoisie 15 to 20 per cent on their money. In 1700 Nantes was sending 50 ships

[12] This section is based on the work of Jaurès, *Histoire Socialiste de la Révolution Française*, Paris, 1922, pp. 62-84.

a year to the West Indies with Irish salt beef, linen for the household and for clothing the slaves, and machinery for sugar-mills. Nearly all the industries which developed in France during the eighteenth century had their origin in goods or commodities destined either for the coast of Guinea or for America. The capital from the slave-trade fertilized them; though the bourgeoisie traded in other things than slaves, upon the success or failure of the traffic everything else depended.[18]

Some ships took on the way wine from Madeira for the colonists and dried turtle from Cape Verde for the slaves. In return they brought back colonial produce to Nantes whence Dutch vessels took it to Northern Europe. Some made the return journey by way of Spain and Portugal, exchanging their colonial cargo for the products of those countries. Sixty ships from Rochelle and Oberon brought their salted cod to Nantes, to go to the inland market or out to the colonies to feed the slaves. The year 1758 saw the first manufactory of Indian cloth, to weave the raw cotton of India and the West Indian islands.

The planters and small manufacturers of San Domingo were able to establish themselves only by means of the capital advanced by the maritime bourgeoisie. By 1789 the Nantes merchants alone had 50 millions invested in the West Indies.

Bordeaux had begun with the wine industry which gave its ship-builders and navigators an opportunity to trade all over the world; then came brandy, also to all ports, but above all to the colonies. By the middle of the eighteenth century, 16 factories refined 10,000 tons of raw sugar from San Domingo every year, using nearly 4,000 tons of charcoal. Local factories supplied the town with jars, dishes and bottles. The trade was cosmopolitan— Flemings, Germans, Dutchmen, Irishmen and Englishmen came to live in Bordeaux, contributing to the general expansion and amassing riches for themselves. Bordeaux traded with Holland, Germany, Portugal, Venice, and Ire-

[18] Gaston-Martin, *L'Ère des Négriers* (1714-1774), Paris, 1931, p. 424.

land, but slavery and the colonial trade were the fount and
origin and sustenance of this thriving industry and far-
flung commerce.

Marseilles was the great centre for the Mediterranean
and Eastern trade, and a royal decree at the beginning of
the century had attempted to exclude it from the trade
with the colonies. The attempt failed. San Domingo was
the special centre of the Marseilles trade. Marseilles sent
there not only the wines of Provence: in 1789 there were
in Marseilles 12 sugar refineries, nearly as many as in Bordeaux.

In the early years most of this trade had been carried
in foreign-built or foreign-owned ships. But by 1730 the
maritime bourgeois began to build themselves. In 1778
Bordeaux ship-owners constructed seven vessels, in 1784
they constructed 32, with a total of 115 for the six years.
A Marseilles ship-owner, Georges Roux, could fit out a fleet
on his own account in order to take vengeance on the English fleet for the prizes it had taken.

Nantes, Bordeaux and Marseilles were the chief centres of the maritime bourgeoisie, but Orleans, Dieppe,
Bercy-Paris, a dozen great towns, refined raw sugar and
shared in the subsidiary industries.[14] A large part of the
hides worked in France came from San Domingo. The
flourishing cotton industry of Normandy drew its raw cotton in part from the West Indies, and in all its ramifications
the cotton trade occupied the population of more than a
hundred French towns. In 1789 exchanges with the American colonies were 296 millions. France exported to the islands 78 millions of flour, salted meats, wines and stuffs.
The colonies sent to France 218 millions of sugar, coffee,
cocoa, wood, indigo and hides. Of the 218 millions imported only 71 millions were consumed in France. The rest
was exported after preparation. The total value of the colonies represented 3,000 millions, and on them depended the
livelihood of a number of Frenchmen variously estimated
at between two and six millions. By 1789 San Domingo

14 Deschamps, *Les Colonies pendant la Révolution*, Paris, 1898,
pp. 3-8.

was the market of the new world. It received in its ports
1,587 ships, a greater number than Marseilles, and France
used for the San Domingo trade alone 750 great vessels
employing 24,000 sailors. In 1789 Britain's export trade
would be 27 million pounds, that of France 17 million
pounds, of which the trade of San Domingo would account
for nearly 11 million pounds. The whole of Britain's colonial trade in that year amounted to only five million
pounds.[15]

The maritime bourgeoisie would not hear of any
change in the Exclusive. They had the ear of the Minister
and the Government, and not only were the colonists refused permission to trade with foreign countries, but the
circulation of all French currency, except the very lowest,
was forbidden in the islands, lest the colonists use it to purchase foreign goods. In such a method of trade they were
at the mercy of the bourgeoisie. In 1774 their indebtedness
was 200 millions, and by 1789 it was estimated at between
300 and 500 millions.[16] If the colonists complained of the
Exclusive, the bourgeoisie complained that the colonists
would not pay their debts, and agitated for stricter measures against the contraband.

Rich as was the French bourgeoisie, the colonial trade
was too big for it. The British bourgeois, most successful
of slave-traders, sold thousands of smuggled slaves every
year to the French colonists and particularly to San Domingo. But even while they sold the slaves to San Domingo,
the British were watching the progress of this colony with
alarm and with envy. After the independence of America
in 1783, this amazing French colony suddenly made such
a leap as almost to double its production between 1783 and
1789. In those years Bordeaux alone invested 100 millions
in San Domingo. The British bourgeois were the great
rivals of the French. All through the eighteenth century

---

[15] Brougham, *The Colonial Policy of the European Powers*,
Edinburgh, 1803, vol. II, pp. 538-540.
[16] Deschamps, *Les Colonies pendant* . . . , p. 25.

they fought in every part of the world. The French had jumped gleefully in to help drive them out of America. San Domingo was now incomparably the finest colony in the world and its possibilities seemed limitless. The British bourgeoisie investigated the new situation in the West Indies, and on the basis of what it saw, prepared a bombshell for its rivals. Without slaves San Domingo was doomed. The British colonies had enough slaves for all the trade they were ever likely to do. With the tears rolling down their cheeks for the poor suffering blacks, those British bourgeois who had no West Indian interests set up a great howl for the abolition of the slave-trade.

A venal race of scholars, profiteering panders to national vanity, have conspired to obscure the truth about abolition. Up to 1783 the British bourgeoisie had taken the slave-trade for granted. In 1773 and again in 1774, the Jamaica Assembly, afraid of insurrection and seeking to raise revenue, taxed the importation of slaves. In great wrath the British Board of Trade disallowed the measures and told the Governor that he would be sacked if he gave his sanction to any similar Bill.[17] Well-meaning persons talked of the iniquity of slavery and the slave-trade, as well-meaning persons in 1938 talked about the native question in Africa or the misery of the Indian peasant. Dr. Johnson toasted the next slave insurrection in the West Indies. Stray members of parliament introduced Bills for the abolition of the slave-trade which the House rejected without much bother. In 1783 Lord North turned down a petition against the trade:[18] the petition did credit to the Christian feelings, and to the humane breast, etc., etc., but the trade was necessary. With the loss of America, however, a new situation arose.

The British found that by the abolition of the mercantile system with America, they gained instead of losing. It

[17] *House of Commons: Accounts and Papers,* 1795-1796, vol. 100.
[18] *Parliamentary History,* XXIII, pp. 1026-1027.

was the first great lesson in the advantages of free trade. But if Britain gained the British West Indies suffered. The rising industrial bourgeoisie, feeling its way to free trade and a greater exploitation of India, began to abuse the West Indies, called them "sterile rocks," [19] and asked if the interest and independence of the nation should be sacrificed to 72,000 masters and 400,000 slaves.[20]

The industrial bourgeois were beginning their victorious attack upon the agricultural monopoly which was to culminate in the Repeal of the Corn Laws in 1846. The West Indian sugar-producers were monopolists whose methods of production afforded an easy target, and Adam Smith [21] and Arthur Young,[22] the forerunners of the new era, condemned the whole principle of slave-labour as the most expensive in the world. Besides, why not get sugar from India? India, after the loss of America, assumed a new importance. The British experimented with sugar in Bengal, received glowing reports and in 1791 the first shipments arrived.[23] In 1793 Mr. Randle Jackson would preach to the company's shareholders a little sermon on the new orientation. "It seemed as if Providence, when it took from us America, would not leave its favourite people without an ample substitute; or who should say that Providence had not taken from us one member, more seriously to impress us with the value of another." [24] It might not be good theology, but it was very good economics. Pitt and Dundas

[19] *The Right in the West Indian Merchants to a Double Monopoly of the Sugar Market of Great Britain, and the expedience of all monopolies examined.* (n.d.)
[20] Chalmers, *Opinions on Interesting Subjects of Law and Commercial Policy arising from American Independence,* London, 1784, p. 60.
[21] Smith, *Wealth of Nations,* vol. I, p. 123. "It appears from the experience of all ages and nations . . . that the work done by freemen comes cheaper in the end than that performed by slaves."
[22] Young, *Annals of Agriculture,* 1788. Vol. IX, pp. 88-96. "The culture of sugar by slaves is the dearest species of labour in the world."
[23] *East India Sugar,* 1822, appendix I, p. 3.
[24] *Debate on the Expediency of cultivating sugar in the territories of the East India Company,* East India House, 1793

saw a chance of capturing the continental market from
France by East India sugar. There was cotton and indigo.
The production of cotton in India doubled in a few years.
Indian free labour cost a penny a day.

But the West Indian vested interests were strong,
statesmen do not act merely on speculation, and these possibilities by themselves would not have accounted for any
sudden change in British policy. It was the miraculous
growth of San Domingo that was decisive. Pitt found that
some 50 per cent of the slaves imported into the British
islands were sold to the French colonies.[25] It was the British slave-trade, therefore, which was increasing French
colonial produce and putting the European market into
French hands. Britain was cutting its own throat. And even
the profits from this export were not likely to last. Already
a few years before the slave merchants had failed for
£700,000 in a year.[26] The French, seeking to provide their
own slaves, were encroaching in Africa and increasing their
share of the trade every year. Why should they continue
to buy from Britain? Holland and Spain were doing the
same. By 1786 Pitt, a disciple of Adam Smith, had seen the
light clearly. He asked Wilberforce to undertake the campaign.[27] Wilberforce represented the important division of
Yorkshire, he had a great reputation, all the humanity, justice, stain on national character, etc., etc., would sound
well coming from him. Pitt was in a hurry—it was important to bring the trade to a complete stop quickly and suddenly. The French had neither the capital nor the organisation to make good the deficiency at once and he would
ruin San Domingo at a stroke. In 1787 he warned Wilberforce that if he did not bring the motion in, somebody else
would,[28] and in 1788 he informed the Cabinet that he

[25] *Report of the Committee of Privy Council for Trade and
Plantations,* 1789, Part IV, Tables for Dominica and Jamaica.
See also Dundas' statistics, April 18, 1792.
[26] Clarkson, *Essay on the Impolicy of the African Slave Trade,*
London, 1784, p. 29.
[27] Coupland, *The British Anti-Slavery Movement,* London,
1933, p. 74.
[28] Coupland, *Wilberforce,* Oxford, 1923, p 93

would not stay in it with those who opposed.[29] Pitt was fairly certain of success in England. With truly British nerve he tried to persuade the European Governments to abolish the trade on the score of inhumanity. The French Government discussed the proposal amicably, but by May, 1789, the British Ambassador wrote sadly that it seemed as if all the French Government's negotiations had been to "compliment us and to keep us quiet and in good humour." [30] The Dutch, less polite, gave a more abrupt negative. But here a great stroke of luck befell Pitt. France was then stirring with pre-revolutionary attacks on all obvious abuses, and one year after the Abolitionist Society had been formed in Britain, a group of Liberals in France, Brissot, Mirabeau, Pétion, Condorcet, Abbé Grégoire, all the great names of the first years of the revolution, followed the British example and formed a society, the Friends of the Negro. The leading spirit was Brissot, a journalist who had seen slavery in the United States. The society aimed at the abolition of slavery, published a journal, agitated. This suited the British down to the ground. Clarkson went to Paris, to stimulate "the slumbering energies" [31] of the society, gave it money, supplied France with British anti-slavery propaganda.[32] Despite the names that were to become so famous and a large membership, we must beware of thinking that the Friends of the Negro represented a force. The colonists took them seriously, the maritime bourgeoisie did not. It was the French Revolution which, with unexpected swiftness, would drag these eloquent Frenchmen out of the stimulating excitement of philanthropic propaganda and put them face to face with economic reality.

[29] *Fortescue MSS.* (Historical Manuscripts Commission, British Museum). Pitt to Grenville, June 29, 1788. Vol. I, p. 342.
[30] *Liverpool Papers* (Additional Manuscripts, British Museum). Lord Dorset to Lord Hawkesbury. Vol. 38224, p. 118.
[31] R. I. and S. Wilberforce, *Life of Wilberforce,* London, 1838, vol. I, p. 228.
[32] *Cahiers de la Révolution Française,* Paris, 1935, No. III, p. 25.

These then were the forces which in the decade preceding the French Revolution linked San Domingo to the economic destiny of three continents and the social and political conflicts of that pregnant age. A trade and method of production so cruel and so immoral that it would wilt before the publicity which a great revolution throws upon the sources of wealth; the powerful British Government determined to wreck French commerce in the Antilles, agitating at home and intriguing in France among men who, unbeknown to themselves, would soon have power in their hands; the colonial world (itself divided) and the French bourgeoisie, each intent on its own purposes and, unaware of the approaching danger, drawing apart instead of closer together. Not one courageous leader, many courageous leaders were needed, but the science of history was not what it is to-day and no man living then could foresee, as we can foresee to-day, the coming upheavals.[33] Mirabeau indeed said that the colonists slept on the edge of Vesuvius, but for centuries the same thing had been said and the slaves had never done anything.

How could anyone seriously fear for such a wonderful colony? Slavery seemed eternal and the profits mounted. Never before, and perhaps never since, has the world seen anything proportionately so dazzling as the last years of pre-revolutionary San Domingo. Between 1783 and 1789 production nearly doubled. Between 1764 and 1771 the average importation of slaves varied between ten and fifteen thousand. In 1786 it was 27,000, and from 1787 onwards the colony was taking more than 40,000 slaves a year. But economic prosperity is no guarantee of social stability. That rests on the constantly shifting equilibrium between the classes. It was the prosperity of the bourgeoisie that started the English revolution of the seventeenth century. With every stride in production the colony was marching to its doom.

The enormous increase of slaves was filling the colony with native Africans, more resentful, more intractable,

[33] Written in 1938.

more ready for rebellion than the creole Negro. Of the half-a-million slaves in the colony in 1789, more than two-thirds had been born in Africa.

These slaves were being used for the opening up of new lands. There was no time to allow for the period of acclimatisation, known as the seasoning, and they died like flies. From the earliest days of the colony towards the middle of the eighteenth century, there had been some improvement in the treatment of the slaves, but this enormous number of newcomers who had to be broken and terrorised into labour and submission caused an increase in fear and severity. In 1784 the administrators, who visited one of the slave shops which sometimes served as a market-place instead of the deck of the slaver, reported a revolting picture of dead and dying thrown pell-mell into the filth. The Le Jeune case took place in 1788. In 1790 de Wimpffen states that not one article of the Negro Code was obeyed. He himself had sat at table with a woman, beautiful, rich and very much admired, who had had a careless cook thrown into the oven.

The problem of feeding this enormous increase in the slave population was making the struggle between the planters and the maritime bourgeoisie over the Exclusive more bitter than ever, and the planters after 1783 had forced a slight breach in the strait jacket which clasped them. Having tasted blood, they wanted more.

Mulattoes educated in Paris during the Seven Years' War had come home, and their education and accomplishments filled the colonists with hatred and envy and fear. It was these last years that saw the fiercest legislation against them. Forbidden to go to France, where they learnt things that were not good for them, they stayed at home to increase the strength of the dissatisfied.

With the growth of trade and of profits, the number or planters who could afford to leave their estates in charge of managers grew, and by 1789, in addition to the maritime bourgeois, there was a large group of absentee proprietors in France linked to the aristocracy by marriage, for whom San Domingo was nothing else but a source of revenue to be spent in the luxurious living of aristocratic Paris. So far had these parasites penetrated into the French aristocracy that a memoir from San Domingo to the King could say: "Sire, your court is creole," without too much stretching of the truth.

The prosperity affected even the slaves. More of them could save money, buy their freedom, and enter the promised land.

This was the San Domingo of 1789, the most profitable colony the world had ever known; to the casual eye the most flourishing and prosperous possession on the face of the globe; to the analyst a society torn by inner and outer contradictions which in four years would split that structure into so many pieces that they could never be put together again.

It was the French bourgeoisie which pressed the button. This strange San Domingo society was but a garish exaggeration, a crazy caricature, of the *ancien régime* in France. The royalist bureaucracy, incompetent and wasteful, could not manage the finances of France; the aristocracy and the clergy bled the peasantry dry, impeded the economic development of the country, gobbled up all the best places, and considered themselves almost as superior to the able and vigorous bourgeois as the white planters considered themselves superior to the Mulattoes.

But the French bourgeoisie too was proud and no members of it were prouder than the maritime bourgeois. We have seen their wealth. They knew that they were the foundation of the country's prosperity. They were buying up the land of the aristocracy. They built great schools and universities, they read Voltaire and Rousseau, they sent their linen to the colonies to be washed and to get the right colour and scent, they sent their wine for two or three voyages to the colonies and back to give it the right flavour. They, along with the other bourgeois, chafed at their social disadvantages; the chaotic state of French administration and finance handicapped them in their business. A hard

winter in 1788 brought matters to a head. The monarchy
was already bankrupt, the aristocracy made a bid to recover its former power, the peasants began to revolt, and
the bourgeoisie saw that the time had come for it to govern
the country on the English model in collaboration with its
allies, the radical aristocracy. In the agitation which began
the French Revolution, the maritime bourgeoisie took the
lead. The bourgeoisie of Dauphiné and Britanny, with their
ports of Marseilles and Nantes, attacked the monarchy
even before the official opening of the States-General, and
Mirabeau, the first leader of the revolution, was the deputy
for Marseilles.

From all over the country the cahiers, or lists of grievances, poured in. But the French people, like the vast
majority of Europeans to-day, had too many grievances of
their own to be concerned about the sufferings of Africans,
and only a few cahiers, chiefly from clergymen, demanded
the abolition of slavery. The States-General met. Mirabeau,
Pétion, Mayor of Paris, Abbé Grégoire, Condorcet, all
members of the Friends of the Negro, were deputies, all
pledged to abolition. But abolition for the maritime bourgeois was ruin. For the moment, however, the States-General grappled with the King.

While the French bourgeoisie led the assault on the
absolute monarchy at home, the planters followed suit in
the colonies. And, as in France, the geographical divisions
of San Domingo and their historical development shaped
the revolutionary movement and the coming insurrection
of the slaves.

The pride of the colony was the great North Plain of
which Le Cap was the chief port. Bounded on the north by
the ocean, and on the south by a ridge of mountains running almost the length of the island, it was about 50 miles
in length and between 10 and 20 miles in breadth. Cultivated since 1670, it was covered with plantations within
easy reach of each other. Le Cap was the centre of the island's economic, social and political life. In any revolution-

ary upheaval, the planters of the North Plain and the merchants and lawyers of Le Cap would take the lead. (But
the slave-gangs of the North Plain, in close proximity to
each other and the sooner aware of the various changes in
the political situation, would be correspondingly ready for
political action.)

Very different was the West Province, with its isolated
plantations scattered over wide areas. In districts like the
Artibonite, Verrettes, Mirabelais, and St Marc, there were
many Mulatto proprietors, some of great wealth.

The South Province was a sort of pariah, somewhat
sparsely populated, with a majority of Mulattoes. The eastern end, Cape Tiburon, was only some 50 miles from
Jamaica and here the contraband trade was particularly
strong.

Early in 1788 the North Province took the lead. It
formed a secret committee to secure representation in the
States-General. In Paris the group of wealthy absentee
noblemen formed a committee for the same purpose, the
two groups collaborated and the Paris noblemen refused to
accept the veto of the King. At the end of 1788 the colonists summoned electoral assemblies and elected a delegation, some of whom consisted of their allies in Paris. In
their cahier they claimed abolition of military justice and
the institution of a civil judiciary; all legislation and taxes
to be voted by provincial assemblies subject only to the
approval of the King and a Colonial Committee sitting at
Paris but elected by themselves. By restricting political
rights to owners of land the planters effectively excluded
the small whites who took little interest in all this agitation.
Of the slaves and Mulattoes, they said not a word. Slaves
did not count, and the Mulattoes secured permission from
the frightened bureaucracy to send a deputation to Paris
on their own account. But a number of the planters at
home, and quite a few in Paris, the Club Massiac, viewed
this desire to be represented in the States-General with distrust. The agitation for abolition of the slave-trade in England, the propaganda of the Friends of the Negro, the
revolutionary temper of France, filled them with forebod

ing. Representation in the States-General by a few deputies
could effect nothing, and it would bring the full glare of
publicity and awakening political interest on the state of
society in San Domingo, which was exactly what they did
not want. But while the pro-representation group were in
a minority, having a positive aim they were bold and confident. Their opponents, with bad consciences and aiming
only at avoiding trouble, could oppose no effective resistance. Colonial representation in a metropolitian assembly
was an innovation unheard of at that time, but the San
Domingo representatives, profiting by the revolutionary
ferment in Paris, circumvented the objections of the King
and Minister. They petitioned the nobility who cold-shoul-
dered them. But when Louis tried to intimidate the Third
Estate, and the deputies went to the tennis-court and swore
that being the representatives of the people they would
never adjourn, Gouy d'Arsy, leader of the colonists, boldly
led his group of colonial noblemen into this historic meeting. Out of gratitude for this unexpected support, the bourgeoisie welcomed them, and thus France admitted the principle of colonial representation. Full of confidence these
slave owners claimed 18 seats, but Mirabeau turned fiercely
on them: "You claim representation proportionate to the
number of the inhabitants. The free blacks are proprietors
and tax-payers, and yet they have not been allowed to
vote. And as for the slaves, either they are men or they are
not; if the colonists consider them to be men, let them free
them and make them electors and eligible for seats; if the
contrary is the case, have we, in apportioning deputies according to the population of France, taken into consideration the number of our horses and our mules?"

San Domingo was allowed only six deputies. In less
than five minutes the great Liberal orator had placed the
case of the Friends of the Negro squarely before the whole
of France in unforgettable words. The San Domingo representatives realised at last what they had done; they had
tied the fortunes of San Domingo to the assembly of a people in revolution and thenceforth the history of liberty in

France and of slave emancipation in San Domingo is one
and indivisible.

Unaware of these portentous developments the colonists in San Domingo were going from victory to victory.
As in France, the last months of 1788 in San Domingo had
been hard. France had had to prohibit the export of grain,
and under these circumstances the Exclusive was a tyran-
nical imposition threatening the island with famine. The
Governor opened certain ports to foreign ships; the Intendant, Barbé de Marbois, agreed to the first small
breaches but refused to sanction their extension. The matter went to the King's Council who repudiated the Governor, recalled him, and appointed a new Governor, with
the colonists calling for the blood of the Intendant. This
was the situation when on a day in September a boat sailed
into the harbour, and the captain, hurrying ashore, ran
down the streets of Le Cap, shouting the news of July 14th.
The King had been preparing to disperse the Constituent
Assembly by force, and the Paris masses, arming themselves, had stormed the Bastille as the symbol of feudal
reaction. The great French Revolution had begun.

III

Parliament and Property

NEARLY all the creoles in San Domingo donned the red cockade, foremost among the agitators being those planters most heavily indebted to the maritime bourgeoisie. The militia was transformed into a National Guard in imitation of the National Guards of revolutionary France. The colonists gave themselves striking uniforms and military decorations, christened themselves captains, brigadiers and generals. They lynched the few who openly opposed them, and having no enemy to fight against they invented some. A detachment of the National Guard marched out of Le

Cap against some rebel Negroes and after hours of weary tramping returned to the town with one of their number mortally wounded, not by the revolting Negroes (there were none) but by the bullets of his own companions. When, two years later, the insurrection broke out, the first chiefs were the blacks who had served as guides in this idiotic expedition.

To escape lynching, Barbé de Marbois and some of the most unpopular bureaucrats fled to France and, in defiance of the Governor, the Provincial Committee claimed the direction of affairs and began to make preparations for an election in the North Province. In January, 1790, came authority from the Minister to form a Colonial Assembly, and three Provincial bodies summoned this Assembly to meet in the town of St Marc.

De Feynier, the Governor, was an old man and weak, but even a strong man would have been in difficulties. For the absolute monarchy, paralysed by the revolution in Paris, could no longer give support to its representatives in the colonies. The small whites, as soon as they heard of the fall of the Bastille, had deserted their friends the bureaucracy and joined the revolution. There was only one hope for the bureaucrats—the Mulattoes, and the Governor instructed the commandants of the districts to adopt a new attitude towards them. "It has become more necessary than ever not to give them any cause for offence, to encourage them and to treat them as friends and whites." [1] The retreat of race prejudice had begun. Sad though it may be, that is the way that humanity progresses. The anniversary orators and the historians supply the prose-poetry and the flowers.

The plan succeeded admirably and the Mulattoes, in sheer self-defence against the murderous violence of the small whites and the revolutionaries, everywhere supported the royalist bureaucracy and military. Greed fortified prejudice. At the beginning of the agitation when the rich

[1] Michel, *La Mission du Général Hédouville à Saint-Domingue.* Port-au-Prince, Haiti, 1929, Vol. 1, pp. 11-12.

whites controlled the movement, they had made overtures
to the rich Mulattoes. But the entry of the small whites
changed this completely. The fiery (and heavily indebted)
politicians who were now leading the revolution in San
Domingo and the propertyless small whites wanted to exterminate the Mulattoes and confiscate their property. The
whites were only 30,000. The Mulattoes and free blacks
were about the same, and increasing at a far greater rate
than the whites. Embittered by their persecution they
called the whites intruders and themselves nationals. The
revolutionaries spread it that unless the Mulattoes were
held down they would soon outnumber the whites and
drive them out of the colony. And now the Mulattoes had
joined the counter-revolution.

Near the end of the year came the news of Mulatto
success in Paris. On October 22nd, the National Assembly
had received them, and the president in reply to their petition had said that no part of the nation would appeal for
its rights in vain to the assembled representatives of the
French people. On December 4th, one of the leading lights
of the revolution at that time, the Count Charles de Lameth,
in revolutionary enthusiasm uttered the famous words, "I
am one of the greatest proprietors in San Domingo, but
I declare to you that I would prefer to lose all I possess
there rather than violate the principles that justice and humanity have consecrated. I declare myself both for the
admission of the half-castes into the administrative assemblies and for the liberty of the blacks!" Not only political
rights for Mulattoes but the abolition of slavery. The news
of this drove white San Domingo to fury. How could they
know that these words were merely spoken in a Pickwick-
ian sense, that Lameth, a right-wing Liberal, would be one
of the most tenacious enemies of both political rights for
the Mulattoes and abolition. They began to terrorize the
Mulattoes.

Lacombe, a Mulatto, claimed for his people social
and political rights. The whites of Le Cap hanged him on
the spot: giving the reason that in heading his petition "In
the name of the Father, of the Son and of the Holy Ghost,"

he had departed from the established formula. M. de Baudière, a white-haired seneschal, drafted a moderate petition for some Mulattoes seeking to improve their status. The whites from the surrounding district lynched him, paraded his head on a pike and shamefully mutilated his dead body. Leaders in this terror were the small whites: the managers and stewards of the plantations and the mass of the townsmen. In some parishes of the North, white planters had summoned the Mulattoes to the primary assemblies. The small whites refused to have them, and their example gradually spread to the country where these small whites enjoyed sitting in assemblies from which the wealthy coloured proprietors were excluded. One primary assembly of the West Province even declared that the men of colour would not be allowed to take the civic oath without adding to the general formula the promise of respect for the whites.

The Mulattoes of Artibonite and Verrettes, rich and numerous, refused to take any such oath and issued the call for an insurrection to their brothers all over the island. The whites summoned all their forces and the rising petered out. But at this the richer planters were thoroughly frightened. The Mulatto chiefs fled and there were only a few arrests. Despite the shrill clamour of the small whites, the rich planters attempted no reprisals. The planters all over the country, and especially in the West Province, were becoming nervous of the behaviour of the small whites. Formerly respectful, they had been for a moment flattered by being treated as equals. But they were pushing forward, eager to use the revolution for the purpose of becoming officials and masters. In the elections for the new Assembly they used intimidation and violence against the richer whites in order to ensure majorities. The rich planters began to look more to the hitherto hated royal authority, and towards a compromise with the other caste of slave-owners, the rich Mulattoes. San Domingo had received the news of the fall of the Bastille in September. Now, barely six months after, in face of the revolutionary small whites, and the extreme revolutionaries in the Colonial Assembly, wealthy San Domingo was following the bureaucrats and drawing nearer to the rich Mulattoes. God had undoubtedly made the black blood inferior to the white, the Exclusive was a monstrous imposition, the bureaucracy was a burden. But these owners of hundreds of slaves were already prepared to turn a blind eye to these century old tenets of their caste in face of the dangers they saw ahead.

The Colonial Assembly, says Deschamps, sincerely believed itself to be a miniature Constituent Assembly. But the coarse San Domingo whites had no spark of that exalted sentiment which drove the revolutionary bourgeoisie elsewhere to dignify its seizure of power with the Declaration of Independence or the Rights of Man. They wasted no time but struck blow after blow at the Exclusive, repudiated the control of the National Assembly, and acknowledged allegiance only to the King. But here their troubles began.

The Assembly of the North Province was composed chiefly of lawyers and Le Cap merchants who represented the great financial and commercial interests of the maritime bourgeois. For them any break with France would have been ruin. Under this new constitution the men of St Marc would have had the last word on the millions of francs they owed to France. And when the Assembly of St Marc passed a decree condemning the usury of the merchants and lawyers of Le Cap the Provincial Assembly of the North (of course on the highest grounds of patriotism) broke with St Marc instantly, withdrawing its members. But although they were opposed to the Assembly of St Marc, the men of the North Plain were themselves bourgeois, linked to the maritime bourgeois of France and, therefore, supporters of the revolution and enemies of the royalist bureaucracy. San Domingo, therefore, had three white parties: the royalist bureaucracy, in other words the counter-revolution, growing stronger every day as the rich planters continued to withdraw from the Assembly of St

Marc; the Assembly of St Marc itself, the Patriots, as they called themselves; and the Provincial Assembly of the North, watching both sides but for the time being supporting the Government as the link with France. All three despised the bastard Mulattoes, but all three needed them. The Provincial Assembly of the North had begun by making overtures to them. The royalist bureaucracy was openly cultivating good relations. The Assembly of St Marc now made advances in return for support in the struggle for independence.[2] The Mulattoes would not listen to them, whereupon the Patriots returned to the belief that free men of colour were contrary to the laws of God and man and should be exterminated. To them in this ferocious mood came the decree of March 8th, passed by the Constituent Assembly in France.

The French bourgeoisie was bound to face the colonial question some time but it dodged the issue as long as it could.

In September, 1789, the Mulatto delegation went to the Club Massiac and asked white support for the rights it would demand from the National Assembly. The Club Massiac rejected the petition. But these planters also wanted independence and secretly tried to bargain with Raimond, the Mulatto leader: Mulatto rights in return for support of independence.[3] Raimond refused. Everything now depended on the National Assembly. But the colonial whites swore that the granting of rights to Mulattoes meant the ruin of the colonies and the bourgeoisie didn't want the colonies ruined. Suddenly the Paris masses entered again into politics, gave the Mulattoes an unshakable foundation

[2] Commissioner Roume to the Committee of Public Safety, *Les Archives du Ministère des Affaires Étrangères. Fonds Divers, Section Amérique*, No. 14, folio 258. See also in this connection, Garran-Coulon, *Rapport sur les Troubles de Saint-Domingue, fait au nom de la Commission des Colonies, des Comités de Salut Public, de Législation, et de la Marine, Réunis*, 4 volumes, Paris, 1798, Vol. II, pp. 7-8.
[3] Garran-Coulon, *Rapport sur les Troubles de Saint-Domingue* . . . Vol. II, p. 6.

for their claim, and completed the colonial confusion of
the bourgeoisie.

The taking of the Bastille on July 14th had done more
than intimidate the King and the Court. It had frightened
the bourgeoisie, who hastened to form a National Guard,
strictly excluding the poor. But the bourgeoisie hastened
also to profit by the blow against the monarchy. It drew
up the Declaration of the Rights of Man and the Citizen,
claiming that all men were born free and equal, and abolishing the caste distinctions of feudalism for ever. The
Constituent voted the final draft almost unanimously, but
the King would not sign and secretly prepared the counter-
revolution. News of this reached Paris and the masses,
chiefly the women, marched to Versailles. Still trusting in
the King, they brought him to Paris (away, as they
thought, from his evil counsellors) and the Assembly came
with him. Beaten again, and again not by the bourgeoisie
but by the people, the King signed. This was early in October and a fortnight later, on October 22nd, the Mulattoes
appeared at the bar of a House still echoing with the famous declaration, and claimed the Rights of Man. The bourgeoisie did not know what to do, did not know what to
say. Raimond, the leader, was a distinguished Parisian lawyer, Ogé was a member of the Friends of the Negro and
a friend of the Abbé Grégoire, Brissot, the Marquis de
Condorcet, and all that brilliant band. Such were his talents
that it was said of him that there was no position to which
he could not aspire. How could an Assembly which had
just passed the Rights of Man refuse to relieve these men
from the injustices under which they suffered? They based
their claim not only on abstract grounds but on their
wealth, and offered six millions as security for the National
Debt. It was an unanswerable case, and the president gave
them his cordial if careful welcome. But the colonists in
Paris would have none of it. They threatened the bourgeoisie with the spectre of a slave revolt on the one hand
and their own independence on the other, and the maritime bourgeois, frightened for their millions of investments
and their trade, went red in the face and put the Rights of

Man in their pockets whenever the colonial question came up. Unfortunately for itself the bourgeoisie was not homogeneous and the radical wing in the House espoused the cause of the Mulattoes. The Assembly, hitherto unanimous on the Rights of Man, split into two, extreme right and extreme left, with the wobblers in between.

On the right were the colonial deputies, the absentee proprietors, the agents of the colonists, and the representatives of the maritime bourgeois, with all their ramifications. The colonists were seeking independence, or at least a large measure of autonomy, in order to break the Exclusive and rid themselves of the royalist bureaucracy. The maritime bourgeoisie, at one with them in their attack on the bureaucracy, was determined to maintain as much of the Exclusive as it could. Both parties were agreed on the necessity for what they called "order" in the colonies, and the colonists, as men who knew, said that "order" could only be maintained if the Mulattoes were kept in their place. In the Assembly the colonial deputies said as little as possible, abstained from all resolutions, delayed every discussion dealing with the colonies, accused the Friends of the Negro of serving foreign interests, denied that Mulattoes and free Negroes suffered grievances, promised that all the grievances of the Mulattoes and free Negroes would be redressed in colonial assemblies. They conspired with the maritime bourgeois to prevent Mulattoes and Negroes from going back to San Domingo, and even extended this prohibition to whites who were sympathetic to the Mulatto cause. When complaints were made to the Minister, he replied that he had given no orders to prevent free passages but that he had no authority to stop this constraint. Not for the last time in history the counter-revolution and everything wealthy in the revolution found common ground on the colonial question.

On the other side were the radicals, humanitarians and philosophers, the intellectuals of the day, led by the Friends of the Negro. Looked upon as dreamers and unpractical men, the solution they proposed, rights to Mulattoes and gradual abolition of slavery, would have best served the interests of France, and, as time proved, the interests of the colonists themselves. But when did property ever listen to reason except when cowed by violence? Against the wealth, the connections and the unscrupulous intrigues of the vested interests, even the radical propagandists were helpless. Their strength was in the masses, and the Paris masses were not yet interested in the colonial question, though they gave a general support to the demands of the Mulattoes.

But except for a few half-hearted attempts by the Friends of the Negro, everybody conspired to forget the slaves.

At first the Right had it their own way, but the colonial question again and again split the bourgeoisie, made it ashamed of itself, destroyed its morale and weakened its capacity to deal with the great home problems which faced it. With Mirabeau's words ringing in their ears the colonists wanted to get colonial questions removed from general discussion and proposed that they should be handed over to a Colonial Commission, consisting of ten merchants and ten colonists. The session ended in disorder. On December 3rd a great debate began and the motion for the Commission was defeated. The next day, Charles de Lameth made his grandiloquent declaration, and henceforth the granting of rights to the Mulattoes was looked upon as the first step towards the abolition of slavery itself.

On January 30th, 1790, the Mulattoes, sponsored by the Friends of the Negro, petitioned again. "Protestants, comedians, Jews, the relations of criminals," all had received their political rights from the Assembly. Yet Mulattoes were still excluded. The Assembly turned a deaf ear, but by February the news from San Domingo, Martinique and Guadeloupe was so ominous that on March 2nd the Assembly appointed a Commission to go through the documents and report in five days. This was exactly what the Club Massiac, the colonial deputies and the maritime bourgeois were playing for, and they had everything fixed. The

Commission, disinterested in appearance, consisted of 12 members, ten of whom represented some branch of the colonial trade. And in addition the intriguers had Barnave appointed chairman.

Barnave is one of the great figures of the French Revolution. He was bourgeois to the bone, a lawyer with a clear, cold intellect. For him, once the bourgeoisie had gained the Constitution and limited the franchise, the revolution was over. Like a good bourgeois he had an immense respect for royal and noble blood. He was intimate with the Lameths and lived at their house, and through them he was in close relationship with the absentee landlords and noblemen of the Club Massiac. The Club Massiac could have got no better advocate. Barnave was a skilful debater and popular. There still hung about him the revolutionary *réclame* of a few passionate words about those who had died in the days of July. The Club Massiac had had its eye on him for a long time. In February the president of the Club sent Barnave a memorandum on the colonial question that Barnave had asked for, and thus it was that, appointed on March 2nd, he had his report ready by March 8th. On that day, speaking for the Commission, he proposed all that any reasonable colonist could expect. The colonists should be left to work out their own constitution and to modify the Exclusive, both subject to the approval of the National Assembly. In the draft decree the words slaves and Mulattoes were not mentioned, for the Assembly could not bear to hear them. But Barnave put the "colonists and their property" under the special safeguard of the Nation, and slaves were property. The decree also declared guilty of crime against the Nation whoever tried to excite opposition to any branch of commerce with the colonies, direct or indirect. This was a warning to the Friends of the Negro and gave the official quietus to all talk about abolition of the traffic. Carried away by such wisdom and delicacy, the bourgeoisie punctuated the reading of the decree with applause, and Mirabeau, Pétion and other deputies of the Left who tried to invoke the Rights of Man were shouted down. The San Domingo die-hards opposed the decree as not giving them enough, but the Assembly dismissed this contemptuously.

The Friends of the Negro had been beaten, but they got ready for the debate on the instructions to accompany the decree. Barnave in his introductory speech and in the instructions themselves made no reference whatever to the burning question of political rights for the Mulattoes and free blacks. The Assembly was fighting hard to forget this awkward problem, but Abbé Grégoire broke the conspiracy of silence. Article 4 of the instructions gave the vote to "all persons" 25 years of age who fulfilled certain property and residential qualifications. Grégoire said he understood that this included the Mulattoes. A San Domingo deputy protested. Another deputy moved that the discussion be closed. De Lameth, the same who had chirped so noisily three months before, agreed that Grégoire's "indiscreet proposal" should not be discussed, and the House decided not to discuss it. The bourgeoisie would not face the issue, sent this ambiguous decree to San Domingo, and hoped for the best.

The decree of March 8th brought roars of rage from the revolutionaries of St Marc. Article 4 said persons, and they proved that Mulattoes were not persons: if persons meant men, then the decree included slaves. To give rights to these Mulattoes would be signing their own death-warrant, for these friends of the counter-revolutionary bureaucracy would swamp a new Assembly. They swore that they would never grant political rights to a "bastard and degenerate race," and launched a new terror against the Mulattoes. But the bureaucrats were taking courage. Many deputies of St Marc themselves were dropping away, indignant at the pretensions of their fellows and fearful of the consequences. Of the original 212 less than half remained. Feeling their support growing, the royalists decided to finish with the revolution in San Domingo, and

De Mauduit, commander of the troops, marched against the Patriots.

The Assembly of St Marc had no force on which it could depend. In the harbour of Port-au-Prince was a ship, the *Léopard*, the crew of which had been won over to the Patriot Party by the Municipality. Defenceless before De Mauduit's troops and facing annihilation, 85 Patriots, of whom 64 were fathers of families, decided to board the *Léopard* and go to France to plead their cause in person. The bureaucracy, wearing the royalist white cockades, remained for the time being masters of the field, and all parties decided to wait on what France would say. Meanwhile, however, all sharpened their knives. Political justice, it was clear, was on the side of the stronger battalions. The Mulattoes, wishing to wear the royalist white cockade, were prohibited by the triumphant bureaucrats. Rejected in France, humiliated at home, the Mulattoes organised a revolt. It was the quarrel between bourgeoisie and monarchy that brought the Paris masses on the political stage. It was the quarrel between whites and Mulattoes that woke the sleeping slaves.

If not at the instigation of the Friends of the Negro, at least with their consent, Ogé left Paris to lead the insurrection in San Domingo. And in this he was aided and abetted by no less a person than Clarkson.[4]

Ogé went secretly to London where he was met by Clarkson.[5] There he got money and letters of credit to purchase arms and ammunition in the United States. He landed in San Domingo on October 21st, 1790, and accom-

[4] Lacroix, *Mémoires pour Servir à l'Histoire de la Révolution de Saint-Domingue.* Paris, 1819. Vol. 1, pp. 54-55.
[5] Clarkson would not have helped to organise a Mulatto revolt in a British colony. Yet Clarkson was a very sincere man and the sincerity of many abolitionists is not questioned here. The Nonconformist missionaries and their congregations were undoubtedly moved by humanitarian motives, sharpened by their own hostility to factory-slavery and game laws. But without Pitt and the interests he represented how effective would they have been?

panied by his brother and Chavannes, one of the many Mulattoes who had fought in the American War of Independence, he raised the standard of revolt.

But Ogé was a politician, whose gifts were unsuited for the task before him. Thousands of Mulattoes were waiting for a signal from the leader. Instead he addressed two high-sounding proclamations, not to his supporters, but to the authorities in Le Cap, asking for the promulgation of the decree of March 8th. Instead of threatening them with the raising of the slaves, good Liberal as he was, he assured them in advance that he had no intention of doing so and appealed to the common interests of whites and Mulattoes as slave-owners. Ogé committed no crimes, but Chavannes massacred a few whites. Red cockades and white drew together. The Mulattoes all over the country were prevented from concentrating by heavy rains and floods. But the impetuous Ogé threw himself and his few hundred men on Le Cap. He was defeated, and with a few companions fled into Spanish territory, whence he was extradited.

The whites tortured Ogé and his companions with a trial lasting two months. They condemned them to be led by the executioner to the main door of the parish church, bare-headed and in their shirts, tied by a cord round the neck, and there on their knees, with wax candles in their hands, to confess their crimes and beg forgiveness, after which they were to be led to the parade-ground, and there have their arms, legs and elbows broken on a scaffold, after which they were to be bound on wheels, their faces turned to the sky, to remain thus while it pleased God to keep them alive. Their heads were then to be cut off, and their goods and property confiscated. Even in death the racial division was to be maintained. The written judgment decreed that they were to be executed on the side of the square opposite to that where whites were executed. Chavannes the soldier endured without a murmur, but Ogé broke down and begged for mercy. Two days after, Ogé's brother suffered the same fate and 21 others were hanged. Thirteen were sent to the galleys for life. The whole Provincial Assembly of the North attended the executions in state. The brilliant Ogé and his success in Paris had been the pride of all Mulatto San Domingo, and the malevolence of his trial and execution was a searing memory in Mulatto minds.

It was the news of Ogé's torture and death which made France as a whole fully aware of the colonial question. Hitherto the French bourgeoisie had been untroubled by any mass pressure. The Constituent refused to accept the protest of the men from the *Léopard,* broke the Assembly of St Marc, ordered the election of a new assembly, and dispatched two regiments of troops to help the Governor. But in its instructions it still left the fate of the Mulattoes to the colonists. All white San Domingo, pro-independence and anti-, were united on one common ground—the maintenance of slavery. Rights for Mulattoes to-day? It would be rights for slaves to-morrow. They fought the Mulatto question as the first outpost of their precious gangs of slaves. The French bourgeoisie saw their point of view and, by shouting down the Friends of the Negro in the House, intimidated the centre and maintained the colonial *status quo.* Once more the Paris masses broke the front of reaction and drove the revolution forward.

The big bourgeoisie had quite finished with the revolution. The Constitution they elaborated divided the masses into active—those who had a property qualification—and passive—the poor who had fought in the streets. The Districts, associations of the masses, were abolished, and the bourgeois National Guard carried out a stern policing of Paris. The masses were chained and muzzled; and without the masses the radical democrats were merely voices. If the King and Queen had been political abstractions and not flesh and blood, they would have lived and died as constitutional monarchs with immense power. But they looked upon all their concessions as merely temporary, and plotted ceaselessly with foreign powers for armed intervention. The people knew, as the people always know

during a revolution, and by April 1791, the Paris masses
were once more on the offensive. On April 18th Louis and
his family wanted to leave Paris for Saint-Cloud. For two
hours a great crowd refused to let the carriage pass, and
the royal family had to turn back. In these turbulent days
came the news of Ogé's martyrdom. Paris, in a ferment,
greeted it with revolutionary rage. Soon a tragedy with
Ogé as hero would be played to crowded houses. When
on April 7th the colonial question again came before the
House, Abbé Grégoire took the floor and demanded an
adjournment of four days in preparation for a debate.
Moreau de Saint-Méry at once opposed, calling for an
immediate vote in the old way. But that could work no
longer. The proposal for an adjournment was carried and
a date fixed. The bourgeoisie was face to face with the
colonial question at last.

The debate was one of the greatest which ever shook
the Constituent. Robespierre made the deputies aware of
the dangerous game they were playing in so flagrant a
breach of the very principles on which their own position
rested:

"If I should suspect that among those who have opposed rights for the men of colour there was any one who
detested liberty and the Constitution, I would believe that
they are merely seeking ways and means of attacking with
success your decrees and your principles. Whenever a
question arises in which the interest of the metropolis is
directly concerned they will tell you: You urge without
ceasing the Rights of Man, but you believe in them so
little yourselves that you have sanctified slavery constitu-
tionally (there was murmuring in the Assembly). The supreme interest of the nation and of the colonies is that you
remain free and that you do not overturn with your own
hands the foundations of liberty. Perish the colonies
(violent interruptions) if the price is to be your happiness,
your glory, your liberty.[6] I repeat it—perish the colonies

---

[6] Robespierre never said: "Perish the colonies rather than our
principles." That was a typical lie of the reaction and has lasted
to this day.

if the colonists wish by menaces to force us to decree that which is most suitable to their interests. I declare in the name of the Assembly, in the name of those members of this Assembly who do not wish to overturn the Constitution, in the name of the entire nation which desires freedom, that we will sacrifice to the colonial deputies neither the nation nor the colonies nor the whole of humanity."

It was magnificent but it was not abolition. It was only the word slavery Robespierre was objecting to—not the thing. All had agreed to leave that alone, though it was in all minds.

Raimond, admitted to the bar of the House to speak for his people, stated crudely that Mulattoes must be given rights so as to unite with the whites to keep down the slaves.

Hour after hour declamation and argument, abuse and applause, testified to the magnitude of the interests presumed to be at stake and the depths of the passions aroused. Four days it lasted with all political Paris taking sides. Among the spectators the commercial representatives of the maritime bourgeois had a special place. They wrote notes to speakers, made gestures of dissent or approbation, and on account of their prestige and business experience exercised an immense influence on the uninformed and undecided of the deputies. But all the popular bodies, The Jacobins, the Friends of the Constitution, etc., detested the Club Massiac and its disgraceful pro-slavery propaganda; the political rank and file were wildly for the Mulattoes: the defence of the Rights of Man abroad was the defence of them at home. The parties were evenly matched and the voting on resolutions and amendments went now one way, now the other. At last on the evening of the fourth day, with the deputies worn out and unable to arrive at a decision, Rewbell rose and proposed a compromise. Every Mulatto whose parents were both free should have the vote. There were only 400 of these but it seemed a way out. The compromise proposal was carried by an overwhelming majority and the spectators cheered a hard-won victory, small in itself but of far-reaching implications. For once a single coloured man had got his rights, the victory of the rest was only a matter of work and time.

The rich are only defeated when running for their lives. Inexperienced in revolution, the bourgeoisie had not purged the ministerial offices, where the royalist bureaucrats still sat plotting for the restoration of the royal power. The colonial deputies wrote to the Constituent declaring their intention not to attend any more sessions and conspired with the bureaucrats to sabotage the decree. After many weeks the Constituent discovered that, from the day the decree had been passed, the greater part of the Colonial Commission had refused to go on with the work. New deputies appointed to carry out the decision of the House reported that they would not attend a Commission whose main object was to oppose the decision they were supposed to implement. The decree lay cold in the offices of the Minister, and on the night of June 20th the revolution swung backwards, giving Barnave and his friends their chance.

Louis, having completed his plans for invading France at the head of the European counter-revolution, fled to Varennes, leaving behind a document in which he repudiated the Constitution he had sworn to obey. The perjury of the royal family was patent now to every living soul in France—including the masses who, warned by Marat, had known this was going to happen and had done what they could to prevent it. The bourgeoisie had had enough of the masses in politics, and when the King fled they were far more concerned with Paris than with the treacherous monarch. In this great crisis Barnave emerged as their leader and truest representative. He reminded the Assembly of what had happened on July 14th (the day which had unleashed the revolution and put these gentlemen where they were). The bourgeoisie must arm, not against the King, but to put the masses in their place. He called for the arming of the citizens, i.e., the bourgeois National

Guard. Under Barnave's firm guidance the Constituent transferred the executive power into its own hands.

If the people had been guarding Louis, he would never have got away, and now it was the people who caught him before he could make contact with the enemies of his country. Barnave was sent as one of the Commissioners to bring him back to Paris, and this characteristic bourgeois offered his services to the Queen in the coach: revolutionary Paris was the common enemy. On June 22nd a deputy threw out the phrase: "The King and the Royal Family have been abducted . . ." The Constituent preferred the people to believe that the King had gone against his will. The radicals tried to protest. The Constituent would not listen and followed Barnave.

But there are times when you cannot bluff the people, and they crowded into the streets day after day demanding that the perjured King should go. On July 14th, the second anniversary of the taking of the Bastille, the masses gathered together at the Champ de Mars to present a petition for the King's deposition, and the bourgeois National Guard, under Lafayette, shot them down. In the face of the revolutionary people the reaction drew closer together. Marat had to go into hiding. Danton fled to London. Barnave, the brothers Lameth, Malouet and Vaublanc (both of whom we have seen proving that the slaves were happy), comprised the Feuillants or King's party and dominated the Assembly. In August came letters from Governor Blanchelande detailing the violent reception of the May decree by the planters. Blanchelande, who was taking instructions from the Club Massiac, sided with them and foretold the calamities which would ensue if the decree were enforced when it came officially: Barnave and his friends were still holding up its dispatch. A new Minister gave strict orders that it was to be sent at once. The clerks in the office were prevailed upon to disobey, so that in the end the decree never reached San Domingo officially, the Commissioners who were to enforce it never left. Petitions and protests came in from San Domingo. Petitions (many of them fictitious) came also from the maritime towns. With revolu-

tionary Paris cowed into submission outside, the democrats
in the House had lost their influence, the centre was under
the influence of the Feuillants, and in the last week of the
Constituent's existence Barnave, who had not attended the
Colonial Commission since the defeat on May 15th, appeared at the tribune and moved in effect the rescinding
of the May decree. "This régime," said Barnave, "is ab-
surd, but it is established and one cannot handle it roughly
without unloosing the greatest disorder. This régime is
oppressive, but it gives a livelihood to several million
Frenchmen. This régime is barbarous, but a still greater
barbarism will be the result if you interfere with it without the necessary knowledge." Bourgeois hypocrisy is not
seldom the truest wisdom, and a great empire and honest
minds go ill together. Barnave was honest but a fool. Instead of taking a leaf from his friends across the Channel
and boldly stating that the Constituent was withholding
the rights in the truest interests of the Mulattoes themselves, he rubbed the Constituent on the raw with every
word and gave ammunition to his enemies in Paris and in
San Domingo. But the Assembly, on the defensive against
the revolution, yielded and on September 24th rescinded
the decree of May 15th. On September 28th another decree ordered the departure of new Commissioners for San
Domingo, and on the 29th the Constituent ceased to sit.

The colonial question was no subordinate interest of
the Constituent Assembly. Far from being an assembly of
theoreticians and visionaries as conservatives like to represent them, the political representatives of the bourgeoisie
were sober men of business, too sober, for they had no
colour prejudice, were profoundly ashamed of the injustices
they were perpetuating, but, standing to lose so much, allowed themselves to be frightened by the colonial deputies.
For this cowardice they paid heavily—abroad and at
home. It was the colonial question which demoralised the
Constituent. Jaurès, so weak on colonial events, but so
strong on the parliamentary assemblies, has traced this

demoralisation with the profound insight of a great parliamentarian. Hitherto, says Jaurès, the revolutionary bourgeois had been reasonably honest.[7] If they had limited the franchise, at least they had done so openly. But to avoid giving the Mulattoes the Rights of Man they had to descend to low dodges and crooked negotiations which destroyed their revolutionary integrity. It was the guilty conscience of the Constituent on the colonial question that placed it at the mercy of the reactionaries when Louis fled. "Undoubtedly but for the compromises of Barnave and all his party on the colonial question, the general attitude of the Assembly after the flight to Varennes would have been different." But it was not the Mulattoes they feared, it was the slaves. Slavery corrupted the society of San Domingo and had now corrupted the French bourgeoisie in the first flush and pride of its political inheritance.

Reaction triumphed. But phases of a revolution are not decided in parliaments, they are only registered there. The radicals were concentrating their forces in the Jacobin Club which would lead the revolution to its conclusion. Barnave and the Lameths had long been oracles of the club, but on the day after the Constituent ceased to sit the club expelled them for the part they had taken in depriving the Mulattoes of the Rights of Man. The breach imminent since the massacre of the Champ de Mars was now open.

And meanwhile, what of the slaves? They had heard of the revolution and had construed it in their own image: the white slaves in France had risen, and killed their masters, and were now enjoying the fruits of the earth. It was gravely inaccurate in fact, but they had caught the spirit of the thing. Liberty, Equality, Fraternity. Before the end of 1789 there were risings in Guadeloupe and Martinique. As early as October, in Fort Dauphin, one of the future centres of the San Domingo insurrection, the slaves were

[7] Jaurès: *Histoire Socialiste* . . . Vol. II, pp. 225-226.

stirring and holding mass meetings in the forests at night. In the South Province, watching the fight between their masters for and against the revolution, they had shown signs of unrest. In isolated plantations there were movements. All were bloodily repressed. Revolutionary literature was circulating among them. But the colonists were themselves giving a better example than all the revolutionary tracts which found their way to the colony. De Wimpffen asked them if they were not afraid to be perpetually discussing liberty and equality before their slaves. But their own passions were too violent to be restrained. Their quick resort to arms, their lynching, murders and mutilations of Mulattoes and political enemies, were showing the slaves how liberty and equality were won or lost.

Of the men who were to lead their brothers to freedom none of them as far as we know was yet active. Dessalines, already 40, worked as a slave for his black master. Christophe listened to the talk in the hotel where he worked but had no constructive ideas. Toussaint alone read his Raynal. "A courageous chief only is wanted." He said afterwards that, from the time the troubles began, he felt he was destined for great things. Exactly what, however, he did not know; he and his brother slaves only watched their masters destroy one another, as Africans watched them in 1914-1918, and will watch them again before long.[8]

But white San Domingo was not thinking of slaves in 1791, nor too much of Mulattoes, except to lynch and rob. The weakness of the Government had unloosed the rivalries of great whites and small whites, and around the slogans of liberty and equality white cockades and red fought for supremacy, with the special violence of slave-owners and the ardent temperament of the tropics. In March two regiments of soldiers were due in San Domingo to assist the Government to keep the Patriots in order. The inhabitants of Port-au-Prince prepared elaborately to win

[8] Written, it must be remembered, in 1938.

them over from the royalist Government. They opened the cafés to them, greeted them with music and dancing and unlimited food and drinks, told them that the Government was the counter-revolution, as indeed it was. The soldiers refused to obey their commanders and the Governor, and joined the Patriot party. De Mauduit's own soldiers, hitherto loyal, under the cross fire of the population and the new arrivals from France, were caught up in the revolutionary ardour. Turning on De Mauduit they murdered him and mutilated his body, sparing it no indignity. Hostile as the small whites and the Patriots were to the rich Mulattoes, they did not disdain the alliance of the Mulatto Patriots. A Mulatto woman who held De Mauduit's feet so that his head might be more easily cut off was rewarded with the direction of the hospital. Rigaud, a leader of the Mulattoes who had been imprisoned by De Mauduit, was liberated by the crowd. A new Municipality took over the functions of Government and a Maltese deserter, Pralotto by name, assumed command of the artillery. The parishes of the West Province accepted the new Government and de Blanchelande, the Governor, fled to Le Cap, where the merchants and lawyers held him virtually prisoner.

All this took place in March 1791, but something else had also taken place. The French soldiers, on landing at Port au-Prince, had given the fraternal embrace to all Mulattoes and all Negroes, telling them that the Assembly in France had declared all men free and equal. At many places near Port-au-Prince the Negroes were seizing arms and rebelling. At one spot they came out with such force and determination that the *maréchaussée* and all the proprietors in the neighbourhood were needed to suppress them. The colonists had to fire and charge, and the slaves did not surrender until their leaders had fallen. A dozen were hanged. Hanging would settle everything, and the Marquis de Caradeu, wealthy planter, commander of the National Guard of Port-au-Prince, earned the admiration of his fellow slave-owners for his vigour and ingenuity as a hanging propagandist: "If there is any trouble about killing them off, we only have to call Caradeu, who has made fifty heads fly on the Aubry Plantation . . . and in order that every-body should know about it had them fixed on pikes along the hedges of his plantation, palm-tree fashion." To such men the news of the May decree giving rights to 400 Mu-lattoes was a dangerous symptom and outrage unspeakable. They lynched Mulattoes, they stamped upon the French flag, they abjured France, they could not mention France or Frenchmen without oaths and curses. The new Assem-bly which was to replace the broken Assembly of St Marc met at Léogane in early August and passed a series of resolutions designed to ensure independence. In order to be nearer the centre of affairs the members decided to transfer to Le Cap where the Governor was. But some of the deputies never reached there, being killed on the way by the revolting Negroes of the North. These, luckily for themselves, had no deputies in Paris listening to parlia-mentary promises and weakening their will. Neglected and ignored by all the politicians of every brand and persua-sion, they had organised on their own and struck for free-dom at last.

IV

The San Domingo Masses Begin

> Eh! Eh! Bomba! Heu! Heu!
> Canga, bafio té!
> Canga, mouné de lé!
> Canga, do ki la!
> Canga, do ki la!
> Canga, li!

THE SLAVES worked on the land, and, like revolutionary peasants everywhere, they aimed at the extermination of their oppressors. But working and living together in gangs of hundreds on the huge sugar-factories which covered the North Plain, they were closer to a modern proletariat than any group of workers in existence at the time, and the rising was, therefore, a thoroughly prepared and organised mass movement. By hard experience they had learnt that isolated efforts were doomed to failure, and in the early months of 1791 in and around Le Cap they were organising for revolution. Voodoo was the medium of the conspiracy. In spite of all prohibitions, the slaves travelled miles to sing and dance and practise the rites and talk; and now, since the revolution, to hear the political news and make their plans. Boukman, a Papaloi or High Priest, a gigantic Negro, was the leader. He was headman of a plantation and followed the political situation both among the whites and among the Mulattoes. By the end of July 1791 the blacks in and around Le Cap were ready and waiting. The plan was conceived on a massive scale and they aimed at exterminating the whites and taking the colony for themselves. There were perhaps 12,000 slaves in Le Cap, 6,000 of them men. One night the slaves in the suburbs and outskirts of Le Cap were to fire the plantations. At this signal the slaves in the town would massacre the whites and the slaves on the plain would complete the destruction. They had travelled a long, long way since the grandiose poisoning schemes of Mackandal.

The plan did not succeed in its entirety. But it very nearly did, and the scope and organisation of this revolt shows Boukman to be the first of that line of great leaders whom the slaves were to throw up in such profusion and rapidity during the years which followed. That so vast a conspiracy was not discovered until it had actually broken out is a testimony to their solidarity. In early August the slaves in Limbé, then and to the end of the revolution one of the storm-centres, rose prematurely and were crushed. This Limbé rising showed that it was dangerous to delay. Three days after, representatives from parishes all over the plain assembled to fix the day. Deputies on their way to Le Cap for the first session of the Colonial Assembly, to begin on August 25th, met throngs of slaves on the road who

abused and even attacked them. On August 21st some
prisoners were taken and de Blanchelande, the Governor,
examined them himself the next day. He did not get much
from them, but he understood vaguely that there was to
be some sort of rising. He took precautions to safeguard
the city from the slaves within and he ordered patrols to
cover the outskirts. But these whites despised the slaves
too much to believe them capable of organising a mass
movement on a grand scale. They could not get from the
prisoners the names of the leaders, and what precautions
could they take against the thousands of slaves on the hundreds of plantations? Some of the white rabble in Le Cap,
always ready for loot and pillage, were revealed as being
connected with a plot of some sort. De Blanchelande was
more concerned about these than about the Negroes.

On the night of the 22nd a tropical storm raged, with
lightning and gusts of wind and heavy showers of rain.
Carrying torches to light their way, the leaders of the revolt met in an open space in the thick forests of the Morne
Rouge, a mountain overlooking Le Cap. There Boukman
gave the last instructions and, after Voodoo incantations
and the sucking of the blood of a stuck pig, he stimulated
his followers by a prayer spoken in creole, which, like so
much spoken on such occasions, has remained. "The god
who created the sun which gives us light, who rouses the
waves and rules the storm, though hidden in the clouds,
he watches us. He sees all that the white man does. The
god of the white man inspires him with crime, but our god
calls upon us to do good works. Our god who is good to
us orders us to revenge our wrongs. He will direct our arms
and aid us. Throw away the symbol of the god of the whites
who has so often caused us to weep, and listen to the voice
of liberty, which speaks in the hearts of us all."

The symbol of the god of the whites was the cross
which, as Catholics, they wore round their necks.

That very night they began. The slaves on the Gallifet plantation were so well treated that "happy as the Negroes of Gallifet" was a slave proverb. Yet by a phenomenon noticed in all revolutions it was they who led the way.

Each slave-gang murdered its masters and burnt the plantation to the ground. The precautions that de Blanchelande had taken saved Le Cap, but the preparation otherwise had been thorough and complete, and in a few days one-half of the famous North Plain was a flaming ruin. From Le Cap the whole horizon was a wall of fire. From this wall continually rose thick black volumes of smoke, through which came tongues of flame leaping to the very sky. For nearly three weeks the people of Le Cap could barely distinguish day from night, while a rain of burning cane straw, driven before the wind like flakes of snow, flew over the city and the shipping in the harbour, threatening both with destruction.

The slaves destroyed tirelessly. Like the peasants in the Jacquerie or the Luddite wreckers, they were seeking their salvation in the most obvious way, the destruction of what they knew was the cause of their sufferings; and if they destroyed much it was because they had suffered much. They knew that as long as these plantations stood their lot would be to labour on them until they dropped. The only thing was to destroy them. From their masters they had known rape, torture, degradation, and, at the slightest provocation, death. They returned in kind. For two centuries the higher civilisation had shown them that power was used for wreaking your will on those whom you controlled. Now that they held power they did as they had been taught. In the frenzy of the first encounters they killed all, yet they spared the priests whom they feared and the surgeons who had been kind to them. They, whose women had undergone countless violations, violated all the women who fell into their hands, often on the bodies of their still bleeding husbands, fathers and brothers. "Vengeance! Vengeance!" was their war-cry, and one of them carried a white child on a pike as a standard.

And yet they were surprisingly moderate,[1] then and afterwards, far more humane than their masters had been or would ever be to them. They did not maintain this revengeful spirit for long. The cruelties of property and privi-

[1] This statement has been criticised. I stand by it. C.L.R.J.

lege are always more ferocious than the revenges of poverty and oppression. For the one aims at perpetuating resented injustice, the other is merely a momentary passion soon appeased. As the revolution gained territory they spared many of the men, women, and children whom they surprised on plantations. To prisoners of war alone they remained merciless. They tore out their flesh with red-hot pincers, they roasted them on slow fires, they sawed a carpenter between two of his boards. Yet in all the records of that time there is no single instance of such fiendish tortures as burying white men up to the neck and smearing the holes in their faces to attract insects, or blowing them up with gun-powder, or any of the thousand and one bestialities to which they had been subjected. Compared with what their masters had done to them in cold blood, what they did was negligible, and they were spurred on by the ferocity with which the whites in Le Cap treated all slave prisoners who fell into their hands.

As usual the strength of the mass movement dragged in its wake revolutionary sections of those classes nearest to it. Free blacks joined them. A planter of Port Magot had taught his black foreman to read and write, had made him free, had left him in his will 10,000 francs, had given to the foreman's mother land on which she had made a coffee plantation. But this black raised the slaves on the plantations of his master and his own mother, set them on fire, and joined the revolution, which gave him a high command. The Mulattoes hated the black slaves because they were slaves and because they were black. But when they actually saw the slaves taking action on such a grand scale, numbers of young Mulattoes from Le Cap and round about rushed to join the hitherto despised blacks and fight against the common enemy.

They were fortunate in that the troops in Le Cap were few, and de Blanchelande, afraid of the slaves and the white rabble in the town, preferred to act on the defensive. One attack was made by the regulars, who drove the slaves before them, but de Blanchelande, yielding to the nervous fears awakened in the city, recalled the detachment. This left the revolution master of the countryside. Gaining courage the blacks extended their destruction over the plain. If they had had the slightest material interest in the plantations, they would not have destroyed so wantonly. But they had none. After a few weeks they stopped for a moment to organise themselves. It is at this period, one month after the revolt had begun, that Toussaint Bréda joined them, and made an unobtrusive entrance into history.

It seems certain that he had been in secret communication with the leaders, but like so many men of better education than the rank and file, he lacked their boldness at the moment of action and waited to see how things would go. Meanwhile, hating destruction, he kept his master's slaves in order and prevented the revolutionary labourers from setting fire to the plantation. While all the other whites in the neighbourhood made a dash for Le Cap, Madame Bayou de Libertas remained on the plantation, protected by Toussaint. Bayou de Libertas himself was with a camp of planters not far off, on guard against the slaves, but came every day to the plantation. Toussaint, then as always master of himself and of all near to him, maintained this untenable situation for over a month. But as the insurrection grew, worn out by the strain of defending the property, his master and his mistress, and learning that Madame de Libertas' life was now in danger, he decided that the old life was over and a new one had begun. He told Madame de Libertas that the time had come for her to go to Le Cap, packed her and some valuables in a carriage and sent her off under the care of his brother, Paul. He sent his own wife and the two children of the household into a safe spot in Spanish San Domingo. Then he slowly made his way to the camp of the revolted slaves.

The man who so deliberately decided to join the revolution was 45 years of age, an advanced age for those times, grey already, and known to everyone as Old Toussaint. Out of the chaos in San Domingo that existed then and for years to follow, he would lay the foundations of a Negro State that lasts to this day. From the moment he joined the revolution he was a leader, and moved without serious rivalry to the first rank. We have clearly stated the vast impersonal forces at work in the crisis of San Domingo. But men make history, and Toussaint made the history that he made because he was the man he was.

He had had exceptional opportunities, and both in mind and body was far beyond the average slave. Slavery dulls the intellect and degrades the character of the slave. There was nothing of that dullness or degradation in Toussaint.

His post as steward of the livestock had given him experience in administration, authority, and intercourse with those who ran the plantation. Men who, by sheer ability and character, find themselves occupying positions usually reserved for persons of a different upbringing, education and class, usually perform those duties with exceptional care and devoted labour. In addition to this practical education, he had, as we have seen, been able to read a little. He had read Caesar's Commentaries, which had given him some idea of politics and the military art and the connection between them. Having read and re-read the long volume by the Abbé Raynal on the East and West Indies, he had a thorough grounding in the economics and politics, not only of San Domingo, but of all the great empires of Europe which were engaged in colonial expansion and trade. Finally he had had the exceptional experience of the last three years of the revolution in San Domingo. The plantation was only two miles from Le Cap, and his duties took him often into the town. The masses of the people learn much during a revolution, far more a man like Toussaint. His superb intellect had therefore had some opportunity of cultivating itself in general affairs at home and abroad: from the very beginning he manœuvred with an uncanny certainty not only between local parties in San Domingo but between the international forces at work.

An important thing for his future was that his character was quite unwarped. Since his childhood he had probably never been whipped as so many slaves had been whipped. He himself tells us that he and his wife were among the fortunate few who had acquired a modest competence and used to go hand in hand and very happy to work on the little plot of land which some of the slaves cultivated for themselves. Besides his knowledge and experience, through natural strength of character he had acquired a formidable mastery over himself, both mind and body. As a boy he was so frail and delicate that his parents had not expected him to live, and he was nicknamed "Little Stick." While still a child he determined to acquire not only knowledge but a strong body, and he strengthened himself by the severest exercises, so that by the time he was 12 he had surpassed all the boys of his age on the plantation in athletic feats. He could swim across a dangerous river, jump on a horse at full speed and do what he liked with it. When he was nearly 60 he was still the finest rider in San Domingo, habitually rode 125 miles a day, and sat his horse with such ease and grace that he was known as the Centaur of the Savannahs.

As a young man he had run after women. Then he decided to settle down. Refusing to live in the concubinage which was so widely prevalent among all classes in San Domingo, but particularly among the slaves, he married a woman who already had a son. She bore Toussaint one child, and he and his wife lived together in the greatest harmony and friendship, when he was master of all San Domingo just as in the days when he was an ordinary slave. For the life that so many lived in the colony, for the reputation that he had among the blacks and the opportunities that his position offered, this was an unusual thing for a man who had begun life as Toussaint had, and who, in the days of his greatness, was partial to the society of attractive women.

From childhood he had been taciturn, which singled him out among his countrymen, a talkative, argumentative people. He was very small, ugly and ill-shaped, but although his general expression was one of benevolence, he had eyes like steel and no one ever laughed in his presence. His comparative learning, his success in life, his character and personality gave him an immense prestige among all the Negroes who knew him, and he was a man of some consequence among the slaves long before the revolution. Knowing his superiority he never had the slightest doubt that his destiny was to be their leader, nor would those with whom he came in contact take long to recognise it.

Nothing could be imagined more calculated to revolt his orderly mind than the spectacle which the slave camp presented. Many men were entirely naked; others wore filthy rags made out of bits and pieces of silks and satins pillaged from the plantations. Their weapons were a few guns and pistols that they had seized, old rusty swords, agricultural implements, sticks pointed with iron, pieces of iron hoop, in fact anything they could lay their hands on. They were destitute of ammunition and the cavalry were mounted on old horses and mules worn down by fatigue. They were divided into two large bands—one under Biassou, the other under Jean François, while a third leader was Jeannot. Jean François was a native of San Domingo, good-looking, very intelligent, and of a proud spirit which had made him run away from his master and become a maroon long before the revolution. In addition to his exceptional intelligence he was very brave, very sober, and of a tenacity that never admitted defeat. Biassou was a fire-eater, always drunk, always ready for the fiercest and most dangerous exploits. He also had had a life more easy than usual, having belonged to a religious establishment, the Fathers of Charity, not far from Le Cap. Jeannot was the slave who had led the foolish expedition of the San Domingo whites in the early days of the revolution, when, dressed up in their military uiniforms, they had looked around for an enemy on whom to practise.

Like their more educated white masters, the slaves hastened to deck themselves with all the trappings and titles of the military profession. The officers called themselves generals, colonels, marshals, commanders, and the leaders decorated themselves with scraps of uniforms, ribbons and orders which they found on the plantations or took from the enemy killed in battle. Biassou called himself a Brigadier. So did Jeannot. Later Jean François entitled himself (in the fashion of European colonial governors to this day) Admiral, Generalissimo and Chevalier of the Order of St. Louis, while Biassou, after a quarrel with Jean François, assumed the title of "Viceroy of the Conquered Territories."

Yet, despite these absurdities, which served the same purpose of impressing their inferiors as the trappings, gold epaulettes and multifarious commands of twentieth century royalty, Jean François and Biassou were men born to command. Nothing but an iron discipline could have kept order among that heterogeneous body of men just released from slavery, and Biassou and Jean François imposed it with an iron hand. Jeannot was a cruel monster who used to drink the blood of his white victims and commit abominable cruelties. Jean François arrested him, tried him, and had him shot, a conspicuous difference from the behaviour of the white colonists in the case of Le Jeune. Jean François soon foresaw a long war and ordered the planting of provisions. Thus early the slave leaders were showing a sense of order, discipline and capacity to govern. Many emissaries of the royalist counter-revolution found their way to the slaves. The priests, in large numbers, remained among them. But even the Mulattoes failed to oust these black leaders, and Jean François and Biassou who were in command at the beginning of the revolution remained masters of their respective bands to the end. Toussaint joined the band of Biassou. On account of his knowledge of herbs Biassou appointed him Physician to the Armies of the King, and from the very beginning Toussaint was high up in his councils.

Masses roused to the revolutionary pitch need above all a clear and vigorous direction. But the first coup had failed and Jean François and Biassou, though they could keep order, had not the faintest idea what to do next. De Blanchelande sent them a proclamation demanding their submission. They refused, but in their reply called themselves the servants of God and the King, and naïvely invited the whites to take all their possessions and leave the island to those who had watered it with their sweat.

To these bewildered political leaders Toussaint brought his superior knowledge and the political vices which usually accompany it.

The slaves had revolted because they wanted to be free. But no ruling class ever admits such things. The white cockades accused the Patriots and the Friends of the Negro of stirring up the revolt, while the red cockades accused the royalists and the counter revolution in France. The small whites accused the Mulattoes and massacred them at sight in the streets.[2]

The Assembly took charge of the colony. It would not ask France for assistance, but sent envoys to the British at Jamaica, to the Spaniards, and to the United States. It did not fear the revolution. It was more afraid of the slaves in Le Cap, and the city rabble, always ready to foment anarchy for the chance of plunder. These small whites refused to fight unless they were given two-thirds of what they found on the plantations as booty. But the majority of the Mulattoes, anxious about their property, volunteered to serve and offered their wives and children as hostages in token of good faith. The Assembly (knowing nothing as yet of the September 24th reversal) promised not only to enforce the decree of May 15th but to extend it to all Mulattoes whether their parents were free or not. But this could only be done, said the Assembly, after the decree had reached the colony and when the troubles were over.

To deceive the Mulattoes the planters were trying tricks, but against the slaves they knew only one weapon— terror. The blacks had their stockades covered with the heads of white victims. The Colonial Assembly stuck the

[2] Lacroix, *Mémoires pour Servir.* . . , Vol. 1, p. 91.

heads of Negroes on pikes placed all along the roads leading to Le Cap. When Boukman was killed (fighting
bravely) the Assembly stuck up his head in Le Cap with
a placard: "This is the head of Boukman, chief of the
rebels." The whites built three scaffolds in Le Cap and
broke 20 or 30 blacks on the wheel every day. With their
usual disregard of the slave even as property they massacred all they met, even those on plantations which had
not yet revolted. Masters denounced those who had helped
them to escape. Slaves presenting themselves to their masters seeking refuge from the devastation of the countryside
or merely because they were afraid or tired of revolution,
were killed at sight. The result was that all, timid as well
as bold, soon understood that there was no hope except
with the revolution, and they flocked to join its ranks. In
a few weeks the insurgents had grown to nearly 100,000.

To help the slaves and confuse the white planters
came news of a Mulatto revolution in the West. Early in
August, a body of Mulattoes, weary of being persecuted
and lynched by the small whites, now lording it as officials
in the revolutionary Municipalities, crept out of Port-au-
Prince and assembled at La Croix-des-Bouquets, a district
about five miles from the capital. From all parts of the
West Province the Mulattoes began to send contingents
there, and with their education, not so widespread as
among the whites, but immensely superior to the half-wild
blacks, they at once found admirable leadership. The most
famous of them was Rigaud, a genuine Mulatto, that is to
say the son of a white and a black. He had had a good
education at Bordeaux and then learned the trade of a
goldsmith. Unlike Toussaint, Jean François and Biassou, he
was already a trained soldier. He had enlisted as a volun-
teer in the French Army which fought in the American
War of Independence, became a non-commissioned officer,
and had also seen service in Guadeloupe. He hated the
whites, not only for the indignities which he, an educated
and widely-travelled soldier, had to suffer, but also because

they were jealous of his goldsmith's business, in those days an important trade.

A very different type of man was Beauvais. He was a member of a Mulatto family which had long been free and rich. He also had been educated in France, had volunteered for service and fought as a non-commissioned officer in the American War of Independence. On his return home he had taken up teaching. He was not only a man of exceptional personal bravery. Tall, of a fine figure and distinguished presence, he was known as one of the handsomest men in San Domingo, and in that licentious age and country he was distinguished for the severity of his mode of life and the charm of his manners. His own people loved him and it would not be difficult for the whites (when in a corner) to forget his colour.

These were the two soldiers. The politician was Pinchinat, who had studied widely in France. In the first days of the revolution he came back to San Domingo to lead the Mulattoes. In 1791 he was already 60, a man loving play and loose living, and hating the whites with all the hatred of a vicious character. He was a most finished politician and well deserved the qualification of man of genius, given to him by Pamphile de Lacroix.[3] "What a man to write and to make treaties," another Mulatto leader would write of him, "he is unique."

Under such leaders, and trained to fight in the *maréchaussée*, the Mulattoes were a formidable force. For this reason the royalist counter-revolution in the West at once sought to make use of them.

Humus de Jumecourt, Commandant of the district of La Croix-des-Bouquets and Cul-de-sac, proposed an alliance guaranteeing them all their rights in return for support of the counter-revolution, or, as he would call it, the lawful government of the island. Pinchinat refused, but offered instead a united front against their common enemy, the Municipality of Port-au-Prince and the Provincial Assembly of the West. De Jumecourt agreed, and the royalist commandants and the rich whites of the West began to join

[3] *Mémoires pour Servir* . . . , Vol. I, p. 183.

the Mulattoes at La Croix-des-Bouquets. There were a few
free blacks holding high command in this troop, so that
despised blacks were now commanding whites. The Mulattoes also incorporated in their force a body of maroons,
nicknamed "The Swiss" in imitation of the bodyguard of
Louis XVI. Full of contempt for men of colour and hating
them now for their persistent royalism, the Patriots attacked La Croix-des-Bouquets. They were heavily defeated,
"The Swiss" fighting with great bravery. A few days later,
the Mulattoes and the whites of the surrounding districts
had a meeting at La Croix-des-Bouquets, where the Mulattoes put before the whites the draft of a concordat embodying their demands for complete equality. The ninth
and last clause consisted of four words: "If not, civil war."
The whites accepted their demands immediately.

The Patriots of San Domingo were always ready to
forget race prejudice in return for something solid. After
he had been defeated in the field, Caradeu, leader of the
Patriots, offered Beauvais Mulatto rights, in return for an
agreement on independence without the intervention of
the royalists.[4] Beauvais refused. By this time nearly all the
rich planters had deserted the Patriots, and even the rich
merchants in Port-au-Prince would have nothing to do with
them. On October 19th a concordat embodying all the
Mulatto demands was signed by all parties. The Provincial
Assembly of the West was to be dissolved immediately, the
white deputies from the West Province to the Colonial Assembly were to be recalled, two battalions of the National
Guard were to be recruited among the Mulattoes, the
memory of Ogé was to be rehabilitated, and the whole
presented for the ratification of the National Assembly and
the approval of the King. The leader of the whites extended
the hand of friendship.

"We bring you finally words of peace; we come no
longer to bargain with you, we come only to accord to you
your demands, we come animated by the spirit of justice
and peace to give you authentic recognition of your rights,

---

[4] Saintoyant, *La Colonisation Française pendant la Révolution*
(*1789-1799*), Paris, 1930, Vol. I, p. 59.

to ask you to see in the white citizens only friends and brothers whom the colony in danger invites you, begs you, to unite with, in order to bring prompt assistance to our troubles. We accept entirely and without any reserve the concordat that you propose to us. Unfortunate circumstances of which you are doubtless aware made us hesitate for a moment. But our courage has broken all obstacles, and we have imposed silence on all mean prejudices, on the petty desire for domination. May the day on which the torch of reason has enlightened us all be forever memorable. May it be a day of forgetfulness for all errors, of pardon for all injuries. Let us henceforth be combatants only in zeal for the public welfare." [5] The "mean prejudices" and "the petty desire for domination" were the small whites who saw themselves being pushed into the background. But the news of the slave revolution in the North had sobered all who owned slaves, and they wanted peace.

All the 14 parishes of the West Province accepted the terms, and on the 24th of October the great ceremony of reconciliation took place in Port-au-Prince. The leaders of the whites and the leaders of the Mulattoes marched into Port-au-Prince arm in arm, with their troops marching behind, greeted by salvoes of artillery and mutual shouts of "Unity and Fidelity." In the general excitement a captain of the white National Guard jumped on a gun-carriage and proclaimed Caradeu Commander of the National Guard of the West Province. There was loud applause which was renewed when he named Beauvais second in command. Then all went to the Church to celebrate with a Te Deum as stipulated in the concordat. One more difficulty remained —"The Swiss." What was to be done with them? The whites argued that to send them back to the plantations would be bad for the slaves and it was agreed to deport them to a deserted beach in Mexico.[6] Among the leaders, Rigaud and Pétion, Mulattoes, fought for "The Swiss";

[5] Quoted from Deschamps, *Les Colonies pendant . . .* , pp. 257-258.
[6] The captain of the boat took his money but dumped them in Jamaica. The English Governor in great anger shipped them back. The Colonial Assembly had them all murdered except

Lambert, a free black, supported the deportation. "The Swiss" out of the way, peace seemed assured, Mulatto rights guaranteed, and the counter-revolution well placed for action.

But in Le Cap the Assembly foamed with wrath at these goings-on in the West. The royalist commanders of the local forces, M. de Rouvrai and M. de Touzard, urged the Patriots in the North to grant Mulatto rights. "But, you will say, must we yield to the menaces of an inferior caste, admit it to civic rights, as a ransom for the evils which they cause us? . . . One day," said de Rouvrai, "the scornful laughs with which you greet the important truths which I dare to tell you will change into tears of blood. . . . In the war of 1756 England wished to seize Cuba and Lord Albermarle was ordered to besiege Havana. He landed with 18,000 men; six months after he had only 1,800. . . .

"Where, I ask you, is the army capable of fulfilling our aim? . . . Have you any others than the Mulattoes? No. Well, why do you reject the help which they offer you . . . ?

"I am not finished, I have some other truths to tell you, I shall tell them to you. France at this moment has her eyes fixed on San Domingo. . . . It is impossible that the claims of the Mulattoes will not be listened to in France; if even they were unjust, they will be welcomed. The constitutional decree that you suppose irrevocable, that you regard as your palladium, will be inevitably modified. . . ."

The Assembly promised to give the Mulattoes their rights, but after the troubles were over. True, there was a slave revolt. But they had appealed to France by now, and to give rights to Mulattoes who outnumbered them would be to hand over the colony, military and civil, to these bastard upstarts and their allies of the the counter-revolution. They could see the results of that unholy alliance in the

---

about 20, whom they sent back to the West so as to prejudice the blacks against the Mulattoes.

West. They had de Blanchelande, the Governor, in their power and they poured out their wrath on the concordat.

The West would not budge from their unity and repudiated the proclamations of the Assembly and the Governor. But six days after the ceremony of reconciliation, there arrived in the colony the decree of the 24th September, by which the Constituent had withdrawn all rights from the Mulattoes and once more put their fate in the hands of the white colonists. "Mean prejudices" and "the petty desire for domination" reared heads again, and the scarcely healed wounds re-opened. The intrigues of Barnave & Co. were coming home to roost.

The 21st November was fixed for the ratification of the concordat. Port-au-Prince was divided into four sections for the voting and three had already voted in favour of ratification. This for the small whites was ruin, and Pralotto and his band were on the look-out to create some cause for a breach. It came over a free Negro, a member of the Mulatto force, who was either insulted by or insulted some whites. He was immediately captured and hanged. Despite the moderation of the Mulattoes, fighting began in the streets. The Mulattoes, taken by surprise, retreated. Fire broke out in the city, for which they were made responsible. Pralotto and his followers massacred rich white citizens, Mulattoes, men, women and children; and plundered the wealthy quarter of the town, while the flames spread and burned two-thirds of Port-au-Prince to the ground, estimated at a loss of 50 million francs.

The Mulattoes had been very patient and forbearing, but now they seemed to go mad. Pinchinat, the man of proclamations, issued a ringing call for battle.

"Fly, my friends, to the siege of Port-au-Prince and let us plunge our bleeding arms, avengers of perjury and perfidy, into the breast of these monsters from Europe. Too much and too long have we served as sport for their passions and their insidious manœuvres; too much and too long have we groaned under this iron yoke. Let us destroy our tyrants, let us bury with them even the smallest vestige of our degradation, let us tear up by its deepest roots this upas tree of prejudice. Recruit some, persuade others, promise, menace, threaten, drag in your wake the decent white citizens. But above all, dear friends, unity, courage and speed. Bring arms, baggage, cannon, munitions of war, and provisions, and come at once to rally under the common standard. It is there that we all ought to perish, or take vengeance for God, Nature, law and humanity, so long outraged in these climates of horror."

Rigaud's brother wrote to his friends: "I fly to vengeance. . . . If my fate is not death on this expedition, I shall be back soon to join you. . . . Long live liberty, long live equality, long live love." Rich whites and royalist commandants followed the Mulattoes, but the Rigaud brothers, Beauvais, and Pinchinat (despite his treatment of "The Swiss") were genuine revolutionaries, putting liberty before property. In a frenzy of excitation and rage they summoned the slaves of the West Province and drew them into the revolution. In the advanced North the slaves were leading the Mulattoes, in the backward West the Mulattoes were leading the slaves. It does not need much wisdom to foresee the consequences.

In the South, whites and Mulattoes were on the point of forming a concordat on the model of the West. All terms had been agreed upon when Caradeu paid a visit to the South and intrigued so successfully that the unity agreement was broken. As soon as the news of the split in Port-au-Prince reached them, Mulattoes and whites each took to arms. The Mulattoes made themselves masters of Jacmel and other towns. In self-defence the whites in the South, outnumbered by the Mulattoes, raised the slaves.

In the North some Mulatto and white proprietors formed a concordat. The Assembly disallowed it and these Mulattoes joined the slaves.

The whites committed frightful atrocities against the Mulattoes. They killed a pregnant woman, cut the baby out and threw it into the flames. They burnt them alive,

they inoculated them with small-pox. Naturally the Mulattoes retaliated in kind.[7]

But here as everywhere the white planters began it,
and exceeded all rivals in barbarism, being trained in violence and cruelty by their treatment of the slaves.

This was the San Domingo that the three Commissioners, Saint-Leger, Mirbeck and Roume, were to restore
to order when they landed at Le Cap on November 29th,
1791. They were welcomed by the Assembly and installed
with an imposing ceremony. They issued a proclamation
mendaciously announcing the near arrival of large bodies
of troops. To their surprise and joy this seemed as if it
would work a miracle.

Biassou, Jean François and the other Negro leaders,
including Toussaint, after four months of insurrection, had
come to a dead end. An insurrection must win victories,
and the whites were content to hold the line of fortifications
known as the Cordon of the West and prevent the insurrection penetrating into the West Province. The former slaves
could devastate the country around but that very devastation was making it impossible for them to exist. Famine began to kill them off. Frightened at what they considered
their hopeless position, and afraid of being beaten into submission, Jean François and Biassou offered peace to the
Commissioners in return for the liberty of a few hundred
leaders. Jean François knew that it was a betrayal. "False
principles," wrote this four-months-old labour leader, "will
make these slaves very obstinate, they will say that they
have been betrayed." But if the Commissioners granted
liberty to those who were named they would co-operate
with the King's troops and hunt down those who refused
to submit. Jean François knew that the business would be
difficult and dangerous and said as much, proof of the passion for liberty which filled the hearts of the blacks. But
he was prepared to do all that he could to help, and to

[7] For a well-documented summary of these atrocities, see Schoelcher, *Vie de Toussaint-L'Ouverture*, Chapter VI.

soothe his conscience wrote disloyally of his followers as a
multitude of Negroes from Africa who did not know two
words of French. In the long and cruel list of leaders betraying brave but ignorant masses this stands high, and
Toussaint was in it up to the neck. Though working in a
subordinate position he took the leading part in the negotiations, and the masterpiece of diplomatic correspondence
which the envoys of the slaves presented at the bar of the
Assembly showed the distance between the men who a few
weeks before had asked the whites to leave the island and
the already fully-fledged political maturity of Toussaint.
To the end of his days he could hardly speak French, he
literally could not write three words without the grossest
errors in spelling and grammar. Years afterwards when he
was master of San Domingo he wrote thus to Dessalines:
Je vouss a vé parlé pour le forli berté avan theire . . . He
meant to write: Je vous avais parlé du Fort Liberté avant-
hier. . . . He could never do better. But he dictated in the
local bastard French or creole, and his secretaries wrote
and re-wrote until he got the exact meaning he wanted.

The letter[8] begins by emphasizing that the King's
proclamation has formally accepted the French constitution, and "very clearly and precisely" has asked for a spirit
of "justice and moderation" to help in the restoration of a
country which has suffered from the repeated shocks of a
great revolution. This conciliatory spirit should cross the
seas. "We pass now to the law relating to the colonies of
September 28th, 1791. This law gives to the colonies the
right of deciding on the status of the free men of colour
and free blacks." Toussaint and the other traitors wanted
not only freedom but political rights. But promises were
not enough. They would defend the decisions of the Colonial Assembly "to the last drop of their blood," but these
decisions must be "clothed with the requisite formalities."
Followed a long apology for the evils which they had
helped to afflict "on this rich and important colony." But
they had not known of the new laws when they had writ-

8 Lacroix, Mémoires pour Servir . . . Vol. I, pp. 148-152. For
the full correspondence see Les Archives Nationales, DXXV, 1.

ten the first letter. "To-day when we are instructed in the new laws, to-day when we cannot doubt the approbation of the mother-country for all the Legislative Acts that you will decree, concerning the interior régime of the Colony, and the status of citizens, we shall not show ourselves refractory." After another long appeal to the Assembly to seize this opportunity to re-establish order promptly "in so important a colony," the letter touched on the difficult question of the slaves. "The laws which will be in force concerning the status of persons free and not free ought to be the same in the whole colony." This was obviously a finger pointing to the concordats in the West Province. "It would be even to your interest if you declared, by a decree bearing the sanction of the Governor, that it is your intention to concern yourselves with the lot of the slaves, knowing that they are the object of your solicitude." Inasmuch as the slaves had confidence in their chiefs, if the Assembly gave the job of pacification to these chiefs, the slaves would be satisfied, which would facilitate restoration of "the equilibrium which has been broken." The conclusion was a protestation of good faith and desire for a speedy settlement. Freedom for the leaders, however, was "indispensable." The letter was signed by Jean François and Biassou, two others, and two commissioners *ad hoc,* one of whom was Toussaint. In its skilful use of both the moral and political connection between the mother-country and the colony, its dangling before the colonists the chance to restore the former prosperity "of this great and important colony," its firm but delicate insistence on political rights, duly certified by law, for the freed men, its luxuriance whenever it dealt with things that cost nothing such as peace, good-will, etc., the letter could have come from the pen of a man who had spent all his life in diplomacy. The writer, knowing the temper of the colonists, had even taken the trouble to suggest to them exactly how the slaves were to be bluffed back into bondage; no imperialist of to-day with three hundred years of traditional deception behind him could have garlanded his claws with fairer words; "the restoration of the broken equilibrium" as a phrase for slavery would not have disgraced the Mandates Commission of the League of Nations. Jean François had written that the thing was difficult but it could be done, and that they were not only prepared but able to do their Judas work the letter gave ample evidence. Political treachery is not a monopoly of the white race, and this abominable betrayal so soon after the insurrections shows that political leadership is a matter of programme, strategy and tactics, and not the colour of those who lead it, their oneness of origin with their people, nor the services they have rendered.

The high and mighty colonists refused. Treat with these brigands who had murdered and burnt and raped? Impossible. In vain the Commissioners protested. The colonists, supremely confident that they would without difficulty drive these revolted dogs back to their kennels, answered that they would grant pardon only to repentant criminals who returned to work. The message ended with the terse request to the envoys, "Get out!" The white colonists could not understand that Biassou was no longer a slave but a leader of 40,000 men. When he got this message he lost his temper and remembered the white prisoners. "I shall make them pay for the insolence of the Assembly which has dared to write to me with so little respect," and ordered them all to be killed. Toussaint, always a hater of unnecessary bloodshed, calmed his chief.

The disappointed Commissioners arranged an interview with Jean François. The Colonial Assembly accused them of plotting counter-revolution. The Commissioners invited them to send delegates.

At the appointed place and time Jean François appeared, leading his horse by the bridle. At the sight of him, M. Bullet, a colonist, was so overpowered with rage that he struck him with a riding-whip. Jean François, fiercely angry, fell back to his own band and peace hung on a thread. At this dangerous moment Saint-Leger had the quick-wittedness and courage to advance alone among the hostile blacks and speak to them kindly. So moved were they at this unexpected behaviour that Jean François threw himself at the feet of the men from France. He reiterated his promise. For the freedom of 400 of the leaders and forgetfulness of the past he would lead the blacks back to slavery. The Commissioners asked him as a guarantee of good faith to return the white prisoners. He agreed and asked to return for his wife, a prisoner in Le Cap, whom the whites had not dared to execute for fear of reprisals. The interview ended amicably, Jean François assuring the Commissioners that he was "touched to see at last white men who showed humanity."

Next day he sent the promised prisoners to Le Cap. But the blacks had probably got to know that something was in the wind. The prisoners were under a strong escort, including Toussaint, which was scarcely sufficient to save them from the hostility of those they met on the way. The members of the delegation presented themselves at the bar of the Assembly. The president would not even speak to them but communicated with them only by note. "Continue to give proof of your repentance and say to those who send you, to address themselves to the Commissioners: it is only by their intercession that the Assembly can come to a decision on your fate." He wanted to impress on the blacks that the Commissioners were subordinate to the Assembly, and he succeeded. So disdainful was the Assembly that it would not include the negotiations in the minutes. Toussaint had plenary powers, and in a vain attempt to break down the pride of the colonists he secretly reduced the number to be freed from 400 to 60.[9] The colonists would not hear of it. Then and only then did Toussaint come to an unalterable decision from which he never wavered and for which he died. Complete liberty for all, to be attained and held by their own strength. The most extreme revolutionaries are formed by circumstances. It is probable that, looking at the wild hordes of blacks who surrounded him, his heart sank at the prospect of the war and the barbarism which would follow freedom even if it

[9] Toussaint in later years often said this. See Sannon, *Histoire de Toussaint-L'Ouverture*. Port-au-Prince, Haiti, 1933, Vol. III, p. 18.

were achieved. He was ready to go a long way to meet the colonists. He probably hoped for some attempt at better treatment. But having been driven to take his decision, as was his way, he never looked back. On his return he told his chiefs not to look to the Commissioners for anything.[10] They had only a faculty of intercession and their powers were subordinate to those of the Assembly. Biassou, who had demanded an interview, evaded it.

Henceforth it was war, and war needed trained soldiers. Toussaint dropped his post of Physician to the Armies of the King, and assuming the title of Brigadier-General started to train an army. Once only in his political life did he ever fail to meet an emergency with action bold and correct.

In the West Province Rigaud, Beauvais and Pinchinat were using as their agent in the gangs a young slave named Hyacinth. He was only 21 years of age, but he went from plantation to plantation claiming, as most leaders of agricultural revolts, that he was divinely inspired. We can judge the backwardness of the western slaves at the beginning of the revolution from the fact that both Hyacinth, and another men, Romaine the prophetess (*sic*), fortified their authority with divine attributes, while Jean François and Biassou in the North from the very beginning aimed at a social revolution. The blacks flocked to join the confederate army of Mulattoes and whites at La Croix-des-Bouquets, and on March 31st the battle between the Confederates and the Patriots of Port-au-Prince took place. The slaves were nearly all native-born Africans. Armed only with knives, picks, hoes, and sticks with iron points, they went into battle. Led by Hyacinth, they charged the bayonets of the Port-au-Prince volunteers and the French soldiers without fear or care for the volleys from Pralotto's cannon which tore their ranks: if they were killed they would wake again in Africa. Hyacinth, a bull's tail in his hand, ran from rank to rank crying that his talisman would

10 Lacroix. *Mémoires pour Servir* . . . Vol. I, p. 157.

chase death away. He charged at their head, passing un-
scathed through the bullets and the grape-shot. Under such
leadership the Africans were irresistible. They clutched at
the horses of the dragoons, and pulled off the riders. They
put their arms down into the mouths of the cannon in order
to pull out the bullets and called to their comrades "Come,
come, we have them." The cannon were discharged, and
blew them to pieces. But others swarmed over guns and
gunners, threw their arms around them and silenced them.
Nothing could stop their devotion, and after six hours the
troops of Port-au-Prince retired in disorder. They had lost
over a hundred soldiers, but nearly 2,000 slaves lay dead
upon the field. The combined army then invested Port-au-
Prince.

The whites were not only fighting with the Mulattoes,
but were petitioning the Governor to prevent disturbers of
the peace coming from the Colonial Assembly to disrupt
the West. They sent him the concordats, they said they
would stick to them whatever he said. They asked him to
publish them, to send them to the King, to the Legislative
in France, to the merchants of the great ports, to everybody.[11]

Whatever the reservations they had made when they
formed this pact with the bastard Mulattoes, the whites
were now eager to cement the alliance and Roume was
overwhelmed by the number of these appeals. Revolution,
says Karl Marx, is the locomotive of history. Here was a
locomotive that had travelled at remarkable speed, for
in April 1792, not yet three years after the fall of the Bastille, the white Patriots in Port-au-Prince were being besieged by a composite army of royalist commandants, white
planters, brown-skinned Mulattoes, and black slaves, none
of them constrained but all for the time being free and
equal partners. No doubt most of the rich were only awaiting the restoration of "order" to put the slaves back in their
places again, but the mere fact of the revolutionary asso-

11 Memorandum from the *Commissaires Conciliateurs des
Citoyens Blancs de l'Artibonite. Les Archives Nationales*, DXXV,
2. One of eight pieces collected by Roume and sent to France.

ciation and the temporary equality meant that the old spell
was broken and things would never be the same again.

The Colonial Assembly in addition to war with the
slaves and war with the Mulattoes had started a fierce row
with the Commissioners over precedence. In Le Cap the
Patriots actually had the Governor under arrest for some
time and were plotting to murder Mirbeck who sailed for
home on February 30th. Saint-Leger had gone to Port-au-
Prince. The Patriots there, spurred on by the Assembly in
Le Cap, threatened to deport him, and he took refuge with
the Confederates. Saint-Leger and Roume were now seriously alarmed, not at revolting slaves, but at the growth of
the counter-revolution. In the same way as Barnave, the
Lameths and their friends in France, white San Domingo
was growing tired of the red cockade and beginning to
look once more to the royal authority. The Confederate
Army seemed all white cockade. But just at this time
Pinchinat had a meeting with Saint-Leger, and what he
told that gentleman made him fly post-haste to France.
Roume also was due to leave three days after, but in a
chance conversation he smelt a royalist plot and stayed to
ward it off. The royalists indeed thought that San Domingo
was now ripe for the picking. But they were mistaken.
Pinchinat had played an astute game. The royalists had
hoped to use the Mulattoes. Now they found that they had
been used instead. As Beauvais told Roume afterwards,
"We were never the dupes of the white cockades. We had
to conquer our rights, we needed auxiliaries. If the Devil
had presented himself we would have enrolled him. These
gentlemen offered and we used them, while allowing them
to believe that we were their dupes."
    The decree of April 4th now came to clinch the vic-
tory of the Mulattoes and allow them openly to support
the French Revolution—for a time.

The colonial question had frayed the nerves and exhausted the Constituent, all of whose members were excluded by law from the Legislative which met on October 1st. The new deputies were no better off as far as the colonial question was concerned for in addition to the Rights of Man for Mulattoes they now faced a slave revolt.

On the Right were the Feuillants, or King's Party, led on the colonial question by Vaublanc, who approved the condition of slaves, even Mulattoes. The Left was stronger since the elections. But though there were over a hundred Jacobin deputies in the Legislative they were split; on the extreme Left were Robespierre and the Mountain, on the Right were the Brissotins, or followers of Brissot, better known in history as the Girondins. The Paris masses organised in the Commune were following the Jacobins. Robespierre and the Mountain would fight for Mulatto rights. So would Brissot, but Brissot's group was composed of Vergniaud, Guadet, and others, actual deputies of the maritime towns. The Girondins were so called after the Gironde province, whose chief town was Bordeaux. Vergniaud was deputy for Bordeaux and all the maritime towns were still firmly against the Rights of Man for Mulattoes.

What first frightened them was the way the news of the insurrection reached France. Paris heard of it from an English paper. The English Ambassador gave information about the seriousness of the uprising—he had got it from Jamaica through London. The *Moniteur,* day after day, asked, why no news from de Blanchelande? On November 7th the *Moniteur* printed a copy of the letter the colonists had written to the Governor of Jamaica. Only on the 8th was a letter from de Blanchelande asking for troops read in the House. The maritime bourgeois began to look at these colonists with a different eye: the Mulattoes at least were faithful to France, and they were strong supporters of slavery.

The first question was for troops to quell the revolt. But in a revolution the revolution comes first. Right and Left wing of the Legislative wanted to know how many troops were to be sent and who would control them. The King was still head of the Army and Navy. The officers were royalist and centres of the counter-revolution. The King's Ministers and officials were still functioning, in Paris and in San Domingo. To put an army and a fleet into the hands of these people was to be putting weapons which, after the suppression of the insurrection, perhaps before, might be used against the revolution itself, and place the richest colony of France entirely in royalist hands. Jacobins and Feuillants fought it out day after day. But though it was a question of repressing a slave revolt, the Legislative, like the Constituent, would not tolerate the use of the word slave. When a deputy in the course of a speech happened to say "But the slaves are the property of the colonists . . ." there were the usual protests and demands that the speaker be called to order. The Legislative, more to the Left, was, perhaps for this reason, even more sensitive than the Constituent. The Colonial Commission, wishing as usual to have everything settled in the ministry, would not make any report. But the Friends of the Negro were far more powerful now, and Brissot gave warning. If the Commission did not present its report in ten days, he was going to open a debate on December 1st. During the interval delegates from the Colonial Assembly arrived in Paris, and on November 30th one of them, Millet, put the colonists' case. It is probable that never, in any parliamentary assembly, was so much impudent lying and dishonesty packed into any single speech.

Millet's description of slavery proved it to be the happiest form of society known in either ancient or modern times. "We live in peace. gentlemen, in the midst of our slaves. . . . Let an intelligent and educated man compare the deplorable state of these men in Africa with the pleasant and easy life which they enjoy in the colonies. . . . Sheltered by all the necessities of life, surrounded with an ease unknown in the greater part of the countries of Europe, secure in the enjoyment of their property, for they had property and it was sacred, cared for in their illnesses with an expense and an attention that you would seek in vain in the hospitals so boasted of in England, protected, respected in the infirmities of age; in peace with their children, and with their family . . . freed when they had rendered important services: such was the picture, true and not embellished, of the government of our Negroes, and this domestic government perfected itself particularly during the last ten years with a care of which you will find no model in Europe. The most sincere attachment bound the master to the slave; we slept in safety in the middle of these men who had become our children and many among us had neither locks nor bolts on our doors."

This was supposed to be the lot of the slaves up to 1787, the year before the Le Jeune case. Terror, to keep the slaves in subjection, attested in a thousand documents? No such thing. True, there were a small number of hard and ferocious masters. "But what was the lot of these wicked men? Branded by public opinion, looked upon with horror by all honest people, shut out from all society, without credit in their business, they lived in opprobrium and dishonour and died in misery and despair. . . ."

What was it that changed this idyllic state of affairs? At this point enter the villain.

"However, gentlemen, a Society takes shape in the bosom of France and prepares from afar the destruction and the convulsions to which we are subjected. . . . And far from being able to continue with our work, this society forced us to renounce it by sowing the spirit of insubordination among our slaves and anxiety among us."

Having hurled his bomb at the Friends of the Negro, Millet turned to the Assembly itself. He knew the tender spot. "Soon they say this Society will demand that the slave-trade be suppressed, that is to say, that the profits which can result from it for French commerce will be delivered to foreigners, for never will its romantic philosophy persuade all the powers of Europe that it is their duty to abandon the cultivation of the colonies and to leave the inhabitants of Africa a prey to the barbarity of their tyrants rather than to employ them elsewhere. Under kind masters they exploit a territory which would remain uncultivated without them, and of which the rich productions are, for the nation which possesses them, a great source of industry and of prosperity."

The Mulattoes? They and the whites had lived peaceably—nay happily. "The bonds of affection and of good feeling which existed between these two classes of men" would be strengthened by the just and humane laws a Colonial Assembly would pass. But here too the Friends of the Negro falsely represented the attitude of the whites as the pretensions of vanity and an endeavour to resist just claims.

But no man can keep it up for ever, least of all men trained in the French intellectual tradition. Before Millet concluded he suddenly let slip the elegant drapery and gave a glimpse of white San Domingo in all its bloated nakedness.

"These coarse men [the blacks] are incapable of knowing liberty and enjoying it with wisdom, and the imprudent law which would destroy their prejudices would be for them and for us a decree of death."

The Legislature listened in silence. This was no juggling with the word slavery—it was the thing itself, presented to the bourgeoisie for their endorsement through all eternity. Jaurès notes that there was no applause, none even of those disgusted interruptions with which the Legislative was wont to express its disapproval of the mere word slavery. When Millet was finished, the President invited the delegates to the honours of the session. But this was too much. One of the extreme Left jumped up in a rage. "What, Mr. President, you invite to the session men who have just outraged philosophy and liberty, men who have just insulted. . . ." But the profits of the slave trade were too much for the Assembly and the Left itself had no heart for this business.

Next day Brissot took the floor, and on behalf of the Mulattoes made a masterly and celebrated speech. He showed the rich whites anxious to have peace and ready to give political rights to the Mulattoes; the Patriots, for the most part heavily indebted to France and bent on independence, jealous of the Mulattoes who did not owe, and determined to maintain the privilege of race, all the more dear to them in that it rested now on such insecure foundation.

"It is by this that we can explain the existence all at the same time in the heart of the same colonist, of hatred against the man of colour who claims his rights, against the merchant who claims his debts, against a free Government which wishes that justice be done to all."

Once more the bourgeoisie battled over Mulatto rights. This time the contest lasted for weeks, in and out of the House. Vaublanc took the place of the absent Barnave, but the Friends of the Negro had a new argument in the concordats between whites and Mulattoes, and the maritime bourgeois were now convinced that the only way to save the colony was to give the Mulattoes their rights: the negotiations of the Patriots with other countries had opened their eyes as to the real nature of these gentlemen. Vergniaud and Guadet were able to convince their patrons that the old policy was false. The great ship-owners, merchants and traders threw over the colonists. Barnave's group, the Feuillants, formed the governing Ministry, but the revolution was taking courage again. The Feuillants were overthrown on March 10th and a Girondin ministry came in, with Roland at its head, but Madame Roland and Brissot as its leading spirits. On March 24th, by a large majority, the Legislative passed a decree, giving full political rights to the men of colour. Some tried to argue that the decisions of the Constituent were sacrosanct, but a deputy of the Left, to the accompaniment of great applause, challenged the theory that the Legislative was forever bound by the decrees of the Constituent and boldly asserted the sovereignty of the people over the rights of formal assemblies. Three new Commissioners were appointed with supreme powers and large forces to enforce the decree and restore order, and on April 4th the King's signature made the decree law.

But what of the slaves? The slaves had revolted for freedom. The revolt was to be suppressed. But at least there might be a promise of pardon, of kind treatment in the future. Not a word. Neither from Vaublanc on the Right nor Robespierre on the Left. Robespierre made an ass of himself by violently objecting to the word slavery, when proposed as a substitute for non-free. Brissot made a passing reference to them as being unfortunate, and that was all.

"The cause of the men. of colour is then the cause of the patriots of the old Third Estate and finally of the people so long oppressed." So had spoken Brissot, and Brissot, representative of the Third Estate, was prepared to help the Third Estate of the Mulattoes and give the people, in France as well as in San Domingo, phrases. The French peasants were still clamouring for the Assembly to relieve them of the feudal dues. The Brissotins would not do it. They would not touch property, and the slaves were property. Blangetty, a deputy, proposed a motion for gradual enfranchisement. The Legislative would not even discuss it. On March 26th, two days after the decree in favour of the Mulattoes, Ducos dared to propose that every Mulatto child be free, "whatever the status of its mother." The Legislative in wrath voted the previous question, and Ducos was not even allowed to speak on his motion. The Friends of the Negro, good Liberals, were now in power and were as silent about slavery as any colonist. The slaves, ignorant of politics, had been right not to wait on these eloquent phrase-makers. Toussaint, that astute student of French politics, read and noted.

Toussaint alone among the black leaders, with freedom for all in his mind, was in those early months of 1792 organising out of the thousands of ignorant and untrained blacks an army capable of fighting European troops. The insurgents had developed a method of attack based on thei   verwhelming numerical superiority. They did not rush forward in mass formation like fanatics. They placed themselves in groups, choosing wooded spots in such a way as to envelop their enemy, seeking to crush him by weight of numbers. They carried out these preliminary manœuvres in dead silence, while their priests (the black ones) chanted the wanga, and the women and children sang and danced in a frenzy. When these had reached the necessary height of excitement the fighters attacked. If they met with resistance they retired without exhausting themselves, but at the slightest hesitation in the defence they became extremely bold and, rushing up to the cannon, swarmed all over their opponents. At first they could not even use the guns they captured, and used to apply the match at the wrong end. It was from these men "unable to speak two words of French" that an army had to be made. Toussaint could have had thousands following him. It is characteristic of him that he began with a few hundred picked men, devoted to himself, who learnt the art of war with him from the beginning, as they fought side by side against the French troops and the colonists. In camp he drilled and trained them assiduously. By July 1792, he had no more than five hundred attached to himself, the best of the revolutionary troops. These and not the perorations in the Legislative would be decisive in the struggle for freedom. But nobody took much notice of Toussaint and his black followers. Feuillants and Jacobins in France, whites and Mulattoes in San Domingo, were still looking upon the slave revolt as a huge riot which would be put down in time, once the division between the slave-owners was closed.

V

And the Paris Masses Complete

SIX THOUSAND MEN, 4,000 National Guards and 2,000 troops of the line, sailed from France in 15 ships to finish with all this quarrelling between the slave-owners in San Domingo and to suppress the black revolt. The Commissioners were Sonthonax, a right-wing Jacobin, friend of Brissot; Polverel, who had moved the expulsion of Barnave and his friends from the Jacobins and was also a follower of Brissot; and one Ailhaud, a nonentity. For the task in hand the expedition was adequate. But it could not escape the division which was tearing all France after July 1789.

The Commissioners were revolutionaries, the commanding officers were officers of the King. Before the boat left, Desparbes, the commander, quarrelled with the Commissioners about precedence and addressed to the troops "equivocal and unconstitutional" words. They quarrelled so loudly that it was heard by the officers and men. They quarrelled again over the method of landing and they split as soon as they landed. The National Guard were civilians of the revolution. The troops were soldiers of the King. As soon as Desparbes landed, instead of mobilising all his forces for an attack against the slaves, he conspired with the local royalists, and the National Guards were distributed among the various camps under royalist officers. The Commissioners carried the revolution on board with them. They went to meet it. But what was of infinitely more importance for the slaves, they had left it behind them.

They had sailed from Rochefort in the middle of July. Before they reached San Domingo the Paris masses, tired of the equivocations and incompetence of the parliamentarians, had taken matters into their own hands and dragged the Bourbons off the throne.

To escape from the demands of the peasants, the wish of the workers that a maximum price be fixed for foodstuffs, and the other burning questions of the revolution, the Girondins, 17 days after the decree of April 4th, plunged the country into war with Austria. The army was half-royalist, half-revolutionary. Marie Antoinette was sending the war plans to the enemy. Revolutionary France seemed unable to organise itself, and the royalists in France were awaiting the entry of the foreigners to rise and massacre the revolution. The Girondins, afraid of the counter-revolution, but more afraid of the Paris masses, would not take steps against the royalists, and the people of Paris, goaded to exasperation, stormed the Tuileries on August 10th. They imprisoned the royal family, the Legislative was dissolved, and a new parliament, the National Convention, was summoned. The masses administered a rough justice to the royalist plotters in the September massacres, and took the defence of France into their own dirty but strong and honest hands. The Girondin Government proposed to leave Paris. The workers forbade it. They armed 2,000 volunteers a day, and, with the royalists in their rear quiet for a long time to come, went singing happily to drive the counter-revolution from the soil of France. If revolutionary France was saved it was due to them.

What has all this to do with the slaves? Everything. The workers and peasants of France could not have been expected to take any interest in the colonial question in normal times, any more than one can expect similar interest from British or French workers to-day. But now they were roused. They were striking at royalty, tyranny, reaction and oppression of all types, and with these they included slavery. The prejudice of race is superficially the most irrational of all prejudices, and by a perfectly comprehensible reaction the Paris workers, from indifference in 1789, had come by this time to detest no section of the aristocracy so much as those whom they called "the aristocrats of the skin." [1] On August 11th, the day after the Tuileries fell, Page, a notorious agent of the colonists in France, wrote home almost in despair. "One spirit alone reigns here, it is horror of slavery and enthusiasm for liberty. It is a frenzy which wins all heads and grows every day." [2] Henceforth the Paris masses were for abolition, and their black brothers in San Domingo, for the first time, had passionate allies in France.

The National Convention would be elected and would deliberate under the influence of these masses. The slaves in San Domingo by their insurrection had shown revolutionary France that they could fight and die for freedom; and the logical development of the revolution in France had brought to the front of the stage masses who, when they said abolition, meant it in theory and in practice.

[1] Garran-Coulon, *Rapport sur les Troubles* . . . , Vol. IV, p. 21.
[2] *Débats entre les accusés et les accusateurs dans l'affaire des Colonies*, 6 volumes, Paris, 1798. The official report of the trial of Sonthonax and Polverel. Published by Garran-Coulon. Vol. II, p. 223.

But it takes organisation and time to translate mass feeling into action, and for the moment the revolution had more urgent matters than slavery to deal with.

Neither the new Commissioners nor the people of San Domingo knew anything about August 10th when the Commissioners landed on September 18th.

They had come mainly to deal with the Mulatto question. To their pleased surprise they found that settled. Three years of civil war, one year of the slave revolution, had taught these white planters some sense at last. As soon as the news of the decree arrived all the whites, North, West and South, accepted it. On July 14th, 1792, the whites gave the men of colour a dinner, a few days later the men of colour returned it. The Governor, the commander of the naval station, the Treasurer, all wrote to the Commissioners to say that all the whites had agreed to accept the decree.[3] Naturally there was still race prejudice.

[3] Enclosures in report of the Commissioners to the Minister of Marine, September 30th, 1792, *Les Archives Nationales* DXXV.

(a) D'Augy, President of the Colonial Assembly, in a speech to the Commissioners on their arrival. ". . . to leave you no doubt on our perfect submission to the law of April 4th last in favour of the men of colour and free Negroes."

(b) Letter of Girardin, Commandant of the naval station: "You ask me, Gentlemen, what are the feelings of the soldiers and the sailors relative to the law of April 4th. Their feelings towards the execution of this law are excellent for this law as for all others. When the law speaks they know how to obey, provided that no one seeks to corrupt them. . . ." Girardin warned the Commissioners against the "factious" in Le Cap who wished to disrupt "the harmony which exists between the respectable inhabitants, white and coloured. . . ." He suggested that the Commissioners land at St Marc where "unity between all the citizens is perfect."

(c) Letter of de Blanchelande, the Governor, to the Commissioners: "The Law of April 4th has been published and accepted in the whole colony."

Letter of Souchet, the Treasurer, to the Commissioners: "You will find here the law of April 4th universally accepted. . . ."

Letter of Delpech, another official: "You will see . . . that the first object of your mission, that of assuring the execution of the law of April 4th, will cause you little trouble, but you will have to take many precautions. . . ."

That cannot be destroyed in a day or in a year. But the whites wanted peace, and at the ceremonial reception the white President of the Assembly, the white Mayor of Le Cap, all treated the quarrel with the Mulattoes as a thing of the past. Two things troubled them. One was slavery. "We have not brought half-a-million slaves from the coasts of Africa to make them into French citizens," said the President of the Assembly to Sonthonax, and Sonthonax reassured him. I recognise, he said, only two classes of men in San Domingo, the free, without distinction of colour, and the slaves. But the second question was the revolution. White cockades and red, each hoped for help from the Commissioners. The royalists saw in the Commissioners officials appointed by the King, the revolutionaries saw in them members of the Jacobin Club. Sonthonax, as was inevitable in a Jacobin and a Brissotin, sided with the revolution. He reorganised the Government to concentrate power in the hands of the Commission and included in his council both Mulattoes and a free black. The next step was now obviously the attack on the slaves before the troops began to feel the effects of the climate. But that vigorous attack was never made.

Early in October San Domingo heard the news of August 10th. This was no mere matter of loyalty to a monarch. The bourgeosie throws over its king for a republic quickly enough if thereby it can save its skin and its goods. August 10th was more than that. It was the bid of the masses for power not with speeches but with arms. There could be no truce anywhere on French territory after August 10th. Royalists under Desparbes and revolutionaries under Sonthonax sprang at each other's throats. The Mulattoes fought for Sonthonax, who was victorious, and de-

---

Sonthonax himself writes to the Minister that Roume sent the same news from South and West.

Yet Mr. Lothrop Stoddard, frantically pursuing his racial theories, goes so far as to say on p. 187 of *The French Revolution in San Domingo* (Boston & New York, 1914) that the Governor and the Commander of the station wrote special memoirs stating that the soldiers and sailors "shared the colonists' repugnance to the law of April 4th."

ported Desparbes and the other royalist leaders to France. The revolution was triumphant. But Sonthonax was determined to abolish Mulatto discrimination, and the small whites and the rabble, although revolutionary, were furious at seeing the rich people of colour high in favour with Sonthonax. They raged with jealousy and race prejudice. Sonthonax called them "aristocrats of the skin" and stood by the spirit and letter of the April 4th decree. Once more the division between the rulers had given a further breathing space to the ruled.

Yet this apparent good fortune was fundamentally no accident. The first sign of a thoroughly ill-adjusted or bankrupt form of society is that the ruling classes cannot agree how to save the situation. It is this division which opens the breach, and the ruling classes will continue to fight with each other, just so long as they do not fear the mass seizure of power. The insurrection nevertheless now seemed at its last gasp. Laveaux, the French commander, even with his few soldiers, defeated Toussaint and drove the revolting slaves from their positions. Famine and disease were decimating their forces. Then it was that 15,000 men, women and children, starving, with their soldiers defeated and driven into the mountains, came begging to be taken back. Toussaint and his trained band of a few hundred, little more than a year old, were helpless in the crowd, and Jean François and Biassou though superior in numbers were weaker than he. Candy, who led a band of Mulattoes, had deserted the blacks and joined the Commissioners, beginning that Mulatto vacillation which was to have such disastrous consequences in the future. Early in 1793 Laveaux was preparing a final assault to complete the rout of the insurrection, when he was recalled by the Commissioners.

The revolution had overflowed the boundaries of France. On January 21st, 1793, the King was executed. The revolutionary armies were now winning successes and the ruling classes of Europe armed against this new monster—democracy. In February came war with Spain, then with Britain, and it was to defend the coasts against the foreign enemy that Sonthonax recalled Laveaux. The rev-

olutionary tide flowed down into the plain once more, never
again to lose heart, and Toussaint begins to emerge as the
man of the future.

For the moment the blacks did not know where their
true interests lay. And if they did not, it was not their
fault, because the French Revolution, being still in the
hands of Liberals and "moderates," was clearly bent on
driving the blacks back to the old slavery. Thus, when the
Spaniards in San Domingo offered the blacks an alliance
against the French Government, naturally they accepted.
Here were white men offering them guns and ammunition
and supplies, recognising them as soldiers, treating them as
equals and asking them to shoot other whites. All trooped
over to join the Spanish forces and Jean François and Biassou were appointed lieutenants-general of the armies of the
King of Spain. Toussaint went also, but he made his terms
with the Spaniards as an independent leader, and not as a
subordinate of Biassou. He had 600 men, well-trained and
absolutely devoted to him, and he received an official title
of colonel.[4] Like all the other blacks, Toussaint attacked
the godless kingless republic and fought in the name of
royalty, both Spanish and French. But for him, already,
these slogans were merely politics, not convictions.

It is his maturity that is so astonishing. Jean François
and Biassou were perfectly satisfied with their new official
positions. But Toussaint proposed to the Marquis d'Hermona, his immediate chief, a plan for conquering the
French colony by granting freedom to all the blacks.[5]
D'Heamona agreed but Don Garcia the Governor refused.
Foiled here, before June he wrote to Laveaux[6]—he had not

[4] Maréchal-de-camp.
[5] Sannon, *Histoire de Toussaint-L'Ouverture*, Port-au-Prince,
1933, Vol. II, p. 220. Toussaint mentions the plan without giving details but it could not have been otherwise than as stated,
for it was immediately after this that he wrote to Laveaux.
[6] Toussaint himself in a letter of May 18th, 1794, reminds
Laveaux of this offer made before the disasters of Le Cap

yet been with the Spaniards four months—offering to join the French and fight against the Spaniards if Laveaux would recognise the liberty of the blacks and grant a plenary amnesty. Laveaux refused and Toussaint, baffled, remained with the Spaniards.

But things went from bad to worse with the French, and on August 6th, Chanlatte, a Mulatto officer, one of Sonthonax' creations, offered Toussaint "the protection" of the Republic if he would bring his forces over. In politics all abstract terms conceal treachery. Toussaint refused and blandly replied that "the blacks wished a King and that they would lay down their arms only when he had been recognised." Doubtless Chanlatte thought him to be an ignorant and fanatical African, for many historians, even after studying Toussaint's career, have still continued to believe that he had some "African" faith in kingship. Nothing was further from Toussaint's mind. Though allied to the Spaniards he continued boldly to rally the blacks on the slogan of liberty for all. On August 29th he issued a call:

"Brothers and friends. I am Toussaint L'Ouverture, my name is perhaps known to you. I have undertaken vengeance. I want Liberty and Equality to reign in San Domingo. I work to bring them into existence. Unite yourselves to us, brothers, and fight with us for the same cause, etc.

"Your very humble and very obedient servant.
"(Signed) TOUSSAINT L'OUVERTURE,
"General of the Armies of the King, for the Public Good." [7]

which took place in June, 1793. The letter is found in *La Bibliothèque Nationale*, MSS. Department. Toussaint's letters to Laveaux and kindred documents arranged in chronological order fill three volumes. They are of the first importance. Schoelcher's *Vie de Toussaint-L'Ouverture* quotes heavily from these letters, and should be consulted for convenience. See pp. 98-99.
[7] *Lettres de Toussaint-L'Ouverture, La Bibliothèque Nationale.* (MSS. Dept.)

This curious document shows that already Toussaint
had changed his name from Bréda to L'Ouverture,[8] and
already had reason to expect that his name was known. But
what is most noteworthy is the confidence with which he
is riding two horses at once. He uses the prestige of his
position as general of the armies of the King, but he calls
on the Negroes in the name of liberty and equality, the
watchwords of the French revolution, of which royalty was
the sworn enemy. Neither would help his aims, so he was
using both.

Sonthonax continued to rule with sternness in the
North, the whites sullenly accepting the victory of the revolution, the Mulattoes grabbing greedily at all Government
posts. Sonthonax, though later he would be disgusted with
this greediness, leaned on them and deported for trial in
France all who smelt of counter-revolution. Just at this
time there arrived from France, Galbaud, appointed Governor in place of de Blanchelande, arrested and sent to
France by Sonthonax. When Galbaud reached Le Cap,
Sonthonax was at Port-au-Prince visiting Polverel. The
whites of Le Cap, nearly all for the counter-revolution, gave
Galbaud, who had property in San Domingo, a tumultu-
ous welcome. Sonthonax and Polverel knew what this
meant and hurrying from Port-au-Prince dismissed Galbaud
and his staff and put them on a vessel to be taken to France.
But Galbaud was not going so easily. The sailors in the fleet
took his part. He landed with a force, the whites of the
counter-revolution joined him, and together they drove the
Commissioners and their forces out of the city. Sonthonax,
facing defeat and extermination, gave orders that the slaves
and prisoners of Le Cap should be armed; at the same
time, promising pardon and freedom to the insurgent

---

[8] L'Ouverture means "the opening." Either Laveaux or Polverel is
said to have exclaimed at the news of another victory by Toussaint: "This man makes an opening everywhere," whence the
new name began. It is not improbable that the slaves called him
L'Ouverture from the gap in his teeth. Later he dropped the
apostrophe.

slaves who surrounded the city, he unloosed the lot at Galbaud and the whites. Galbaud's sailors, drunk with victory and with wine, had just turned from fighting to pillage when 10,000 blacks swooped down from the hills on to the city. The road from the heights ran along the sea-shore, and the sailors who remained on the ships in the harbour could see them hour after hour swarming down to Le Cap. The counter-revolution fled for the harbour leaving all behind them. Galbaud had to throw himself into the sea to get to a boat, and to complete the royalist discomfiture, fire broke out and burnt two-thirds of the city to the ground, destroying hundreds of millions' worth of property. Ten thousand refugees crowded on to the vessels in the harbour and set out for the United States of America, the great majority of them never to return. It was the end of white domination in San Domingo.

That is how white San Domingo destroyed itself. The current legend that the abolition of slavery resulted in the destruction of the whites is a shameless lie, typical of the means by which reaction covers its crimes in the past and seeks to block advance in the present. In May 1792 the whites were all tumbling over each other to give rights to the Mulattoes, and Roume says that when the decree of April 4th arrived, they published it the day after.[9] It was too late. If they had done it a year before, at the outbreak of the slave revolution, they would have been able to master it before it spread. Why didn't they? Race prejudice? Nonsense. Why did not Charles I and his followers behave reasonably to Cromwell? As late as 1646, two years after Marston Moor, Mrs. Cromwell and Mrs. Ireton had tea with Charles at Hampton Court. Cromwell, great revolutionary but great bourgeois, was willing to come to terms. Why did not Louis and Marie Antoinette and the court behave reasonably to the moderate revolutionaries before August 10th? Why indeed? The monarchy in France had to be torn up by the roots. Those in power never give way,

[9] Roume to the Committee of Public Safety. Report of 18 Ventôse (1793), *Les Archives du Ministère des Affaires Étrangères.* A document of great value.

and admit defeat only to plot and scheme to regain their lost power and privilege. Had the monarchists been white, the bourgeoisie brown, and the masses of France black, the French Revolution would have gone down in history as a race war. But although they were all white in France they fought just the same. The struggle of classes ends either in the reconstruction of society or in the common ruin of the contending classes. The French Revolution laid the basis of modern France, the country as a whole being strong enough to stand the shock and profit by it, but so corrupt and rotten was the slave society of San Domingo that it could not stand any strain and perished as it deserved to perish.

Sonthonax returned to Le Cap, a town half-ruined. To his surprise, the pillage over, the revolted slaves did not stay with the Commissioners. Gathering up their plunder they went back to their roving life in the hills and to their Spanish allies. The French sent envoys to win them over, but all of them, Toussaint included, replied that they could only obey a King and they would only recognise the Commissioners when they had a King, which piece of sophistry had been carefully taught them by the Spaniards. The royalist officers were deserting Sonthonax for the Spaniards, and now, to complete the difficulties of the Commissioners, the slaves who had not yet revolted, kindled by the revolutionary ferment around them, refused to be slaves any longer. They crowded the streets of Le Cap, exalted as at a revivalist meeting, and called for liberty and equality. On plantations which had hitherto escaped destruction it was the same. The white slave-owners who remained in San Domingo had learnt much in the last two years. One of them who owned hundreds of slaves told Sonthonax that it would be best to declare abolition. Sonthonax learnt that Jean François was about to rally the blacks to his standard by calling them all to liberty. Hemmed in on all sides and looking for support against the enemy at home and the enemy abroad, Sonthonax declared the abolition of slavery on August 29th, 1793. It was his last card and he could not help himself.

In the West Province, Polverel, although dissastified, accepted the decree and persuaded the whites who remained not to oppose it. For the time being, having no other alternative, they accepted. But the decree was a failure. Those freed by Sonthonax remained always faithful to him; but Jean François, Biassou and the other experienced soldiers remained in alliance with the Spaniards, and Toussaint, though not faithful to the Spaniards, still refused to go over to the French.

In the South the slaves had revolted against both whites and Mulattoes, and were winning great victories. But in the West the Mulattoes were still dominant. Rigaud and Beauvais with their white allies had long since captured Port-au-Prince. Chasing the royalists away, the Mulatto army established a Mulatto domination. But when the fighting was over they chose some of the bravest slaves and offered them freedom if they would lead the rest back to slavery and keep them in order. The offer was accepted, and 100,000 slaves were led back to their plantations—the inevitable fate of any class which allows itself to be led by another. Sure of their slaves, many of the Mulatto proprietors in the West, though having the Government in their hands, were furious at the decree of abolition and abandoned the revolution to which they owed so much. Property, white and Mulatto, had come together again under the flag of the counter-revolution.

Sonthonax tried desperately to win over the black slaves. But despite all the overtures by Laveaux, urging the decree of abolition as evidence of good-will toward the blacks, Toussaint would not join the French. His band was growing fast now, not only in numbers but in quality. Many of the deserting royalist officers, instead of joining the Spanish forces, preferred to join a troop of blacks who had formerly been French, hoping to gain influence over them and use them for their own purposes. They joined Toussaint's band. From them he learnt the orthodox military art: used them to train his troops, and organised an efficient staff. There were no maps of the district. He called together the local inhabitants: learnt from them the geography of their neighbourhood and from his early dabblings in geometry was able to construct useful maps. One of his guides was Dessalines, unable to read or write, his body scarred with strokes from the whip, but a born soldier, soon to hold high command.

Toussaint's forces grew, as much by his fearless fighting as by his mastery of politics and intrigue. Lieutenant-Colonel Nully having deserted to Toussaint, the French appointed Brandicourt in his place. With 300 picked men Toussaint prepared an ambush for Brandicourt. As Brandicourt's men approached they were not fired upon but challenged: "Who goes there?" "France." "Then let your general come and speak to ours—no harm shall befall him." Brandicourt who was in the centre ordered an attack, but his men begged him to parley with Toussaint. As soon as Brandicourt went forward he was seized and brought before Toussaint, who commanded him to write an order to his forces to yield. In tears, Brandicourt wrote to Pacot his second-in-command that he was a prisoner and left it to him to do what he thought fit. Toussaint tore up the letter and insisted that Brandicourt should write a direct command to lay down arms. Brandicourt wrote, and on getting the letter, Pacot (who was secretly in touch with Toussaint) said to the other officers, "Do what you like, I shall surrender." The three detachments joined Toussaint's forces without a blow. When Toussaint returned to camp leading these white troops, his own men were so startled that he had difficulty in assuring them that the newcomers were allies, and his chief d'Hermona was equally astonished.

This bloodless victory gave him Dondon. He marched on Marmelade, where a stern engagement lasted all day. Vernet, the Mulatto commander, called a coward by Polverel, found himself in difficulties, and soon he deserted to Toussaint with 1,200 men. Toussaint took Ennery and the commander of that fort joined him. There remained only

Plaisance between him and Gonaïves; but he was driven back by a Mulatto legion from the West, which recaptured Ennery. After a short respite to gather his forces he re-took Ennery, and in December 1793 he marched into Gonaïves. Going back he took Plaisance, and Chanlatte, the commander, joined him with all his troops. All the garrisons at St Marc, Verrettes, Arcahaye, in hopeless isolation, surrendered to Toussaint and joined his forces. The abolition of slavery, the basis of property in San Domingo, had weakened the morale of the republican commanders, and between joining the counter-revolution under Toussaint, and being massacred by his forces, the choice was easy, especially as the black general already had a great reputation for humanity, a very singular thing in the San Domingo of those days. Thus in the early months of 1794 Toussaint held the Cordon of the West from the Spanish colony to the sea, and had isolated the North Province from the West and South. The Spaniards held every fortified post in the North Province except Le Cap itself and two others, and all knew it was Toussaint's doing. Toussaint was still subordinate to Jean François and Biassou, but he now had 4,000 men and under him were blacks, Mulattoes and whites, former officers of the *ancien régime* and former republicans. But the majority were black, and Dessalines, Christophe and Moïse had been slaves. Toussaint was in undisputed command, already a master of the art of war, and a skilful negotiator. But although he had fought under the flag of the counter-revolution, he knew where his power lay, and under the very noses of the Spanish commanders he continued to call the blacks to freedom.

Jean François and Biassou, his rivals, were now the idols of the refugee French colonists. Two years before they would not even speak to them, but revolution is a great teacher and these French planters, "the new subjects of the King of Spain," [10] as they called themselves, compared

[10] *Lettres de Toussaint-L'Ouverture, La Bibliothèque Nationale.* This and the other passages quoted are from a complaint by the émigré colonists to the Spanish Governor, dated April 4th. 1794. See Schoelcher, p. 92.

Jean François and Biassou to the "great generals of an-
tiquity" and looked to them to clear the mountains, "re-
establish order," and then take Le Cap. Biassou, Jean
François and d'Hermona formed a plan of campaign and
Biassou began to group his forces, suppressing some of
the camps Toussaint had instituted. Toussaint replaced the
camps and raised the blacks. To the wrath and disgust of
the colonists he persisted in violating the "sacred promises"
of the Spanish King by promising "general freedom to all
the slaves who had gone back to their duty" and were preserving order. The colonists praised Biassou, "whose conduct merited general admiration," but they cursed Toussaint and his liberty for all, called him a traitor to the
King, and demanded his head. Toussaint exercised an extraordinary domination over all men with whom he
worked, and the Marquis d'Hermona, who admired him
greatly, either could not or would not do anything.

And while Toussaint performed these miracles in the
North, the British added to the complications by making
an armed bid for San Domingo, now apparently without
defence.

From the very beginning of the revolution, the planters had been throwing out threats that they would seek the
overlordship of Britain, and after the slave revolt in 1791
they offered the colony to Pitt. But San Domingo was
hardly Africa or India where one raided at will. Interference would mean war with France. The British therefore
refused, but busied themselves with schemes and plans of
conquest. In December 1792, Lieutenant Colonel John
Chalmers, an expert on West Indian affairs, wrote a memorandum to Pitt on what he called the "vast, vast importance" of San Domingo.[11] "The deplorable situation of the
French West Indies," said Chalmers, "seems loudly to crave
the protection of Great Britain." And oddly enough this
protection promised to be most profitable. "The advantages

[11] Chatham Papers, G.D. 8/334. Miscellaneous papers relating
to France, 1784-1795. (Public Record Office.)

of San Domingo to Great Britain are innumerable and would give her a monopoly of sugar, indigo, cotton, and coffee. This island for ages would give such aid and force to industry as would be most happily felt in every part of the Empire. It would prevent all migration from all the three kingdoms to America, which (without such acquisition) will keep pace and augment with the prosperity of America so as to become truly alarming and detrimental."

Chalmers shared advanced British opinion on the decline of the British West Indies. "The West Indian possessions of Great Britain are comparatively deficient, diminutive, widely extended and, therefore, little capable of defence." Here was a chance to remedy this sad state of affairs. By an alliance with Spain, "offensive and defensive," the two countries could keep France and America out of the West Indies, and secure themselves there. Britain should try to get the whole of San Domingo, but should circumstances or the united powers decide the whole to be "too ponderous for her political scale," she must at all events retain the North part of the island.

The patriotic Colonel ended on a characteristic note. "Gloomy and perilous as the present state of Europe is, yet, from these evils, the greatest and most lasting benefits may arise from a brief well-conducted war, terminated by a happy pacification. . . . It is, therefore, humbly hoped that the belligerents will see the strong necessity of confining her [France] to limits as established at the death of Henry the Fourth, adding thereunto all her foreign dominions, San Domingo and the isle of Bourbon, excepting."

Colonel Chalmers's anxiety about the "vast, vast" importance of San Domingo was quite unjustified. Those were Pitt's sentiments exactly. The moment war seemed imminent, Dundas despatched four French colonists to Williamson, the Governor of Jamaica, with a letter of introduction. Immediately after the declaration of war, negotiations were begun and on September 3rd, 1793, capitulations were signed.[12] The colony would accept the pro-

[12] Colonial Office Papers, Jamaica. C.O. 137/91, February 25th, 1793.

tection of Great Britain until the peace. Modifications would be introduced in the Exclusive, but the *ancien régime* would be re-established, slavery, Mulatto discrimination, and all. Clarkson and Wilberforce were left to bewail and bemoan[13] the peculiar lukewarmness Pitt now showed for the cause he had advocated so urgently a few years before.

If ever there was a good thing, this looked like one. Petitions from all parts of the island assured the British that they would be welcomed by all persons possessing property, and who else in San Domingo mattered? All expenses were to be repaid from the revenues of San Domingo. General Cuyler told Dundas that he entertained "no apprehensions of our successes in West Indies." [14] Pitt and Dundas pressed the expedition on, with a reckless disregard even for the safety of Britain. Dundas was "very nearly out of temper" [15] at some delay. For Pitt "the West Indies was the first point to make certain." [16] What San Domingo meant in those days can be judged from the fact that though a French invasion threatened Britain, even that was not to delay the despatch of the expedition. "Additional exertions will then be necessary to make the country take care of its own internal defence." [17] Two years later this same Dundas would tell Parliament that the war in the West Indies was "on the part of this country . . . not a war for riches or local aggrandisement but a war for security." [18] Dundas knew that not a single member of Parliament would believe him. But Parliament has always agreed to

---

[13] James Stephen to Wilberforce: "Mr. Pitt, unhappily for himself, his country and mankind, is not zealous enough in the cause of the negroes to contend for them as decisively as he ought, in this cabinet any more than in parliament." July 17th, 1797. R. I. and S. Wilberforce, *Life of Wilberforce,* London, 1838, Vol. II, pp. 224-225.
[14] Fortescue MSS. (Historical Manuscripts Commission). Vol. II, p. 405. July 17th, 1793.
[15] Fortescue MSS., Dundas to Grenville, October 12th, 1793, Vol. II, p. 444.
[16] *Ibid.* To Grenville, July, 1793, Vol. II, pp. 407-408.
[17] *Ibid.* Dundas to Grenville, October 11th, 1793, Vol. II, p. 443.
[18] February 18th, 1796.

speak in these terms in order to keep the people quiet.

On September 9th the British expedition of 900 men left Jamaica and landed at Jérémie on the 19th. Property-owners are the most energetic flag-waggers and patriots in every country, but only so long as they enjoy their posses-sions: to safeguard those they desert God, King and Coun-try in a twinkling. All propertied San Domingo rushed to welcome the British, the defenders of slavery. Soldiers like the brothers Rigaud and Beauvais and the detachments they commanded, politicians like Pinchinat, stayed with the French, but the Mulatto proprietors, particularly those of the West Province, preferred their slaves to liberty and equality. All the fighting round Port-au-Prince was forgot-ten. When Beauvais remonstrated with Savary, Mulatto Mayor of St Marc, Savary did not disguise his views. "So long as the proclamations of the Civil Commissioners as-sured a happy and prosperous future, I carried out all their instructions; but from the moment I saw that they were preparing the thunder-bolt which is bursting on all sides, I took measures to safe-guard our fellow citizens and pre-serve our property." Ogé's brother went with Savary.

With such a welcome nothing could stop the British. By the beginning of 1794 they were in possession of the whole sea-board of the Gulf of Port-au-Prince, excepting the capital; the whole of the West Province; most of the South, except for a small territory held by Rigaud's troops; and the important fortress of Môle St Nicholas. From the other West Indian islands came even more startling news of the triumph of Britain and the counter-revolution. On February 3rd a British force of 7,000 men and 19 vessels sailed from Barbados and in two months had captured Martinique, Saint Lucia, and Guadeloupe. Williamson, Governor of Jamaica, had information that in Le Cap itself "all the people of property" [19] (the phrase is his own) were waiting to receive them. He wrote to Dundas of the "pro-digious" [20] trade they were now doing with San Domingo

[19] Colonial Office Papers, Jamaica. C.D. 137/91. To Dundas, July 13th, 1793.
[20] *Ibid.* C.D. 137/92. To Dundas, February 9th, 1794.

and hoped that the trade would correspondingly improve British revenues. Dundas congratulated him heartily on this surprisingly quick success.[21]

It was a crucial moment in world history. If the British could hold San Domingo, the finest colony in the world, they would once more be a power in American waters. Instead of being abolitionists they would be the most powerful practitioners and advocates of the slave-trade,[22] on a scale excelling anything they had ever done before. But there was another more urgent issue. If the British completed the conquest of San Domingo, the colonial empire of revolutionary France was gone; its vast resources would be directed into British pockets, and Britain would be able to return to Europe and throw army and navy against the revolution.

Sonthonax, Polverel and Laveaux knew this and fought to save San Domingo for the revolution. "If it is necessary to hide in a double and triple range of hills," said Sonthonax to his followers in Le Cap, "I will show you the way. We shall have no other asylum than cannons, no other food than water and bananas, but we shall live and die free." The British tried to bribe Laveaux, for revolutionaries were of course low fellows who act as they do for money or ambition. Laveaux, a nobleman under the old régime, called out Major James Grant who, however, declined. "Let us perish, citizen," wrote Sonthonax to one of his officers. "Yes, let us perish a thousand times rather than permit the people of San Domingo to fall again into enslavement and servitude. If we are defeated we shall leave for the English only bones and ashes." The British called on him to surrender Port-au-Prince. With a handful of men he disdainfully refused and the British retired. But at the end of May a united force of British soldiers and French

---

[21] *Ibid.* C.D. 137/91. December 13th, 1793.
[22] On new land which was good, such as San Domingo still offered, and later Brazil, the slave even though expensive still gave good profit, and was often the only labour available.

émigrés attacked the town. Traitors let them into an important fort on the outskirts, and Sonthonax and Polverel, escorted by Beauvais and a small detachment of blacks, fled to Jacmel. It was June 4th and the English celebrated the capture of the capital on the birthday of the King. The rest now was only a matter of days.

Toussaint, a Spanish officer and therefore ally of the British, saw all his secret hopes being wrecked by the British victories. He was following the progress of abolition in England.[23] But from the time there seemed a real possibility of getting San Domingo, the Abolition Bill began its long career as a hardy annual. French republic, British constitutional monarchy, Spanish autocracy, though one might smile and another frown according to the exigencies of the moment, none troubled to disguise that in the last analysis the Negro could expect either the overseer's whip or the bayonet. Once the British were masters of San Domingo, then Spaniards and British would turn on the blacks and drive them back into slavery. Sonthonax had abolished slavery, but he had no authority to do so. It was the republican Government in France alone which could decide this, and the republican Government spoke no word.

Despite the feeling for the slaves in France, the Convention did nothing for over a year. As long as Brissot and the Girondins remained in power no word would be said about the slaves. But Brissot and his party could not last. They would not check the speculations of the bourgeoisie with the currency, they would not fix maximum prices for food, they would not tax the rich to pay for the war, they would not pass the legislation necessary to abolish the feudal dues, they would not ratify the seizure of the land by the peasants. Being afraid of Paris they would not bring the whole country under a strong central government, and despite incessant royalist insurrection and plotting they

[23] Saintoyant, *La Colonisation Française* . . . , Vol. II, p. 148.

stuck to a federal system whereby the bourgeoisie in the provinces would be beyond the control of revolutionary Paris. They it was, and not Robespierre and the Mountain, who instituted the revolutionary tribunals aimed, not against the counter-revolution, but against all who proposed any "agrarian law or any other law subversive of territorial, commercial or industrial prosperity." Robespierre was no Communist but he was prepared to go further than the Girondins, and the masses, who by now knew what they wanted, turned from the Girondins and gave their support to Robespierre and the Mountain—the extreme Left. Dumouriez, the Girondin general commanding in the field, deserted to the counter-revolution. The Paris masses, deserting the Paris Commune, hitherto the real revolutionary centre of Paris, organised an independent centre of their own, the famous Evêché; and on May 31st and June 2nd, with firmness but great moderation, made the Girondin leaders retire from the Convention, placing them only under house arrest, and offering hostages out of their own ranks as guarantees for their safety. When history is written as it ought to be written, it is the moderation and long patience of the masses at which men will wonder, not their ferocity. The Girondins escaped and, going to the provinces, joined the counter-revolution.

In those difficult days Robespierre and the Mountain gave France a strong government. The Convention abolished the feudal laws at last, put an end to the most crying abuses, and won the confidence of the people. Despite the political intrigues of the leaders, the Government (while hostile to Communism) took the people into its confidence, for it had nobody else to depend upon. A rare exaltation of sacrifice and devotion moved through revolutionary France and Paris. As in Russia under Lenin and Trotsky, the people were told honestly of victory or of defeat, errors were openly acknowledged, and where to this day reaction can only see a few thousand people who fell under the guillotine, Paris between March 1793 and July 1794 was one of the supreme epochs of political history. Never until 1917 were masses ever to have such powerful influence—for it was no more than influence—upon any government. In these few months of their nearest approach to power they did not forget the blacks. They felt towards them as brothers, and the old slave-owners, whom they knew to be supporters of the counter-revolution, they hated as if Frenchmen themselves had suffered under the whip.

It was not Paris alone but all revolutionary France. "Servants, peasants, workers, the labourers by the day in the fields" [24] all over France were filled with a virulent hatred against the "aristocracy of the skin." There were many so moved by the sufferings of the slaves that they had long ceased to drink coffee, thinking of it as drenched with the blood and sweat of men turned into brutes.[25] Noble and generous working-people of France and those millions of honest English Noncomformists who listened to their clergymen and gave strength to the English movement for the abolition of slavery! These are the people whom the sons of Africa and the lovers of humanity will remember with gratitude and affection, not the perorating Liberals in France nor the "philanthropy plus five per cent" [26] hypocrites in the British Houses of Parliament.

This was the France to which, in January 1794, three deputies sent by San Domingo to the Convention arrived, Bellay, a Negro slave who had purchased his freedom, Mills, a Mulatto, and Dufay, a white man. On February 3rd they attended their first session. What happened there was quite unpremeditated.

The Chairman of the Committee on Decrees addressed the Convention, "Citizens, your Committee on Decrees has verified the credentials of the deputies from San Domingo. It finds them in order, and I move that they be admitted to their places in the Convention." Camboulas rose. "Since 1789 the aristocracy of birth and the aristocracy of religion have been destroyed; but the aristocracy of the skin still

[24] F. Carteau, *Les Soirées Bermudiennes,* Bordeaux, 1802. Authentic, because Carteau was a colonist, opponent of abolition, and relates his own experiences.
[25] *Ibid.*
[26] Cecil Rhodes: "Pure philanthropy is very well in its way, but philanthropy plus five per cent is better."

remains. That too is now at its last gasp, and equality has been consecrated. A black man, a yellow man, are about to join this Convention in the name of the free citizens of San Domingo." The three deputies of San Domingo entered the hall. The black face of Bellay and the yellow face of Mills excited long and repeated bursts of applause.

Lacroix (of Eure-et-Loire) followed. "The Assembly has been anxious to have within it some of those men of colour who have suffered oppression for so many years. To-day it has two of them. I demand that their introduction be marked by the President's fraternal embrace."

The motion was carried amidst applause. The three deputies of San Domingo advanced to the President and received the fraternal kiss while the hall rang with fresh applause.

Next day, Bellay, the Negro, delivered a long and fiery oration, pledging the blacks to the cause of the revolution and asking the Convention to declare slavery abolished. It was fitting that a Negro and an ex-slave should make the speech which introduced one of the most important legislative acts ever passed by any political assembly. No one spoke after Bellay. Instead Levasseur (of Sarthe) moved a motion: "When drawing up the constitution of the French people we paid no attention to the unhappy Negroes. Posterity will bear us a great reproach for that. Let us repair the wrong—let us proclaim the liberty of the Negroes. Mr. President, do not suffer the Convention to dishonour itself by a discussion." The Assembly rose in acclamation. The two deputies of colour appeared on the tribune and embraced while the applause rolled round the hall from members and visitors. Lacroix led the Mulatto and the Negro to the President who gave them the presidential kiss, when the applause started again.

Cambon drew the attention of the House to an incident which had taken place among the spectators.

"A citizeness of colour who regularly attends the sittings of the Convention has just felt so keen a joy at seeing us give liberty to all her brethren that she has fainted (applause). I demand that this fact be mentioned in the min-

utes, and that this citizeness be admitted to the sitting and
receive at least this much recognition of her civic virtues."
The motion was carried and the woman walked to the front
bench of the amphitheatre and sat to the left of the President, drying her tears amidst another burst of cheering.

Lacroix, who had spoken the day before, then proposed the draft of the decree. "I demand that the Minister
of Marine be instructed to despatch at once advices to the
Colonies to give them the happy news of their freedom,
and I propose the following decree: The National Convention declares slavery abolished in all the colonies. In consequence it declares that all men, without distinction of colour, domiciled in the colonies, are French citizens, and
enjoy all the rights assured under the Constitution."

Gone was all the talking and fumbling, the sabotage
of the Barnaves, the convenient memory of the Brissots. In
1789 Grégoire had proposed equality for Mulattoes and
gradual abolition. He had been treated as anyone would be
treated who for the Union of South Africa to-day proposed
merely social and political equality for educated Africans
and relief from the slavery of the pass-laws for the rest. Like
Grégoire he would be denounced as a Bolshevik and would
be lucky to escape lynching. Yet when the masses turn (as
turn they will one day) and try to end the tyranny of centuries, not only the tyrants but all "civilisation" holds up its
hands in horror and clamours for "order" to be restored. If
a revolution carries high overhead expenses, most of them
it inherits from the greed of reactionaries and the cowardice
of the so-called moderates. Long before abolition the mischief had been done in the French colonies and it was not
abolition but the refusal to abolish which had done it.

At that time slavery had been overturned only in San
Domingo of all the French colonies, and the generous spon-
taneity of the Convention was only a reflection of the over-
flowing desire which filled all France to end tyranny and
oppression everywhere. But the generosity of the revolutionary spirit was at the same time the soundest political
policy. Robespierre was not present at the session and did
not approve of the step. Danton knew that the Convention

had been swept off its feet by an excess of feeling, and thought that it ought to have been more cautious. But that master of revolutionary tactics could not fail to see that the decree, by ratifying the liberty which the blacks had won, was giving them a concrete interest in the struggle against British and Spanish reaction. "The English are done for," he shouted, "Pitt and his plots are riddled."

But while the revolution swelled with justifiable pride, the rich fumed, remaining shameless and obstinate. As soon as the decree was passed the maritime bourgeois sent to the deputies of the Convention an "address . . . on the occasion of the enfranchisement of the Negroes."

"Bravo! One hundred times bravo, our masters. This is the cry with which all our places of business resound when the public press comes each day and bring us details of your great operations. Certainly, we have all the time to read them at leisure since we have no longer any work to do. There is no longer any ship-building in our ports, still less any construction of boats. The manufactories are deserted and the shops even are closed. Thus, thanks to your sublime decrees, every day is a holiday for the workers. We can count more than three hundred thousand in our different towns who have no other occupation than, arms folded, to talk about the news of the day, of the Rights of Man, and of the Constitution. It is true that every day they become more hungry, but whoever thinks of the stomach when the heart is glad!"

The Convention, bourgeois itself, was not too happy after the first excitement was over,[27] but the masses and the radicals hailed the decree as another "great clearance in the forest of abuses." [28]

It is not known exactly when the news reached the West Indies. But on June 5th, the day after the celebrations of the King's birthday and the capture of Port-au-Prince,

[27] Saintoyant, *La Colonisation Française* . . . , Vol. I, pp. 330-333.
[28] The phrase is Grégoire's.

the English commanders at St Kitts heard that seven French
ships had escaped the British fleet and landed at Guadeloupe. In command was Victor Hugues, a Mulatto, "one
of the great personalities of the French revolution to whom
nothing was impossible," [29] taken from his post as public
prosecutor in Rochefort and sent to the West Indies.
Hugues brought only 1,500 men, but he brought also the
Convention's message to the blacks. There was no black
army in the Windward islands as in San Domingo. He had
to make one out of raw slaves. But he gave them the revolutionary message and dressed them in the colours of the
Republic. The black army fell on the victorious British, began to drive them out of the French colonies, then carried
the war into the British islands.

Toussaint got the news of the decree sometime in May.
The fate of the French in San Domingo was hanging by a
thread, but now that the decree of Sonthonax was ratified
in France, he did not hesitate a moment but at once told
Laveaux that he was willing to join him. Laveaux, over-
joyed, accepted the offer and agreed to make him a Brigadier-General, and Toussaint responded with a vigour and
audacity that left all San Domingo gasping. He sent to the
destitute Laveaux some good ammunition from the Spanish
stores. Then he persuaded those of his followers who were
with him to change over, and all agreed—French soldiers,
ex-slaves of the rank-and-file and all his officers, blacks and
white royalists who had deserted the Republic to join him.
His demeanour at Mass was so devout that d'Hermona
watching him communicate one day commented that God
if he came to earth could not visit a purer spirit than Toussaint L'Ouverture. One morning in June, Toussaint, having
communicated with his usual devotion, fell on the startled
Biassou and routed his troops. Then in a campaign as brilliant as the one by which he had captured the line of camps
for the Spaniards, he recaptured them for the French, either conquering them or winning over commanders and
men, so that when he joined the French he had 4,000

[29] Sir Harry Johnston, *The Negro in the New World*, London,
1910, p. 169.

troops, the North Province was almost recaptured, and the Spaniards, Biassou and Jean François were not only routed but demoralised. The British, having received some over- due reinforcements, were already calculating how much of the conquered San Domingo they could wangle from their allies, the Spaniards. In these matters the more we have the better our pretensions, wrote Dundas to Williamson. On them just about to swallow the prize Toussaint turned with one of his tigerish leaps. He captured all their positions on the right bank of the Artibonite, drove them across the river, and but for a succession of unexpected misfortunes would have taken their stronghold of St Marc.

VI

The Rise of Toussaint

THE RELATION of forces in San Domingo was now completely changed and although few recognised it fully at the time, Toussaint and the blacks were henceforth the decisive factors in the revolution. Toussaint was now a French officer in command of an army of some 5,000 men, holding a line of camps or fortified positions between the North Province and the West, and had pushed his way into the West Province as far as the right bank of the Artibonite.

Rigaud in the South had taken the lead over Beauvais and was occupied with his own campaign against the Brit-

ish. The Republic, weak on the sea, could send no assistance. Both British and Spaniards, thanks to the British fleet
and British wealth, were well supplied with money and
arms. The British were in possession of some of the most
fertile districts in the colony and the formerly rich North
Plain, though now held again by the French, was practically devastated. The owners of property betrayed the
Republic at every turn. All that the Republic had to offer
was liberty and equality. But they were enough. For years
Pitt and Dundas continued to pour men and money into
the West Indies against what they were pleased to call
brigands. Helped by the climate, the black labourers so recently slaves, and the loyal Mulattoes, led by their own
officers, inflicted on Britain the severest defeat that has befallen a British expeditionary force between the days of
Elizabeth and the Great War. The full story remained hidden for over a century, until it was unearthed in 1906 by
Fortescue, the historian of the British Army. He puts the
blame on Pitt and Dundas "who had full warning that on
this occasion they would have to fight not only poor, sickly
Frenchmen, but the Negro population of the West Indies.
Yet they poured their troops into these pestilent islands, in
the expectation that thereby they would destroy the power
of France, only to discover, when it was too late, that they
had practically destroyed the British Army." [1]

Laveaux was now in sole charge of the colony, Sonthonax and Polverel having been recalled, accused of treason and all other crimes by some of the émigré colonists.
These had abandoned the monarchy, embraced the Jacobins, and managed to achieve this much before the decree
of February 4th. But though Toussaint dutifully informed
his chief of every step, he was practically in unchecked
command of the bulk of the forces and of his district. Everything depended on the army. The majority of Toussaint's
rank-and-file were Africans born out of the colony, unable

[1] Fortescue, *History of the British Army*, London, 1909, Vol.
IV, Part 2, p. 385.

to speak two words of French, in Jean François' scornful phrase. The chief officers also were, like Toussaint himself, ex-slaves. Besides Dessalines, there was Christophe who had left the hotel to seek Toussaint's band in the mountains, his brother, Paul L'Ouverture, and Moïse who had crossed the Atlantic as a child and was adopted by Toussaint, passing as his nephew. The army, except for a few white officers, was a revolutionary army through and through, and that was its greatest strength.

If the Republic, liberty and equality gave the army its morale, its centre was Toussaint himself. He had had his first command in October 1792, and in less than two years we find him writing more than once that a long experience has taught him the necessity of being himself on the spot, otherwise things never go well.[2]

His presence had that electrifying effect characteristic of great men of action. "I put before them the position of the enemy and the absolute necessity of driving him off. The brave republicans, Moïse, J. B. Paparet, Dessalines and Noel answered in the name of all the chiefs that they would brave any sort of danger, that they would go anywhere and that they would follow me to the end." The ranks, although exhausted, responded in the same way and marched against musket and cannon shot "without drawing a single weapon, guns in bandoliers." "Nothing," said Toussaint, "could resist the valour of the sansculottes." On one occasion when ammunition had given out they fought with stones. He lived with the men and charged at their head. If cannon was to be moved, he himself helped, once getting a hand badly crushed in the process. All knew him from the few months before when he was merely old Toussaint. He shared all their toils and dangers. But he was self-contained, impenetrable and stern, with the habit and manner of the born aristocrat.

"I have received your letter, as well as the minutes of your meeting," he writes to some of his officers. "I have noted with pleasure the manner in which you have repulsed

[2] This and the two succeeding chapters are based chiefly on the correspondence with Laveaux. See Note 6 on p. 124.

the enemy, and I have only praise for the way in which you
have exterminated him with a courage worthy of good republicans.

"But I see, Citizens, with much pain, that the orders
which I have given you three times running to move on to
the territory of our enemies and drive them from it, have
not been put into execution. If you had condescended to
execute the orders which I had sent to you . . . all the
camps on the other side of the Artibonite would have been
destroyed. . . . You have trampled my orders into the
dust."

His extraordinary abilities, his silence, the sharpness
of his tongue when he spoke, kept even his most trusted
officers at a distance. They worshipped him, but feared
rather than loved him. Even Dessalines, the Tiger, was
afraid of Toussaint, and this excessive reserve and aloof-
ness, though they grew on him and would one day have
their full consequences, were of inestimable value in those
early undisciplined days.

The troops often were without even food and had to
go looking for sugar-cane. Even when some arms did arrive
in August, they were no good. "I have received two thousand guns, but they are in bad condition. . . . I shall get
them repaired, many are too short and these I shall give
to the dragoons. . . . Many of the guns in the 7th and 8th
regiments are no good."

The British and Spaniards, having all they wanted and
knowing the condition of Toussaint's men, sent agents
among them offering them arms and accoutrements and
good pay. From Laveaux to the labourers the British made
their offers of money. But there is no record of any notable
success with Toussaint's men. The morale of the revolutionary army was too high.

Toussaint had the advantage of liberty and equality,
the slogans of the revolution. They were great weapons in

an age of slaves, but weapons must be used and he used them with a fencer's finesse and skill.

Bands of maroons infested the war-area, the most powerful a band of 5,000 under Dieudonné. Rigaud and Beauvais were trying to get him to co-operate with them, but Dieudonné distrusted them, said he did not want to obey any Mulatto, and entered into negotiations with the British. The British had made all arrangements to buy him over, but the millstone around their necks in this campaign was their reactionary policy. They could not even lie on a large scale: it was too dangerous, and their rich allies would have deserted them at once. They had to be so careful even about making arrangements with Dieudonné that he got suspicious and withdrew. Beauvais and Rigaud heard about Dieudonné's negotiations with the British and begged Toussaint to use his influence. With a single one of his dictated letters, Toussaint changed the whole situation.

". . . I cannot believe the painful rumours that are spread about you, that you have abandoned your country to ally yourself with the English, sworn enemies of our liberty and equality.

"Can it be possible, my dear friend, that at the very moment when France triumphs over all the royalists and recognises us for her children by her beneficent decree of the 9 Thermidor, accords us all our rights for which we are fighting, that you should let yourself be deceived by our ancient tyrants who are only using one-half of our unhappy brothers in order to load the other with chains. For a time the Spaniards had blinded my eyes, but I did not take long to recognise their rascality. I abandoned them and have beaten them well. I returned to my country which received me with open arms and has recompensed my services well. I beg of you, my dear brother, to follow my example. If special reasons prevent you from having confidence in Generals Rigaud and Beauvais, Governor Laveaux who is a good father to all of us and in whom our mother-country has placed its confidence, should at least deserve yours. I hope that you will not refuse me, who am a black as yourself, and, I assure you, wish nothing more than to see you happy, you and all our brothers. As far as I am concerned I believe that our only hope of this is in serving the French Republic. It is under its flag that we are truly free and equal. That is how I see it, my dear friend, and I do not believe that I am making a mistake. . . ." The letter is worth an immediate second reading; every sentence hits home.

"If it is possible that the English have succeeded in deceiving you, believe me, my dear brother, abandon them. Unite yourself to honest republicans, and all together let us chase these royalists from our country. They are rascals who wish to burden us again with those shameful chains that we have had so much trouble to break." He begged for unity. "Remember, my dear friend, that the French Republic is one and indivisible and it is that which gives it its strength and has made it victorious over all its enemies."

Time would show to what degree Toussaint was sincere in these constant references to the French Republic.

His envoys took this letter to Dieudonné's camp and read it to the assembled troops. When the blacks heard it they burst out into invectives against Dieudonné and his friends, conclusive proof that though they were ignorant and unable to pick their way among the mass of proclamations, lies, promises, and traps which surrounded them, yet they wanted to fight for liberty. Laplume, Dieudonné's second-in-command, profiting by this disillusionment, arrested Dieudonné and two of his followers on the spot. This also was the work of Toussaint, who had instructed his men that if Dieudonné was completely won over by the British they were to take some of the other chiefs aside and "with the utmost energy" show them that they were being deceived. Dieudonné was thrown into prison, but Laplume instead of joining Rigaud or Beauvais joined Toussaint's forces with 3,000 men. Toussaint wrote hastily to Laveaux begging him to make Laplume a colonel. "I assure you that this will produce the best effect," and Laveaux sanctioned the appointment. Rigaud and Beauvais could hardly have been too pleased. A force of 3,000 men was an immense acquisi-

tion, and Toussaint had won them by a letter and a deputation.

If the army was the instrument of Toussaint's power,
the masses were its foundation and his power grew with his
influence over them. Just out of the degradation of slavery
they had come into a world of indiscriminate murder and
violence. The Spaniards invited 800 French back from the
United States to Port-au-Prince. After a church sermon the
priest, Vasquez, gave the signal to Jean François who had
spent the morning with him in the confessional box. The
Spanish soldiers joined with Jean François' bands and
quietly murdered over a thousand French people, men,
women and children. They at least would never claim their
property again. Such were the models of civilisation for the
ex-slaves. Great tracts of the West Province were continually being fought over, devastated and burnt. In the
war areas rich and poor, black and white, all starved. Little
wonder that the black labourers were constantly in a state
of insurrection.

Fear of the restoration of slavery was always the cause
of the trouble. The British had no intention of abolishing
slavery, neither had the Spaniards. Permission to form
black regiments was only given in 1795,[3] and even then it
was most positively forbidden that any who served with
the British should be promised freedom.[4] But they could
not keep that up, and the British got blacks to fight on their
side by paying them. All parties confused the ignorant
Negroes by playing on their fears and accusing every other
party—the French and Toussaint himself, of wishing to
restore slavery. The British and Spaniards could second
their propaganda with offers of money and guns. Jean
François told the blacks that only a King had authority to
make them free and therefore they must fight for the Spanish King. Some planters hid the decree from their slaves.
The blacks already distrusted the white planters. Now the

[3] Fortescue, *History of the British Army*, Vol. IV, Part 2, p. 452
[4] *Ibid.*, p. 469.

machinations of British and Spaniards were teaching those who were learning to understand politics that nearly all whites in the colonies were the same, birds of prey feeding on the ignorance and inexperience of the great masses of the black labourers.

For these blacks, lacking civic discipline, running wild in a country torn by revolution and war, knowing only that they wanted to remain free, yet confused and deceived by all parties, for them Toussaint had a deep and passionate sympathy. "O you Africans, my brothers!" he addresses them in a proclamation, "you who have cost me so many fatigues, so much labour, so much worry, you whose liberty is sealed with more than half of your own blood! How long will I have the mortification of seeing my misled children fly the counsels of a father who idolises them!" Autocrat though he was, that is the way he felt about his people. "It is always the blacks who suffer the most," was an expression often on his lips; and one can feel his spontaneous horror at the news of a rising provoked by the British among the cultivators of a district in the North Province. "You will not have much difficulty in divining whence has come this terrible blow. Is it then possible that the labourers will always be the plaything and the instruments of vengeance of those monsters whom hell has loosed upon this colony? . . . The blood of so many victims cries for vengeance, and human and divine justice cannot delay to confound the guilty."

At the first hint of insurrection he would go himself. The most difficult districts were around Limbé, Plaisance, Marmelade and Port-de-Paix, the early centres of the revolt in the North Province and destined to hold the first place to the end. Early in 1796, for instance, he hears one day that the labourers of Port-de-Paix have taken arms and massacred some whites. In one night he covers the long distance from Verrettes to Port-de-Paix. He calls the blacks together and gives them an address on the way they should conduct themselves. If they have grievances, assassination is not the way to have them redressed. One of them speaks

for the rest. "Alas! general. They want to make us slaves
again. There is no equality here as it seems there is in your
part of the world. They look at us with a bad eye, they persecute us. . . ." Their provisions are taken for less than
they were worth, the whites take their chickens and pigs.
If they protest they are thrown into prison, and to get out
of prison they have to pay.

"The reasons you have given me seem justified," says
Toussaint, "but if even you had a house full of them, you
have rendered yourself wrong in the sight of God." They
begged him to organise them. "Fix everything, we shall be
so good that everybody will be forced to forget what we
have just done."

Next day Toussaint calls a meeting of all the blacks in
the district. He makes them swear to work hard and be
obedient. He appoints a commander. The labourers cried:
"Long live the Republic! Long live liberty, long live equality, long live Governor Laveaux, long live Toussaint
L'Ouverture!" They danced, and cheered Toussaint when
he left.

Unfortunately there was another insurrection soon
after, and the leader and 12 of his friends were tried by
military tribunal and shot the same day. Toussaint went
again, and discovered that the British had been intriguing
among them, had given them guns and ammunition. Toussaint arrested no one, fired no shot, but talked to them and
was able to lead them back to work.

He wasn't always so successful. "I went myself to
speak to them and try to make them see reason. . . . They
armed themselves and I received as thanks for my pains a
bullet in my leg from which I still feel some lively pain."

But these years 1795 and 1796 marked the growth of
confidence in him by the labourers in the North Province,
not only as a soldier, but as a man devoted to their interests, whom they could trust in all the difficulties that surrounded them, the man who was on their side in the struggle against slavery. By his incessant activity on their behalf
he gained their confidence, and among a people ignorant,

starving, badgered, and nervous, Toussaint's word by 1796
was law—the only person in the North whom they could
be depended upon to obey.

But despite the ignorance and confusion there was a
new spirit abroad. Black San Domingo had changed and
would never be the same again, whether fighting with English, Spanish or French. Even Jean François, royalist, dismissed Laveaux' overtures with incisive scorn. "Until I see
M. Laveaux and other French gentlemen of his quality
giving their daughters in marriage to Negroes, only then
will I believe in all your pretended equality."

All the French blacks, from the labourers at Port-de-
Paix demanding equality, to the officers in the army, were
filled with an immense pride at being citizens of the French
Republic "one and indivisible" which had brought liberty
and equality into the world. Officers of different colours
would not accept invitations offered to one group;[5] as good
republicans they refused to bow and scrape before the
Spanish Marquis, who raged at the impertinence of these
blacks.[6] Five years of revolution had wrought these astonishing changes. Toussaint always addressed the blacks as
French citizens: what will France think if she learns that
your conduct was not worthy of true republicans?

Devotion to the Republic and a hatred of royalty and
all that it stood for fills the documents of the time. Jean
François had issued a proclamation "In the name of the
King, his Master," offering his "brothers" in Dondon provisions, arms, all that they needed from the moment they
joined the Spanish side. The municipality of Dondon made
a withering reply.

Some republicans have offered to surrender? "If there
were among us men low enough to resume their chains, we
abandon them to you with a good heart. . . .

"The liberty that the republicans offer us you say is
false. We are republicans and, in consequence, free by nat-

---

[5] *Lettres de Toussaint-L'Ouverture. La Bibliothèque Nationale.*
[6] *Ibid.*

ural right. It can only be Kings whose very name expresses
what is most vile and low, who dared to arrogate the right
of reducing to slavery men made like themselves, whom
nature had made free.

"The King of Spain furnished you abundantly with
arms and ammunition. Use them to tighten your chains.
. . . As for us, we have need for no more than stones and
sticks to make you dance the Carmagnole. . . .⁷

"You have received commissions and you have guarantees. Guard your liveries and your parchments. One day
they will serve you as the fastidious titles of our former
aristocrats served them. If the King of the French who
drags his misery from court to court has need of slaves to
assist him in his magnificence, let him go seek it among
other Kings who count as many slaves as they have subjects.

"You conclude, vile slaves as you are, by offering us
the protection of the King, your Master. Learn and say to
Casa Calvo [the Spanish Marquis] that republicans cannot
treat with a King. Let him come and you with him, we are
ready to receive you as republicans should. . . ."

That was the style, the accent of Toussaint and his
men. The British and the Spaniards could not defeat it. All
they could offer was money, and there are periods in human history when money is not enough.

A growing army and the confidence of free black
labourers meant power. But Toussaint saw early that political power is only a means to an end. The salvation of San
Domingo lay in the restoration of agriculture. This was an
almost insuperable task in a disorganised society, depending on the labour of men just out of slavery and surrounded
on every side by the rabid greed and violence of French,
Spaniards and British. Toussaint addressed himself to this
from the first days of his command.

"Work is necessary," he proclaimed, "it is a virtue, it

⁷ An expression in a famous French song of the Revolution, the
Ça Ira.

is for the general good of the state." His regulations were harsh. The labourers were sent to work 24 hours after he assumed control of any district, and he authorised the military commandants of the parishes to take measures necessary for keeping them on the plantations. The Republic, he wrote, has no use for dull or incapable men. It was forced labour and restraint of movement. But the need brooked no barriers. He retained the confidence of the labourers because he insisted that wages should be paid, and was equally stern with the white proprietors. All, "whether proprietors or others," were ordered to their respective parishes and plantations. If the proprietors did not obey, their property would be confiscated. From the very beginning of his career as administrator Toussaint had his policy towards the whites clear in his mind, and he never shifted from it.

He knew these owners of property, French to-day, British to-morrow, royalists, republicans, utterly without principles except in so far as these helped to preserve their plantations. But they had the knowledge, education and experience which the colony needed if it was to be restored to prosperity. They had travelled in France and in America. They had culture, which only a section of the Mulattoes had and none of the slaves. Toussaint therefore treated them with the utmost forbearance, being helped by an unwarped character which abhorred the spirit of revenge and useless bloodshed of any kind. "No reprisals, no reprisals" was his constant adjuration to his officers after every campaign. It was their plantations these whites wanted and he gave them their plantations, always ready to forget their treachery if they would work the land. Once on taking Mirabelais from the British he found there more than 300 white émigrés from the North Province. It would have been the simplest thing to have these traitors to their country and upholders of slavery shot out of hand. They would certainly not have spared him. He called them before him and made them take the oath of fidelity to the Republic. Some who wanted to return to their parishes asked him for passports and he obliged them. Their plantations had of course been sequestrated. Toussaint made investigations and enquiries seeking to get them restored.

He appointed whites to government posts with the confidence of the old royalist governors. "I have made Guy military commandant, and Dubuisson his Adjutant. These are two brave Frenchmen who have contributed very much to converting their fellow citizens. . . . I have confided the administration to Jules Borde who I believe is a good republican and who possesses the necessary ability to carry out this duty. He has the good will of his fellow citizens who approve of my choice." He recommends another white creole who accompanied him in an expedition ". . . and has conducted himself honourably. I feel fairly certain of his civism." What these whites (with their memories of the past) thought at being looked over, examined and granted posts with such assurance by a former slave is not known. But there is no record of any disrespect or open hostility. They may have hated it in private, but it would have been difficult to get any response. Toussaint had his army of ex-slaves with its ex-slave officers which he kept intact and free of possible disruptive elements. But he was so genuinely kind to the whites in their distressful condition that they could not fail to appreciate it. "My heart," he writes to Laveaux at the news of an insurrection, "my heart is torn at the fate which has befallen some unhappy whites who have been victims in this business." That was the way he felt about all people, blacks and whites. The whites grew to recognise that he could always be depended upon to protect them from the labourers ready to massacre them at the slightest hint of any return to slavery. As they learned to trust him, many of them came back to their plantations. White women told Laveaux the attentions and the assistance that they had received from this "astonishing man," called the old ex-slave, with his despised black skin, their father. In Laveaux' own words, the parish of Petite-Rivière, where he visited Toussaint, offered the satisfying spectacle of more than 15,000 labourers back to work, all full of gratitude to the Republic: blacks, whites, Mulattoes, labourers, proprietors—all blessing the "virtuous chief" whose care maintained among them order and peace.

What must Laveaux have thought, ex-count of the *ancien régime* and a cultivated Frenchman of a cultivated age, as he received week after week these letters from Toussaint the ex-slave? Very wonderful letters some of them are. Toussaint was equally master of a proclamation, a delicate piece of manœuvring as his epistle to Dieudonné, or a military despatch.

"The enemy had not taken the precaution to establish on the St Marc road reserve camps to protect his retreat. I used a trick to encourage him to pass by the highway, this is how. From the town of Verrettes he could see all my movements, so I made my army defile on the side of Mirabelais where he could see it, so as to give him the idea that I was sending large reinforcements there; while a moment after I made it re-enter the town of Petite-Rivière behind a hill without his perceiving it. He fell right into the snare; seeming even to hasten his retreat. I then made a large body of cavalry cross the river, putting myself at the head of it in order to reach the enemy quickly and keep him busy, and in order to give time to my infantry, which was coming up behind with a piece of cannon, to join me. This manœuvre succeeded marvellously. I had taken the precaution to send a four-inch piece of cannon from Petite-Rivière to the Moreau plantation at Detroit in order to batter the enemy on the right flank during his passage. While I harassed him with my cavalry, my infantry advanced at great speed with the piece of cannon. As soon as it reached me I made two columns pass to right and to left to take the enemy in the flank. As soon as these two columns arrived within pistol shot, I served the enemy in true republican fashion. He continued his way showing all the time a brave front. But the first cannon shot that I caused to be fired among his men, and which did a great deal of damage, made him abandon first a waggon and then a piece of cannon. I redoubled the charge and afterwards I captured the other three pieces of cannon, two waggons full of munitions, and seven others full of wounded who were promptly sent to the rear. Then it was that the enemy began to fly in the greatest disorder, only for those at the head of the retreat to find themselves right in the mouth of the piece of cannon which I had posted at Detroit on the Moreau plantation. And when the enemy saw himself taken in front, behind, and on all sides, that fine fellow, the impertinent Dessources, jumped off his horse and threw himself into the brushwood with the debris of his army calling out 'Every man for himself.' Rain and darkness caused me to discontinue the pursuit. This battle lasted from eleven in the morning to six in the evening and cost me only six dead and as many wounded. I have strewn the road with corpses for the distance of more than a league. My victory has been most complete and if the celebrated Dessources is lucky enough to re-enter St Marc it will be without cannon, without baggage, in short what is called with neither drum nor trumpet. He has lost everything, even honour, if vile royalists are capable of having any. He will remember for a long time the republican lesson which I have taught him.

"I have pleasure in transmitting to you, General, the praises which are due to Dessalines. . . . The battalion of the sansculottes above all, which saw fire for the second time, showed the greatest courage."

Here is not only the born soldier but the born writer. The despatch has the authentic ring of the great captains. Dessources' corps was a famous corps of white creoles, and the news of this victory of the black sansculottes over the old planters spread over the colony, lifting the prestige of the blacks and concentrating attention on Toussaint.

In administration as in war it was the same. Laveaux from the beginning seems to have allowed Toussaint carte-blanche, and Toussaint made himself into a whole cabinet like a fascist dictator, except that he actually did the work. The British have made a breach in the Artibonite river

in order to flood the lower part of the plain and prevent his
soldiers from advancing further. The rains had so widened
this breach that it was at least two hundred feet wide. He
is blocking it with roots, wood and rocks. He has had more
than eight hundred men working at it for eight days already, and he will keep them at it until they are finished,
because if he leaves it in this state, when the rainy season
comes the country would be devastated by the over-flowing
of the river, and cultivation ruined.

It seems to me, he warns Laveaux, that you should
send some boats with cannon to cruise before Caracol,
Limonade, etc., so as to prevent neutral vessels landing in
any of these ports. "It is to our interest to intercept the provisions and the help that they can receive by sea."

Spain and France made peace at the Treaty of Bâle in
September, 1795. Toussaint warns Laveaux not to think
that the Spaniards will observe neutrality. He knows them
well. They hate liberty for the blacks, they will certainly
continue to keep contact with the British, and Laveaux
should continue to guard the communications.

He moves the town of Verrettes. It is in a bad position
for defence, being dominated by neighbouring ground. He
traces the plan of a new town in the middle of a superb
level savannah absolutely open.

War, politics, agriculture, international relations, long-
range problems of administration, minor details, he dealt
with them as they came, took decisions and gave advice to
Laveaux, but, characteristic of his tact, always as a subordinate. When Laveaux, neglecting to take his warning
of Spanish treachery, reaped his reward, Toussaint gave
him a gentle "I told you so." Even after decisions that he
must have known were irrevocable, he submits them as
subject to Laveaux' approval. In no letter does he find it
necessary to explain any charge or complaint made against
him by Laveaux, yet he writes: "I shall always receive with
pleasure the reprimands that you address to me. When I
deserve them it will be a proof of the friendship that you
have for me." A strong personal friendship grew up between the two men, so diverse in origin, brought together

by the revolution. Laveaux was kind-hearted, upright and
devoted to Negro emancipation. Toussaint, infinitely suspicious and very reserved, had absolute faith in Laveaux
and never trusted any other man, black, white or brown.
Laveaux had the same feelings towards him, and a letter of
Laveaux to Toussaint that remains is addressed to his "most
intimate friend, Toussaint." Amidst all the military, political
and other problems there is this note of strong mutual
attachment. "Here is something important. I send you some
truffle. Be so kind as to accept them from him who wishes
you the best of health, and who embraces you with all his
heart. All my officers assure you of their respect and fidelity.

"P.S. General, our impatience to see you grows every
day—shall we be long deprived of this pleasure?"

Seven days afterwards it seems that the visit will take
place: "I see with pleasure that you will not delay to come
to see us here. I await you with the utmost impatience as
do all my men, who ardently desire to see you and, at the
same time, to demonstrate to you their attachment."

Laveaux, it is obvious from Toussaint's replies, wrote
in a similar strain. Toussaint gracefully acknowledged his
commander's graciousness. "I do not know how to express
my thanks for all the pleasant things that you have said to
me, and how happy I am to have so good a father who
loves me as much as you do. Be sure that your son is your
sincere friend, that he will support you until death. My
army thanks you for your kind regards, and charges me to
assure you of its attachment and its submission. . . .

"I embrace you with all my heart and be sure that I
share with you your difficulties and your cares."

Yellow fever killed off the English troops in thousands,
but reinforcements always came and money poured in to
finance bodies of French slave-owners, white and Mulatto,
and black troops. At times internal intrigues and British
money made Toussaint's position very weak. But liberty
and equality triumphed as Danton had known they would
triumph. Toussaint and Rigaud held the English in check.
Victor Hugues beat them in engagement after engagement:
1795, says Fortescue, is the most disgraceful year in the

history of the British Army. It was the decree of February 4th which had done it. Toussaint, careful of everything, sent a personal deputation to the Republic in France to attest his loyalty and inform them of the care with which he was performing his duties as soldier and protector of cultivation, also no doubt to explore French politics. Nothing escaped him. He had joined the French and assumed his command in May 1794. By the beginning of 1796 he was proconsul of his district, governing and fighting as if he had done nothing else all his life.

Before such ability, energy and charm, Laveaux capitulated completely. In the early months of 1796, all San Domingo knew that Toussaint L'Ouverture, the black general, stood first in the councils and affection of the Governor.

VII

The Mulattoes Try and Fail

EMINENCE ENGENDERS ENEMIES. The white revolutionary royalists had long ago marked down Toussaint as enemy No. 1. After giving a list of the most dangerous republicans, one of them singled him out for special attention, "As for Toussaint, he is the great papa." But the whites were no longer a force in San Domingo. The potential rulers were the Mulattoes, and the Mulattoes saw in this growing reputation and friendship of the black leader with Laveaux a threat to the domination they considered theirs by right. Mulattoes and some free blacks filled most of the important posts in the troops (other than those commanded by Toussaint), in the Municipalities, and in the general administration. Villate, the commandant of Le Cap, was a Mulatto. The Mulattoes of the South were under the leadership of Rigaud, Beauvais and Pinchinat, who were harassing the British and building up a Mulatto State. The Mulatto ex-slaves were glad to attach themselves to the leaders of their caste who needed numbers.

In the West Province, however, the Mulattoes were a problem. Most of the rich proprietors joined the British, but the French planters who negotiated with Williamson had abjured the decree of April 4th (after all the oratory and the pamphleteering, who cared about that now?); nothing would satisfy these but the colony as it was before. Williamson hinted to the British Government that if he could only be given authority to enforce the provisions of the Negro Code, he would conquer the colony at once.[1] Dundas refused.[2] Williamson, on the spot, no doubt felt that you could make the promises, conquer the colony, and then get out of obligations. Dundas seemed to think that a few thousand reinforcements would be sufficient to defeat the black brigands without promising any dangerous concessions.

But despite these rebuffs the Mulatto proprietors remained on the whole uneasily pro-British. Whenever Toussaint captured an area, following his usual policy, he welcomed them if they took the oath of allegiance to the Republic. But as soon as his back was turned, they would intrigue and plot to get the British back. The first great attack on St Marc suffered from the treachery of the Mulattoes, and in St Marc, Mirabelais, Verrettes and the whole Artibonite district, they were the chief support of the British, who without them would have been driven out long before 1798. They caused Toussaint to lose many of his most important captures. "What has been my surprise to-day to learn that the rebels of St Marc with those of

[1] To Dundas, January 17th, 1794. Colonial Office Papers, Jamaica, C.D. 137/92.
[2] *Ibid.*, C.D. 137/93. July 5th, 1794.

Mirabelais have taken from us Verrettes and several other posts, and obliged our people to fall back. . . . This reverse has befallen us only owing to the perfidy of the men of colour of this district. Never have I experienced so many treasons. And I take an oath that henceforth I shall treat them in a manner very different to that which I have done hitherto. Whenever I have made them prisoners, I have treated them like a good father. The ungrateful wretches have replied by seeking to deliver me to our enemies." After a great deal of intrigue with republicans inside the large and beautiful district of Mirabelais, Toussaint was successful and informed Laveaux with great joy that he was now in possession "without any shedding of blood"—always a great point with him. Alas! A few weeks afterwards his garrison is driven out. The Mulattoes have deceived him again. In time he lost his patience. "These rascals conspire more than ever . . . there is a conspiracy. . . . You must know that a man of colour is at the head of it." The Mulattoes would abandon Toussaint's army during an engagement and join the enemy. "Scoundrels," "rogues," "rascals," Toussaint does not restrain himself. They spread the news that Toussaint wished to deliver the country to the English. "All the hatred of these scoundrels is directed against me. It is by such impostures that they excite the people." But later a new note crept into his complaints. "The enemies of liberty and of equality have sworn to do away with me. . . . I am to perish in some ambush that they propose to lure me into. Let them trap me well, for if they miss me I will not spare them. . . . These gentlemen say that it is necessary at all costs to get rid of me." One conspiracy, he says, has Chanlatte at its head, and Chanlatte was an officer in the republican army. Toussaint, ex-slave, with his army of ex-slaves led by ex-slaves, the most powerful force in San Domingo, was essentially the man of the black labourers, and not only the Mulattoes who were hanging around the British, but even the Mulattoes who were republicans were watching this threat to themselves in the close intimacy between Toussaint and Laveaux and Laveaux' interest in and popularity with the black

masses. This was no question of colour, but crudely a question of class, for those blacks who were formerly free stuck
to the Mulattoes. Persons of some substance and standing
under the old régime, they looked upon the ex-slaves as
essentially persons to be governed.

Laveaux loved the blacks for their own sake, and he
loved Toussaint for the services he had rendered and because he was Toussaint. His reports to the Minister are
filled with their praises. But he loved them too because he
was afraid of the Mulattoes and saw in them a counterweight to Mulatto power.

The Mulattoes felt that they could govern the country
themselves, they were aiming at independence and some
of the local whites conspired with them. These Mulatto
citizens, Laveaux warned the Minister,[3] wish to dominate
all, wish to have all places, wish to enjoy everything themselves. The Mulattoes and the former free blacks of Le Cap
could not bear to see an ex-slave do well in business or
hold any position.[4] Villate filled the National Guard of Le
Cap with Mulattoes, put former slaves into prison, disregarded Laveaux' orders, wrote him insulting letters, and
intrigued with the Mulattoes in the South. "Ah! If Rigaud
would have communicated with me the colony would have
been saved a long time ago." Laveaux heard of these
and similar remarks by Villate, and begged the Minister
for help.

"The chiefs who were formerly slaves are the support
of liberty and of the Republic. I am firmly of the opinion
that without them there would have already been large
movements for independence." The constant threat of the
Mulattoes while having to fight against the British was
wearing Laveaux down. "I have been compelled through
love of my country, for my Fatherland, to stand it all with

---

[3] Reports to the Minister of Marine. *Les Archives Nationales*,
DXXV, 50.
[4] *Ibid*. Report of 17 Messidor An IV.

a patience beyond the human." But he could not stand it much longer.

His headquarters were at Port-de-Paix. In July 1795, the Convention concluded peace with Spain, and in October instructed Laveaux to make Le Cap his headquarters; Villate had been master of Le Cap for three years and now Laveaux, Governor and Commander-in-Chief, was coming to reduce him and his fellows to a subordinate position. When Laveaux arrived he liberated the Negroes from the prisons. Many Mulattoes were living without paying rent in houses deserted by former owners. Perrod, the Treasurer, assessed the houses and made them pay, and they raised the cry of tyranny. Things were coming to a head. Early in 1796, Pinchinat and a colleague on their way to Paris came to Le Cap. Instead of going on to Paris, Pinchinat busied himself in Le Cap, was introduced to the barracks where he addressed the soldiers, wrote numerous letters to the South, and then went back to the South to establish an alibi.

If Laveaux' intimacy with Toussaint and admiration for him had a sound political basis, Toussaint's intimacy with Laveaux and admiration for him had the same. Nothing ever escaped Toussaint. He had been watching the manœuvres of the Mulattoes and of Villate for a long time, from the very beginning of his association with Laveaux. After he had been appointed commander of the West Cordon, he had banteringly asked Colonel Pierre Michel, an ex-slave, why he had not kept him informed of Villate's intrigues at Le Cap. During the next two years Toussaint and Villate clashed. Villate complained to Laveaux that Toussaint prohibited the proprietors from selling their coffee to Le Cap. Toussaint indignantly denied the charge and enclosed a batch of correspondence to prove its falsehood. "I believe you too just, General, not to suspend your judgment . . . and I hope that you do not believe me capable of having committed such a fault. . . . If Villate had been one of my true friends he would also have acquainted me with the charges which were brought to him against me. In spite of the fact that my brothers in Cap François intrigue against me in this way, I have nothing to say against them. I regard them always as brothers and friends. By the grace of God, time will make you know the right." Toussaint was always careful of his reputation. If he did not have a virtue he assumed it. Yet in this case his indignation and sanctimoniousness seem justified. When the Mulattoes betrayed, Toussaint called them scoundrels, he cursed the royalists, the British and the Spaniards, but despite the intrigues going on all round, and the intimacy of the letters, there is not a single malicious insinuation against anybody. All his life he strove for conciliation with enemies and peaceful settlements in all disputes.

But he was not the man to be caught napping. He had his agents in Le Cap. In early March he knew that the Mulatto conspiracy was ripe and might burst at any moment. Why else should he write Laveaux the following letter, two days before the 20th? "Yes, General, Toussaint is your son. You are dear to him. Your tomb will be his, and he will support you at peril of his life. His arm and his head are always at your disposal, and if ever it should happen to him to fall, he will carry with him the sweet consolation of having defended his Father, his virtuous friend, and the cause of liberty."

Yet it is pretty certain that he told Laveaux nothing of his suspicions, for Laveaux, though aware of the tension, was taken quite by surprise.

At ten o'clock in the morning of March 20th Laveaux was sitting in his bedroom at Le Cap talking to another officer. Suddenly six or eight persons rushed in, all Mulattoes, "not a Negro, not a white man." He thought it was some quarrel that they wanted him to judge. Instead the intruders showered curses and blows upon him. His aide-de-camp rushed to his assistance, but the attackers arrested Laveaux, the other officer and the aide-de-camp. Laveaux was in slippers, and in the struggle they slipped off his feet. Barefooted and bareheaded as he was, the Mulattoes dragged the Governor by the hair and by the arm to the prison. Perrod, the Treasurer, was already there. For two days they stayed in prison without seeing anyone and without any assistance. At eight o'clock on the second day the Municipality came to Laveaux, said that it was in a state of despair at his arrest, which was abominable, etc., etc., and that it hoped to get him out in a short while.

But the Municipality was in the plot also. As soon as Laveaux was arrested it decreed that Laveaux and Perrod had "lost public confidence." It named Villate Governor of San Domingo. Villate wrote to Pageot, the military commander of the North, and to Casa Calvo of Spanish San Domingo to inform them of his new appointment.

But the conspiracy never had the slightest chance of success. The ubiquitous Toussaint had been watching it develop and had his men on the spot. Pierre Michel commanded a battalion at Fort Liberté near Le Cap. Pierre Michel had come from Africa in a slave ship and worked as a slave. He had been released by the revolution, could not read or write, but had risen from the ranks to become a colonel. He was a good soldier, dictated clear and concise reports, and then traced over in ink the signature which had been written for him in pencil. He was a man of great promptitude, daring and ambition, with a gift for intrigue. While keeping in touch with Toussaint against Villate, he was himself plotting against Toussaint, aiming at mastery of the North himself. Such were the men created by five years of revolution.

As soon as Michel heard the news of Laveaux' arrest he understood what was afoot. He grouped those officers who were faithful to the Government under himself. He wrote at once to inform Toussaint, who was at Gonaïves, 75 miles away, and instructed all the black chiefs in the neighbourhood to call out the armed labourers and march on Le Cap to deliver "their friend, Laveaux." He arrested a courier of Villate's, found on him a list of six names, and sent the list for Toussaint, his superior officer, to take action. The black masses in the town called out by the friends of the Government, ran through the streets crying "Power to the law! Power to the law!"

Toussaint was at Gonaïves when he got the news of the *coup d'état.* "What!" he wrote to Laveaux, "They have the audacity to threaten you and take up arms against you. What are they aiming at? They will go back to their duty or I shall take a thousand lives for one."

He despatched two battalions to march on the city, one of them under the dreaded Dessalines. He wrote menacing letters to places where he suspected that Villate might have supporters, and these letters were sufficient to keep the would-be revolutionaries quiet.

He addressed one of his flaming proclamations to the citizens of Le Cap. " . . . In disrepecting the Governor you disrespect France. What will the mother-country say when she learns of your irregular proceedings towards her representative. . . . Cast a glance, cast a glance at the district of the Artibonite and see the unheard-of cruelties which the English practise on your brothers. Some are embarked on boats and drowned in the sea, and the rest branded on the cheeks and chained as galley slaves. Even the women of colour are obliged to abandon their homes and hide in the woods to save themselves from the barbarity of our enemies. You, on the contrary, you can live peaceably in your houses. But no, you sow confusion. . . ." A few days after he himself arrived in Le Cap at the head of his personal cavalry-guard. But by this time the insurrection was half over. Laveaux had been released, and Villate had fled from Le Cap with a small body of personal supporters. The black masses in town and country were solid for Laveaux. Toussaint, triumphant, fought for peace. He sent a deputation to Villate inviting him to come back to Le Cap, and the deputies left accompanied by a hundred black women. Villate told them that he hoped Laveaux would be murdered by those very blacks to whom he was showing so many favours. However, he agreed to meet Toussaint but wanted Toussaint to come out to him. Toussaint, suspecting an am-

bush, refused to go. Meanwhile, the black women who accompanied the deputation had listened to the insinuations
of Villate's soldiers, and hurrying back to Laveaux' headquarters outside Le Cap, they ran all over the town shouting that Laveaux and Perrod had two ships in the harbour
loaded with chains to throw the Negroes again into slavery.
Immediately the soldiers who had supported Laveaux surrounded his house, calling for his blood. They were going
to murder him when Toussaint appeared before the crowd,
led it towards the main store-house, opened the doors,
showed them that there were no chains. The blacks were
satisfied, as much by the practical demonstration as by their
confidence in Toussaint, a general, a black, and ex-slave
like themselves.

But although the insurrection was stifled, Laveaux,
knowing the weakness of his position, would not take puni-
tive measures. Blockading Le Cap were twelve British and
two American ships. The Mulatto leaders were obviously
still ready for insurrection. Laveaux suspected a plot, and
had to do all he could to prevent an insurrection which
might have had the collusion of the British. The Mulattoes
were clamouring that the power should be shared—one
man should not have all of it.

On the first of April Laveaux, accompanied by Toussaint, went into Le Cap and assembled the people and
the army on the parade-ground. He knew that the Mulattoes were expecting him to make some alteration to the
Government in their favour, re-instating Villate with greater
powers. To the astonishment of all and the unbounded joy
of the blacks he proclaimed Toussaint Assistant to the
Governor and swore that he would never do anything
without consulting him. He called him the saviour of constituted authority, the black Spartacus, the Negro pre-
dicted by Raynal who would avenge the outrages done to
his race. Toussaint, overwhelmed with gratitude, coined
one of his flying phrases, "After God, Laveaux."

French historians date the elevation of Toussaint
above Mulattoes and French representatives in the minds
of the blacks from this memorable day, and not without a

condemnation of Laveaux. It is the privilege of historians to be wise after the event, and the more foolish the historian the wiser he usually aims to be. Laveaux could not help himself. Toussaint wanted him to dismiss Villate. "The Dominican Catechism says to pardon our offenses, Lord, as we shall pardon those who have offended us. But in an army, no subordination no discipline, and no discipline no army. If the lieutenant is not subordinate to his captain, the sub-lieutenant, the sergeant and the soldier will not be subordinate either. That at any rate is what I think, General." Laveaux would not take the step. He was afraid that civil war might lead to the loss of the colony. But he wrote to the Minister explaining what he had done. By nominating Toussaint "he had checked the plans of these evilly-disposed men." Laveaux was certain that Rigaud was in the conspiracy also. The Mulattoes had been blocked for the moment, but French authority in the colony was in danger and Laveaux was very near a break-down.

"Ah, Citizen," he pleaded with the Minister. "Do not lose time. Send troops, a powerful force, send Commissioners, send laws and all that is needed to make them respected. Any more delay will make France lose the four years of labour and of fatigue that we true republicans have suffered."

The French Government, alarmed at the growth of Mulatto aspiration, hastened to send a Commission which landed at Le Cap on May 11th, 1796. It consisted of five men, Giraud and Leblanc, and three who had played a part in San Domingo history, Raimond the Mulatto, Roume, who was sent to take possession of Spanish San Domingo, handed over to France by Spain at the Treaty of Bâle, and our old friend, Sonthonax. Sonthonax luckily for himself had arrived in Paris just after the fall of Robespierre. He had stood his trial and had been triumphantly acquitted of the charges brought against him by the colonists. He was known to be a lover of the blacks, and France was now afraid not of the blacks but of the Mulattoes. Sonthonax came therefore with the special injunction to keep the Mulattoes in check. He brought only 1,200 men but plenty of arms and ammunition. On August 17th, four months after Sonthonax landed, the Directory confirmed Toussaint's promotion by Laveaux to the rank of general of division, and that of Pierre Michel and other ex-slaves as generals of brigade. France, still engaged in a life and death struggle in Europe, was leaning on the blacks, not only against the British, but against the threat of Mulatto independence. Thus the stock of Toussaint as leader of the blacks was rising steadily.

VIII

The White Slave-Owners
Again

SONTHONAX, as dictatorial and self-willed as ever, dominated the Commission and began a pronounced pro-black
policy. He loved the blacks, said that he wished he was a
black man, and lived openly with a Mulatto woman.

If all the whites had been like Sonthonax, the labourers would have lost their anti-white feelings by which they
meant only anti-slavery. For Laveaux and Sonthonax they
would have done anything. But the blacks could not trust
the old slave-owners; the British bribed, intrigued, and
gave money and guns, and the insurrections all over the

colony continued. Sonthonax wrote secretly to the Directory that the blacks hated the whites, but he understood the reason for their hate. Three weeks after he landed he published a proclamation in creole which declared that everyone who was convicted of saying in the markets or elsewhere that the Negroes had not acquired their liberty for ever, or that a man could be the property of another man, was a traitor to his country and would be punished accordingly. To reassure a people so sensitive to freedom he abolished restraint for debt and put at liberty all those who were in prison for this offence.

He worked hard to instil into them the necessity for labour. Everybody is free in France, he said, but everybody works. Yet he stood firmly against coercion. Work hard, was his advice, but do not forget that no one has the right of forcing you to dispose of your time against your will. He rigorously forbade beating on the plantations. He instituted schools where blacks were given an elementary education and learnt Greek and Roman history. He sent the sons of the blacks and Mulattoes to France to be educated in a special school that the Republic opened for them. He announced that he would not deliver a commission to anyone who could not sign his name. And thus in every house in Le Cap could be seen blacks, men and women, some of 50 years of age, learning to read and write. In the country districts the labourers begged Sonthonax to send them as teachers even young European children who knew how to read and write. The blacks knew their ignorance and were willing to learn from the whites, to be guided by men from France, men like Laveaux and Sonthonax, to learn from the white children. All they asked was to be rid for ever of the fear of slavery. But the British were there spending millions to enslave them once more. They knew that the old slave-owners for whom they worked now as free men would make them slaves again at the first opportunity. Their hope was Toussaint, a black man, ex-slave, with his army of black men, ex-slaves. All the black labourers of San Domingo had their eyes on him.

Toussaint, when Sonthonax arrived, was second in

military rank to Laveaux. He had the confidence of the
French Government who sent him presents and letters of
congratulation, and undertook the education of his sons
in Paris. With Laveaux and Sonthonax, its representatives
in San Domingo, he was on the best of terms. The Mulattoes in the North were discredited, and Toussaint with his
army and mass support was the most powerful man in San
Domingo. Is it from this moment that dates his tentative
ambition to become master of the island? Many are convinced of this, but it is certainly a false view. What is certain is that Toussaint wanted to become commander-in-
chief, and now with extreme delicacy he suggested to
Laveaux that he could help him to get back to France if
he wished.

The French Constitution of the Year III had given
San Domingo seven deputies in the two Houses. The elections were to take place in September 1796, and in August
Toussaint told Laveaux that he could get him elected as a
representative: Laveaux had sacrificed his health, his wife,
his children, and he needed a rest from the intrigues and
factions of San Domingo. The excuse offered was perfect.
Laveaux had laboured in San Domingo through the years
of the revolution and the invasion by the British. Without
one trip to France, he had borne the brunt of the fighting,
first against the slaves and then against Spaniards and British, as Governor and Commander-in-Chief. His letters to
the Minister show how much he felt the strain and he leapt
at the chance. He at any rate did not suspect Toussaint's
motives, or if he did bore him no grudge. They remained
the closest of friends after Laveaux' return to France, their
intimate correspondence continued, and Laveaux was always Toussaint's staunchest defender.

But Sonthonax too at this same election, though it
took place only a few months after his arrival, had himself
elected as a representative of the colony in the French
Parliament. One of Toussaint's reasons for suggesting Laveaux' return was to have a trustworthy representative of
the blacks in France. And this was the very reason why
Sonthonax wanted to go back. The political situation had

shifted in France since the abolition of slavery without a debate, and the supporters of Negro liberty had good cause to be nervous.

Robespierre and the Mountain had maintained power until July 1794. The Terror had saved France, but long before July Robespierre had gone far enough and was now lagging behind the revolutionary masses. In the streets of Paris, Jacques Varlet and Roux were preaching Communism; not in production but in distribution, a natural reaction to the profiteering of the new bourgeosie. Robespierre, however, revolutionary as he was, remained bourgeois and had reached the extreme limit of the bourgeois revolution. He persecuted the workers—far more working-men than aristocrats perished in this phase of the Terror. In June 1794, the revolutionary armies won a great victory in Belgium; and at once the continuation of the terror was seen by the public as factional ferocity and not a revolutionary necessity. Right-wing and left in the Convention combined to strike at this sinister dictator, and when he sent out the call to the people he could not get the old response. Some of the sections came, but there was a delay, rain fell, and they went back home again. The revolutionary ardour which had inspired them since August 1792 was gone, killed by Robespierre himself. He seems to have been in constant fear of a split between the extreme revolutionism of Paris and the rest of the country but destroyed his own Left-wing and thereby sealed his own doom.

The tragedy was that the Paris masses, in leaving him to his fate, were opening the door to worse enemies. Robespierre's successors were the new officialdom, the financial speculators, the buyers of church property, all the new bourgeoisie. They were enemies of royalty (which would guillotine them all if it came back) and avid of social equality, but were determined to keep the masses in their place and willing to ally themselves with the old bourgeoisie, and even some of the aristocracy, in a joint exploitation of the new opportunities created by the revolution. When the masses grasped the trend of affairs they tried, twice in 1795, to reassert their old power. But the new bourgeois France was too strong for them. They were defeated, reaction increased, and as it grew the old slave-owners, crawling out of their prisons and hiding-places, held up their heads again and clamoured for "order" to be restored in San Domingo and the colonies.

On the morning after, the Convention had not been too happy over abolition. Robespierre seems to have doubted the utility of colonies at all, and probably with the idea of bargaining with Britain had let it be known that he did not want the colonial question raised, whereat all kept quiet.[1] The lucky Sonthonax, a Brissotin and there-fore enemy of Robespierre, had arrived back in France before Robespierre fell, and was once more in danger of the guillotine. But with the death of Robespierre, the co-lonial question came to the fore again. Before the Con-vention was dissolved, Boissy d'Anglas praised the mag-nificent defence of San Domingo by Toussaint and Rigaud and their armies, and said that they deserved well of the country. Gouly, a colonial deputy, opposed this resolution without success. But he delivered a long address, between the lines of which one could see the claws of restoration, and the Convention had this document printed.

The new Constitution gave France the Directory of five members and two Houses, the Council of Elders, and the Council of Five Hundred. The two bodies elected on a restricted franchise met in November 1795. The new bourgeoisie dominated both Houses. The Jacobins, weary and discredited, were in a minority. Vaublanc, who had fled after August 10th, and a strong clique were members of the Council of Five Hundred, and the émigré colonists kept up a ceaseless agitation inside and outside parliament

---

[1] Saintoyant, *La Colonisation Française* . . . , Vol. I, pp. 229-230.
There was a curious alliance between Robespierre, Fou-quier-Tinville, head of the revolutionary tribunals, and some of the émigré colonists. See in particular a report of Dufay, the white member of the first three representatives to San Domingo. *Les Archives Nationales*, DXXV, 57.

for the "restoration of order" in the colonies. What was this "order"? The blacks had no doubt as to the kind of "order" that the émigré colonists wished to restore. They did not say "slavery" openly—the revolution was still too near—but black San Domingo began to hear that Page (who had written the letter of August 11th) and his friend Bruley, Vaublanc, and other notorious enemies of colonial liberty were once more active in France. The blacks could deal with local whites whose speech or actions hinted at any return to slavery. The Republic they had always looked upon as their friend. But now, as they heard what was happening in France and heard who were in the new Parliament and what they were saying, their doubts grew and they began to ask all strangers arriving in the colony from France if the Republic was sincere in giving them liberty.

The Republic of 1794 had been sincere in giving them liberty but the Republic of 1796 might be equally sincere in taking it away. In addition to their clamour for the restoration of "order" (while blacks and Mulattoes under Toussaint and Rigaud drained away the blood of Britain, the Republic's chief enemy) the maritime bourgeois and the colonists directed their fire on Sonthonax, as the executioner of the whites and the origin of all the troubles.

Sonthonax reached San Domingo in May 1796, but by the time preparations were being made for the San Domingo elections in August, the colonial reaction was making such headway in France that he felt, both in his own defence and for the sake of the blacks, that it would be better if he went back to France as a deputy.

The maritime bourgeois and the planters had made an infinite deal of mischief on the colonial question until the Paris masses gave the colony a chance to adapt itself to the new conditions. Now, as soon as they were coming into power again, they began with their old greed, dishonesty and tricks. The mischief that they would cause this time would be as nothing to what they had done between July 14th, 1789, and August 10th, 1792. When it was all over they would blame the revolutionaries.

Sonthonax easily had himself elected, but though he wanted to go everybody begged him to stay. San Domingo was still unsettled and his influence was strong. With the blacks his name was already a talisman, and in an insurrection which took place in the revolutionary centre of Port-de-Paix, where whites were massacred, the labourers had risen to cries of "Long live Sonthonax! Long live Sonthonax!" Obviously the blacks, like horses, dogs, cats and some wild animals, judged a man not by the colour of his skin but by the way he behaved. British agents, well supplied with money, were always moving among them stirring up strife and encouraging disorder. French royalists were doing the same. The situation was extremely uncertain and all classes, white and black, asked Sonthonax not to go. The Municipality of Le Cap, Mulatto and black officers, Clairveaux,[2] Moïse and Christophe begged him to remain. Moïse, supposed to be an implacable hater of the whites, told Sonthonax that if he left he would resign, as the colony would most certainly be thrown into disorder,[3] and at a meeting of the Commissioners, Raimond, Leblanc and Giraud told him that if he went they would not remain behind.[4] They feared for their lives. Thus pressed, Sonthonax stayed.[5] Portrayed in France as the executioner of the whites and disrupter of the colony, he was in reality a rallying centre for blacks and whites so long as they were republicans. But he was without mercy against the old slave-owners, and these were the ones who

---

[2] Clairveaux, Maurepas and 100 other signatories to Sonthonax, September 30th, 1796. *Correspondance du Citoyen Sonthonax.* Vol. II, p. 370, *La Bibliothèque Nationale.*

[3] *Ibid.* Moïse to Sonthonax. September 21st 1796. *Correspondance du Citoyen Sonthonax,* Vol. II, p. 372.

[4] Report of Deliberations of the Commission by Pascal, the Secretary, 25 Vendémiaire, AN V. *Les Archives Nationales,* DXXV, 45.

[5] Copy of minutes of the Electoral Assembly, 20 Fructidor, AN IV, and following days. *Les Archives Nationales,* DXXV, 45.

The long-held belief that Toussaint engineered the election of Sonthonax to get rid of him is therefore directly contrary to the facts.

were most clamorous in France. Toussaint too pressed him to stay, and far from having arranged the election of Sonthonax in order to get rid of him, as is commonly urged, Toussaint told the Directory that the safety of the colony depended upon Sonthonax being left as Commissioner, at least until peace with Britain was declared.

Unfortunately Sonthonax, true representative of the revolution, was also the agent of the French Republic, sent to ensure that France and not the Mulattoes should rule the colony.

The Mulatto stronghold was the South under Rigaud who carried on the war against the British with such skill and vigour as to draw again and again praise even from an English Tory historian.[6] By 1797 Rigaud was master of a large part of the South. He had 6,000 men and a detachment of cavalry. Each battalion chief commanded a cantonment, with absolute power, carrying out all civil and political functions. No black held rank above that of captain, and, unlike Toussaint, Rigaud kept the whites in rigid subjection, excluding them from every position of importance.

Rigaud was undoubtedly narrow-minded. He wore always a brown wig with straight hair to give him an appearance as close to that of a white man as possible. This sensitiveness to colour is usually accompanied in active men by great bitterness against the oppressing race, and the narrowness of Rigaud's organisation and his exclusion of whites and blacks from all positions of power undoubtedly owed something to his personal character. But fundamentally it lay in the very circumstances of the Mulattoes. They were hopelessly outnumbered by the blacks. They, more than the illiterate blacks, knew about the émigré propaganda and intrigues for the restoration of white supremacy. Toussaint did not trust the whites at all, but the blacks were so backward that he had to use whites. The

[6] Fortescue, *History of the British Army*, London, 1906, Vol. IV, pt. 1.

Mulattoes were better equipped. Though not all of them were educated, yet there were enough of them to govern. And if they established a Mulatto oligarchy, not only past events but future were to prove that the whites at least were the last persons whose complaints should have been listened to.

Rigaud and his followers had abandoned slavery but they were hard on the black labourers. They made them understand that their freedom was due to the Mulattoes, they confined them to the plantations, and Rigaud's prisons were filled with whites and blacks in irons, but never a single Mulatto. He had as his chief adviser Pinchinat, and they restored cultivation to such an extent that Rigaud never asked for any financial assistance from the French Government and paid for his own ammunition. Yet he was a true friend of the Republic. He dismissed all the bribes the British offered him and, unlike Toussaint, shot without mercy all, even Mulattoes, who intrigued with the British. Whatever Sonthonax' instructions, he should have left Rigaud alone, at least until the peace. But, overconfident, he tackled Rigaud without the means to enforce his will. He had not been long in the colony when he despatched to the South a Commission of three, General Desfourneaux and Rey, two white men, and Leborgne, a Mulatto. Desfourneaux was to bring Rigaud's army under his own control, the Commission was to restore equality among citizens of all colour (Sonthonax' instructions were particularly stringent on this). It was to investigate whether the plot of March 20th had any roots in the South, and it was to arrest Pinchinat and bring him to Le Cap to account for his share in that conspiracy—Pinchinat who was the idol of the South and of the Mulattoes all over the colony. Toussaint told Sonthonax not to attempt such a thing. He and Rigaud respected and indeed had an admiration for each other. Rigaud never had any personal jealousy of Toussaint because Toussaint was a Negro,[7] and co-operated

[7] This is another of the tenacious legends now exploded by the mass of documents reproduced in Michel, *La Mission du Général Hédouville*. . . .

against the British under Toussaint's orders. Toussaint thought that Sonthonax should begin by having a conference. Above all he warned Sonthonax against sending Rey, who was an enemy of Rigaud's and had tried to assassinate him in Les Cayes. Sonthonax would not listen.

Never was an expedition more certain of failure, and its adventures give a useful idea of the social chaos with which Toussaint had to deal.

Rigaud, though suspicious, welcomed the Commissioners and treated them with the greatest respect. The Commissioners duly noted the power which Rigaud and his officers exercised. But unmindful of this, wherever they journeyed they stirred up the labourers against Rigaud's government, telling them that the Mulattoes were oppressing them. Unrest among labourers and soldiers began wherever the Commissioners passed.

Their private conduct was unsatisfactory. They piled up great expenses, gambled for hours in the private homes at which they stayed, and entertained loose women in a loose way. Rigaud was engaged to a young woman, Marie Villeneuve. Rey seduced her, and when Rigaud came to see him told him smilingly, "Rigaud, I am going to introduce you to the most beautiful girl in Les Cayes, but promise me to tell no one!" Taking him into the bedroom he drew the curtains of the bed and showed him Marie Villeneuve. Rigaud, a man of notoriously violent temper, threw himself on Rey, knocked him down, and was about to hurl him over the balcony into the street when the servants rushed in and saved him. One of the Commissioners stupidly asked Rigaud what he thought would happen if they arrested Pinchinat. Yet Rigaud and the Mulattoes continued to show an exemplary patience. The delegation attempted an expedition against enemy territory. Desfourneaux, acting as chief officer, would not take the advice of the local officers, and his column was badly beaten. Coming back in a temper he arrested the Treasurer of the South, as he had been ordered to do, and also arrested a Mulatto officer for some offence. While this officer was being conducted towards the harbour he met a group of his own soldiers. He made a dash for safety, got safely among his own men, and the simmering insurrection began.

The European soldiers and the National Guard stood by the Government delegation, but the Mulattoes all took the part of Rigaud. That night Rigaud's brother raised the black labourers who, however hard their lot, would always follow anyone who they thought was for them against slavery. Beauvais, knowing that the Commissioners were severely to blame but recognising their authority as representatives of the Government, tried to make peace between the two parties. The Mulattoes refused to listen to him and said they would wait for Rigaud. Rey and Desfourneaux fled, and the Mulattoes and the blacks in full insurrection massacred scores of whites, who of course were all for the Commission. Leborgne and Kerverseau, another European officer, were only saved because Beauvais, although powerless to stop the excitement, never left them for a single moment.

Rigaud was the only man who could have restored calm, but Rigaud would not come. He was fond of an expression, "How terrible is the rage of the people!", and when he heard of the massacre in Les Cayes, all he would do was to say this over and over again. At last Kerverseau and Leborgne gave authority to Rigaud to re-establish quiet. Rigaud issued a proclamation stating that he had been officially put in control of the government, and immediately calm was restored. Leborgne and Kerverseau left, and Rigaud remained master of the South. He and his people had been grossly provoked, but they were guilty of rebellion. Sonthonax refused to receive the delegations that the Municipality of Les Cayes sent to him to explain the unfortunate occurrences. The South tried Roume, the other Commissioner. Roume also refused to listen. The Municipality sent two whites to Paris to plead its case. When after some delay these two reached Paris, they turned against Rigaud and became his accusers instead of his defenders. Sonthonax reorganised the geographical division of San Domingo so as to bring two districts of the

South within the jurisdiction of the government. The inhabitants, spurred on by Rigaud, drove out the officers whom Sonthonax sent to take charge. Sonthonax sent a condemnatory proclamation. The citizens of Les Cayes dragged it through the streets at the tail of an ass. Pinchinat, elected among others as representative to the French Parliament for the South, was refused permission to sit when he reached Paris. The breach between the South under Rigaud and the Government, both in San Domingo and in France, was complete. But Rigaud sent a representative to put his case to Toussaint. Sonthonax heard of it and wanted to have him arrested. Toussaint refused and protected Rigaud's man. Thus in the last months of 1796 and at the beginning of 1797 Toussaint was in close relationship with Rigaud who was in a very uncertain position. The British had a good opportunity during all this confusion and might have conquered the colony then. They have even claimed that about this time Rigaud entered into negotiations with them. However that may be, the Mulattoes, repelled by the Republic, drew nearer to the blacks under Toussaint, but while Rigaud and his people looked upon Sonthonax as their worst enemy, Toussaint maintained the friendliest relations with the Commissioner. Sought after by blacks, Mulattoes and whites, the suave and discreet Toussaint was gradually becoming the one man in San Domingo on whom everything hinged.

Sonthonax continued to rule with energy. His other colleagues except Raimond left him. Roume was in Spanish San Domingo. Sonthonax intrigued among the black generals, but solely for his own power and without any designs against their liberty. Rochambeau, a white general, objected to the wealth and dominance of the black generals and Sonthonax sent him home at once. Against white arrogance or the white émigrés Sonthonax was as fierce an enemy as any black labourer. He wanted to sweep the aristocrats off the face of the earth. Toussaint used to send assistance to his old master in America, Bayou de

Libertas. He wanted to get him back but bowed to the law against émigrés and Sonthonax was especially pleased at this instance of Toussaint's civism. Sonthonax held frequent revolutionary demonstrations, and made the children in the schools spend many hours singing revolutionary hymns.

But he worked also at the restoration of the colony. Le Cap was partially rebuilt, and cultivation began to flourish. On a plantation in the North Plain a little Negro named Brossard had the confidence of both blacks and whites. He got the labourers to work on a promise of a fourth part of the produce and he raised the capital to begin production again. The experiment was a great success and plantations were farmed out by the Government on this new principle. Toussaint encouraged his generals and other notabilities to adopt this system by which everybody including the state profited. Dessalines in time had 30 plantations farmed out to him. Toussaint popularised certain slogans by repeating them over and over again. "I do not wish to be any Coast Negro" was one of them, referring to the primitive needs of the Africans from the slave coast. "The guarantee of the liberty of the blacks is the prosperity of agriculture" was another saying always on his lips which spread among the blacks. Banditry, idleness, murder, these things still continued as they continued in France until the advent of Bonaparte; but torn and devastated as San Domingo still was, the colony had definitely taken an upward turn by the early months of 1797. Toussaint was appointed Commander-in-Chief and Governor on the recommendation of Sonthonax, who installed him in Le Cap with an imposing ceremony.

The name of Sonthonax was in the mouth of every black. Here, astonishing sight, was a white man who protected the liberties and privileges of all, labourers and generals alike, as if he had once been a slave himself.

On the 17th of August, 1797, Toussaint went into Le Cap and called on Sonthonax. After a few minutes there he visited the Commissioner Raimond and told him that the colony would be in serious danger if Sonthonax did not leave at once. He did not wish to use violence against Sonthonax, because of his official position, but Raimond being his brother Commissioner should ask him to leave for Paris to take up his post as deputy. He said he could not give his reasons.

Raimond was thunder-struck, as well he might be. Toussaint and Sonthonax were the best of friends. What had happened? He was also frightened. This was a very serious step with incalculable consequences. Next day Toussaint told Raimond that Sonthonax was preparing a catastrophe, that the whites who were still in San Domingo would be murdered. He accused Sonthonax of wishing to raise the blacks against the whites. They argued with Toussaint fruitlessly, and tried to point out to him the gravity of the step, which might lead to disorder and civil war in a colony which was peaceful at last. Raimond and Pascal, general secretary of the Commission, went to Sonthonax and told him what they had heard. Toussaint then came, but Sonthonax said he preferred to speak to Toussaint alone. Why? Sonthonax failed to convince Toussaint and finally agreed to go, if Toussaint would give him a valedictory letter.

Next day Raimond and Pascal came again, and Toussaint, still keeping silence as to his reasons, told them of the proposed letter. The two went to Sonthonax and came back with a draft, which they asked Toussaint to sign and to get his staff to sign also. Toussaint summoned his officers and the letter was read to them. Some, whom Sonthonax had already got at, refused to sign; others wondering what this was all about said they would wait to hear what were the intentions of the Commissioner himself. Pascal ran to Sonthonax and begged him to clear the air by saying what he intended to do. But Sonthonax, on learning the attitude of these officers, refused to say anything and even seemed disposed to resist. Toussaint then told the officers they could sign if they wanted to or not, as they pleased. Sonthonax, he said, wanted to go to France to take up his duty as a deputy and had asked for this letter. He had called them together to sign it, not to deliberate over it, as that would be against the law. Some signed, including Moïse and Christophe. Others went away, of whom a few came back afterwards and wanted to sign. Toussaint would not allow it. He said that he was not begging them to oblige him, he was ready to sign the letter alone and take full responsibility. This was typical of Toussaint, who had been trained as a slave and then as a soldier. He never troubled to explain overmuch to subordinates. Their business was to obey.

The letter was full of compliments to Sonthonax for his work and of the urgency of someone like him being in France to defend the liberty of the blacks. Raimond took the letter with the signatures to Sonthonax, who replied with another complimentary epistle. Toussaint, who always carried on a diplomatic intrigue in the most ceremonial manner, replied with yet another. Sonthonax had been given three days, but he sought to gain time, stirring up the officers friendly to him. One morning at four o'clock Toussaint had the alarm cannon fired, and sent General Agé to tell Raimond that if Sonthonax did not leave at once, he would enter the town and embark him by force. It was the end of Sonthonax. Accompanied by his mistress, Raimond, and some officers friendly to him, Sonthonax traversed the streets of Le Cap on his way to the boat. The population watched him go dumb with sorrow and bewilderment. He was immensely popular with all the blacks, but Toussaint had said he was to go and after that nothing could save him.

What was behind this extraordinary episode, an unsolved enigma to this day? Toussaint's explanation, the secret that he guarded, was that since the end of 1796 Sonthonax had at various times suggested to him that he should massacre the whites and declare the colony independent. This was what Toussaint wrote in a long letter[8]

8 Report of 18 Fructidor, An V, (September 5th) 1797. *Les*

to the Directory in which he gave an account in dramatic form of the various interviews in which Sonthonax had made this proposal to him.

Here is part of Toussaint's story. He was installed as Commander-in-Chief on May 2nd, 1797. On that day, after the ceremony, he was mounting his horse to go back to Gonaïves when Sonthonax stopped him, asked him into his house and again broached the subject.[9]

"I am very, very pleased, I am enchanted at seeing you Commander-in-Chief of the armed forces of the colony. We are in a position now to do exactly what we want. You have influence on all the inhabitants. It is imperative for us to execute our project. This is the most suitable moment, circumstances were never more favourable, and no one is better able to act than you and I."

Toussaint replied.

"That is to say, Commissioner, that you wish to destroy me . . . to kill all the whites and make ourselves independent. Yet you had promised me that you would not speak to me again about these projects."

"Yes, but you see that it is absolutely indispensable."

Thus goes on page after page this curious dramatic dialogue, with the same actors, the same theme, but only time and place differing. How much truth was there in it? Nobody knows for certain. When Sonthonax defended himself against this charge in Paris, he said that he had left San Domingo of his own free will, which was a lie. He claimed to have discovered a plot by priests and émigrés, of which Toussaint was the instrument, to get rid of the Commission. This was nonsense. He also accused Raimond of conspiring with Toussaint, to invite him by means of the letter to leave for France. But both Pascal and Raimond could easily refute this statement. If anyone should be accused of independence, said Sonthonax, it should be Toussaint, and he charged Toussaint with being surrounded by émigré whites, with organising the revolt of

---

Archives Nationales, A.F. III, 210. Reproduced in part in Sannon, *Histoire de Toussaint-L'Ouverture*, Vol. II, pp. 24-40.
[9] *Ibid.*

1791, with fighting for the Spanish King and leaving him only when he heard of negotiations for peace and knew that the King of Spain would not need him any longer. All this was partly lies, partly nonsense. If Sonthonax were not guilty, his defence was a poor one.

But it is no easier to understand Toussaint's side either. He was certainly lying when he portrayed himself as being angry with Sonthonax for making such treacherous proposals. Up to a few days before his visit to Le Cap, he and Sonthonax were and had been close friends. He said that since the end of 1796 Sonthonax had made these proposals to him. On February 1st, 1797, he had written to the Minister asking him not to believe insinuations that Sonthonax and Raimond were betraying the interests of France, and asking that Sonthonax should remain: "the safety of San Domingo, its entire restoration, demands that the Directory should not permit him to return. . . . My attachment to France, the love of the Fatherland, and of my brothers, oblige me to make the request of you." On June 15th in a letter to Sonthonax Toussaint signed himself "friendship without end." On June 16th he wrote to Mentor, another black, that the measures of the Commission had been all approved. "How joyful Sonthonax will be! I would be glad to be near him to embrace him and to tell him my satisfaction. This satisfaction makes me forget for a moment my vexations." [10]

Yet, a few weeks after, to the astonishment of everyone he was insisting with all the strength of his unbreakable will that Sonthonax was to go. Nothing that happened in San Domingo can explain this. The explanation, as with so much in the history of San Domingo, must be sought in France. What was happening there changed Toussaint's views and with them the course of the black revolution.

The planters in the Paris of 1797 were nearly as noisy if not quite as powerful as they had been in 1791. The

[10] *Les Archives Nationales*, A.F. 1212. Quoted from Schoelcher, *Vie de Toussaint-L'Ouverture*, p. 194.

revolution in France was dead. Babeuf had arrived at the
conclusion that political equality could only be achieved
by a drastic change in economic organisation. The Directory's police reported that working men and women were
eagerly reading Babeuf's writings. But the fighting enthusiasm of the old days had been broken by defeat and disappointment. Babeuf's attempt failed miserably, and the bourgeoisie took advantage of the reaction to stabilise itself.
Respectable Jacobin deputies, who had probably never
heard the name of Babeuf until he was captured, were
accused of terrorism and anarchism, and of 216 former
members of the Convention who were due to retire in
March 1797 scarcely a dozen were re-elected. So far had
reaction gone that the president of the Elders was Barbé
de Marbois, the Intendant who had been chased from San
Domingo by the Patriots in 1789.

Vaublanc and his party, therefore, immensely reinforced after the new elections, carried on as in the good
old days. Why are the blacks armed, asked Bourdon? To
destroy all parties? The unfortunate white colonists had de-
creased from 40,000 to 25,000. Some days later Bourdon
gave a new message to the Directory about massacres and
denounced the official report as lies. Why were the whites
in San Domingo suffering? The Directory was pardoning
royalists in France: of 1,500 requests for restoration of
rights from émigrés only 166 had been rejected. Yet in the
colonies this persecution was going on. At last in May the
Directory was able to send a message from San Domingo.
It was from Toussaint.

Hatred of the English, he said, had united all parties.
The English had put the crown on their atrocities by in-
venting cuirasses studded with sharp-pointed pieces of
steel which they threw among the republican soldiers when
it came to hand-to-hand fighting, knowing that most of the
blacks were barefooted. But this hateful device has only
turned out to their shame: "Our soldiers have defied these
weapons with an unconquerable rage and have proved that
no obstacle is able to stop men carrying arms for liberty."

At this stirring message, an echo from an age that

still lingered faintly in their ears, the deputies broke into enthusiastic applause and demanded that it should be printed. But Vaublanc raged and stormed, said the whole was a pack of lies, nothing could be more ridiculous, and on May 27th, he made the fiercest attack yet made on Sonthonax. "He is covered with the blood of the whites. He has made atrocious laws, which the tigers of Libya would not make if tigers had the misfortune to need laws. He has raised impositions; he has pocketed vast sums of which he has given no account." All of this was untrue. If Sonthonax had had whites killed, it had been in defence of the Republic. He had not stolen any money; to the end of his days he remained a poor man. It was his legislation in favour of the blacks that was driving Vaublanc and the colonists wild. Vaublanc blamed Sonthonax and Laveaux as having contributed most to the spirit of insubordination among the blacks. Day after day he abused Sonthonax and the blacks (those blacks without whom the colony would assuredly have been British). Barbé accused the labourers of being the passive and servile instruments of Sonthonax' crimes. Delahaye said that San Domingo needed new agents with an imposing force.

On June 1st the Directory sent a message to the House from Raimond describing all that was being done for cultivation. Bourdon said it was a pack of lies, that the proprietors were being chased away, and that the Commissioners were putting the money in their pockets. Vaublanc said that the same boat which brought Raimond's despatch had brought Martial Besse, a creole general, who said that the colony was in the wildest disorder. He asked for the recall of Sonthonax. Garran-Coulon defended Sonthonax, but finally a motion proposed by Vaublanc and Villaret-Joyeuse was carried by an enormous majority, and on June 3rd the House decided on the recall of Raimond, Roume, and Sonthonax. In the course of his speech Villaret-Joyeuse said that the military régime was the only one which would save San Domingo and save the unhappy whites from the daggers of the Negroes. He and Vaublanc demanded that San Domingo should be put in a state of siege until the peace. On June 12th the Council of Elders approved the motion for the recall.

Sonthonax most certainly had friends in France who kept him informed. Toussaint, we know, had his private agents. But even without these special sources of information San Domingo knew, for the news was appearing day by day in the *Moniteur*, the official journal. The *Moniteur* of June 12th carried an announcement of a letter from Lord G . . . to the Directory requesting a passport for an English representative to Paris to discuss terms of peace. Peace had been in the air for a long time. If terms of peace were being discussed, then France might soon be able to devote attention to San Domingo and to send troops. Sonthonax knew the strength of the counter-revolution in France. He could see exactly where the steady growing reaction would end. He himself would lose his head and the colony would ultimately be restored to slavery. He might not have expressed himself so freely to Toussaint as Toussaint described in his despatch. But it is not impossible that, sick and tired of the reaction and fearing for the future, he had proposed to Toussaint that they should seize the colony, purge it of the white slave-owners, and make it independent. Toussaint, very careful, would reject these advances while bearing Sonthonax, friend of the blacks, no ill-will for them. But some time in July Toussaint got news of the decree recalling Sonthonax and of the reception which the speeches of Vaublanc, Barbé and the others had got. There was obviously a terrific struggle ahead, and he and his ally, Rigaud, in disgrace with the Directory, would have to fight. With his usual decision he made up his mind to throw Sonthonax to the wolves at once. What other reason can be assigned for his violent *volteface?*

Whatever the reasons for his dismissal of Sonthonax, the fact itself was of enormous significance. Henceforth the French Government suspected Toussaint of a design to make the colony independent, and Toussaint feared the intention of the French to restore slavery. The Directory itself had no intention of restoring slavery. But the Directory might not continue in power, and no one knew what its successors would do. It is from this time that Toussaint, driven by events, envisaged the necessity of holding on to power even at the cost of defying France.

How acutely he had foreseen the course of French politics was proved by the events of the next few months. For the men who were now reaping the fruits of the revolution, the restoration of "order" in San Domingo was only one item in a general wave of reaction they were forcing on France as fast as they could. They admitted deputies hitherto ineligible, suppressed the revolutionary clubs, revoked the laws relating to the deportation and dismissal of priests who would not take the oath to the Republic, reorganised the National Guard in such a manner as to exclude the more democratic elements. But they were going too fast. Some of their chiefs were even intriguing with royalty, and the new bourgeoisie did not want royalty and feudalism back again; even the weary and cheated masses would support their new masters against those outworn and discredited creeds. The Directory was watching this tide of reaction and, itself rotten with corruption, was powerless to stop it. Suddenly it got the proofs of a royalist conspiracy and decided to use them against these brazen relics of the *ancien régime*, whether royalist or no. On the night of the 18 Fructidor (September 3rd), they were arrested. A *coup d'état* banished 65 of them to the Guianas and checked for a time the descent of the revolution. Among the 65 were Vaublanc, Villaret-Joyeuse, Barbé de Marbois, Bourdon, Delahaye, and Dumas, all of them implacable enemies of the new régime in San Domingo. Black freedom was saved for a time, but Toussaint had had a serious shock.

On November 5th he addressed a letter to the Directory which is a milestone in his career.[11] He did not know

11 Report of 14 Brumaire, AN VI. *Les Archives Nationales*, A.F. III, 210. Reproduced in part in Sannon, *Histoire de Toussaint-L'Ouverture*, Vol. III, p. 36.

then of the *coup d'état* of the 18th Fructidor, when Vaublanc and his band had got their deserts. He wrote still under the belief that the reactionary group of old slave-owners had strong influence in the legislature. The Directory itself he did not accuse openly. But he let it see that he no longer had confidence in it, and that henceforth the blacks were going to watch every party in France.

"The impolitic and incendiary discourse of Vaublanc has not affected the blacks nearly so much as their certainty of the projects which the proprietors of San Domingo are planning: insidious declarations should not have any effect in the eyes of wise legislators who have decreed liberty for the nations. But the attempts on that liberty which the colonists propose are all the more to be feared because it is with the veil of patriotism that they cover their detestable plans. We know that they seek to impose some of them on you by illusory and specious promises, in order to see renewed in this colony its former scenes of horror. Already perfidious emissaries have stepped in among us to ferment the destructive leaven prepared by the hands of liberticides. But they will not succeed. I swear it by all that liberty holds most sacred. My attachment to France, my knowledge of the blacks, make it my duty not to leave you ignorant either of the crimes which they meditate or the oath that we renew, to bury ourselves under the ruins of a country revived by liberty rather than suffer the return of slavery.

"It is for you, Citizens Directors, to turn from over our heads the storm which the eternal enemies of our liberty are preparing in the shades of silence. It is for you to enlighten the legislature, it is for you to prevent the enemies of the present system from spreading themselves on our unfortunate shores to sully it with new crimes. Do not allow our brothers, our friends, to be sacrificed to men who wish to reign over the ruins of the human species. But no, your wisdom will enable you to avoid the dangerous snares which our common enemies hold out for you. . . .

"I send you with this letter a declaration which will acquaint you with the unity that exists between the pro-

prietors of San Domingo who are in France, those in the
United States, and those who serve under the English banner. You will see there a resolution, unequivocal and carefully constructed, for the restoration of slavery; you will
see there that their determination to succeed has led them
to envelop themselves in the mantle of liberty in order to
strike it more deadly blows. You will see that they are
counting heavily on my complacency in lending myself to
their perfidious views by my fear for my children. It is not
astonishing that these men who sacrifice their country to
their interests are unable to conceive how many sacrifices
a true love of country can support in a better father than
they, since I unhesitatingly base the happiness of my children on that of my country, which they and they alone
wish to destroy.

"I shall never hesitate between the safety of San Domingo and my personal happiness; but I have nothing to
fear. It is to the solicitude of the French Government that
I have confided my children. . . . I would tremble with
horror if it was into the hands of the colonists that I had
sent them as hostages; but even if it were so, let them know
that in punishing them for the fidelity of their father, they
would only add one degree more to their barbarism, without any hope of ever making me fail in my duty. . . .
Blind as they are! They cannot see how this odious conduct
on their part can become the signal of new disasters and
irreparable misfortunes, and that far from making them
regain what in their eyes liberty for all has made them lose,
they expose themselves to a total ruin and the colony to its
inevitable destruction. Do they think that men who have
been able to enjoy the blessing of liberty will calmly see it
snatched away? They supported their chains only so long
as they did not know any condition of life more happy than
that of slavery. But to-day when they have left it, if they
had a thousand lives they would sacrifice them all rather
than be forced into slavery again. But no, the same hand
which has broken our chains will not enslave us anew.
France will not revoke her principles, she will not withdraw from us the greatest of her benefits. She will protect

us against all our enemies; she will not permit her sublime morality to be perverted, those principles which do her most honour to be destroyed, her most beautiful achievement to be degraded, and her Decree of 16 Pluviôse which so honours humanity to be revoked. *But if, to re-establish slavery in San Domingo, this was done, then I declare to you it would be to attempt the impossible: we have known how to face dangers to obtain our liberty, we shall know how to brave death to maintain it.*[12]

"This, Citizens Directors, is the morale of the people of San Domingo, those are the principles that they transmit to you by me.

"My own you know. It is sufficient to renew, my hand in yours, the oath that I have made, to cease to live before gratitude dies in my heart, before I cease to be faithful to France and to my duty, before the god of liberty is profaned and sullied by the liberticides, before they can snatch from my hands that sword, those arms, which France confided to me for the defence of its rights and those of humanity, for the triumph of liberty and equality."[13]

Pericles on Democracy, Paine on the Rights of Man, the Declaration of Independence, the Communist Manifesto, these are some of the political documents which, whatever the wisdom or weaknesses of their analysis, have moved men and will always move them, for the writers, some of them in spite of themselves, strike chords and awaken aspirations that sleep in the hearts of the majority in every age. But Pericles, Tom Paine, Jefferson, Marx and Engels, were men of a liberal education, formed in the traditions of ethics, philosophy and history. Toussaint was a slave, not six years out of slavery, bearing alone the unaccustomed burden of war and government, dictating his thoughts in the crude words of a broken dialect, written

[12] Toussaint's emphasis.
[13] Probably a quotation from one of the Directory's letters to him.

and rewritten by his secretaries until their devotion and his will had hammered them into adequate shape. Superficial people have read his career in terms of personal ambition. This letter is their answer. Personal ambition he had. But he accomplished what he did because, superbly gifted, he incarnated the determination of his people never, never to be slaves again.

Soldier and administrator above all, yet his declaration is a masterpiece of prose excelled by no other writer of the revolution. Leader of a backward and ignorant mass, he was yet in the forefront of the great historical movement of his time. The blacks were taking their part in the destruction of European feudalism begun by the French Revolution, and liberty and equality, the slogans of the revolution, meant far more to them than to any Frenchman. That was why in the hour of danger Toussaint, uninstructed as he was, could find the language and accent of Diderot, Rousseau, and Raynal, of Mirabeau, Robespierre, and Danton. And in one respect he excelled them all. For even these masters of the spoken and written word, owing to the class complications of their society, too often had to pause, to hesitate, to qualify. Toussaint could defend the freedom of the blacks without reservation, and this gave to his declaration a strength and a single-mindedness rare in the great documents of the time. The French bourgeoisie could not understand it. Rivers of blood were to flow before they understod that elevated as was his tone Toussaint had written neither bombast nor rhetoric but the simple and sober truth.

IX

The Expulsion of the British

TOUSSAINT sent a white man, Colonel Vincent, an officer of
Engineers and a close friend, to the Directory to explain
his action against Sonthonax. Rigaud congratulated Toussaint on the expulsion of Sonthonax, and Toussaint, in undisputed command, prepared to sweep the British completely out of San Domingo.

Pitt and Dundas for years hung grimly on to their
hope of getting the island. In November 1795, in an attempt most probably to win Rigaud, Dundas authorised
Forbes to grant the same privileges to Mulattoes as to

whites.[1] But he still forbade the promise of freedom to Negro troops. That would have been selling the horse to preserve the stable. But the attempt to win Rigaud failed.

On February 18th, 1796, Dundas addressed the House of Commons. He was speaking in opposition to a motion for the abolition of slavery and the slave trade. In principle Dundas agreed with the movers of the motion; this agreement in principle was routine, but, continues Dundas,

"With those who argued on the general principle of the slave trade—as inexpedient, impolitic and incompatible with the justice and humanity of the British constitution— he had always, and must still, agree. . . .

"He opposed it because he thought were it agreed to by the House, it would endanger the peace of the country. Such a resolution, if passed into a law in the present distracted state of the colonies, would throw them entirely into the power of the enemy." The foolish Barnave had not learnt to argue that slavery was maintained for the benefit of the slaves. Dundas went even further.

"The war in the West Indies on the part of this country was not a war for riches or local aggrandizement, but a war for security."

But the drain of men and money was too great. By the end of 1796, after three years of war, the British had lost in the West Indies 80,000 soldiers including 40,000 actually dead, the latter number exceeding the total losses of Wellington's army from death, discharges, desertion and all causes from the beginning to the end of the Peninsular War.[2] The cost in San Domingo alone had been £300,-000 in 1794, £800,000 in 1795, £2,600,000 in 1796, and in January 1797 alone it was more than £700,000.[3] Early in 1797 the British Government decided to withdraw and maintain control only of Môle St Nicholas and the island of Tortuga. Toussaint did not know this, however, and he and Rigaud, close allies since the expulsion of Sonthonax, or-

---

[1] Fortescue, *History of the British Army*, Vol. IV, pt. 1, p. 468.
[2] Fortescue, Vol. IV, pt. 1, p. 496.
[3] Fortescue, Vol. IV, pt. 1, p. 546.

ganised the final campaign. In January 1798 he was ready for the decisive attack on Mirabelais, while Beauvais, Rigaud and Laplume were to attack at different points in the South to prevent the concentration of the British forces.

Toussaint, wishing to win back for the colony those white and Mulatto proprietors who were living in territory controlled by the English, rigorously forbade all pillage and destruction by his own soldiers, and addressed to the traitors a series of proclamations promising them forgiveness and full rights as French citizens if they would be faithful to the Republic. Always a firm adherent of the rules of civilised warfare, he found it necessary to rebuke General John White for the barbarities of the troops under his command.

"I feel that though I am a Negro, though I have not received as fine an education as you and the officers of His Britannic Majesty, I feel, I say, that such infamy on my part would reflect on my country and tarnish its glory." [4]

Combining military superiority with propaganda, Toussaint won seven victories in seven days. Maitland saw that the game was up, and asked Toussaint for a truce. He would evacuate the West Province completely in return for the protection of the lives and property of the inhabitants under British rule. That was exactly what Toussaint wanted, and negotiations were already taking place when Toussaint learned that General Hédouville had arrived in Spanish San Domingo, appointed sole Agent for the colony by the Directory.

The five men, who under the name of the Directory ruled France, had been seriously perturbed by the arrival in France of the deported Sonthonax. They never wished to restore slavery, and had warmly approved of the steps

[4] Sannon: *Histoire de Toussaint-L'Ouverture,* Vol. II, pp. 57-58. Vol. II, Chaps. 3 and 4, contains a fully documented account of the last phase of the war, with long extracts from Toussaint's correspondence with Maitland, Hédouville, etc. Except where otherwise stated, the passages quoted in this chapter are reproduced from these chapters.

Sonthonax had taken to educate the black labourers. But
the émigré colonists gave them no rest, and in July 1797,
after the Houses had voted for the recall of Sonthonax,
they appointed General Hédouville their special Agent in
San Domingo. Hedouville, an experienced soldier, had
shown notable diplomatic gifts in his pacification of La
Vendée, the most dangerous and persistent centre of counter-
revolution in France. The events which preceded 18 Fructidor had left the Directors very much occupied, and those
events themselves had sent the most obstreperous of the
colonists to Guiana. Had Sonthonax arrived in France before Vaublanc and his friends had been deported, he would
have been lucky to escape imprisonment. But once again
he reached home just after the fall of his enemies, and met
with a sympathetic reception. The Directors themselves,
however, were now thoroughly alarmed. Toussaint had de-
posed their representative, there were charges and counter-
charges of plots for independence. Then came Toussaint's
letter warning them that the blacks would fight to the
death at any hint of restoring the old régime. Here was a
new complication. It was now not so much the Mulattoes
who were to be feared, but the blacks, their black army
and this black general. At once the attitude to Rigaud
changed. Hédouville was instructed to leave, and to do all
that he could to check Toussaint's power until France
could send troops. He might have to use Rigaud against
Toussaint. The Directory did not know. So it gave Hédouville a free hand to pardon or arrest Rigaud as might seem
suitable and possible to him. The Directory pretended willingly to accept Toussaint's deportation of Sonthonax, and
maintained good relations with him. Yet so doubtful was
Hédouville of the reception he would get from Toussaint
that he landed at Santo Domingo, the headquarters of
Roume. He arrived late in April, just in time to hear of the
further successes of the irresistible Negro.

Hédouville had gathered from all sources information
about the men he was going to meet, and particularly about

Toussaint. And nobody left him in any doubt about the kind of man Toussaint was. General Kerverseau, an able soldier of strong and upright character, indicated to him the only possible line of policy.

"He is a man of great good sense, whose attachment to France cannot be doubted, whose religion guarantees morality, whose firmness equals his prudence, who enjoys the confidence of all colours, and who has on his own an ascendancy which nothing can counter-balance. With him you can do all; without him you can do nothing."

It is important for us to remember two sentences in Kerverseau's tribute. First, Toussaint was devoted to France. Secondly, Toussaint in 1798, after four years, had the confidence of whites, Mulattoes and blacks. He had set himself this aim, despite all provocation he had fought for it, and had achieved complete success.

What did Hédouville intend to do? Toussaint did not know, but he ordered that Hédouville should be welcomed with every distinction. In his letters to the new Agent, he was polite but reserved. "Permit me to make an observation to you as officer of the Republic. . . . There are men who appear outwardly to love liberty for all, but who are inwardly its sworn enemies. . . . What I say is true, I know it from experience." Toussaint was cold even in his reference to Roume, a sincere friend of the blacks, as his private correspondence shows.[5] "If the Commissioner Roume esteems me, I reciprocate it in my esteem for him and respect his virtues." Toussaint trusted none of them.

But as soon as he heard that Hédouville had arrived, he hastened to let Rigaud know. Though reassured by Pinchinat in Paris, Rigaud did not exactly know what steps Hédouville intended to take against him. He asked Toussaint for support against Hédouville, and sent him a confidential agent to discuss things he dared not write down.[6] The black leader and the Mulatto were in complete solidarity.

[5] Roume's correspondence for this period is to be found in *Les Archives Nationales*, A.F. III, 210.
[6] Michel, *La Mission du Général Hédouville* . . . , p. 135.

Continuing his negotiations with Maitland, Toussaint
granted an amnesty to all the planters who had submitted
to the British, and to all the labourers who had fought for
British pay. The only persons excepted were those planters
who had actually fought in the British ranks, or those royalists who had come to San Domingo from elsewhere. It was
a typical gesture by a man who all his life seemed quite
untouched by the ordinary human passion of revenge, and
never let anything divert him from his aim, the restoration
of San Domingo and the reconciliation of all the inhabitants, white, brown and black. He submitted the terms of
the amnesty to Hédouville, who ratified them. Maitland
tried to distinguish between Toussaint and Rigaud. Toussaint would have none of it, reminding Maitland that he
was Rigaud's superior officer. But he did not press Maitland hard. All he wanted was that he should leave San
Domingo. All proposals and counter-proposals were sent
to Hédouville for his approval, and on April 30th the Convention was signed whereby the British entirely evacuated
the West Province.

The soldier émigrés, Dessources and some others,
vicomtes and chevaliers, broke the terms of the amnesty,
destroyed cannon and ammunition dumps, killed all the
animals, and set plantations on fire. Toussaint's Africans,
on the other hand, starving and half-naked, marched into
the towns, and such was their discipline that no single act
of violence or pillage was committed. So admirable was the
conduct of his brother, Paul L'Ouverture, and his troops at
La Croix-des-Bouquets, that a number of citizens of all
colours wrote to Toussaint expressing their satisfaction at
having such an officer in command of their district. They
begged for a visit from Toussaint himself.

The entry into Port-Républicain[7] was a Roman triumph. The black labourers, so long made to understand
that they were born to serve, came out to see a black army

[7] Formerly Port-au-Prince.

hailed as the saviours of San Domingo, and the whites hastened to abase themselves before him whom they called their liberator. First came the clergy, with cross and banner and censers of burning incense, and then the erstwhile subjects of His Britannic Majesty. In the middle of the road a huge triumphal arch had been erected. The richest white women, riding on horseback or in open carriages, escorted by a guard of honour composed of young white creoles, came out to welcome the Commander-in-Chief. Young white girls threw over him flowers and garlands. Always a model of politeness, he descended from his horse and thanked them for their kindness. Four of the richest white planters of Cul-de-Sac carried with pride a dais, and others of them bowed at his feet, begging him to ascend. Toussaint could see among them men who had been his most relentless enemies, and indignant and humiliated he refused. "A dais and incense," he said, "belong only to God."

That night the town was illuminated. In all the great houses there was dancing, and one hundred and fifty sat down to a banquet. Next day the Mayor presented an address praising Toussaint's work as "a masterpiece of policy, wisdom and humanity." Toussaint's reply was characteristic.

"Learn, citizens, to appreciate the glory of your new political status. In acquiring the rights that the Constitution accords to all Frenchmen, do not forget the duties it imposes on you. Be but virtuous and you will be Frenchmen and good citizens. . . . Work together for the prosperity of San Domingo by the restoration of agriculture, which alone can support a state and assure public wellbeing. Compare in this respect the conduct of the French Government, which has not ceased to protect, with that of the English Government, which has destroyed. The appearance of your countryside which I passed through on my way here has filled me with grief. Its condition should have convinced you long ago that in joining the English you had embraced only a chimera. You thought you would gain, you have only lost. . . .

"The liberty without licence which the labourer will enjoy, the reward which the law accords to his labour, will attach him to the soil he cultivates. . . .

"The age of fanaticism is over. The reign of law has succeeded to that of anarchy. . . . Wise by experience, the Directory has just sent here a single Agent whom it has chosen from among its most trustworthy citizens. The glory which he has justly acquired in Europe, the virtues which characterise him, assure us of happiness. Let us aid him in his important mission by absolute obedience, and while he lays the foundations of the felicity which he meditates, I shall look over your safety, your tranquillity and your happiness, so long as you observe the solemn oaths that you have made to remain faithful to France, to cherish its Constitution and respect its laws. . . ."

Man of action, Toussaint habitually wrote and spoke like a philosopher. This comprehensive and concise speech was a programme for the country, and a personal gesture to Hédouville.

Before Toussaint could reach Le Cap, the British, still eager to possess a portion at least of this wonderful island, suddenly opened a strong attack on Rigaud in the South. For the moment Rigaud was in danger, and he appealed to Toussaint for help. Before Toussaint's reinforcements arrived, Maitland made an attempt to detach Rigaud from Toussaint. Rigaud replied that he would make war on him to the last extremity.

Toussaint interviewed Hédouville at Le Cap, then hurried down to meet Rigaud at Port-Républicain, and the two men saw each other for the first time. Rigaud, who had long wanted to meet "this virtuous man," treated Toussaint with the deference due to the Commander-in-Chief, and Toussaint, who always had perfect tact, addressed Rigaud as his old comrade. With the help of Toussaint's reinforcements the British attack had been beaten off, and the two set off in Toussaint's carriage to meet Hédouville. The tradition (which has all the facts in its favour) is that they reached Le Cap each agreeing to support the other against any intrigues by the Agent of the Directory.

What happened at this interview between Hédouville and Rigaud is one of the great tragedies of San Domingo. Hédouville overwhelmed Rigaud with attentions, promised that France would give him proofs of high consideration, bewailed the evils of the colony, told him that the surest way to assuage them was to help him to achieve his secret instructions—the withdrawal of supreme power from Toussaint L'Ouverture. Rigaud seized the chance to put himself right with France—and ruined himself, his caste, and his country for a generation.

Between the French bourgeoisie and the black labourers the Mulattoes, from August 1791, wavered continuously. Mulatto instability lies not in their blood but in their intermediate position in society. The pity was that Rigaud, dictator in the South, had not the sense to see that the French would use him against Toussaint and then inevitably turn on him.

It is said in San Domingo that Toussaint (whose methods were always oblique) had hidden himself where he could hear the interview between Rigaud and Hédouville. It was not necessary. During this very visit Hédouville began to show a changed attitude to Toussaint. The captain of the boat which had brought Hédouville told Toussaint how pleased he would be to take him back to France in the same vessel. "Your ship is not big enough for a man like me," said Toussaint. Still another pressed him about this trip to France, how honoured and welcome he would be. "I shall go when this," and he touched a shrub in the garden, "is big enough to take me."

Toussaint was warning Hédouville and his friends that no liberties were to be taken with him. Full of diplomatic tricks himself, he affected to be extremely impressed by the courtesies Maitland had shown and would show him. Over and over again he said that the French would never have treated him in this distinguished way. This was not true and he knew it. Laveaux and Sonthonax and the people of Port-Républicain had showered on him honours and dignities. But Toussaint wanted this to go to Hédouville. He even wrote to Hédouville about Maitland's honours, hoped that Hédouville had no objections to these courtesies being paid to an officer of the Republic. So that, while doing his duty and paying every necessary attention to Hédouville, he let him know by direct and indirect means that he was not going to be trifled with, and demanded in his turn the respect and consideration due to his rank. Hédouville, conceited and superior, seemed unable to realise that he was dealing with a man who was in command of a victorious army, had the great mass of the people in two provinces behind him, and had nothing to learn from any Frenchman in subtlety and diplomatic finesse. He continued with his baiting of the uneducated old Negro who spoke French so badly.

Rigaud had deserted him, Hédouville was just waiting his chance to strike at him. But Toussaint continued with his self-imposed mission of driving the British out with the least damage to the colony. Maitland's forces were now concentrated at Môle St Nicholas in the North and at Jérémie in the South. Toussaint, while massing troops to take them by assault if necessary, now brought off one of his most brilliant pieces of diplomatic negotiation.

All the whites in the West Indies, quaking at the bad example Toussaint and his blacks were setting, viewed with dismay the idea of Maitland coming to terms with a black, and none more so than the Earl of Balcarres, Governor of Jamaica. All through the negotiations he was petitioning Maitland not to evacuate Môle St Nicholas. But Toussaint wanted to get Môle St Nicholas without bloodshed, and he wanted a trade agreement with America, which he could get only if the British fleet allowed it. So while he negotiated, he sent message after message to the fractious Balcarres, warning him that Jamaica was very near to San Domingo and that he could easily send some blacks across in canoes to burn down the plantations and start a revolt.[8] Balcarres would naturally inform Maitland of this and Maitland, the soldier, could appreciate these threats. Either the British must conquer Toussaint or they must conciliate him, and Maitland knew that Toussaint could not be conquered. He therefore informed Toussaint that he wanted to communicate with him on "some important subjects." Toussaint left him in no doubt as to what was wanted: "I hope it is to announce the definitive evacuation of the points that the English still occupy in this portion of the Republic . . . it would be the only means of stopping or retarding my march. . . . Although Jérémie is so strong, I promise you to upset its fortifications; if it cost me 2,000 men, I shall take it."

On this Maitland agreed to evacuate Jérémie. Toussaint secured from Hédouville authority to carry on these new negotiations and sent his representative to Maitland to treat at first for all the districts except Môle St Nicholas. But Maitland now gave up hope of retaining even that fortress and offered to evacuate San Domingo completely. Toussaint accepted, keeping Hédouville scrupulously informed.

Toussaint, though carefully polite with Maitland, was at his most masterful. Maitland proposed to him that, as part of the price for evacuation, the fortifications should be dismantled. Toussaint refused, and demanded them in the condition in which Maitland had found them. "I flatter myself that you will adhere to this demand, if not I shall be constrained to break off negotiations." Maitland agreed.

But Maitland, after sending his envoy to Toussaint, sent another to Hédouville to make special arrangements, not for terms of evacuation but for the acutal transfer of Môle St Nicholas. Maitland may or may not have meant mischief. A few days afterwards without the slightest trouble a similar instrument was signed for the rendition of the fortress of Tiburon, after the entry of Rigaud's troops into Jérémie. Hédouville said afterwards that Maitland did this

[8] Lacroix, *Mémoires pour Servir* . . . , Vol. II, pp. 334-335.

to excite the jealousy of Toussaint.[9] If so his own conduct was all the more open to question.

He knew that Toussaint was carrying on negotiations for the evacuation of the Môle with Maitland, but anxious to increase his own prestige, he sent a personal representative to the British commander of the fort and issued a proclamation granting an amnesty in the Toussaint manner. But the terms arranged were not satisfactory to Maitland. He repudiated them, and informed Toussaint, who thus learned that Hédouville was carrying on negotiations with the enemy Commander-in-Chief behind his back. Toussaint, conscious that his own conduct had been faultless, attacked Hédouville without mercy.

"My frankness prevents me, Citizen Agent, from concealing that I have been sensibly affected by this lack of confidence. . . .

"In direct contradiction of your authorisation, without regard to my position as Commander-in-Chief of the army of San Domingo, without reflection, without even thinking it necessary to inform me, you send junior officers to treat . . . and you give them powers which annul my own. It seems to me, however, that according to military hierarchy it is I, as first Chief of the Army, who should have transmitted your orders to junior officers . . . I would have preferred that you had declared to me openly that you thought me incapable of treating with the English. . . . You would then have saved me from the disagreeable necessity of contracting written engagements and giving my word of honour. . . .

"General Maitland, in asking to treat with me, has understood the military hierarchy; if he addressed himself to me as Commander-in-Chief, I recognised in you the representative of the nation, for I have only treated after having demanded your approval. What have I done to merit this mistrust?"

He had Hédouville in a corner and he did not spare him. But even then he did not want a breach, and con-

[9] Report to the Directory of Frimaire, An VII. *Les Archives Nationales*, A.F. III, 210.

cluded by saying that if only Hédouville would have confidence in him, together they could save the colony and make agriculture prosper. Hédouville blustered, boasted of all the things he had done and the army staffs on which he had worked, said that Toussaint could not teach him his duty. He did not know how dangerous a game he was playing. Had Toussaint been merely an ambitious chief of brigands, France would have lost the colony in August 1798. Even while Hédouville was so thoughtlessly prodding at the man on whose army and influence everything depended, the British, having failed to conquer Toussaint by force of arms, made a supreme effort to get him by that species of lies and deception known as diplomacy.

Maitland, a prejudiced Englishman, did not think Toussaint very intelligent.[10] But Maitland had seen that the blacks in San Domingo, now that they had military experience, organisation and leaders, were a match for any European expedition. The French were certain to send an expedition to restore French authority, and a French army would bleed to death in the island. Maitland therefore saw it as his business to make Toussaint as strong as possible in order that he might the more thoroughly defeat the French. He invited Toussaint to an interview, embraced him, paid him full military honours, reviewed the troops for him, gave him magnificent gifts (in the name of George III), and then proposed to him to make the island independent and rule it as King.[11] He assured him of British protection, "a strong squadron of British frigates would be always in his harbours or on his coasts to protect them," [12] and asked in return for the exclusive trade with the island. The Americans also were building up a good trade with San Domingo, Maitland had sent an American envoy to Toussaint, and it was certain that they would come in with the British.

[10] Maitland to Dundas, Dec. 26, 1798, Public Record Office, War Office Papers, W.O. 1/170 (345).
[11] Lacroix, *Mémoires pour Servir* . . . , Vol. I, p. 346. Lacroix says that he saw the proposals himself among Toussaint's papers.
[12] *Ibid.*

Sharp as was the divergence between himself and Hédouville, Toussaint refused. He, like Rigaud, had enough power to sway his supporters to his will. France was powerless, and he would have got all the support and resources he needed from Britain. His refusal is the measure of the difference between himself and Rigaud. The British, he knew, would make the alliance, and then when he had broken with France either come to terms at his expense with France, or, with their strong squadron of frigates designed for Toussaint's protection, blockade the island, overthrow him, and restore slavery. Toussaint would have none of it. Maitland's letters show, it is true, that he realised, as so many of the French who knew the island realised, that the Negroes in San Domingo were a power. The British were going to keep their bargain for the sake of British honour, but also because they could not do otherwise. But as soon as peace was declared it would be a different story. This is not in any way speculative. Before the end of the year Maitland actually wrote this to Dundas to be quite sure that the intended treachery should not miscarry. "It may not be necessary for me to add that the instant peace takes place my whole view of this subject would at once be changed." It was not necessary. Dundas would understand. To avoid any shadow of misunderstanding Maitland continued.

"To diminish the French power and to stop the greater evil of the French Directory getting into its hands the means Saint Domingo would afford them of annoying us; it may be well to submit to the smaller evil of (during the war) supporting the assumed power of Toussaint, but on the restoration of peace and anything like a settled government in France; both with a view to the restoration of the original colonial system if that is practicable, and with a view to let France waste her means in men and money in this attempt . . ." [13] It was in the best tradition of the way in which the higher civilisation uplifts the backward peoples. But Toussaint merely expressed his regrets and declined with thanks.

[13] Maitland to Dundas, Dec. 26th, 1798. See note 10, p. 211.

Such is history. But if that were all, it would be un-readable. Along with the material resistance to Maitland's debased concept of human life and the unashamed savagery of himself and his highly placed instructors, is to be noted the elevated principles by which the ex-slave guided his profoundly practical life. Toussaint was then as always devoted to the French Republic. This devotion will in the end lead him to an untimely and cruel death. But it gave him a splendid life. To all the blacks, revolutionary France, which had decreed equality and the abolition of slavery, was a beacon among the nations. France was to them indeed the mother-country. Toussaint, looking always to the development of the blacks as a people, did not want to break with France, its language and tradition and customs, to join the slave-holding British. He would be faithful to France as long as France was faithful to the blacks.

But the war prevented France from sending supplies to the colony, and he arranged a secret convention with Maitland whereby goods should come to certain selected ports in British and American ships, to be paid for by San Domingo produce. More he would not do.

When Balcarres learned that Maitland was evacuating San Domingo completely, he wrote to the Home Government protesting. The reply was a masterpiece. After detailing at great length the various advantages of the evacuation, it concluded with unanswerable resignation: there was nothing else to be done.[14]

Both on the battlefield and in the Council Chamber Toussaint had out-manœuvred the British generals as he had out-manœuvred the Spaniards, getting all that he required at the least possible cost to himself.

This was the end of the ill-fated expedition to San Domingo. "After long and careful thought and study," says Fortescue, "I have come to the conclusion that the West Indian campaigns, both to windward and to leeward, which were the essence of Pitt's military policy, cost England in Army and Navy little fewer than one hundred thou-

[14] Portland to Balcarres, January 6th, 1799. Public Record Office, C.O. 137/101.

sand men, about one-half of them dead, the remainder permanently unfitted for service." [15] For the sake of a few barren islands still held by the British "England's soldiers had been sacrificed, her treasure squandered, her influence in Europe weakened, her arm for six fateful years fettered and paralysed." [16]

Fortescue does not seem to realise that Pitt and Dundas were playing for the finest colony in the world and a rich market for the otherwise unprofitable slave trade.

Fortescue blames everything and everybody, Pitt and Dundas for incompetence, the climate, the fever. The fever killed many more men than the blacks and Mulattoes did, but we have seen with what poor resources and against what internal intrigues Toussaint fought. San Domingo was not the first place where European invaders had met fever. It was the decree of abolition, the bravery of the blacks, and the ability of their leaders, that had done it. The great gesture of the French working people towards the black slaves, against their own white ruling class, had helped to save their revolution from reactionary Europe. Held by Toussaint and his raw levies, singing the *Marseillaise* and the *Ça Ira*, Britain, the most powerful country in Europe, could not attack the revolution in France. "The secret of England's impotence for the first six years of the war may be said to lie in the two fatal words, St Domingo." [17]

Hédouville knew all this, none would know it better than he, but for him the expulsion of the British was merely another good reason why Toussaint should be got rid of at once. France wanted her authority restored in the colony. That was politics, and there is no gratitude in politics. But Toussaint was a Negro and a former slave, and now that he had won back the colony for them, Hédouville and his staff not only intrigued against him, but grossly insulted him. Toussaint often wore a handkerchief tied round his

[15] Fortescue, *History of the British Army*, Vol. IV, pt. 1, p. 565.
[16] *Ibid.*, p. 565.
[17] *Ibid.*, p. 325.

head, and some of them boasted that with four men they could go into the camp of the old monkey with the hand-kerchief and capture him. Not only did Toussaint hear it, but it began gradually to be rumoured among the black masses that the Agent and his staff were hostile to Tous-saint, and whoever was hostile to Toussaint was hostile to the blacks. And yet it is curious and characteristic of Tous-saint that the most bitter subject of quarrel was the émigré whites, with Toussaint the ex-slave taking their side, and Hédouville, a former nobleman, attacking Toussaint for protecting them.

Roume also recommended conciliation with the émi-grés, but he advised the Directory to scrutinise carefully all the planters, and allow only those who had rid them-selves of their former prejudices to come back to the colony. Toussaint, however, invited back all who would take the oath of fidelity. Perhaps in addition to their valu-able knowledge and education he felt that they would cease to intrigue and plot for the restoration of slavery only if they came back and found it possible to enjoy their property. He needed them now more than ever to counter-balance the power of the Mulattoes. Some of these émi-grés commanding Negro troops hired by the British had been excluded from the original amnesty. But Toussaint knew that San Domingo cultivation needed these blacks, knew too that Maitland was going to take the blacks straight to Jamaica where they would find themselves en-slaved. Maitland was prepared to treat for them if their officers were also accepted, and Toussaint agreed. Hédou-ville accused him of protecting the enemies of the Republic. Toussaint referred to the amnesty authorised by him and the special circumstances of these émigré officers.

Toussaint, a sincere Catholic, had pardoned some émi-grés who swore fidelity after a Church service. Hédouville accused him of breaking the republican law which forbade official association with religion. The bickering being con-tinuous, Toussaint resigned his post as Commander-in-Chief.

What his feelings were we can judge from his letter

to Hédouville when the latter refused to pronounce on the resignation. This is, with perhaps one exception, the most astonishing of the voluminous and astonishing correspondence of this uneducated ex-slave, who until he was 45, six years before, had probably never received a letter, far less written one.

"There was no need for you to quote me your instructions to recall to me your worth and dignity. It is sufficient for me to know that you are sent by France to hold you in veneration. I respect too much the Directory of which you are the Agent not to respect you in person and covet your approbation; the proofs of confidence with which the Directory has honoured me are too precious not to make me desire yours to the same degree. But it is because these sentiments are profoundly engraved in my heart, it is because your esteem and your confidence are infinitely precious to me, that, justly alarmed at the fear of losing them, I found it necessary to show you my despair. Faithful to my duty and my principles, I could only attribute the misfortune which has befallen me to the perfidious manœuvres of intriguers against me, personally, and against peace and order. . . . If I have asked permission to retire, it is because, having honourably served my country, having snatched it from the hands of powerful enemies who fought for possession of it, having extinguished the fires of intestine war to which it was for long a prey, having too long forgotten a cherished family to which I have become a stranger, having neglected my own interests, sacrificed my time and my years to the triumph of liberty, I wish now to save my old age from an insult which would shame my children. I would feel it the more inasmuch as I shall know that I have not deserved it, and I shall certainly not survive it. I do not conceal from you that, as you seem to be delaying indefinitely to accede to my request, I shall make it to the Directory itself. Men in general are so inclined to envy the glory of others, are so jealous of good which they have not themselves accomplished, that a man often makes himself enemies by the simple fact that he has rendered great service. The French Revolution has furnished many ex-

amples of this terrible truth. Many great men have expiated
in exile or on the scaffold the services that they have rendered to their country, and it would be imprudent for me
to remain any longer exposed to the shafts of calumny and
malevolence.

"An honourable and peaceable retreat in the bosom of
my family is my sole ambition. There, as at the head of my
armies, I shall always be ready to show a good example
and give the best advice. But I have learnt too much of the
heart of man not to be certain that it is only in the bosom
of my family that I shall find happiness."

These words surely came from the heart. Vaublanc
and the others being in Guiana, he had no immediate fear
of slavery. He saw that Hédouville might dismiss him. To
resist would have meant civil war, against Rigaud also.
"My conduct for some time, and above all since your interview with General Rigaud, has been a continual infraction
of the law." And rather than face a civil war purely for his
personal position he preferred to go. Hédouville had been
rubbing it in to him that though Commander-in-Chief he
was subordinate to the Agent. "I know your powers," wrote
Toussaint. "That is why I addressed my resignation to you,
and if I had not known them you would have taught them
to me by ceaselessly reminding me that you can dismiss me,
which makes me think you very much want to do so."

It was no bluff. He sent a secretary to the Directory
to arrange the terms of his retirement. The English were
not yet six months out of San Domingo. Toussaint was
drinking the cup to the dregs, but even then, as the letter
shows, he was not thinking in any way of the independence
of the colony. He would retire. If any attempt were ever
made on liberty for all, he would be there.

It was the San Domingo masses that saved him. Hédouville was making arrangements with the Directory to
supersede him and the black generals and put three white
generals in their place,[18] but he dared not do it, so great
was the unrest in the country and in the army. Hédouville

[18] Sannon, *Histoire de Toussaint-L'Ouverture*, Vol. II, p. 116-
117.

tried to introduce a system of apprenticeship of the labourers to the owners for periods of six and nine years, a stupidity which the British were to repeat with a resounding ill-
success after the emancipation of the slaves in their own
colonies in 1833. The blacks might have taken that from
Toussaint or Sonthonax, not from Hédouville. The army
had not been paid, despite Toussaint's urgent pleas, and it
resented its neglect and the attacks on its general. Fears
for black liberty began to grow. Hédouville claimed that
Toussaint and the generals were spreading calumnies
against him among the labourers. He wanted them like
good French citizens to sit quietly while now that he had
no use for them he arranged for their dismissal and once
more put black men where they belong.

The unrest increased. Hédouville began to realise
where he would find himself without Toussaint. He asked
Toussaint to address a circular to the commandants of the
districts to quiet the blacks and turn them from their al-
leged intention to rise and massacre the whites. Toussaint
repudiated this aspersion on the character of the labourers,
and while he addressed the required circular he dissociated
himself from the idea that the blacks were only awaiting
an opportunity to massacre the whites. Hédouville now
tried to recover lost ground with Toussaint. He made overtures through friends. Toussaint replied in kind but held
himself stiffly aloof.

Hédouville wanted to restore the civil authority as the
controlling force, and was naturally in immediate conflict
with Toussaint's generals. Toussaint had disbanded some
of the troops. They had gone back to work willingly, but
Hédouville was disbanding Negro troops and confiding the
care of the coasts only to white troops. The blacks looked
on this with intense suspicion. Hédouville was not Laveaux
or Sonthonax. The blacks did not care for anything he had
done in La Vendée. He addressed a sharp reprimand to
Moïse, unjustly; Moïse replied as sharply. The country was
in that state of tension when any incident could cause an
insurrection. Toussaint would not go to Le Cap. He told
Hédouville that he had been informed that his life was not

safe there. Hédouville asked him to go to Fort Liberté, where Moïse was stationed, to quiet unrest. Toussaint found an excuse for delay. If Hédouville wanted to govern, well, let him govern.

Suddenly a private quarrel broke out among the garrison at Fort Liberté while Moïse, the commander, was away. The soldiers, representatives of the labourers, got into conflict with the Municipality, consisting chiefly of Mulattoes and the old free blacks. A word from Toussaint would have restored order. Instead Hédouville sent another Negro, Manginat, with authority to depose Moïse and assume command. Certainly in law Hédouville had every right to dismiss Moïse. But not only was the action unjustified, it was stupid, for Moïse was, after Toussaint, the most popular man in the army, and was also Toussaint's nephew.

Moïse, returning to the fort, found Manginat proclaiming his new commission. "You cannot make war as I can, citizen Manginat," he told him. "Take care." But Manginat, with Hédouville's commission, insisted on his rights. The National Guard and a detachment of European troops opened fire, one of Moïse's brothers was killed, the other was captured, and Moïse had to ride for his life. As soon as Hédouville heard of this, he dismissed Moïse from the service, and ordered that he should be captured, dead or alive. When Toussaint heard that Hédouville had dismissed Moïse, he gave Dessalines orders to march on Le Cap and arrest Hédouville.

Toussaint had given the Agent ample rope, and Hédouville had hanged himself. At first he maintained a bold front, but Moïse raised the black labourers on the plain, and as Hédouville felt the noose tightening about his neck he sent Colonel Vincent and a priest to Toussaint seeking to patch up the quarrel. But Toussaint's mind was now made up, and he acted with his usual rapidity and decision. Intimate as he was with Vincent, he arrested and imprisoned him. He ordered a detachment to intercept three of Hédouville's officers who served under Rigaud and were bringing letters. They attempted resistance and were killed. Toussaint then marched on Le Cap. Hédouville did not wait for him. Already Dessalines' troops were pushing into the outskirts of the town. Hédouville issued proclamations denouncing Toussaint as a traitor and fled on board a boat in the harbour. Toussaint, arriving in Le Cap, invited Hédouville to come ashore, but Hédouville declined and left for France, with about a thousand functionaries, whites, Mulattoes and former free blacks, who detested Toussaint and his ex-slave generals. The Municipality and the citizens hastened to welcome Toussaint and thank him for restoring order.

The Rubicon had been crossed, and next day in a public speech at Fort Liberté, Toussaint boldly asserted his own authority. "At the very moment when I have chased the English from the colony . . . Hédouville chooses a Negro to destroy the brave General Moïse and the Fifth Regiment who have so much contributed to the evacuation of our enemies from the colony. It is they whom you wished to kill. And when you killed them, do you not know that there are thousands of brave blacks behind you who would have taken vengeance for this brave General Moïse and the Fifth Regiment, don't you see that you expose all these unhappy Europeans and your wives and children to massacre? . . . What would France say? . . .

"I reinstate Moïse in his former functions. . . . Who reverts to the sword will perish by the sword. . . . Hédouville says that I am against liberty, that I want to surrender to the English, that I wish to make myself independent; who ought to love liberty more, Toussaint L'Ouverture, slave of Bréda, or General Hédouville, former Marquis and Chevalier de Saint-Louis? If I wished to surrender to the English, would I have chased them away? . . . Remember that there is only one Toussaint L'Ouverture in San Domingo and that at his name everybody must tremble."

This was the new Toussaint. He had no wish to break with France, but Hédouville, France's representative, had been a source of nothing but unrest and disorder. Henceforth he would govern. That night he dined with Moïse and in a long monologue he expressed himself fully. It is one of the few occasions on which we get a glimpse into his mind.

"Hédouville has spread it that he is going to France to seek forces to come back. . . . I do not want to fight with France, I have saved this country for her up to the present, but if she comes to attack me, I shall defend myself.

"General Hédouville does not know that at Jamaica there are in the mountains blacks who have forced the English to make treaties with them? Well, I am black like them, I know how to make war, and besides I have advantages that they didn't have; for I can count on assistance and protection."

Toussaint clearly meant the British. But although he knew that the English would leap at the chance to ally themselves with him, he would only form an alliance if the French attacked him.

"Finally," he told Moïse and the others, "I have done what I ought to do. I have nothing to reproach myself with. I laugh at whatever Hédouville says and he can come when he wants to."

There is the same note of personal responsibility as when Sonthonax was embarked. He worked alone, making his decisions without the advice or assistance of anyone, and his officers, soldiers and labourers followed him blindly.

Where was he heading for? He did not know. His powerful mind, unaided by precedent or education, was slowly working out a satisfactory relationship with France whereby the connection would be maintained with benefit to both, and yet he would govern as all these Commissioners, Agents and others could not govern. He would find it before long. But meanwhile he sent Vincent to Roume in Santo Domingo, asking him to assume the position vacated by Hédouville until instructions came from Paris. But Roume was already Commissioner. When Hédouville left France the Directory was so uncertain of his reception and his future fate that a member of his staff was entrusted with a sealed packet to be opened only in case of his death or enforced absence from the island. When it was opened it

contained Roume's appointment. Roume was therefore installed as Hédouville's successor. The faithful Vincent, who
thoroughly approved of Hédouville's expulsion, was sent
to Paris to present Toussaint's despatches and explana-
tions.[19] In his report Toussaint accused Hédouville of serving the interests of the party which had been defeated on
the 18th Fructidor. Over and over again he referred to this
coup d'état. The machinations of Vaublanc and the émigrés
haunted him and the black labourers of San Domingo.

Hédouville naturally reached Paris before Vincent.

From him the Directory learned[20] that the colony
was practically lost to France, and that there was only one
chance of saving it:

"The export of sugar and coffee by English and American boats will make money flow in the colony, and he
(Toussaint) will not fail to attribute this state of things to
the wisdom of his government.[21] I am no less convinced
that sooner or later this precious island will escape from
French domination. I do not take it on myself to propose
the measure you will take to weaken the power of those
who dominate it, but if the moment is not yet ripe for
taking vigorous measures, it will perhaps appear to you
important to create germs of division between them, to
embitter the hate which exists between the Mulattoes and
the blacks, and to oppose Rigaud to Toussaint. I do not see
my way to guarantee the purity of the intentions of the
first, but in justice to him I can assure you that I have only
praise for his conduct. You will have proof in his correspondence. If I had been able to count entirely on him I
would not have hesitated to go to the South in spite of the
uncertainty of sailing there without being interrupted by
the English. . . ."

Although race feeling remained, there was no hostility
between Toussaint and Rigaud. Hédouville's own words
show that he deliberately created it, and even then was not

[19] *Les Archives Nationales*, A.F. III, 210.
[20] Report of Frimaire, An VII. *Les Archives Nationales*, A.F. III,
210.
[21] Why not? *C.L.R.J.*

sure of Rigaud. Before he laid the plan in front of the
Directory he had acted; he had written a letter to Rigaud
absolving him from all obedience to Toussaint and author-
ising him to take possession of the districts of Léogane and
Jacmel, incorporated in the South by a previous decree not
yet carried into effect. That, he hoped, would start the
conflagration and keep it going until France was ready.
Hédouville and his superiors belonged to the same breed
as Maitland and his. Uninhibited, they wallowed with zest
in the filth and mire of their political conceptions and
needs, among the very leaders of their society, but nevertheless the very dregs of human civilisation and moral
standards. A historian who finds excuses for such conduct
by references to the supposed spirit of the times, or by
omission, or by silence, shows thereby that his account of
events is not to be trusted. Hédouville after all was a
product of the great French Revolution. Voltaire and Rousseau were household words and died before the Revolution began. Jefferson, Cobbett, Tom Paine, Clarkson and
Wilberforce had already raised banners and were living
lives which to Maitland and his kind made them into subversive enemies of society. They had their reasons. So have
their counterparts of to-day. They fill our newspapers and
our radios. The type is always with us, and so are their
defenders.

X

Toussaint Seizes the Power

TOUSSAINT in his twelve years of politics, national and international, made only one serious mistake, the one which ended his career. Strategic necessities he always saw early, and never hesitated in carrying out whatever policies they demanded. Now that he had dismissed Hédouville, the official representative of the French Government, and his acknowledged superior, he saw that he had now to crush the Mulatto state of Rigaud. The great danger now was a French expedition and it was suicidal to allow Rigaud and his Mulattoes to remain in control of the South and West. They would most certainly welcome a French force and ensure the ruin of the black state.

It is easy to misjudge Rigaud. For him France was the mother-country still, who had made free men of Mulattoes and blacks. "I grieve to see this, the most cruel blow that has ever been struck against those of us in San Domingo whom the Revolution has made to live again. The Directory will see its authority nullified in this colony. The whole of France will believe that we wish *to make ourselves independent*,[1] as a crowd of fools already say and believe."

Rigaud sent in his resignation to Toussaint. If it were accepted, then inevitably Beauvais would succeed him, and Beauvais, Toussaint and Roume would be able perhaps to make unity a reality. Rigaud pleaded: "He [Roume] will no doubt consult you as to the choice of my successor. I once more assure you, Citizen General, of my fidelity to France and my respect and untarnished regard for your person." The waste, the waste of all this bravery, devotion and noble feeling on the corrupt and rapacious bourgeois who were still, in the eyes of the misguided Rigaud, the banner-bearers of liberty and equality.

Roume refused to accept Rigaud's resignation and thenceforth civil war was inevitable. With the packet that contained Roume's appointment were two other packets. What did they contain? We do not know. But it may well have been instructions to keep the two parties apart at all costs. Roume did not want war, but he acted as if his business was to prevent a close understanding.

Rigaud's effort to resign—he intended to retire to France—and the tone of his letters to Toussaint show how uncertain he was. But the French Government did its diabolical work with skill. Hédouville suggested that the Directory should even place the blame for the breach on him publicly so as not to alarm Toussaint. The Directory expressed its regret to Toussaint at seeing Hédouville re-

[1] Rigaud's emphasis.

turn, but professed to retain confidence in Toussaint. Yet Bruix, the Colonial Minister, wrote cordially to Rigaud.[2] Talleyrand, Minister for Foreign Affairs, wrote encouragingly both to Toussaint[3] and to Rigaud.[4] Thus France kept the pot boiling merrily.

Maitland left San Domingo in October or November 1798 and on December 12th the following appeared in the *London Gazette.*

"No event has happened in the history of the present war of more interest to the cause of humanity or to the permanent interests of Great Britain than the treaty which General Maitland has made with the black general Toussaint upon the evacuation of San Domingo.

"By this treaty the independence of that most valuable island is in fact recognised and will be secured against all the efforts which the French can now make to recover it. Not merely without the expense to England of fortifications or of armies but with the benefit of securing to us its exclusive commerce.

"Toussaint L'Ouverture is a negro and in the jargon of war has been called a brigand. But according to all accounts he is a negro born to vindicate the claims of this species and to show that the character of men is independent of exterior colour. The late events in San Domingo will soon engage the public attention. They are such as are calculated to please all parties. It is a great point to rescue this formidable island from the grasp of the Directory, from whence, if they had regained their footing, they might have incessantly menaced and perhaps assailed the most favourite of our West Indian possessions; and on the other hand it is a great point gained to the cause of humanity that a negro domination is in fact constituted and organised in the West Indies under the command of a

---

[2] 4 Ventôse An VII (Feb. 22nd, 1799). *Les Archives du Ministère de la Guerre.* B.[7] 1.

[3] Sannon: *Histoire de Toussaint-L'Ouverture,* Vol. II, p. 148.

[4] 19 Germinal An VIII (April 8th). *Les Archives du Ministère de la Guerre.* B.[7] 1.

negro chief or king. That the Black Race whom the Christian world to their infamy have been accustomed to degrade. . . . Every Liberal Briton will feel proud that this country brought about the happy revolution. . . ."

The British, after having been driven out of the island in September, were posing in December as the authors of "the happy revolution," and rejoicing at the freedom of a people, to enslave whom they had just lost 100,000 men. In addition to soothing the national vanity this lying notice would also, of course, be read by the Directory. Having thus driven another wedge between Toussaint and the French, Maitland then set out for America to negotiate the division of the trade with that country.

Harcourt was sent on in advance to San Domingo but Toussaint did not want to negotiate with the British at all. He challenged Harcourt about the notice which had appeared in the Press. Harcourt returned an evasive answer, and had the unbelievable stupidity to tell Toussaint that the British were making these arrangements with him "not so much for any military or commercial advantage, but to witness to him their satisfaction at his good faith and punctuality in the execution of his engagements. . . ."[5]

When Maitland got to America he found that Toussaint had been making his own arrangements with the American Government. The President had already authorised a trade agreement and appointed a trade representative to San Domingo. From no classes of people have Negroes suffered more than from the capitalists of Britain and America. They have been the most pertinacious preachers of race prejudice in the world. Yet the Americans vied with the British in compliments to black Toussaint and San Domingo trade. John Hollingsworth of John Hollingsworth and Co. wrote to Toussaint that "in you I place the most implicit confidence and have moreover the pleasure to add that, as far as my information goes, I find the same to be prevalent, which to me is no small consola-

[5] For these negotiations see the correspondence of Toussaint seized by the French. *Les Archives du Ministère de la Guerre*, B.[7] 1.

tion as I have advocated the proposed negotiation with my utmost endeavour." [6]

When the British agents learned how far Toussaint had gone with the Americans, they forgot their protestations of negotiating only to please Toussaint, turned nasty, and threatened that if their ships were not allowed in the harbours on the same terms as the Americans, British cruisers would blockade the island. That was Toussaint's dilemma. France was at war with Britain. Like all the French blacks he detested the British. But the San Domingo economy was on the verge of collapse. And though he tried to evade a trade agreement with the enemies of France, he had in the end to admit British ships flying the American or Spanish flag into the San Domingo harbours. Roume suggested that he should arrest Maitland, as would have been very easy. Toussaint refused. Instead he read Roume's letter to Maitland and read him also his own reply to Roume indignantly repelling the base suggestion. Maitland was much impressed.

This whole Convention was in every way irregular. Maitland knew that Toussaint had no authority. Toussaint knew that he had none. At the peace all these problems would be resolved. In any case to treat thus with Britain, actually at war with France, was a dangerous thing to do, but it was an act of wise and courageous statesmanship. Even Roume, the Agent of the French Government, whom it placed in a very difficult position, had to admit that Toussaint was justified. The Directory itself approved of the arrangement with the United States in the *Moniteur* of 26 Vendémiaire, An VIII (October 19th, 1799).[7] Toussaint attempted no secrecy. He openly admitted there were secret clauses in the Convention [mutual promises not to attack each other], but that these secret clauses were necessary for the salvation of San Domingo and were no treason to France.[8] Even Rigaud joined the chorus of praise: "Al-

[6] *Les Archives du Ministère de la Guerre*, B.[7] 1.
[7] Ardouin, *Études sur l'histoire de Haïti* (Paris, 1853), Vol. IV, p. 46.
[8] Sannon, *Histoire de Toussaint-L'Ouverture*, Vol. II, pp. 151-

though my enemies, always active to harm me, have managed to diminish your friendship for me, I am not the less an admirer of your talent and of your merit. . . . I offer my tribute of praise which you deserve."

But the trade with America could not have been arranged without the consent of the British. Rigaud, however, said nothing about this. Toussaint, on the other hand, excluded the ports of the South from the agreement. And even before he actually signed with Maitland on June 13th, 1799, he once more took the offensive against Rigaud.

In a public proclamation Rigaud defended himself with moving passion against the charge that he did not wish to obey Toussaint because Toussaint was a Negro.

"Indeed, if I had reached the stage where I would not wish to obey a black, if I had the stupid presumption to believe that I am above such obedience, on what grounds could I claim obedience from the whites? What a grievous example would I be giving to those placed under my orders? Besides, is there so great a difference between the colour of the Commander-in-Chief and mine? Is it a tint of colour, more or less dark, which instils principles of philosophy or gives merit to an individual? And if one man is a little lighter in colour than another, does it follow that one must obey him in everything? I not willing to obey a black! Why, all my life from my cradle I have been obedient to blacks. Isn't my birth the same as that of General Toussaint? Isn't my mother who brought me into the world a Negro? Have I not a black elder brother for whom I have always had a profound respect and whom I have always obeyed? Who has given me the first principles of education? Is it not a black who was schoolmaster in the town of Les Cayes? Isn't it clear that I have been accustomed to obedience to blacks all my life? And everyone knows that first principles remain eternally graven in our hearts. I have consecrated my life to the defence of the blacks.

152. The Convention is printed in full in Schoelcher, *Vie de Toussaint-L'Ouverture*, pp. 416-419.

From the beginning of the revolution I have braved all for the cause of liberty. I have not betrayed my principles and I shall never do so. Besides, I am too much a believer in the Rights of Man to think that there is one colour in nature superior to another. I know a man only as a man."

These words could not have been written before July 14th, 1789. A true son of the revolution, Rigaud was hurt in his soul that people might think his quarrel with Toussaint was due to Toussaint's colour. Toussaint was equally emphatic, and though he accused the Mulatto class of con- spiring against him, yet he disdained the charge of hating Mulattoes by pointing to the great number of them who were fighting in his army against Rigaud.

"Without doubt the susceptibilities, the jealousies born of the differences of colour, manifested themselves sometimes to an unreasonable degree, but the exigencies of the service and a severe discipline had more than ever fused the three colours in the ranks of the army. The same state of things existed in the civil administration and this was one of the happiest consequences of political equality consecrated by the principles of the revolution. The rival- ries of colour were not then the initial cause of the conflict which was beginning. They complicated it and became one of its elements, when many officers of colour, in sev- eral parts of the country, took Rigaud's side, and Toussaint had to treat them as traitors. . . ." [9]

This is the opinion of M. Pauléus Sannon, himself a Haitian, and no one has written more wisely and pro- foundly on the San Domingo revolution and Toussaint L'Ouverture. Very clearly also he sees the Mulattoes as a typical intermediate class with all the political instability of that class.

"There was always also more of a political tradition among the men of colour, and a peculiar disposition, often noticed, which tended to make them particularly suscep- tible to all the hopes or anxieties which grew out of public events. It is this mental attitude which caused the struggle

[9] *Histoire de Toussaint-L'Ouverture*, Vol. II, p. 140.

between the military chiefs to assume all the tendencies of a war of colour."

And he concludes: "Toussaint L'Ouverture did not detest the Mulattoes any more than Rigaud hated the blacks. And if each of them defended himself badly from the contrary sentiments which they attributed to each other in this respect, it was because they needed, each of them, the united force of a party in a conflict where the parties were confounded with the classes and the classes with the colours."

Toussaint for a moment seems to have thought of winning over Beauvais to his side and through Beauvais of binding the colony together. He published a proclamation attacking Rigaud and praising Beauvais. Beauvais, through the very amiability of character which made him so beloved by everybody, played a miserable rôle in this crisis. Had he declared boldly for Toussaint, such was his influence and the strategic importance of his command that Rigaud could hardly have fought at all. Had he declared for Rigaud, Toussaint would have been in serious danger. But so slight was the class bitterness and colour feeling at the beginning of the struggle that Beauvais, a Mulatto of the Mulattoes, could not decide. Finally he threw up his command and sailed for France, honest to the last and unable to take sides in this fratricidal struggle maliciously kindled by the eternal enemies of peace in San Domingo.

Rigaud struck first and took Petit-Gôave. But this fine soldier, so brilliant against the English, at once audacious, tenacious and careful, was at his worst in this crucial campaign.

Where Rigaud hesitated and looked to France, Toussaint looked to France for nothing. Sending Dessalines into the South, he travelled North to crush the revolts. Free blacks of the North were revolting for Rigaud and even Pierre Michel, ancient slave, joined the revolt against

Toussaint and was shot. Before the speed of Toussaint's movements and his ruthless execution of traitors, the rebels quailed. "Punish even with death those who attempt the least movement."

Despite Rigaud's vacillation, the Mulatto South fought magnificently at first. All their pride was roused, and their bitterness can be understood. There was all the old hatred between Mulattoes and blacks. Toussaint had striven to moderate it, but it still remained. The Rigaud brothers and the other Mulatto leaders had a great record of military and administrative success from the very first days of the revolution. Rigaud's achievements against the British were nearly as fine as Toussaint's. The morale of the Mulatto population was high: when towns were besieged by the British, the women ran along the ramparts assisting the men with a fearlessness and disregard that showed their revolutionary temper. All the Mulattoes were devoted to the Republic. Rigaud had shot without mercy Mulattoes who were traitors, even though Mulatto women begged him on their knees to spare them. He had deported the émigré whites. To them it seemed that Toussaint, deceived by the old whites whom they hated, and sold to the British, against whom they had shed so much blood, was at once a traitor to the Republic and a tyrant seeking to establish a black domination. They fought like tigers.

The war at last rested on the fate of Jacmel, blockaded by land and sea. For five months Jacmel held out under Pétion, an unusually able officer who had deserted from Toussaint. The besieged ate horses, dogs, cats, rats, old leather, the grass in the streets, until there was nothing more to eat. Rigaud, strangely inactive, fought irresolutely, waiting for France. At last Jacmel could hold out no longer. The starving garrison cut its way through Dessalines' men and Toussaint's ultimate victory grew nearer.

Bonaparte, victorious in the internal struggle of the bourgeoisie for power, was still too busy in Europe to deal with San Domingo. But Hédouville assured him that Toussaint was sold to the British. Toussaint's talk to Moïse had been copied down by Moïse's white secretary[10] and sent to France. Vincent's report,[11] however, was wholly favourable to Toussaint. This did not change Bonaparte's plans, but Toussaint for the time being had to be humoured. Bonaparte appointed a new Commission consisting of Vincent, Raimond, and General Michel, to make peace between the two combatants. Bonaparte had learned from Vincent that Toussaint was the protector of Europeans, and, much more important, the most powerful man in the colony. He confirmed Toussaint in his post as Commander-in-Chief and Governor, but carefully avoided taking any side in the quarrel. He did not write direct to Toussaint, but addressed a letter from the Consuls to the citizens of San Domingo, assuring them of their liberty but notifying them that by the new Constitution he had given to the French, the colonies would no longer be represented in the French Parliament but would be governed by "special laws." He asked that on the flags of the army an inscription should be written telling them that they owed their liberty to France.

When Vincent landed in San Domingo race feeling was high. All over the colony blacks and Mulattoes were saying that the civil war had been kindled by the whites to weaken both sides and restore slavery.[12] The whites had taken Toussaint's side, but they were not pleased when he drafted them into the army and made them go and fight against Rigaud. But the black labourers were heartily sick of Commissioners from France. They said they did not want any white people to govern them, they would be governed by Toussaint. Moïse, who did not like Vincent, arrested him, and Vincent suffered great privations and was nearly shot by his guards. Toussaint apologised to Vincent, but the arrest could hardly have taken place without

[10] Sannon, *Histoire de Toussaint-L'Ouverture*, Vol. II. See notes on pp. 121 and 126.
[11] *Précis sur l'état actuel de la colonie de Saint-Domingue. Les Archives Nationales*, A.F. III, 1187.
[12] *Précis de mon voyage à Saint-Domingue*, 20 Pluviôse, AN X. *Les Archives Nationales*, A.F. IV, 1212.

his orders, though the indignities were probably due to
spontaneous race feeling.

Toussaint was glad to get confirmation of his post
as Commander-in-Chief from the new régime. In the war
of proclamations that he was waging with Rigaud it was
an unanswerable argument against the charge that he was
a traitor to France. But the vagueness of the letter confirmed his worst suspicions. What were these "special
laws"? Why had not Bonaparte written to him personally?
He refused to inscribe the words on the banner.

The first thing, however, was the war. The inhabitants of the South were tiring of the struggle. Toussaint
said that someone ought to go to Rigaud, and asked Vincent whether he would dare. But when Vincent said yes,
Toussaint was embarrassed. He feared a trap. It was on
this visit that, for the first time, Vincent noticed that his
presence was distasteful to Toussaint.[13]

Yet Vincent did go to Rigaud. The ruler of the South,
for so many years second in San Domingo history to Toussaint alone, was like a man distracted. During the interview
hatred for Toussaint overmastered his reason, and he
seemed on the verge of committing suicide. How could
France confirm the traitor Toussaint in his command? He
would continue his resistance. But Rigaud no longer had
the confidence of his followers. Vincent was not only Toussaint's envoy. He was the representative of France, and
the population welcomed his coming. Why should they go
on fighting? Why had they ever fought at all? Even during
the truce which Vincent arranged, the inhabitants of one
town, St Louis, admitted Dessalines and his officers and
entertained them to dinner. Vincent at one time feared
for his own life, so violent were the rage and despair of
the cheated and deceived Rigaud. Rigaud planned to blow
up Cavaillon, the official capital of the South, but the captain of the garrison refused to allow it. Realising at last
that all was over, the unfortunate Rigaud set sail for
France, refusing to meet Toussaint. He was shipwrecked
and reached Paris only on April 7th, 1801. He sought an

13 *Précis de mon voyage.*

interview with Bonaparte, who listened in silence to his lengthy recital, then told him, "General, I blame you for only one thing, not to have been victorious."

In the years of its history as an independent State the Mulattoes and blacks of San Domingo have fought the unceasing struggle of the classes, sometimes rising to civil war, as is common to all societies whether homogeneous in colour or not. But at the slightest threat of foreign invasion they have always presented a solid front to the enemy. This lesson they were to learn by hard experience. Yet never was there so favourable an opportunity for a working arrangement as at the very beginning of their history under two such men as Toussaint and Rigaud, between whom there was such mutual admiration and understanding until Hédouville's arrival in the island. Hédouville's rôle does not concern us. The fatal error was Rigaud's. He could not see as far as Toussaint saw when he politely but firmly declined to play the fly to Maitland's spider.

With victory, by August 1800, Toussaint had only half-solved his problem. Hitherto he had been distinguished for his humanity toward beaten opponents and his conciliatory policy toward enemies, even the émigré whites whom all republican San Domingo hated and distrusted. But the garrisons in the South, the officials, were still mainly Mulatto. To leave them as they were, after the bitterness of the civil war, meant that if a French expedition landed they would welcome it even more eagerly than when under Rigaud. Seven hundred of Rigaud's finest soldiers left the South and went to Cuba rather than serve under Toussaint. He asked Clairveaux, one of his Mulatto commanders, to govern the South. It was a concession to Mulatto sentiment, but Clairveaux refused. Thus the task of pacification fell unfortunately to Dessalines.[14]

Toussaint did not confiscate property, not even the property of those who had followed Rigaud and aban-

[14] He was commander of the West Province but the South was subordinate to him.

doned the colony. One-fourth of the revenue from these plantations he gave to the labourers, one-half he turned over to the public treasury, and the other quarter was kept for the owners. Mulatto women had conspired against him, but even during the war he said that he did not make war on women, would not pay much attention to their "cackle"; if they were proved guilty he would merely imprison them and see that no harm befell them. All through the privations of the war and immediately after he treated them with special care. But he could not trust the army that Rigaud had made, which was as loyal to Rigaud as his own army was to him. Despite the amnesty, therefore, he commanded Dessalines to purge the troops. Three hundred prisoners in Léogane were shot, and 50 others in Port-Républicain, nearly all officers. Toussaint had to put a stop to it. "I said to prune the tree, not to uproot it." All things considered he had been singularly humane.[15] But the population of the South had made peace on Toussaint's word, which he had the reputation of never breaking. He had fought the British and the Spaniards and strictly observed all the rules of war. Many white émigrés, traitors to their country, now enjoyed their plantations and lived happily and peacefully under his protection after four years' service in the British Army; while the South saw the brothers Rigaud driven away and men who had shed their blood against these same whites for the Republic shot down in cold blood by Toussaint's soldiers. A great bitterness against Toussaint and Dessalines smouldered in the hearts of the Mulattoes of the South. Toussaint knew what he had done and the danger. But he could not help it. At all costs he

[15] It is often stated that Toussaint had thousands of Mulattoes massacred. It is a godsend for historians inimical to the Negro race. Unfortunately for them it is not true. If ever a man hated Toussaint, it was the Mulatto historian Saint-Remy, who collected everything evil that he could find about Toussaint in the biography of him which he wrote. Yet Saint-Remy, himself a Haitian, who wrote in 1850, records that the "moderation of L'Ouverture was astonishing after the triumph that he had just won." Lacroix's figure of 10,000 Mulattoes murdered is just nonsense. For a discussion of this often-repeated lie see Schoelcher, *Vie de Toussaint-L'Ouverture*, pp. 268-269.

had to have an army in the South on which he could depend when a French expedition landed.

The South was now under control. The next danger-spot to be safeguarded was Spanish San Domingo. Bonaparte had expressly forbidden Toussaint to annex that colony. Toussaint would then be master of the whole island, all its resources and all its forts. But this was exactly the reason why Toussaint was going to take it. He was not going to leave his flank exposed to the French expedition.

Roume had hitherto supported Toussaint against Rigaud. Even when the Commission of Vincent, Raimond, and Michel was on its way, Roume had written privately to them[16] expressing his admiration for and faith in Toussaint, his fear lest power might turn his head, but his confidence that Toussaint would not embark on the mad adventure of independence. Roume had had secret instructions to encourage Toussaint to make an attack on Jamaica.[17] This would still further tie Toussaint's hands and cause a clear breach with Britain. Roume proposed the scheme to Toussaint, but Toussaint, though he did not oppose it,[18] was not going to entangle himself with Britain to please France. Emissaries were sent to Jamaica to stimulate a revolt, though it is not certain whether they went from Roume or from Rigaud. The British, however, were so incensed that they seized armaments which Toussaint was transporting by sea for the siege of Jacmel. Immediately Toussaint protested, the British paid him a million and a half francs in compensation, and good relations were restored.[19] Toussaint was determined not to quarrel with the British, and the British were determined not to quarrel with Toussaint. The scheme to embroil Toussaint with

[16] Michel, *La Mission du Général Hédouville* . . . , p. 139.
[17] Letter of Ventôse, AN VII. *Les Archives du Ministère des Colonies.*
[18] Schoelcher, *Vie de Toussaint-L'Ouverture.* Notes on pp. 270-271.
[19] Sannon. *Histoire de Toussaint-L'Ouverture*, Vol. II, p. 207.

Jamaica had failed. It was over Spanish San Domingo that the clash came.

The Spaniards still retained control; Roume, before he succeeded Hédouville as Commissioner, had been merely a sort of resident minister. In the last days of December, while still besieging Jacmel, Toussaint asked Roume for authority to annex the colony. The Spaniards, he said, were stealing Negroes from the French part of the island and selling them as slaves. This was true but obviously only a pretext. Roume had done his best, but he could support Toussaint no longer, for Bonaparte's orders were rigid. Roume had to defend himself, and Toussaint having allowed British trade representatives in San Domingo, Roume published a proclamation calling on him to chase them from the colony and prove that the accusations of infidelity to France were untrue. Toussaint refused, and Roume demanded permission to return to France. Toussaint could have marched into Spanish San Domingo, but he had to the full that care of dictators to legalise their most arbitrary acts. He wanted Roume's authority. Suddenly some thousands of blacks, set in motion by Toussaint's agents, chiefly Moïse, marched on Le Cap, threatening to pillage the town if Roume did not sign the decree which would save their brothers from slavery. Roume refused. For nearly a fortnight Le Cap stood in fear of destruction. To get him out of the way, Moïse commanded Vincent to go to Môle St Nicholas. The labourers, though adamant, were disciplined and maintained perfect order. At last Toussaint came and demanded that Roume sign. "My choice is made," Roume replied. "France will avenge me." Toussaint threatened him: "If you do not sign the decree . . . it means the end of all the whites in the colony, and I shall enter Spanish territory with fire and sword." Roume signed, but he wrote secretly to the Spanish Governor encouraging him not to hand over the colony to Toussaint's agents. Toussaint arrested Roume and sent him to Dondon, where with his wife and two

daughters he was kept under supervision. Then with
Roume's official authority he and Moïse marched on Spanish San Domingo. The Spanish troops were routed, and
on January 21st, 1800, the Spanish Governor formally
handed over the colony.

Toussaint used his usual conciliatory methods. He appointed Clairveaux the Mulatto to be ruler of the province and his brother Paul to be commander of the garrison
at Santo Domingo. He addressed proclamations to the
inhabitants promising full amnesty and these were scrupulously observed.

He was now complete master of the whole island, a
territory nearly as large as Ireland, and he had become
so in less than ten years. "I found the colony dismem-
bered, ruined, over-run by the bandits of Jean François,
by the Spaniards and by the English, who fought over the
bits. It is to-day purged of its enemies, quiet, pacified, and
advances toward its complete restoration." He had made
the boast after the departure of Maitland. Now it was more
than ever true.

But there was still Bonaparte with his "special laws."
Before he left Santo Domingo he wrote to Bonaparte asking for approval of what he had done. He accused Roume
of intriguing against him and impeding his wish to take
possession of the former Spanish colony. "Having decided
to take possession by force of arms I found myself obliged
before setting out to invite Citizen Roume to desist from
the performance of his duties and retire to Dondon until
further orders. . . . He awaits your commands. When
you want him, I will send him to you."

This was defiance. Toussaint attempted no defence:
"Whatever may be the calumnies that my enemies have
seen fit to write to you against me, I shall abstain from
justifying myself; but although delicacy enforces silence
upon me my duty prescribes that I prevent Roume from
doing harm." This was more than defiance. It bordered
perilously on impertinence, and Bonaparte was the last
man in the world to be trifled with.

Toussaint had burnt his boats. With vision, courage

and determination he was laying the foundations of an independent nation. But, too confident in his own powers, he was making one dreadful mistake. Not with Bonaparte nor with the French Government. In nothing does his genius stand out so much as in refusing to trust the liberties of the blacks to the promises of French or British Imperialism. His error was his neglect of his own people. They did not understand what he was doing or where he was going. He took no trouble to explain. It was dangerous to explain, but still more dangerous not to explain. His temperament, close and self-contained, was one that kept its own counsel. Thus the masses thought he had taken Spanish San Domingo to stop the slave traffic, and not as a safeguard against the French. His silence confused them and did not deceive Bonaparte. Dessalines, his fearless lieutenant, had no such scruples. After the war with Rigaud, Dessalines told his soldiers, "The war you have just won is a little war, but you have two more, bigger ones. One is against the Spaniards, who do not want to give up their land and who have insulted your brave Commander-in-Chief; the other is against France, who will try to make you slaves again as soon as she has finished with her enemies. We'll win those wars." That was and still is the way to speak to the masses, and it is no accident that Dessalines and not Toussaint finally led the island to independence. Toussaint, shut up within himself, immersed in diplomacy, went his tortuous way, overconfident that he had only to speak and the masses would follow.

XI

The Black Consul

SO LONG as the war lasted between France and Britain Toussaint was safe. But peace might come at any moment now, and with the peace would come Bonaparte's "special laws."

The colony was devastated by 12 years of civil and foreign war. Of the 30,000 whites in the colony in 1789, only 10,000 remained. The rest had been killed or had emigrated. Of the 40,000 free Mulattoes and free blacks there were still about 30,000, while of the 500,000 Negro slaves perhaps one-third had perished. Plantations and cultivation had been destroyed far and wide. For nearly ten years the population, corrupt enough before, had been trained in bloodshed and soaked in violence. Bands of marauders roamed the countryside. The only disciplined force was the army, and Toussaint instituted a military dictatorship.

The ultimate guarantee of freedom was the prosperity of agriculture. This was Toussaint's slogan. The danger was that the blacks might slip into the practice of cultivating a small patch of land, producing just sufficient for their needs. He would not allow the old estates to be broken up, but bound the interests of the labourers to their work by giving them their keep and a fourth of the produce. The generals in command of the districts were responsible for the industry of the labourers and the prosperity of cultivation. He confined the blacks to the plantations under rigid penalties. He was battling with the colossal task of transforming a slave population, after years of licence, into a community of free labourers, and he was doing it in the only way he could see. On behalf of the labourers he saw to it that they were paid their quarter of the produce.[1] This alone was sufficient to mark the change from the old to the new despotism.

For behind this despotism the new order was vastly different from the old. The black labourers were free, and though there might be dissatisfaction with the new régime, as in the Paris of 1800, there was no regret for the old. Where formerly the labourers had worked from dawn until far into the night, now work began at five and ended at five. No employer dared to beat them. Dessalines whipped blacks in his province, and Toussaint threatened to take away his command at the least complaint.[2] It was not only humanity. Any régime which tolerated such practices was doomed, for the revolution had created a new race of men.

[1] This was admitted by General Leclerc in the decree of July 4th, 1802. *Les Archives du Ministère de la Guerre*, B⁷5.
[2] Gragnon-Lacoste, *Toussaint-L'Ouverture*, Paris and Bordeaux, 1877, p. 194.

The change had first expressed itself in August 1791. Roume, who knew the black labourers as well as any other Frenchman, has traced it in detail.[3] In the North they came out to sustain royalty, nobility and religion against the poor whites and the Patriots. But they were soon formed into regiments and were hardened by fighting. They organised themselves into armed sections and into popular bodies, and even while fighting for royalty they adopted instinctively and rigidly observed all the forms of republican organisation. Slogans and rallying cries were established between the chiefs of the sections and divisions, and gave them points of contact from one extremity of the plains and towns of the North to the other. This guaranteed the leaders a means of calling out the labourers and sending them back at will. These forms were extended to the districts in the West Province, and were faithfully observed by the black labourers, whether fighting for Spain and royalty or for the republic. Roume assured Bonaparte that he recognised these slogans, even during the insurrection which forced him to authorise the taking of Spanish San Domingo.

In 1911, Hilaire Belloc, writing of the French Revolution, claimed that this instinctive capacity of the masses for revolutionary organisation was something peculiarly French.[4] It was an error. At the same time as the French, the half-savage slaves of San Domingo were showing themselves subject to the same historical laws as the advanced workers of revolutionary Paris; and over a century later the Russian masses were to prove once more that this innate power will display itself in all populations when deeply stirred and given a clear perspective by a strong and trusted leadership.

The people were strongly disciplined. Even when they crowded into Le Cap and threatened Roume, their conduct was orderly, they destroyed nothing, merely pre-

[3] Reports to the Minister, 19 and 22 Prairial, An VIII. *Les Archives Nationales*, A.F. IV, 1187.
[4] Hilaire Belloc, *The French Revolution*, Home University Library.

sented their demands that the slave traffic to Spanish San Domingo be stopped, and waited.[5]

At bottom the popular movement had acquired an immense self-confidence. The former slaves had defeated white colonists, Spaniards and British, and now they were free. They were aware of French politics, for it concerned them closely. Black men who had been slaves were deputies in the French Parliament, black men who had been slaves negotiated with the French and foreign governments. Black men who had been slaves filled the highest positions in the colony. There was Toussaint, the former slave, incredibly grand and powerful and incomparably the greatest man in San Domingo. There was no need to be ashamed of being a black. The revolution had awakened them, had given them the possibility of achievement, confidence and pride. That psychological weakness, that feeling of inferiority with which the imperialists poison colonial peoples everywhere, these were gone. Roume and the other Frenchmen who lived in San Domingo and knew the people created by the revolution never ceased to warn the French Government of the catastrophe that would follow any attempt to restore slavery, or indeed impose its will on these people in any way by force. The Mulattoes and the old free blacks resented Toussaint's despotism, but the masses at first gave him their fullest confidence.

Sure of himself, Toussaint reorganised the administration with boldness and skill. He divided the island into six departments, and the boundaries that he fixed remain to this day. He created ordinary courts of law and two courts of appeal, one in the French part of the island and one in the Spanish part, and a Supreme Court of Appeal in the capital. There were also special military courts to deal quickly with robberies and crimes on the high road, plentiful since the years of revolution and war.

[5] Roume, Despatch of 19 and 22 Prairial, AN VIII. *Les Archives Nationales*, A.F. IV, 1187.

The finance of the old régime was complicated and irksome. Toussaint demanded first an "exact inventory of our resources";[6] then abolished the numerous duties and taxes which were only a source of fraud and abuses. He gave the *gourde,* the local unit of money, a uniform value for the whole island. All merchandise and produce imported or exported paid a duty of 20 per cent. All fixed property paid the same. There was the same duty on everything manufactured for consumption in the colony.

Thus he was able to get rid of the numerous officials whom the old system demanded; each taxpayer knew how much he had to pay, and the simplicity of the system and his strict supervision raised the standard of probity.

In his taxation he was feeling his way. He lowered the tax on fixed property from 20 to 10 per cent, and on the advice of Stevens, the United States Consul, abolished it altogether soon afterwards. The 20 per cent tax on imports acted as a check on the purchases of the merchants, and Toussaint lowered it to 10 per cent; later, to encourage the poor, he lowered the duty on articles of the first necessity to 6 per cent. He was learning quickly. All this was taking place in the course of the year 1801.

Contraband had been a feature of the old régime. Toussaint organised a maritime police. Merchants who traded abroad were carefully scrutinised; their names were placed on a list in the customs house, and they could be struck off for dishonesty. For a similar offence the customs officials could be sent to the military tribunals. Against all defaulting officials Toussaint was merciless.

Against Raimond, who had sided with Roume against him, Toussaint bore no grudge. Raimond had ability, and Toussaint appointed him Administrator of the National Estates, an important source of revenue.

[6] Nemours, *Histoire Militaire de la Guerre d'Indépendance de Saint-Domingue,* Paris, 1925, Vol. I, pp. 67-93. A summary and analysis of the better known facts with some additional material

Spanish San Domingo presented a special problem. It was backward, and the Spaniards hated Toussaint and his black generals. He trusted to wise administration and his conciliatory policy to win them over. He gave them their own Appeal Court. He repaired the old roads and built a splendid new one from Santo Domingo to Laxavon, 200 miles long. There were only 22 sugar factories in the whole of the Spanish part, and little cultivation, the inhabitants depending on timber and cattle-breeding for their few wants. He invited them to embark on cultivation in the French style. He lowered their import and export duty to 6 per cent in consideration of the poverty of the country. To encourage cultivation he prohibited the export of timber, but modified this ruling later. He was struck with the potential wealth of Spanish San Domingo, and issued a glowing description of it inviting settlers and offering concessions.

Toussaint knew the backwardness of the labourers; he made them work, but he wanted to see them civilised and advanced in culture. He established such schools as he could. A sincere Catholic and believer in the softening effect of religion on manners, he encouraged the practice of the Catholic religion, and wrote to that old friend of the blacks, the Abbé Grégoire, for advice. He favoured legitimate children and soldiers who were married, and forbade his officials and commandants to have concubines in the houses of their wives, a legacy of the old disreputable white society. He was anxious to see the blacks acquire the social deportment of the better class whites with their Versailles manners. Struck by the carriage and bearing of a French officer, he said to those around him, "My sons will be like that."

Around himself as Governor he instituted social "circles," great and small. All who were invited to a "great circle" had to attend. He himself wore the undress uniform of a regimental officer, contrasting with the brilliance of the uniforms around him. When he appeared the whole company, men and women, rose. He went round the hall speaking to everyone, and then retired by the same door at which he had entered, bowing right and left to the company.

The "small circle" was in the nature of a public audience. All the citizens entered the grand hall of the governor's palace, and Toussaint spoke to them as was convenient. After a time he retired to a small apartment in front of his bedroom which he used as a study, inviting those persons with whom he wanted to talk. These were usually the more distinguished whites, men who had the knowledge and experience that he needed and that were so sadly lacking in the labourers and some of his generals. There they talked of France, which he had never seen, of religion, agriculture, commerce. When he wished to conclude this audience he rose and the company retired, Toussaint accompanying them to the door.

He erected fine buildings in Le Cap and built a huge monument to commemorate the abolition of slavery.

Personal industry, social morality, public education, religious toleration, free trade, civic pride, racial equality, this ex-slave strove according to his lights to lay their foundations in the new State. In all his proclamations, laws and decrees he insisted on moral principles, the necessity for work, respect for law and order, pride in San Domingo, veneration for France. He sought to lift the people to some understanding of the duties and responsibilities of freedom and citizenship. It was the propaganda of a dictatorship, but not for base personal ends or the narrow interests of one class oppressing another. His government, like the absolute monarchy in its progressive days, balanced between the classes, but his was rooted in the preservation of the interests of the labouring poor. With the growth of a black ruling class, complications were arising already. But for the period his form of government was the best.

Success crowned his labours. Cultivation prospered, and the new San Domingo began to shape itself with astonishing quickness. At Le Cap was built a hotel, the Hotel de la République, of a style which would compare

with the finest that existed in any part of the world. It was
frequented by blacks, local whites, and Americans, all on
a footing of equality. At the same table sat private individuals, the generals and officers of every rank, and high
officials. Toussaint went there regularly, taking his place
in any vacant seat like any of the rest; he said often that
distinctions of rank had no place outside the public service.

Race prejudice, the curse of San Domingo for two
hundred years, was vanishing fast. Some of the Americans
were marrying Mulatto women. The stigma of colour
could not flourish when so many Negroes and Mulattoes
filled the highest positions in the country. Travellers who
saw Le Cap during that wonderful year agreed that a new
spirit was in the country.[7] The theatres began to play
again, and some of the Negro players showed a remarkable talent. No doubt the poor sweated and were backward so that the new ruling class might thrive. But at least
they too were better off than they had been. While on the
one hand the authority, social ease and culture of those
who, a dozen years before, had been slaves, amazed all
observers, the success of Toussaint's administration can be
judged by the fact that in a year and a half he had restored
cultivation to two-thirds of what it had been in the most
flourishing days of the old régime.[8]

Those were the ideas and the methods of government
of Toussaint. The revolution had made him; but it would be
a vulgar error to suppose that the creation of a disciplined
army, the defeat of the English and the Spaniards, the defeat of Rigaud, the establishment of a strong government
all over the island, the growing harmony between the
races, the enlightened aims of the administration—it would

[7] Beard, *Life of Toussaint L'Ouverture*, p. 138.
[8] Nemours, *Histoire Militaire de la Guerre* . . . , Vol. I, pp. 17-
19. Nemours summarises the evidence. Idlinger the treasurer
(white) of the island under Toussaint also states the same in a
memoir written for the French Government in 1804. See *Les
Archives du Ministère des Affaires Étrangères. Fonds divers,
Section Amérique*, No. 14, folio 202.

be a crude error to believe that all these were inevitable. At a certain stage, the middle of 1794, the potentialities in the chaos began to be shaped and soldered by his powerful personality, and thenceforth it is impossible to say where the social forces end and the impress of personality begins. It is sufficient that but for him this history would be something entirely different. It is therefore essential for us to consider what sort of man he was.

It was his prodigious activity which so astonished men. Nobody ever knew what he was doing: if he was leaving, if he was staying, whither he was going, whence he was coming. He had hundreds of thoroughbred horses scattered in stables all over the country, and he habitually covered 125 miles a day, riding far in advance of his guards and arriving at his destination alone or with one or two well-mounted attendants. The inspection of agriculture, commerce, fortifications, Municipalities, schools, even the distribution of prizes to successful scholars—he was tireless in performing these duties all over the country, and none knew when and where the Governor would appear. He deliberately cultivated this mysteriousness. He would leave a town in his carriage surrounded by his guards. Then some miles away he would step out of it and ride in the opposite direction. And after these lightning dashes across country he was able to go into his cabinet and dictate hundreds of letters until far into the early morning. He dictated to five secretaries at once,[9] and as he told Hédouville during one of their quarrels, he took full responsibility for anything that bore his signature, signing nothing that he did not read himself. He carried into his correspondence the same methods that he used in his administration. One secretary would write down half of an important letter, Toussaint would then send him 60 miles away and conclude it by means of another.

He was as completely master of his body as of his mind. He slept but two hours every night, and for days would be satisfied with two bananas and a glass of water.[10]

[9] Nemours, *Histoire Militaire de la Guerre* . . . , Vol. I, p. 126.
[10] Lacroix, *Mémoires pour Servir* . . . , Vol. I, p. 406.

Physically without fear, he had to guard against being poisoned, and in the various villages where he stayed he had old black women prepare for him callaloos, a kind of vegetable broth. He could trust these old women. They had no ambitions and were too proud of him to do him any harm. In the field he slept dressed, booted and spurred; in the towns he always kept near to his bed a pair of trousers. At all hours of the night couriers and officers found him ready to receive them with becoming dignity.

His control over his soldiers was not due only to his skill as a general. He had that reckless physical bravery that makes men follow a leader in the most forlorn causes. From the beginning of his career to the end he charged at the head of his men whenever a supreme effort was required. In one battle he chased the Spanish commander alone for nearly a mile and brought back two prisoners, and in ten years was wounded 17 times. Even on his ordinary trips he took all sorts of risks. When he was already Commander-in-Chief he was nearly drowned in trying to cross a swollen river on horseback, and escaped only by getting rid of his sword. He could make soldiers accomplish the seemingly impossible. In the march on Spanish San Domingo, when he wanted speed, the men were doing over 40 miles a day and had to be checked to wait for the cavalry.[11]

He seemed to bear a charmed life. During the civil war against the South his enemies tried to ambush him twice. The first time his doctor, who was sitting in the carriage with him, was killed at his side, several of his officers were unmounted, and the plume of his hat was cut away by a bullet. A little later on the same journey his coachman was killed and his carriage riddled with bullets. Only a few minutes before, he had left the carriage and was at the time riding some distance away. No wonder he came in the end to believe in himself as the black Spartacus, foretold by Raynal as predestined to achieve the emancipation of the blacks. The labourers in their turn worshipped him as a direct servant of God.

[11] Nemours, *Histoire Militaire de la Guerre* . . . , Vol. I, p. 146.

His aides were Negroes, one of them his nephew. Despite the broadness of his views and his conciliatory aims, Toussaint kept his army overwhelmingly black and ex-slave. But his personal advisers were all white men: Vincent, Pascal who had come as secretary to the Commission in 1796, and two Italian priests. He liked to talk to the rich white planters. But no person, man nor woman, ever had any influence on him. He seems to have had one friend in all his life, Laveaux. Impenetrable, he trusted no one, confided in no one. If he had a weakness it was in keeping people mystified. Yet he guarded his reputation and was careful in his contacts with people. He had the extraordinary faculty of satisfying all who came to see him, and was known all over the island as a man who never broke his word. Even Sonthonax, the Jacobin lawyer and a very finished intriguer himself, said in the French Chamber that Toussaint was incapable of telling lies. But this was before Toussaint accused him of plotting independence.

Despite his awkwardness of build and ugliness of feature he managed in the end to make a strong impression upon all with whom he came in contact. He had in the last years an unusual distinction of carriage. His step was martial, his manner commanding. Simple in his private life, he wore resplendent uniforms on state occasions, and his aides-de-camp followed his example in elegance and display. He knew how to listen to a subordinate officer with dignity and yet with affability. He could acknowledge marks of public respect and affection while avoiding them with easy good nature. With all classes of people he found instinctively the right method.

When the black labourers came to him, nervous about their liberty and white domination, he would take a glass vase and fill it with grains of black maize, then put in a few grains of white maize. "You are the black maize; the whites who would enslave you are the white maize." He then shook the glass and showed it to them. "See, the white ones only here and there." The blacks went away reassured. They came to him saying that they did not wish to obey either whites or Mulattoes (due in all probability to some insults or injustices meted out to them by these former masters). Toussaint took a glass of wine and a glass of water, mixed them together and showed the result. "How can you tell which is which? We must all live together." They went away satisfied.

A Negro who wanted the post of judge came to see Toussaint. He was unfitted for the post, but Toussaint did not want to hurt his feelings. "You know Latin, of course," said Toussaint. "Latin!" Toussaint reeled off a string of cheap Latin phrases that he had picked up, probably from official documents and the church service. The applicant retired, satisfied that he was incompetent, and marvelling at the knowledge of the Governor.

He was absolutely at home with the masses of the people and yet, at the same time, men like Maitland and the local whites were astonished at the singular courtesy and charm of his manners. There was nothing of the rough diamond about Toussaint. Three white women of the ancient régime, living abroad, wrote to him asking for the restoration of their properties. Toussaint's reply showed some of the secret of his success with all classes of people.

"I have received the letters with which you have been so kind as to honour me. . . . I have always done as much as lies in my power to preserve the property of each and every one; yours, citizens, . . . has not suffered from the unhappy events inevitable in a revolution; it is intact. The power to remove the sequestration under which it lies does not rest with me; that is in the hands of the Agent of the Directory. I can only assure you that his decision will be punctually executed.

"For more than three years, citizens, I have asked the Citizen Descheaux, your mother, to come back to her property; my advice, unhappily for her and for you, has not prevailed over that of her brother. There was still time to profit . . . by a proclamation carrying the name and authorisation of the French Government. Your mother has, however, preferred to follow the fate of her brother, Cockerel, rather than remain at St Marc to profit by the advantages of the amnesty and retake possession of her property. She has left with her brother; it no longer depends on me to get her to come back home.

"In regard to the husband of the Citizen Fontanges, I can no longer prevent him from being written down as an émigré. That would be to place myself above the law, and that has never entered my mind nor my principles. When the Agent decides to raise your sequestration . . . I shall neglect nothing to put the Citizen Fortier, whom you recommend to me, in a position to look after your interests in the most advantageous manner. If my advice can be of any use to him, I shall give it to him, if he wishes it, with the greatest pleasure, being happy to seize the opportunity to witness the infinite value which I attach to your goodwill, on every occasion that it is in harmony with my duty.

"Accept, citizens, the assurance of my respect and regards. I sincerely wish the happiness of you all and the return of your mother to your arms." [12]

Perhaps it is in his correspondence that we can most easily grasp the range and sensitivity of Toussaint's untaught genius. In his letter to the Commissioners in 1791, his correspondence with Laveaux, his overtures to Dieudonné, his letter to the Directory in 1796, his speech at Port-Républicain after the expulsion of the English, his letters to Hédouville and his resignation, in all these, as here in this gracious but careful letter, his vision of precisely what is required is unerring, his taste is faultless, and the constantly varying approach is always suffused with revolutionary passion, a large humanity and a never-failing personal distinction. These letters more than anything else show that whatever the task that faced him he did it to the manner born.

[12] Schoelcher, *Vie de Toussaint-L'Ouverture*, p. 289.

In a community where so many were still primitive
and simple-minded, the personal character and conduct of
the leader, sprung from the people, was not without social
significance. Despite Toussaint's despotism, his ruthlessness,
his impenetrability, his unsleeping suspicion of all around
him, his skill in large-scale diplomacy and petty intrigue,
to the end of his life he remained a man of simple and
kindly feelings, his humanity never drowned by the rivers
of blood which flowed so plentifully and so long. His "no
reprisals" sprang from a genuine horror of useless bloodshed. Women and children in particular he hated to see
suffer. While his army starved in the campaign against the
British, he gave food to the destitute white women of the
district. After the civil war he paid the same careful attention to the Mulatto women and children. He was incapable
of meanness, pettiness or vindictiveness of any kind. Biassou, his old enemy and rival, had been murdered, and left
a widow in Spanish San Domingo. Toussaint gave her a
pension, and when he went to Santo Domingo he saw that
she returned to her home with honours and dignities. To
the widow of Chavannes, the Mulatto who had perished
with Ogé, he gave a pension of 6,000 francs a year. Often,
where a modern dictator would shoot, he preferred to deport. He had that curious detachment and inward scorn of
men which distinguished Bonaparte, who forgave his family
over and over again when they deceived him, and without
any personal bitterness watched Murat, Talleyrand and
Fouché intriguing and plotting against him. Toussaint
could strike without mercy at men like Rigaud who im-
perilled his plans, but when one day a white officer who
had deserted to the English was captured and brought
back, he merely smiled at him: "Ah, I see that we are too
good friends for fortune to keep us apart any longer," and
did no more.

He was fortunate in his family, and they helped to
give him prestige. His brother Paul was a distinguished
officer. Moïse and Belair, his nephews, were famous for
their bravery. His nephew, Chancy, was his aide-de-camp.
No one could say that any of them owed his position to

anything but conspicuous ability. His wife lived on a plantation in the interior, and devoted herself to the cultivation of coffee. Whenever Toussaint could escape from his duties he went there. Visitors saw them sitting hand in hand as in the old days when they were slaves together. Her sister married a French officer; old Pierre Baptiste, who lived to be over a hundred, would not accept any honours or riches but lived simply in Le Cap. Whenever Toussaint went to the town, his first visit was always to the old man who had given him the rudiments of an education.

He loved children and they loved him. Riding one day from Gonaïves to Ennery, a little orphan named Rose, ten years of age, ran after him calling, "Papa, papa, take me away with you." He dismounted, took her up and carried her home to his wife. "Here is an orphan who has just called me her father. I have accepted the title. Accept also the title of her mother." And Rose became a member of the L'Ouverture household. This was the sort of thing that bound him to a simple agricultural people. He did not do it for propaganda. It came naturally to him, as did also his respect for old people, to whom he always gave way in the street. He loved music, and always had flowers in his room.

The basis of his power was the support of the black labourers. Its framework was the army. But from the simplest black labourer to the French generals and the best educated and most travelled and experienced of the local whites, all recognised that both in his work and personal idiosyncracies he was the first man in San Domingo, and such a man as would have been in the first rank in any sphere. He demanded, and they gave, unquestioned obedience. He had his advisers, but his proclamations, laws and addresses have his own personal quality and all accounts of him and tradition agree that he left nothing to anybody, working at everything himself, consulting friends and well-wishers, but evolving his schemes in his own secretive manner and then checking every small detail himself.

After a time he never questioned the future. Of unbounded energy and will, he had the fatalism of men who know that their cause is equipped to meet whatever dan-

gers impend. For himself he expected the usual end of revolutionaries. An impudent Spaniard of Spanish San Domingo once pointedly referred to the fate of Columbus in
an answer to a question. Toussaint did not deny the parallel.

"I know very well that Columbus suffered ingratitude
from Spain, and that such is the destiny of men who serve
their country well; they have powerful enemies. As for me,
it is the fate which is reserved for me, and I know I shall
perish a victim of calumny." In this Roman stoicism he
was, despite his Catholicism, a typical representative of the
French Revolution.

With the exception always of Bonaparte, no single
figure in the whole period of the French Revolution travelled so fast and so far.

But Toussaint was no phenomenon, no Negro freak.
The same forces which moulded his genius had helped to
create his black and Mulatto generals and officials. Agé,
his Chief of Staff, was a white man, but all the senior generals were black or Mulatto, chiefly black. There were two
Generals of Division, one Dessalines, the other Clairveaux,
a Mulatto. Dessalines was the most famous of the black
generals. By some he was thought to excel Toussaint in
military genius; yet it was late in life before he learned to
sign his name. He governed the Department of the West
with a rod of iron, and though having no constructive
capacity for government he had a shrewdness, cunning and
ruthless determination which were to be of inestimable
service to his people before long. He had no sympathy with
Toussaint's policy of reconciliation with the whites, but
dazzled by Toussaint's gifts he worshipped his chief and
obeyed him implicitly. Late in 1801 he married one of the
most notable women in San Domingo, a Negro of remarkable beauty and intelligence, the former mistress of a
planter who had given her a good education. She was very
sympathetic toward the whites, and she and Toussaint kept
Dessalines in check.

Of the other seven Generals of Brigade, Vernet was a Mulatto, the last to be appointed. All the others were blacks. Toussaint's favourite was his nephew, Charles Belair, and it was believed that he destined Belair to be his successor. In 1801 he was only 23, and had been aide-de-camp to Toussaint when he was only 18. He had fought with distinction against the British and in the civil war against the South. Handsome, with distinguished manners, he loved military parade and display. He did not like the whites, and Sanite, his wife, hated them and encouraged him to treat them harshly.

Moïse was a different type, a "bonny lad," a dashing soldier, fond of women, the most popular soldier in the army, beloved by the blacks of the North for his ardent championship of them against the whites. He stood high in Toussaint's favour until he refused to carry out Toussaint's severe labour legislation in the North. Cultivation in his district suffered, and Toussaint sent observers to watch his administration and listen to the criticisms Moïse indiscreetly made of Toussaint's policy toward the whites. At first it was thought he would be the successor, and the whites decided that if Moïse ever ruled they would leave.

In one way the most remarkable of the black generals was Maurepas. He was the only one who had not been a slave, and came from an old free family. He read widely, was a man of great culture, and knew the military art to the last point. He governed his district with justice and fairness to all.

Christophe, ex-waiter, could neither read nor write, but he also astonished the French by his knowledge of the world and the ease and authority with which he ruled. He was an English Negro, but unlike Toussaint he learned to speak French with remarkable fluency. He loved luxury, was friendly with the whites, and governed well.

Laplume (the same who had arrested Dieudonné) was an old incompetent, a poor soldier, but easy-going and beloved by all in the South, blacks and whites alike.

They lived in houses costing millions, which would have been beautiful in Paris. When Maurepas entertained

General Ramel, the Frenchman could not believe his eyes at his manners, conversation and patent ability.[13] French generals, officials and colonists who wrote reports and memoirs about these generals and other officials when at the height of their power, all noted the ease and quickness with which they had learned to command. Pamphile de Lacroix said of these old slaves that they had learned more quickly than French workers or peasants in a similar position could have done.[14] This was probably true, and it was because the black leaders were not so permeated by the ideas of the ruling class as a French worker or peasant would have been. Mass support had elevated them and maintained them in supreme power, and the responsibility gave them confidence. In one report drawn up for Hédouville's private use, the author noted the colour of each officer and official in a long list, and good, bad and indifferent soldiers and administrators are divided equally among the three colours.[15] But many of the blacks, illiterate, had to have white secretaries. Toussaint was sending black and Mulatto children to France at the public expense to be educated, so that they might return and govern. All he wanted was time.

But San Domingo was not destined to have peace. The white slave-owners were a cause of discord at home, while the maritime bourgeois in France remembered always the fabulous profits of the slave trade. The whites, having no other choice, accepted Toussaint's régime. With

[13] Reminiscences of General Ramel. See introduction to *Toussaint L'Ouverture,* a play by Lamartine, Paris, 1850, p. xxiv.
[14] After 400 years of carrying civilisation to the Native the British and Dutch in South Africa cannot find one Native to represent the Africans in the Cape Parliament. In 1936 the South African whites deprived the Native of the vote which he had had in Cape Province for generations.
[15] Notes of a colonist for the use of Hédouville. Reprinted in Michel, *La Mission du Général Hédouville* . . . , pp. 85-103.
For notes and memoranda on the black generals by white men, French and colonials, who knew them well, *see also* Gaston Nogerée, Report to the French Government, 1801. *Les Archives Nationales,* F. 7, 6266; Lamartine, *Toussaint L'Ouverture,* pp. xvi-xxviii; Lacroix, *Mémoires pour Servir* . . . , Vol. II, pp. 308-345; Idlinger, *Les Archives du Ministère des Affaires Etrangères. Fonds divers, Section Amérique,* No. 14.

the sensitiveness of property-owners they saw that as long as Toussaint was there their lives were safe, and they talked and behaved as if they were devoted to him. When he came back to Le Cap after the campaign in the South they took the leading part in the celebrations. He was welcomed by a great triumphal arch, verses composed in his honour were read by a white woman of great beauty who placed on his head a crown of laurel. Old Toussaint, always gallant, embraced the charming diseuse. There were also other embracings of a less public nature. The creole ladies of San Domingo, members of some of the most distinguished families of the old régime, were carried away by his singular personality and his power. In less than a dozen years they had managed to overcome the cast-iron prejudices in which they had been reared. They fought among each other for his notice and sent him passionate letters, locks of hair, and keepsakes of all kinds. Toussaint was not averse, although with discretion. Open immorality in high places, he told his generals, had an evil effect on public morals.[16] It was exactly the sort of thing Toussaint would say and think.

And yet, despite all this intimacy between whites and the new black ruling class, Toussaint knew that, unlike Sonthonax, Laveaux, Roume, and Vincent, all the revolutionaries of the first period, these old slave-owners and their women did not like the labourers, whatever the pre-

[16] When the French captured Port-au-Prince in 1802, Lacroix, who was left in command, found among Toussaint's effects, "locks of hair of all colours, rings, golden hearts crossed by arrows, latchkeys . . . and an infinity of love-letters . . ." (*Mémoires pour Servir . . .* , Vol. II, p. 105). This does not suit Mr. Lothrop Stoddard's racial theories. On p. 388 of his book, *The French Revolution in San Domingo*, he writes as follows about the relations of white women with the black generals: "The negro generals had greatly abused their power in this respect. For Toussaint's gross misconduct in this regard, see Lacroix II, 104-105." How many will look up Lacroix? Naturally they believe after reading Stoddard that Toussaint and his generals raped white women or forced them to sleep with them through fear. Thiers, in his famous *History of the Consulate and the Empire*, actually says so. It is a typical example of the cloud of lies which obscure the true history of imperialism in colonial countries.

tended devotion of the men and the liking the women might have for him as an individual. It was in 1798 that he wrote so courteously to the white women who asked for a return of their property, and all through that year he and Hédouville quarrelled about the policy to be adopted toward the white émigrés. Yet at that very period when the whites of Port-au-Prince were bowing and scraping before him, an incident took place which lets us see what Toussaint thought of the whites as whites.

A white colonist wanted a post as storekeeper and asked Toussaint for it. Toussaint said no. The colonist's wife tried many times to approach Toussaint, but was unsuccessful. Some time after she gave birth to a son and asked Toussaint to be the godfather. Toussaint, usually so suave and conciliatory, for some reason or other, decided to let this woman know his mind.

"Why, Madame, do you wish me to be godfather of your son—your approach to me has no other aim than to get me to give a post to your husband, for the feelings of your heart are contrary to the request that you make of me."

"How can you think so, General? No, my husband loves you, all the whites are attached to you."

"Madame, I know the whites. If I had their skin—yes, but I am black and I know their aversion to us. Have you reflected well on the request which you make of me? If I accept, how do you know that when he reaches the age of reason, your son may not reproach you for giving him a Negro as godfather?"

"But, General . . ."

"Madame," Toussaint interrupted her, pointing to the sky, "He who governs all is alone immortal. I am a general, it is true, but I am black. After my death, who knows if my brothers will not be driven back into slavery and will yet perish under the whip of the whites. The work of men is not durable. The French Revolution has enlightened Europeans, we are loved and wept over by them, but the white colonists are enemies of the blacks. . . . You wish your husband to get a post Well, I give him the employment that he demands. Let him be honest and let him remember that I cannot see everything, but that nothing escapes God. I cannot accept your offer to be godfather to your son. You may have to bear the reproaches of the colonists and perhaps one day that of your son." [17]

These were his views; he never changed them. Yet he set his face sternly against racial discrimination. He guarded his power and the rights of the labourers by an army overwhelmingly black. But within that wall he encouraged all to come back, Mulattoes and whites. The policy was both wise and workable, and if his relations with France had been regularised he would have done all he hoped to do. But San Domingo did not know where it stood in relation to France. There were still fears for liberty, and the black labourers did not approve of Toussaint's policy. They felt that he showed too much favour to their old enemies.[18]

These anti-white feelings of the blacks were no infringement of liberty and equality, but were in reality the soundest revolutionary policy. It was fear of the counter-revolution. They had loved Sonthonax, called down blessings on his head, and made their children pray for him at night. Fifty years afterwards their old eyes would glow as they told travellers of this wonderful white man who had given them liberty and equality, not only in words but in deeds. But men like Sonthonax, Vincent, Laveaux, and Roume were few and with the decline of the revolution in France had come a man like Hédouville. The black labourers had their eyes fixed on the local whites and resented Toussaint's policy. It was not the whites at home whom Toussaint feared. It was the counter-revolution in France. But the blacks could see in the eyes of their former owners the regret for the old days and the hatred. Shortly after Toussaint issued one of his stern proclamations confining the blacks to the plantations, some of these whites issued a

[17] Malenfant, *Des Colonies et particulièrement de celle de Saint-Domingue*, Paris, 1819.
[18] Proclamation of Christophe I, 1814, Printed in Beard, *Life of Toussaint L'Ouverture*, p. 326.

proclamation of their own to the labourers. "You say that you are free. Yet you are going to be forced to come back to my house and there I shall treat you as before and shall show you you are not free." [19] This was the spirit which so constantly provoked massacres of the whites. Toussaint fined the culprits heavily, ordered that all who could not pay should be imprisoned, even women, and reduced such officers as were concerned to the ranks. But he still continued to favour the whites. Every white woman was entitled to come to all "circles." Only the wives of the highest black officials could come. A white woman was called madame, the black woman was citizen. Losing sight of his mass support, taking it for granted, he sought only to conciliate the whites at home and abroad.

What would Bonaparte do? Toussaint, pursuing his policy, made gestures of friendship to all abroad. Madame de Beauharnais, Josephine's mother, had a plantation at Léogane. After the evacuation by the British, Josephine wrote to Toussaint about the plantation, which was in ruins. A correspondence began. Toussaint repaired and restored the plantation at the expense of the colony, and sent the revenues to Madame Bonaparte. Josephine befriended his two boys, and they went often to luncheon and dinner at her house. But Toussaint wanted his sons back and Bonaparte would not send them. Toussaint prepared for the inevitable war. That was one of the reasons which drove him to demand that his generals be mercilessly strict with the labourers.

He bought 30,000 guns from America. He armed the labourers. At reviews he would snatch a gun, wave it, and shout, "Here is your liberty!" He was not afraid to arm the masses. He trusted them for he had no interests apart from theirs. He hid stocks of ammunition and supplies in secret places in the interior. He called up the able-bodied for military training, and drilled the regular army. Bold in innovation, he introduced a system of commands by whistles. In every conceivable way (except one) he prepared. The blacks would have to fight. This war would devastate San

[19] Ardouin. *Études sur l'histoire* . . . , Vol. IV, p. 256.

Domingo as no war had ever devastated it before, ruin his work and let loose barbarism and savagery again, this time on an unprecedented scale. But any large expedition could have no other aim than the restoration of slavery. In that cruel dilemma he worked feverishly, hoping against hope, writing to Bonaparte, begging for skilled workmen, teachers, administrators, to help him govern the colony.

Bonaparte would not answer, and Toussaint could guess why. If Bonaparte wrote a personal letter he would have either to accept or condemn. If he accepted, then Toussaint's position would receive the final sanction. If he condemned, then Toussaint would openly declare independence and perhaps clinch a bargain with the British if one were not made already.

Toussaint, however, immediately after the victory in the South, had decided to regularise his own position and put an end to internal troubles for the future by giving San Domingo a Constitution. For this purpose he summoned an assembly of six men, one from each province, consisting of rich whites and Mulattoes: there was not one black. As always now, he was thinking of the effect in France, and not of the effect on his own masses, feeling too sure of them. The members of his assembly were merely figureheads. The Constitution is Toussaint L'Ouverture from the first line to the last, and in it he enshrined his principles of government.[20] Slavery was forever abolished. Every man, whatever his colour, was admissible to all employments, and there was to exist no other distinction than that of virtues and talents, and no other superiority than that which the law gives in the exercise of a public function. He incorporated in the Constitution an article which preserved their rights to all proprietors absent from the colony "for whatever reason" except if they were on the list of émigrés proscribed in France. For the rest, Toussaint concentrated all power in his own hands.

[20] The Constitution is printed in full in Nemours, *Histoire Militaire* . . . , Vol. I, pp. 95-112.

Every municipal administration was composed of a mayor and four administrators. They were nominated by the Governor for two years from a list of 16 submitted to him.

The Church was strictly subordinate to the State. The Governor apportioned to each minister of religion the extent of his administration, and the clergy were not allowed under any pretext whatever to form an association in the colony. Laws were to be preceded by this formula: "The Central Assembly of San Domingo, on the proposal of the Governor . . ." They were to be promulgated with the formula: "The Governor commands . . ." Every department of administration, finance, police, army, was confided to him, and he corresponded directly with France on everything relating to the colony. He had the censorship of all printed matter.

The Central Assembly could accept or reject laws, but the Assembly was in the hands of the Governor, being elected by the principal administrators, whom he nominated. The Constitution appointed Toussaint Governor for life, with power to name his successor.

Constitutions are what they turn out to be. France in 1802 could have no quarrel with Toussaint over this Constitution on the score of despotism. What would strike any Frenchman, however, was that the Constitution, though swearing allegiance to France, left no room for any French official. Toussaint wanted them to come out and help govern, but under the local government. It was virtual independence, with France as elder brother, guide and mentor. He had no precedents to guide him, but he knew what he wanted. When remonstrated with as to where was the place of France in such a government, he replied, "The French Government will send Commissioners to speak with me." Absolute local independence on the one hand, but on the other French capital and French administrators, helping to develop and educate the country, and a high official from France as a link between both Governments. The local power was too well safeguarded for us to call the scheme a protectorate in the political content of that dishonest word. All the evidence shows that Toussaint, working alone, had reached forward to that form of political allegiance which we know to-day as Dominion Status.

Firm as was his grasp of reality, old Toussaint looked beyond San Domingo with a boldness of imagination surpassed by no contemporary. In the Constitution he authorised the slave-trade because the island needed people to cultivate it. When the Africans landed, however, they would be free men. But while loaded with the cares of government, he cherished a project of sailing to Africa with arms, ammunition and a thousand of his best soldiers, and there conquering vast tracts of country, putting an end to the slave-trade, and making millions of blacks "free and French," as his Constitution had made the blacks of San Domingo. It was no dream. He had sent millions of francs to America to wait for the day when he would be ready.[21] He was already 55. What spirit was it that moved him? Ideas do not fall from heaven. The great revolution had propelled him out of his humble joys and obscure destiny, and the trumpets of its heroic period rang ever in his ears. In him, born a slave and the leader of slaves, the concrete realisation of liberty, equality and fraternity was the womb of ideas and the springs of power, which overflowed their narrow environment and embraced the whole of the world. But for the revolution, this extraordinary man and his band of gifted associates would have lived their lives as slaves, serving the commonplace creatures who owned them, standing barefooted and in rags to watch inflated little governors and mediocre officials from Europe pass by, as many a talented African stands in Africa to-day.[22]

Too much importance has been attached to the Constitution. It was merely a formal embodiment of the position to which Toussaint had been moving steadily since his expulsion of Hédouville. His method of publishing it was his usual one of mystery. He summoned his white and Mu-

[21] Saint-Anthoine, *Vie de Toussaint-L'Ouverture*, p. 325.
[22] Written in 1938.

latto Assembly to prepare the document. He then left them to it, and set off to capture Spanish San Domingo. On his return the Constitution was ready. Nobody knew its contents except himself and his Assembly. He suddenly told Vincent that he would allow him to leave for France if he would take the Constitution to Bonaparte. Vincent agreed, because there seemed no chance of getting away otherwise. Toussaint told him to go to Gonaïves and bid Madame L'Ouverture good-bye, Vincent being very friendly with the family. As soon as Vincent left, Toussaint published the Constitution, in July, 1801. There was a religious ceremony, a great banquet, and illuminations and public rejoicings. Toussaint's Constitution was a despotism, and the Mulattoes and the free blacks did not like it. But what cared those thousands who sang and danced?

When Vincent returned he went to Toussaint and reproached him for publishing so far-reaching a document without the sanction of the French Government and when he saw the details he was horrified. He consulted Pascal, and both agreed that Toussaint ought to withdraw it. They might as well have asked the island of San Domingo to withdraw itself from the Caribbean Sea and attach itself to France.

Toussaint listened very patiently. "There is no room in it for any official from France," said Vincent. "France will send Commissioners to speak with me," said Toussaint.[23] "What is really required is that France send you chargés d'affaires and ambassadors, as the Americans and the Spaniards will certainly do. And even the British."

This was a crude innuendo. Even Vincent (at times) suspected Toussaint. How difficult it was for them to understand that Toussaint was using the British and playing the diplomatic game with them, but detested these bulwarks of European reaction just as much as any other true son of the revolution.

"I know that the English Government is the most dangerous for me and the most perfidious for France. It did all it could to get the sole right of trade with the island, but I

23 *Précis de mon voyage.* . . .

gave it only what I could not help giving. I needed it."
Why doesn't Bonaparte write to me? he asked Vincent: he
writes to the King of England.

Pascal, until this time another devoted follower, also
disapproved of the Constitution and Toussaint dropped
him. Vincent complained to Moïse and Christophe: they
also condemned it. Christophe said Toussaint had gone too
far, and Moïse called Toussaint an old fool. "He thinks he
is King of San Domingo!"

The printing of the Constitution particularly startled
Vincent. To have had it printed meant (in those days) that
an irrevocable decision had been taken. Toussaint agreed.
It would have cost him nothing to send a written copy. But
he was going his way. There was one last painful interview
between the two men. Vincent did all he could to make
Toussaint reconsider his action. All the blacks were free.
He could not withdraw the right of governing the island
from France.

"Give me a list of your comrades in arms, who have
contributed most to driving out the English and restoring
cultivation. The Government, I am certain, will prove to
them its gratitude."

Toussaint, usually calm, was violently agitated. He
replied that he would see with infinite pleasure some of his
comrades rewarded. But when Vincent asked him what he
wanted for himself, he replied sharply that he wanted nothing; that he knew his destruction was the ultimate aim,
that his children would never enjoy the little that he had
amassed, but that he was not yet the victim of his enemies.
To this personal outburst he added some reflections which
so hurt the conscience of the sensitive Vincent that he
would not even write them down. But we can guess what
they were. Bitterness at the insults and neglect which he
felt were caused by his colour, the impossible position in
which he and his people were placed: submission, which
would mean the restoration of slavery; or defiance, which
would mean war and the complete devastation of the island; his isolation, white and black friends against him;
all these must have wrung the words out of him who ordi-

narily never spoke but when he thought it necessary, and then said only what he wanted to say. He turned abruptly from Vincent, and evading about a hundred persons who were waiting for him, he sprang on his horse and rode away so quickly that even his guard was taken by surprise.

For these fews weeks Vincent seems to have doubted Toussaint. Vincent was a white man. He could never dread slavery as a black man could, never have that unsleeping fear of white treachery so strong in that generation of San Domingo Negroes. Honest himself, Vincent took it for granted that the rulers of France would act with common decency toward those black men whose services to France he had witnessed. To him it seemed that Toussaint was merely pursuing a personal ambition. Before he left he sounded Christophe. Would he leave Le Cap, where he commanded, and go to St Iago to welcome the French expedition which would certainly come? It would save a great deal of trouble. Christophe, evasive, said he would do his best for peace. With this equivocal answer Vincent had to be satisfied. He did not know what to do. He went home via America and from Philadelphia he wrote to Toussaint, warning him against projects of independence.

Vincent did all that a man could do. Even in trying to detach Christophe from Toussaint he was acting, as he thought, in the best interests of France and of San Domingo. To him the restoration of slavery was unthinkable. He expected it as little as millions of British people expected the intrigues of Baldwin, Hoare and Eden with Laval and Mussolini after the denial of arms to Abyssinia and the grandiose promises of fidelity to the League of Nations and the idea of collective security. Many an honest subordinate has in this way been the unwilling instrument of the inevitable treachery up above; the trouble is that when faced with the brutal reality he goes in the end with his own side, and by the very confidence which his integrity created does infinitely more harm than the open enemy.

XII

The Bourgeoisie Prepares to Restore Slavery

TOUSSAINT was perfectly right in his suspicions. What is the régime under which the colonies have most prospered, asked Bonaparte, and on being told the *ancien régime* he decided to restore it, slavery and Mulatto discrimination.

Bonaparte hated black people. The revolution had appointed that brave and brilliant Mulatto, General Dumas,[1] Commander-in-Chief of one of its armies, but Bonaparte

---

[1] Father of Alexandre père and grandfather of Alexandre fils. France has erected a monument to these three in the Place Malesherbes, Paris.

detested him for his colour, and persecuted him. Yet Bonaparte was no colonist, and his anti-Negro bias was far
from influencing his major policies. He wanted profits for
his supporters, and the clamorous colonists found in him a
ready ear. The bourgeoisie of the maritime towns wanted
the fabulous profits of the old days. The passionate desire
to free all humanity which had called for Negro freedom
in the great days of the revolution now huddled in the
slums of Paris and Marseilles, exhausted by its great efforts
and terrorised by Bonaparte's bayonets and Fouché's police.

But the abolition of slavery was one of the proudest
memories of the revolution; and, much more important, the
San Domingo blacks had an army and leaders trained to
fight in the European manner. These were no savage tribesmen with spears, against whom European soldiers armed
with rifles could win undying glory.

Occupied with his European campaigns, Bonaparte
never lost sight of San Domingo, as he never lost sight of
anything. His officers presented plan after plan, but the
British fleet and the unknown strength of the blacks prevented action. Yet early in March 1801, a shift in his policy
nearly compelled him to leave Toussaint in complete charge
of San Domingo.

French and British bourgeoisie were in the middle of
that struggle for world supremacy which lasted over twenty
years and devastated Europe. Bonaparte aimed at India,
and having missed his first spring by way of Egypt, he won
over the Tsar Paul, and these two arranged to march over-
land and steal from the British what these had stolen from
the Indians. Bonaparte could not fight in two hemispheres
at once, and on March 4th he wrote a letter to Toussaint,
a letter beaming with goodwill.[2] He had been busy, but
now that peace was near he had had time to read Toussaint's letters. He would appoint him Captain-General of
the island. He asked Toussaint to develop agriculture and
build up the armed forces. "The time I hope will not be far
when a division from San Domingo will be able to contrib-

[2] Correspondence of Napoleon.

ute in your part of the world to the glory and the possessions of the Republic."

But the British bourgeoisie, driven out of America, now fully realised the importance of India. Pitt, in collusion with Paul's son Alexander, organised the murder of the pro-French Paul.[3] Seven days after the letter to Toussaint was written, Paul was strangled, and on the following day the British fleet sailed into the Baltic. When Bonaparte heard he knew at once that Pitt had beaten him, and the Indian raid was off. The letter and instructions to Toussaint were never sent, and Bonaparte prepared to destroy Toussaint. It is Toussaint's supreme merit that while he saw European civilisation as a valuable and necessary thing, and strove to lay its foundations among his people, he never had the illusion that it conferred any moral superiority. He knew French, British, and Spanish imperialists for the insatiable gangsters that they were, that there is no oath too sacred for them to break, no crime, deception, treachery, cruelty, destruction of human life and property which they would not commit against those who could not defend themselves.

When Vincent arrived in Paris preparations were well under way, but the Constitution gave Bonaparte a convenient excuse. Poor Vincent had attempted to persuade Toussaint to give way to Bonaparte by condemning the Constitution as treason. Now he tried to persuade Bonaparte to give way to Toussaint by denying that the Constitution was treason. Bonaparte accused Toussaint of being sold to the British. Stoutly Vincent defended him. Bonaparte swore at Vincent, cursed the "gilded Africans," said that he would not leave an epaulette on the shoulders of a single nigger in the colony. Vincent put it to him that Britain might assist Toussaint. Bonaparte boasted that Britain had shown some inclination to oppose the expedition, but when he threatened to clothe Toussaint with unlimited powers and acknowledge his independence, the

[3] Eugene Tarlé, *Bonaparte*, London, 1937, pp. 116-117.

British had kept silence. (Bonaparte thought that they dreaded the effect of an independent San Domingo on their own slave colony of Jamaica. But Pitt, Dundas and Maitland were laughing in their sleeves and rubbing their hands in anticipation.) Vincent tried to point out the dangers of the expedition. Bonaparte called Toussaint a "revolted slave," called Vincent a coward and drove him from his presence. Vincent was appalled at Bonaparte's violence. If this was the spirit in which the French were going to San Domingo, they were heading for a fall. As anxious now for France as for San Domingo, he took the bold step of addressing a memoir to the Minister, in which he tried to paint the strength of the colony and the extraordinary genius of the man who ruled there.

"At the head of so many resources is a man the most active and tireless of whom one can possibly have any idea; it is the strictest truth to say that he is everywhere and, above all, in that spot where a sound judgment and danger make it essential for him to be; his great sobriety, the faculty accorded to him alone of never taking a rest, the advantage he enjoys of being able to start at once with the work in his office after wearisome journeys, of replying to a hundred letters a day and tiring out his secretaries; more than that, the art of tantalising and confusing everybody even to deceit: all this makes of him a man so superior to all around him that respect and submission reach the limits of fanaticism in a vast number of heads. He has imposed on his brothers in San Domingo a power without bounds. He is the absolute master of the island and nothing can counteract his wishes, whatever they may be, although some distinguished men, but very few blacks among them, know what are his plans and view them with great fear."

Vincent described Toussaint as superior to everyone in San Domingo, but if one reads that extract again it becomes clear that this brave, honest, intelligent, and experienced officer was obviously describing the most extraordinary human being he had ever met in his life, with powers beyond what he thought possible. In the writings of contemporaries describing the great figures of the French

Revolution and Napoleonic era, one finds this note of astonishment, this "I can't believe my own eyes" attitude, in writings about only three men, Bonaparte, Nelson the sailor and Toussaint.

Bonaparte was so angry that he banished Vincent to the island of Elba.

Personally loved and respected by all their contemporaries, Vincent and Beauvais failed, as will fail all who do not understand that in a revolution each must choose his side and stick to it.

But though Bonaparte might shout "nigger" in the best slave-owning manner, more than anyone in France he divined the difficulties. At first he had thought it easy. The colonists who had fled in the early days of the revolution thought of the slaves as a motley crowd of black brigands who would fly at the first sight of white men. How could such cowed and trembling niggers ever be anything else? They had defeated the British? Nonsense. That was fever. General Michel of the last Commission, who had not seen Toussaint's armies in action, called his officers a collection of conceited incompetents.

But Roume, Pascal, and Vincent, all of whom liked the blacks and therefore knew what they were capable of, were against any expedition. Pascal said that the more enlightened of the blacks, i.e. those who had been free before the revolution, did not love Toussaint, but forty-nine-fiftieths of the population followed him blindly, regarding him as being inspired by God. Roume's attitude was most astonishing. Roume was not even a Frenchman, but a creole from Tobago. Yet, despite his rough treatment at the hands of Toussaint, he still retained his belief in Toussaint's devotion to France. He wrote that Toussaint had acted irregularly because of his fear of slavery. Let Bonaparte clothe him with full civil and military power and reassure him about the future. At the end of the war he would hand back the colony.[4]

4 To the Minister. *Les Archives Nationales.* AF. IV, 1187.

Malenfant, an old colonist who was now an official in San Domingo, was offered a post in the expedition. He drafted a memorandum full of praise for Toussaint and the labourers, and warned Bonaparte against the catastrophe he was preparing. When he met Leclerc, the Captain-General, a few days before the fleet sailed, Leclerc accused him of cowardice. "All the niggers, when they see an army, will lay down their arms. They will be only too happy that we pardon them."

"You are misinformed, General . . ."

"But there is a colonist who has offered to arrest Toussaint in the interior of the country with 60 grenadiers."

"He is bolder than I, for I would not attempt it with 60,000."

"He is very rich, Toussaint. He has more than 40 millions."

Patiently Malenfant pointed out to him that it was impossible for Toussaint to have this sum. Malenfant shared Roume's opinion of Toussaint. He said afterwards that if Bonaparte had sent Laveaux to San Domingo with 3,000 men all would have been well. Toussaint was an eminently reasonable man, and he and Laveaux would have worked out a *modus vivendi* whereby French capital would have had full opportunity in the island. It was not to be. Leclerc pooh-poohed Malenfant's remonstrances and dismissed him.

Bonaparte never had any such foolish ideas. Vincent had told him of the strength of Toussaint's army, with its soldiers and officers tried and experienced by ten years of constant fighting, and the great soldier added more and more men to the force. So as to avoid too much talk, he distributed his preparations in every harbour in France, Holland and Belgium. The preliminaries of peace were signed on October 1st, 1801. Eight days after Bonaparte gave the word, and even the delay of adverse winds held up the expedition only until December 14th.

It was the largest expedition that had ever sailed from France, consisting of 20,000 veteran troops, under some of Bonaparte's ablest officers. The Chief of Staff was Dugua, whom Bonaparte had left in charge of Egypt when he set out on the march to Palestine. Boudet had commanded the advance-guard of Dessaix, whose last minute attack had saved Bonaparte from a disastrous defeat at Marengo. Boyer had commanded the mobile guards which patrolled Upper Egypt; Humbert had commanded the expedition against Ireland. There were men who had experience of guerrilla warfare in La Vendée. General Pamphile de Lacroix, who sailed with the expedition and wrote a valuable history of the campaign and the San Domingo revolution, has left us his opinion. "The army of Leclerc was composed of an infinite number of soldiers with great talent, good strategists, great tacticians, officers of engineers and artillery, well educated and very resourceful." [5] At the last moment Bonaparte changed the command, putting his brother-in-law, Leclerc, at the head, a sign of the importance he attached to the venture. Pauline, Leclerc's wife, and their son went with the expedition. She carried musicians, artists, and all the paraphernalia of a court. Slavery would be re-established, civilisation restarted, and a good time would be had by all.

And in these last crucial months, Toussaint, fully aware of Bonaparte's preparations, was busy sawing off the branch on which he sat.

In the North, around Plaisance, Limbé, Dondon, the vanguard of the revolution was not satisfied with the new régime. Toussaint's discipline was hard, but it was infinitely better than the old slavery. What these old revolutionary blacks objected to was working for their white masters. Moïse was the Commandant of the North Province, and Moïse sympathised with the blacks. Work, yes, but not for whites. "Whatever my old uncle may do, I cannot bring myself to be the executioner of my colour. It is always in the interests of the metropolis that he scolds me; but these interests are those of the whites, and I shall only love them when they have given me back the eye that they made me lose in battle."

[5] *Mémoires pour Servir* . . . . Vol. II, p. 319.

Gone were the days when Toussaint would leave the front and ride through the night to enquire into the grievances of the labourers, and, though protecting the whites, make the labourers see that he was their leader.

Revolutionaries through and through, those bold men, own brothers of the Cordeliers in Paris and the Vyborg workers in Petrograd, organised another insurrection. Their aim was to massacre the whites, overthrow Toussaint's government and, some hoped, put Moïse in his place. Every observer, and Toussaint himself, thought that the labourers were following him because of his past services and his unquestioned superiority. This insurrection proved that they were following him because he represented that complete emancipation from their former degradation which was their chief goal. As soon as they saw that he was no longer going to this end, they were ready to throw him over.[6]

This was no mere riot of a few discontented or lazy blacks. It was widespread over the North. The revolution-

[6] Georges Lefebvre: *La Convention*, Volume I., p. 45, mimeographed lectures delivered at the Sorbonne (see Bibliography, p. 379). "The Jacobins, furthermore, were authoritarian in outlook. Consciously or not, they wished to act with the people and for them, but they claimed the right of leadership, and when they arrived at the head of affairs they ceased to consult the people, did away with elections, proscribed the Hébertistes and the Enragés. They can be described as enlightened despots. The sansculottes on the contrary were extreme democrats: they wanted the direct government of the people by the people; if they demanded a dictatorship against the aristocrats they wished to exercise it themselves and to make their leaders do what they wanted."

The sansculottes, of Paris in particular, saw very clearly what was required at each stage of the revolution at least until it reached its highest peak. Their difficulty was that they had neither the education, experience nor the resources to organise a modern state if only temporarily. *This was pretty much the position of the revolutionaries of Plaisance, Limbé and Dondon in relation to Toussaint. Events were soon to show how right they were and that in not listening to them Toussaint made the greatest mistake of his career.*

For a balanced account of the way in which the sansculottes themselves worked out and forced upon an unwilling Robespierre the great policies which saved the revolution, see Lefebvre (mimeographed lectures), *Le Gouvernement Revolutionnaire* (2 Juin 1793-9 Thermidor II), Folio II.

aries chose a time when Toussaint was away at Petite-Rivière attending the wedding of Dessalines. The movement should have begun in Le Cap on September 21st, but Christophe heard of it just in time to check the first outbursts in various quarters of the town. On the 22nd and 23rd the revolt burst in the revolutionary districts of Marmelade, Plaisance, Limbé, Port Margot, and Dondon, home of the famous regiment of the sansculottes. On the morning of the 23rd it broke out again in Le Cap, while armed bands, killing all the whites whom they met on the way, appeared in the suburbs to make contact with those in the town. While Christophe defeated these, Toussaint and Dessalines marched against the rising in Marmelade and Dondon, and it fell to pieces before him and his terrible lieutenant. Moïse, avoiding a meeting with Toussaint, attacked and defeated another band. But blacks in certain districts had revolted to the cry of "Long Live Moïse!" Toussaint therefore had him arrested, and would not allow the military tribunal even to hear him. The documents, he said, were enough. "I flatter myself that the Commissioners will not delay a judgment so necessary to the tranquillity of the colony." He was afraid that Moïse might supplant him.[7]

Upon this hint the Commission gave judgment, and Moïse was shot. He died as he had lived. He stood before the place of execution in the presence of the troops of the garrison, and in a firm voice gave the word to the firing squad: "Fire, my friends, fire."

What exactly did Moïse stand for? We shall never know. Forty years after his death Madiou, the Haitian historian, gave an outline of Moïse's programme, whose authenticity, however, has been questioned. Toussaint refused to break up the large estates. Moïse wanted small grants of land for junior officers and even the rank-and-file. Toussaint favoured the whites against the Mulattoes. Moïse sought to build an alliance between the blacks and the Mu-

[7] Toussaint himself admitted this not very long afterwards. See Poyen, *Histoire Militaire de la Révolution de Saint-Domingue*, Paris, 1899, p. 228.

lattoes against the French. It is certain that he had a strong sympathy for the labourers and hated the old slave-owners. But he was not anti-white. He bitterly regretted the indignities to which he had been forced to submit Roume and we know how highly he esteemed Sonthonax. We have very little to go on but he seems to have been a singularly attractive and possibly profound person. The old slave-owners hated him and they pressed Toussaint to get rid of him. Christophe too was jealous of Moïse and Christophe loved white society. Guilty or not guilty of treason, Moïse had too many enemies to escape the implications of the "Long Live Moïse" shouted by the revolutionaries.

To the blacks of the North, already angry at Toussaint's policy, the execution of Moïse was the final disillusionment. They could not understand it. As was (and is) inevitable, they thought in terms of colour. After Toussaint himself, Moïse, his nephew, symbolised the revolution. He it was who had led the labourers against Hédouville. He also had led the insurrection which extorted the authority from Roume to take over Spanish San Domingo, an insurrection which to the labourers had been for the purpose of stopping the Spanish traffic in slaves. Moïse had arrested Roume, and later Vincent. And now Toussaint had shot him, for taking the part of the blacks against the whites.

Toussaint recognised his error. If the break with the French and Vincent had shaken him from his usual calm in their last interview, it was nothing to the remorse which moved him after the execution of Moïse. None who knew him had ever seen him so agitated. He tried to explain it away in a long proclamation: Moïse was the soul of the insurrection; Moïse was a young man of loose habits. It was useless. Moïse had stood too high in his councils for too long.

But so set was Toussaint that he could only think of further repression. Why should the blacks support Moïse against him? That question he did not stop to ask or, if he did, failed to appreciate the answer. In the districts of the insurrection he shot without mercy. He lined up the labourers and spoke to them in turn; and on the basis of a stumbling answer or uncertainty decided who should be shot. Cowed by his power they submitted.

He published a series of laws surpassing in severity anything he had yet decreed. He introduced a rigid passport system for all classes of the population. He confined the labourers to their plantations more strictly than ever, and he made the managers and foremen responsible for this law under pain of imprisonment. Anyone fomenting disorder could be condemned to six months' hard labour with a weight attached to his foot by a chain. He prohibited the soldiers from visiting a plantation except to see their fathers or mothers, and then only for a limited period: he was now afraid of the contact between the revolutionary army and the people, an infallible sign of revolutionary degeneration.

And while he broke the morale of the black masses, he laboured to reassure the whites. Some of them rejoiced openly at the rumours of the expedition, and Toussaint, instead of treating them as he had treated the labourers, merely deported them. There were others, we need not doubt, who, holding the same views, thought it wiser to keep their mouths shut. A substantial number, however, accepted the new order, and viewed with dismay the violence and destruction which they knew were inevitable if a French expedition came. Some began to leave, and asked for passports. One of the most notable creoles in San Domingo, a man of good education and judgment, who fully accepted the new San Domingo,[8] came to Toussaint and asked him for a passport. Here was what Toussaint dreaded: the break-up of the unstable régime before it had had a chance to acquire cohesion. He went quickly to the door to see that he was not likely to be overheard (a char-

[8] We know this from his report to Bonaparte. *Les Archives Nationales*, F. 7, 6266.

acteristic action). Then coming back, he looked de Nogerée full in the face and asked him: "Why do you want to go away, you whom I esteem and love?"

"Because I am white, and notwithstanding the kindly feelings you have for me, I see that you are about to become the irritated chief of the blacks."

With some injustice he accused Toussaint of deporting those whites who had rejoiced at the coming of the expedition. Toussaint justified his action with warmth:

"They have had the imprudence and folly to rejoice at such news, as if the expedition was not destined to destroy me, to destroy the whites, to destroy the colony."

With a mind such as his, essentially creative and orderly, this was the prospect which preoccupied him and warped his judgment.

"In France I am represented as an independent power, and therefore they are arming against me; against me, who refused General Maitland's offer to establish my independence under the protection of England, and who always rejected the proposals which Sonthonax made to me on the subject."

He knew that the expedition was on its way, but still he hoped that somehow the coming catastrophe might be averted.

"Since, however, you wish to set out for France, I consent, but at least let your voyage be useful to the colony. I will send letters to the First Consul by you, and I will entreat him to listen to you. Tell him about me, tell him how prosperous agriculture is, how prosperous is commerce; in a word, tell him what I have done. It is according to all I have done here that I ought and that I wish to be judged. Twenty times I have written to Bonaparte, to ask him to send Civil Commissioners, to tell him to dispatch hither the old colonists, whites instructed in administering public affairs, good machinists, good workmen: he has never replied. Suddenly he avails himself of the peace (of which he has not deigned to inform me and of which I learn only through the English) in order to direct against me a formidable expedition, in the ranks of which I see my·

personal enemies and people injurious to the colony, whom I sent away.

"Come to me within twenty-four hours. I want,—oh, how I want you and my letters to arrive in time to make the First Consul change his determination, to make him see that in ruining me he ruins the blacks—ruins not only San Domingo but all the western colonies. If Bonaparte is the first man in France, Toussaint is the first man in the Archipelago of the Antilles."

He had no false modesty as to what he meant to San Domingo.

He reflected for a moment, then said in a firm tone that he had been making arrangements with the English to get 20,000 blacks from Africa, but not for treachery, to make them soldiers of France. "I know the perfidy of the English. I am under no obligation to them for the information they gave me as to the expedition coming to San Domingo. No! Never will I arm for them!"

But reality forced itself on him again.

"I took up arms for the freedom of my colour, which France alone proclaimed, but which she has no right to nullify. Our liberty is no longer in her hands: it is in our own. We will defend it or perish."

This strange duality, so confusing to his people who had to do the fighting, continued to the very end. And yet, in this moment of his greatest uncertainty, so different from his usual clarity of mind and vigour of action, Toussaint showed himself one of those few men for whom power is a means to an end, the development of civilization, the betterment of his fellow-creatures. His very hesitations were a sign of the superior cast of his mind. Dessalines and Moïse would not have hesitated. He issued another proclamation, and devoted most of it to reassuring the white proprietors who "will always find in us ardent protectors, true friends, zealous defenders. . . ."

What did all this mean to the former slaves? When he touched the expedition, the confusion of his mind was evident in every line. "Men of good faith . . . will not be able any longer to believe that France, who abandoned

San Domingo to herself at a time when her enemies disputed possession . . . will now send there an army to
destroy the men who have not ceased to serve her will. . . ."

After thus sowing doubt in the minds of the people
as to the intentions of the French, he continued: "But if
it so happens that this crime of which the French Government is suspected is real, it suffices for me to say that a
child who knows the rights that nature has given over it
to the author of its days, shows itself obedient and submissive toward its father and mother; and if, in spite of
its submission and obedience, the father and mother are
unnatural enough to wish to destroy it, there remains no
other course than to place its vengeance in the hands of
God."

So God was to defend the blacks from slavery. What
of the army and the people and himself, their leader?

"Brave soldiers, generals, officers, and rank and file,
do not listen to the wicked . . . I shall show you the road
you ought to follow . . . I am a soldier, I am afraid of no
man and I fear only God. If I must die, it shall be as a soldier of honour with no fear of reproach."

Toussaint could not believe that the French ruling
class would be so depraved, so lost to all sense of decency, as to try to restore slavery. His grasp of politics
led him to make all preparations, but he could not admit
to himself and to his people that it was easier to find decency, gratitude, justice, and humanity in a cage of starving tigers than in the councils of imperialism, whether in
the cabinets of Pitt or Bonaparte, of Baldwin, Laval or
Blum.

Criticism is not enough. What should Toussaint have
done? A hundred and fifty years of history and the scientific study of revolution begun by Marx and Engels, and
amplified by Lenin and Trotsky, justify us in pointing to
an alternative course.

Lenin and the Bolsheviks after the October Revolution
faced much the same problem as Toussaint. Russian bour-

geois culture was a relatively poor thing, but Lenin admitted frankly that it was superior to that of the proletariat and would have to be used until the proletariat had
developed itself. He rigidly excluded the bourgeoisie from
political power, but he proposed that they should be given
important posts and good salaries, higher than those of
Communist Party members. Even some Communists who
had suffered and fought under Tsarism were after a time
dismissed and replaced by competent bourgeois. We can
measure Toussaint's gigantic intellect by the fact that,
untrained as he was, he attempted to do the same, his black
army and generals filling the political rôle of the Bolshevik
Party. If he kept whites in his army, it was for the same
reason that the Bolsheviks also kept Tsarist officers. Neither
revolution had enough trained and educated officers of its
own, and the black Jacobins, relatively speaking, were far
worse off culturally than the Russian Bolsheviks.

The whole theory of the Bolshevik policy was that the
victories of the new régime would gradually win over those
who had been constrained to accept it by force. Toussaint
hoped for the same. If he failed, it is for the same reason
that the Russian socialist revolution failed, even after all
its achievements—the defeat of the revolution in Europe.
Had the Jacobins been able to consolidate the democratic
republic in 1794, Haiti would have remained a French
colony, but an attempt to restore slavery would have been
most unlikely.

It was in method, and not in principle, that Toussaint
failed. The race question is subsidiary to the class question
in politics, and to think of imperialism in terms of race is
disastrous. But to neglect the racial factor as merely incidental as an error only less grave than to make it fundamental. There were Jacobin workmen in Paris who would
have fought for the blacks against Bonaparte's troops. But
the international movement was not then what is it to-day,
and there were none in San Domingo. The black labourers
saw only the old slave-owning whites. These would accept
the new régime, but never to the extent of fighting for it
against a French army, and the masses knew this. Tous-

saint of course knew this also. He never trusted Agé, his Chief of Staff who was a Frenchman, and asked Agé's junior, Lamartinière, to keep an eye on him. But whereas Lenin kept the party and the masses thoroughly aware of every step, and explained carefully the exact position of the bourgeois servants of the Workers' State, Toussaint explained nothing, and allowed the masses to think that their old enemies were being favoured at their expense. In allowing himself to be looked upon as taking the side of the whites against the blacks, Toussaint committed the unpardonable crime in the eyes of a community where the whites stood for so much evil. That they should get back their property was bad enough. That they should be privileged was intolerable. And to shoot Moïse, the black, for the sake of the whites was more than an error, it was a crime. It was almost as if Lenin had had Trotsky shot for taking the side of the proletariat against the bourgeoisie.

Toussaint's position was extraordinarily difficult. San Domingo was, after all, a French colony. Granted that, before the expedition was a certainty, plain speech was impossible; once he understood that it was coming, there should have been no hesitation. He should have declared that a powerful expedition could have no other aim than the restoration of slavery, summoned the population to resist, declared independence, confiscated the property of all who refused to accept and distributed it among his supporters. Agé and the other white officers should have been given a plain choice: accept or leave. If they had accepted, intending to be traitors, the black officers would have been on guard against them, the men would have known where they stood and would have shot them at the slightest vacillation before the enemy. The whites should have been offered the same choice: accept the black régime which has guaranteed and will guarantee your property, or leave; traitors in war-time would be dealt with as all traitors in war. Many of the planters favoured independence. They would have stayed and contributed their knowledge, such as it was, to the new State. Not only former slaves had followed Toussaint. Lamartinière was a Mulatto so white that

only those who knew his origins could tell that he had
Negro ancestry, but he was absolutely and completely devoted to the cause of Toussaint. So was Maurepas, an old
free black. With Dessalines, Belair, Moïse and the hundreds of other officers, ex-slave and formerly free, it would
have been easy for Toussaint to get the mass of the population behind him. Having the army, some of the better
educated blacks and Mulattoes and the labourers who had
supported him so staunchly in everything, he would have
been invincible. With the issue unobscure and his power
clear, many who might otherwise have hesitated would
have come down on the side that was taking decisive action. With a decisive victory won it was not impossible to
re-open negotiations with a chastened French government
to establish the hoped-for relations.

It was the ex-slave labourers and the ex-slave army
which would decide the issue, and Toussaint's policy
crippled both.

He left the army with a divided allegiance. There
were Frenchmen in it whose duty would be to fight for
France. They, the Mulattoes and the old free blacks had
no fears about their liberty.

Instead of bringing the black labourers nearer he drove
them away from him. Even after the revolt it was not too
late. Lenin crushed the Kronstadt revolt with a relentless
hand, but, in a manner so abrupt as to call forth protests
from sticklers for party discipline, he proposed the New
Economic Policy immediately afterwards. It was this quick
recognition of danger that saved the Russian Revolution.
Toussaint crushed the revolt as he was bound to do. But
instead of recognising the origin of the revolt as springing
from the fear of the same enemy that he was arming
against, he was sterner with the revolutionaries than he
had ever been before. It happened that the day on which
Moïse was executed, November 21st, was the very day
fixed by Bonaparte for the departure of the expedition.

Instead of reprisals Toussaint should have covered
the country, and in the homely way that he understood so
well, mobilised the masses, talked to the people, explained

the situation to them and told them what he wanted them to do. As it was, the policy he persisted in reduced the masses to a state of stupor.[9] It has been said that he was thinking of the effect in France. His severity and his proclamation reassuring the whites aimed at showing Bonaparte that all classes were safe in San Domingo, and that he could be trusted to govern the colony with justice. It is probably true, and is his greatest condemnation.

Bonaparte was not going to be convinced by Toussaint's justice and fairness and capacity to govern. Where imperialists do not find disorder they create it deliberately, as Hédouville did. They want an excuse for going in. But they can find that easily and will go in even without any. It is force that counts, and chiefly the organised force of the masses. Always, but particularly at the moment of struggle, a leader must think of his own masses. It is what they think that matters, not what the imperialists think. And if to make matters clear to them Toussaint had to condone a massacre of the whites, so much the worse for the whites. He had done everything possible for them, and if the race question occupied the place that it did in San Domingo, it was not the fault of the blacks. But Toussaint, like Robespierre, destroyed his own Left-wing, and with it sealed his own doom. The tragedy was that there was no need for it. Robespierre struck at the masses because he was bourgeois and they were communist. That clash was inevitable, and regrets over it are vain. But between Toussaint and his people there was no fundamental difference of outlook or of aim. Knowing the race question for the political and social question that it was, he tried to deal with it in a purely political and social way. It was a grave error. Lenin in his thesis to the Second Congress of the Communist International warned the white revolutionaries —a warning they badly need—that such has been the effect of the policy of imperialism on the relationship be-

9 Idlinger, Treasurer to the Colony. Report to the French Government, *Les Archives du Ministère des Affaires Etrangères. Fonds divers, Section Amérique*, No. 14.

tween advanced and backward peoples that European Communists will have to make wide concessions to natives of colonial countries in order to overcome the justified prejudice which these feel toward all classes in the oppressing countries. Toussaint, as his power grew, forgot that. He ignored the black labourers, bewildered them at the very moment that he needed them most, and to bewilder the masses is to strike the deadliest of all blows at the revolution.

His personal weakness, the obverse side of his strength, played its part also. He left even his generals in the dark. A naturally silent and reserved man, he had been formed by military discipline. He gave orders and expected them to be obeyed. Nobody ever knew what he was doing. He said suddenly that Sonthonax must go and invited his generals to sign the letter or not, as they pleased. When Vincent spoke to Christophe and Moïse about the Constitution, they knew nothing about it. Moïse's bitter complaint about Toussaint and the whites came obviously from a man to whom Toussaint had never explained the motives of his policy. They would not have needed much persuasion to follow a bold lead. Moïse was feeling his way towards it, and we can point out Toussaint's weakness all the more clearly because Dessalines had actually found the correct method. His speech to the army was famous, and another version—he probably made it more than once—ran this way: "If France wishes to try any nonsense here, everybody must rise together, men and women." Loud acclamations greeted this bold pronouncement, worth a thousand of Toussaint's equivocal proclamations reassuring the whites. Dessalines had not the slightest desire to reassure whites.

The whites were whites of the old régime. Dessalines did not care what they said or thought. The black labourers had to do the fighting—and it was they who needed reassurance. It was not that Toussaint had any illusions about the whites. He had none whatever. When the war had actually begun, he sent a curt message to his commanders: "Leave nothing white behind you." [10] But the mischief had been done.

Yet Toussaint's error sprang from the very qualities that made him what he was. It is easy to see to-day, as his generals saw after he was dead, where he had erred. It does not mean that they or any of us would have done better in his place. If Dessalines could see so clearly and simply, it was because the ties that bound this uneducated soldier to French civilisation were of the slenderest. He saw what was under his nose so well because he saw no further. Toussaint's failure was the failure of enlightenment, not of darkness.

In the last days of December, the fleet of Admiral Villaret-Joyeuse, bearing on board the first detachment of 12,000 men, sailed into the harbour of Samana Bay. Toussaint, standing alone on a neighbouring peak, watched the vessels. Unaccustomed to naval armaments, he was overwhelmed by their number; as he returned to his staff he uttered the words, "We shall perish. All France is come to overwhelm us." It was not fear. He was never afraid. But certain traits of character run deep in great men. Despite all that he had done he was at bottom the same Toussaint who had hesitated to join the revolution in 1791 and for one whole month had protected his master's plantation from destruction. Only this time it was not a plantation and a few score slaves but a colony and hundreds of thousands of people.

[10] Mauviel, Bishop of San Domingo, memorandum to Napoleon, *Les Archives Nationales*, AF. IV. 1187.

XIII

The War of Independence

THE DEFEAT of Toussaint in the War of Independence and his imprisonment and death in Europe are universally looked upon as a tragedy. They contain authentic elements of the tragic in that even at the height of the war Toussaint strove to maintain the French connection as necessary to Haiti in its long and difficult climb to civilisation. Convinced that slavery could never be restored in San Domingo, he was equally convinced that a population of slaves recently landed from Africa could not attain to civilisation by "going it alone." His tergiversations, his inability to take the firm and realistic decisions which so distinguished his career and had become the complete expression of his personality, as we watch his blunders and the inevitable catastrophe, we have always to remember that here is no conflict of the insoluble dilemmas of the human condition, no division of a personality which can find itself only in its striving for the unattainable. Toussaint was a whole man. The man into which the French Revolution had made him demanded that the relation with the France of liberty, equality, fraternity and the abolition of slavery without a debate, should be maintained. What revolutionary France signified was perpetually on his lips, in public statements, in his correspondence, in the spontaneous intimacy of private conversation. It was the highest stage of social existence that he could imagine. It was not only the framework of his mind. No one else was so conscious of its practical necessity in the social backwardness and primitive conditions of life around him. Being the man he was, by nature, and by a range and intensity of new experiences such as is given to few, that is the way he saw the world in which he lived. His unrealistic attitude to the former masters, at home and abroad, sprang not from any abstract humanitarianism or loyalty, but from a recognition that they alone had what San Domingo society needed. He believed that he could handle them. It is not improbable that he could have done it. He was in a situation strictly comparable to that of the greatest of all American statesmen, Abraham Lincoln, in 1865: if the thing could be done at all, he alone could do it. Lincoln was not allowed to try. Toussaint fought desperately for the right to try.

If he was convinced that San Domingo would decay without the benefits of the French connection, he was equally certain that slavery could never be restored. Between these two certainties, he, in whom penetrating vision and prompt decision had become second nature, became the embodiment of vacillation. His allegiance to the French Revolution and all it opened out for mankind in general and the people of San Domingo in particular, this had made him what he was. But this in the end ruined him.

Perhaps for him to have expected more than the bare freedom was too much for the time. With that alone Dessalines was satisfied, and perhaps the proof that freedom alone was possible lies in the fact that to ensure it Dessalines, that faithful adjutant, had to see that Toussaint was removed from the scene. Toussaint was attempting the impossible—the impossible that was for him the only reality that mattered. The realities to which the historian is condemned will at times simplify the tragic alternatives with which he was faced. But these factual statements and the judgments they demand must not be allowed to obscure or minimise the truly tragic character of his dilemma, one of the most remarkable of which there is an authentic historical record.

But in a deeper sense the life and death are not truly tragic. Prometheus, Hamlet, Lear, Phèdre, Ahab, assert what may be the permanent impulses of the human condition against the claims of organised society. They do this in the face of imminent or even certain destruction, and their defiance propels them to heights which make of their defeat a sacrifice which adds to our conceptions of human grandeur.

Toussaint is in a lesser category. His splendid powers do not rise but decline. Where formerly he was distinguished above all for his prompt and fearless estimate of whatever faced him, we shall see him, we have already seen him, misjudging events and people, vacillating in principle, and losing both the fear of his enemies and the confidence of his own supporters.

The hamartia, the tragic flaw, which we have constructed from Aristotle, was in Toussaint not a moral weakness. It was a specific error, a total miscalculation of the constituent events. Yet what is lost by the imaginative freedom and creative logic of great dramatists is to some degree atoned for by the historical actuality of his dilemma. It would therefore be a mistake to see him merely as a political figure in a remote West Indian island. If his story does not approach the greater dramatic creations, in its social significance and human appeal it far exceeds the last

days at St Helena and that apotheosis of accumulation
and degradation, the suicide in the Wilhelmstrasse. The
Greek tragedians could always go to their gods for a dramatic embodiment of fate, the *dike* which rules over a
world neither they nor we ever made. But not Shakespeare
himself could have found such a dramatic embodiment of
fate as Toussaint struggled against, Bonaparte himself; nor
could the furthest imagination have envisaged the entry
of the chorus, of the ex-slaves themselves, as the arbiters
of their own fate. Toussaint's certainty of this as the ultimate and irresistible resolution of the problem to which
he refused to limit himself, that explains his mistakes and
atones for them.

    Like Toussaint, Bonaparte did everything himself and
he wrote out the plan of campaign with his own hand.
    He divided it into three periods. In the first Leclerc
was to promise Toussaint everything he asked for, in order that Leclerc might establish himself in the principal
points of the country.
    "As soon as this is done, you will then be firmer. Com-
mand him to reply without equivocation to me, the proclamation and my letter." Toussaint was to come to Le Cap
and swear fidelity to the Republic. "On that very day" he
and all his supporters, white and black, were to be shipped
to France without being disgraced but with honour and
consideration. (This was merely to avoid irritating the population unnecessarily: no epaulette was to be left on the
shoulders of a single nigger.) Raimond (with no mass
following) was to be arrested and sent to France as a
criminal. During this first period Leclerc was to treat
Moïse, Dessalines, and Toussaint well, and every attempt
was to be made to win over men like Christophe, Clairveaux, and Maurepas who were "favourable to the whites,"
in other words men who had carried out Toussaint's policy
and treated them with fairness and consideration. This was
the first period, to last about 15 or 20 days.

But Bonaparte had his doubts about Toussaint, Moïse, and Dessalines. If they did not come to swear fealty (and be politely but firmly deported), they were to be declared traitors, hunted down by "a war to the death," and if captured shot within 24 hours. This would end the second period. "On the same day" at all points "all doubtful persons, whatever their colour, were to be arrested, and all the black generals whatever their status deported." The last stage was the disarming of the population. The National Guard and *gendarmerie* were to be "reorganised," in other words, made all white, and San Domingo would then be ready for the "special laws."

The first thing was to break the military power of the blacks: no black above the rank of captain was to be left in the island.

The second thing was prestige. Bonaparte knew the imperialist importance of a proper respect for white women among natives. The ancients never thought a conquest completed until the victor had slept with the wife or daughter of the conquered monarch. It is difficult to inculcate the proper sentiment of inferiority in a man who sleeps with your sister. Bonaparte ordered that all white women who had "prostituted themselves" to Negroes, were to be sent to Europe, whatever their rank. Leclerc was not to tolerate from anyone any talk about the "rights of those blacks who had shed so much white blood." [1] Whatever his rank or services he was to be shipped to France.

The "special laws" were not specified, but the Mulattoes, too, were to be suitably dealt with. Rigaud, Pétion, Villate and other officers, having no fears for their own rights and thinking to supplant Toussaint and his generals, had obtained permission to come with the expedition. Bonaparte had them all put on one ship, the *Vertu*. If Toussaint welcomed the expedition they were not even to be allowed to land, but were to be deported at once to Madagascar. If there was fighting to be done, however,

[1] The instructions are printed in full in *Die Kolonialpolitik Napoleons I*, by Roloff (Munich, 1899), as an appendix.

then they would be allowed to shed their share of blood.[2]

Bonaparte in these instructions repudiated the idea of restoring slavery. He was lying. But he was still posing as the heir of the revolution, and he dared not commit this reactionary policy to black and white lest it fall into the hands of Leclerc's successor (if Leclerc needed one) and for fear of the effect on the army. Even when he did give Leclerc authority to restore slavery, Leclerc kept it from his second-in-command, Rochambeau. Many officers, and all the soldiers, believed that they were fighting for the revolution against Toussaint, a traitor sold to priests, émigrés, and the British.

It is on colonial peoples without means of counter-publicity that imperialism practises its basest arts, and what is staggering in this document is not its duplicity. It is the calm assumption of stupidity and trustfulness on the part of the black generals. Bonaparte seemed to have had fears of only three, Toussaint, Moïse, and Dessalines.

But the most bewildering fact in all this history, and the testimony to Bonaparte's knowledge of men, is that Pétion and Rigaud knew that they would be deported to Madagascar if there was no resistance. Yet so strong is the pull of authority that they were prepared to accept even this grudging recognition.[3] The apparently impudent assumptions of Bonaparte were really sound policy. That calm confidence in its capacity to deceive is a mark of the mature ruling class. This accounts for its wild fury when it runs up against the type which never pays any attention to its most solemn protestations. Bonaparte was wise in singling out Toussaint, Dessalines, and Moïse. But for the first two the whole plan would have succeeded.

---

[2] Sannon, *Histoire de Toussaint-L'Ouverture*, Vol. III, p. 48. This is not in the instructions.
[3] Sannon, *Histoire de Toussaint-L'Ouverture*, Vol. III, p. 48.

On February 2nd Leclerc appeared off the harbour
of Le Cap with 5,000 of his 12,000 men, and instructed
Christophe, commanding the troops in the town, to prepare quarters for his men. Christophe, poor fool, had had
everything ready to receive them, and but for a quarrel between Leclerc and Villaret-Joyeuse and an adverse wind
Leclerc would have had Le Cap intact. But Toussaint,
riding hard from Samana, arrived just in time to stop Christophe. He did not show himself, but allowed Christophe
to carry on negotiations, hiding in a room nearby and
making Christophe speak loudly so that he could hear his
refusal.[4]

On his way to Christophe, Leclerc's envoy as if by
accident let slip some proclamations by Bonaparte calling
on the population to rally round Leclerc, protector of their
liberties, restorer of peace, etc. It was all that the petty-
bourgeois needed. The Municipality and the civil functionaries, Mulattoes and free blacks, always jealous of
Toussaint's illiterate black generals and their low origin,
and resenting Toussaint's despotism, gave demonstrations
of joy and satisfaction. Stupid as only the petty-bourgeois
functionary can be, they implored Christophe to welcome
the French expedition.[5] César Télémaque, Mayor of Le
Cap, old free black and a notably able administrator, led
this folly, gave an official reading of the proclamation, and
pestered Christophe to submit. To add force to the protestations of himself and his friends, he brought a deputation of old men, women and children to Christophe. Whites,
and all the formerly free were radiant, but the officers of
the army, black and Mulatto, were grimly hostile, and
would not speak to the French. Under the watchful eye of
his chief, Christophe remained firm and replied to Leclerc's
threats with counter-threats. Next day, the 4th, Christophe
summoned the garrison, who took the oath to be faithful
to death. They learned that Fort Liberté had been taken

[4] Lacroix, *Mémoires pour Servir* . . . , Vol. II, pp. 69-88.
[5] Lacroix. *Mémoires pour Servir* . . . Lacroix took part in the
negotiations.

by the French. It was war, and Christophe called on the inhabitants to evacuate the town. Men, women and children started the painful journey up into the hills that began almost where the city ended. A few inhabitants remained near César Télémaque at the Municipality, hoping in spite of themselves for some intervention against this last and final misery. All had their eyes fixed on the sea. At last as evening fell a boat detached itself from the squadron, and taking advantage of the growing darkness, moved toward the harbour. Immediately Christophe's scouts on guard gave the dreaded signal by the discharge of cannon, and and at the sound the soldiers, torches in hand, ran through the city. Soon everything was burning. Suddenly with a terrific shock the powder-magazine exploded. Rocks loosened by the explosion came rolling down, crushing women and children hiding in the hills. By Toussaint's orders all in the city, whites and Télémaque and his friends, were compelled to follow the troops. They came unwillingly, bitterly regretting that Leclerc had not been welcomed.

Christophe and his soldiers, guarding the population, retired to the mountains. All night the fire raged, destroying property to the value of 100 million francs. Leclerc's envoys had told him how flourishing the city was, but when he landed the next day he was welcomed by cinders and ashes: of 2,000 houses only 59 remained. It was an indication to the bitterly disappointed Frenchman of the days that were to come, the beginning of a devastation which threw San Domingo back half a century.

But even then Toussaint still hesitated. On his way from Le Cap to Gonaïves he met a French detachment. Stopping to parley he was greeted with bullets and nearly lost his life. His horse was wounded, the hat of one of his officers was carried away by a bullet, and Christophe had to throw himself from his horse and swim across a river to escape capture or death.

War is a continuation of politics by other means, and Toussaint was now reaping the reward of his policy during the previous year. The labourers, hostile to the

French, did not respond to his call. They could not understand why Toussaint should call on them to fight these whites, when all his policy had been towards conciliation of them.[6] It was easy for Toussaint's enemies to represent him as a tyrant, consorting with émigrés and priests—everyone could see him doing this—seeking to hand the colony over to the British for the triumph of his own ambition. Mulattoes and former free blacks were openly for the French. San Domingo was a French colony. Why should they burn down their property for Toussaint's ambition?

The army did not know where it stood. Christophe had nearly let Leclerc in, and now wavering among the commanding officers came to the help of Leclerc and further confused both rank-and-file and masses. Port-Républicain, the capital, was under the command of Agé. Boudet with 3,500 men called on Agé to surrender the town. At a conference of the officers, the white officer in charge of the powder magazine refused to hand over the keys. Lamartinière drew his pistol and shot him dead at the conference table. Another bullet for Agé would have saved an infinite amount of trouble. But before such a demonstration of loyalty and the temper of others of his subordinates Agé temporised. To Boudet's summons he replied that he could do nothing except by the orders of Dessalines, his superior officer, who was at St Marc. What sort of resistance was this? Thus encouraged, Boudet landed his troops and

[6] ". . . he (Toussaint) was favourable to white colonists, especially to those who occupied new possessions; and the care and partiality which he felt for them went so far that he was severely censured as being more attached to them than to his own people. This negro wail was not without reason; for some months previous to the arrival of the French he put to death his own nephew, General Moïse, for having disregarded his orders relative to the protection of the colonists. This act of the Governor, and the great confidence which he had in the French Government, were the chief causes of the weak resistance which the French met with in Hayti." This is an extract from a manifesto published by Christophe in 1814 when Haiti was again threatened. (Reprinted in Beard, *Life of Toussaint L'Ouverture*, London, 1853, p. 326.) Toussaint did not trust the French Government as Christophe says. He would not have armed to the extent and in the manner he did if he had. But he allowed the people to think that he trusted the French.

marched boldly towards the town. Another officer, follower
of Rigaud, delivered an important fort to the advance-
guard. There was some brave fighting at the last moment,
but with such confusion and disloyalty in the command
the garrison could not hold the town. Trying in vain to set
it on fire as they left, Lamartinière and his men retreated.
Not only was the capital gone, with little loss, and all its
supplies intact, but the French captured the treasury with
two and a half million francs.[7]

The next night came an offer of submission from
Laplume, the Negro general commanding in the South.
Officers and men, as they had been accustomed to do in
the political tangles of the revolution, followed their commanders, who in most cases had built their corps themselves. Even at Santo Domingo, where Paul L'Ouverture
was in command, the French had another easy success.
Kerverseau, hitherto in Toussaint's service, had joined Leclerc, and had been put in command of a French detachment. He marched on Santo Domingo and demanded
submission. L'Ouverture refused. A group of French and
Spanish inhabitants attempted to let the French into the
city, but Paul L'Ouverture dispersed them. Yet even Toussaint's own brother, while refusing to admit Kerverseau,
wrote to the Governor asking for orders. Where Toussaint's
own brother was so uncertain, what could the masses do?
Only then did Toussaint write commanding him to defend
to the last and "even to the extent of capturing Kerverseau
and his troops"—a miserable and tell-tale indication of
vacillation. Afraid that his messengers might be captured,
Toussaint gave his couriers another letter counselling Paul
to conciliation. This letter the officers (two blacks and a
white) in case of arrest were to present to their captors,
hiding the genuine instructions. The officers were killed,
and both letters were found on them. Kerverseau sent the
false letter to Paul, who opened the gates and let Kerverseau in. Mauviel, the Bishop of San Domingo, had long
been working on Clairveaux, second in rank of Toussaint's

[7] The commander of Boudet's advance-guard was Pamphile de
Lacroix.

officers. Clairveaux in a few days would yield to Mauviel
and surrender to the French. It was treason, but it was
an easy treason after he had heard that Toussaint's own
brother, his subordinate, had let Kerverseau in, apparently
on Toussaint's instructions. The French welcomed Toussaint's officers and men and treated them as comrades. The
masses looked on, confused, bewildered, not knowing what
to do. Fortunately for these misguided chiefs, Toussaint,
Dessalines, and Maurepas paid no attention to Leclerc's
proclamations. It was this that saved the traitors, for Bonaparte's instructions were explicit, and but for the resistance
of the so-called enemies of France the epaulettes would
have been torn from the shoulders of these stupidly trust-
ful blacks.

On February 10th Maurepas, holding Port-de-Paix,
the strongest position on the North coast, was attacked by
1,500 troops under Debelle and menaced by the guns of
the fleet. Refusing to capitulate he retired from the town
and took up his position in the mountains. But Rochambeau took Fort Dauphin, and thus except for St Marc under
Dessalines nearly the whole littoral was in the hands of
Leclerc.

Toussaint on February 8th did not yet know the full
extent of his reverses, but as the blows fell upon him he
braced himself not for surrender but for resistance. The
dream of orderly government and progress to civilisation
was over. He had held on to the last shred of hope for
peace, but as he saw the enemy closing in, then and then
only did he prepare to fight. Grievous had been his error,
but as soon as he decided to look the destruction of San
Domingo fairly in the face, he rose to the peril, and this,
his last campaign, was his greatest. He outlined his plan to
Dessalines. "Do not forget, while waiting for the rainy
season which will rid us of our foes, that we have no other
resource than destruction and fire. Bear in mind that the
soil bathed with our sweat must not furnish our enemies
with the smallest sustenance. Tear up the roads with shot;
throw corpses and horses into all the fountains, burn and
annihilate everything in order that those who have come

to reduce us to slavery may have before their eyes the image of that hell which they deserve." It was too late. Events were to show that if he had but mobilised the masses before and purged his army, the French attack would have been crippled at the start. His desire to avoid destruction was the very thing that caused it. It is the recurring error of moderates when face to face with a revolutionary struggle.

Dessalines never got the letter. But the superb soldier and revolutionary leader was a man far different from Christophe and the rest. He needed neither instructions nor exhortation to take appropriate action. When he heard that Port-Républicain was taken, he paled through his black skin, turned fiercely to curse those around him and bellowed with wrath. Such a thing should never have happened, and it was all Toussaint's fault.

The French had the initiative, and Dessalines did not wait to be attacked. Marching south to meet them, he made contact with Lamartinière at La Croix-des-Bouquets. Feinting as if to retreat into the Cahos Mountains, he sent the French on a false scent and speeded to Léogane, a town rich in resources and the port of a fertile and flourishing plain. Boudet sent a division after him, but Dessalines got to Léogane first, burnt it to the ground and devastated the plain. He was now in a critical position. He could go no further into the South. Laplume threatened him there. Boudet's pursuing division and Boudet himself at Port-Républicain barred his retreat. And 900 men landed at Arcahaye put that seaport town in the hands of the French. Only the uncharted mountains offered an escape. High over frightful precipices and unknown paths Dessalines led his men. The waiting French never saw him, and after a series of forced marches he got back to St Marc, re-organised his forces and then marched south again to meet the French and check them in their advance on his headquarters. Boudet was attacking by sea and land. Making use of every difficulty of the difficult road, Dessalines made

Boudet fight every inch of the way, and the French advance had continually to be cleared by artillery. In the final engagement Dessalines was defeated; but after such a harassing march and murderous combat, that Boudet's men lay exhausted and could not follow the retreating army. Taking his time, Dessalines retired to St Marc. On the parade ground he had kept a huge fire burning for two days, and he had filled the town and his own recently completed palace with inflammable material. Lighting a torch, with his own hand he applied it to his house, while his soldiers followed his example throughout the town. Boudet, like Leclerc, marched into ruins. But weary and dispirited as were the French, they were to have no peace. For Dessalines, judging that the garrison at Port-Républicain would be depleted, now set off south again at top speed, intending to surprise the town, take it by assault, and burn it to the ground. As he ranged from one part of the island to another, wearing out these inhuman persecutors of his people, this old slave, with the marks of the whip below his general's uniform, was fast coming to the conclusion at which Toussaint still boggled. He would declare the island independent and finish with France. The old slave-owners were everywhere grinning with joy at the French expedition; he would finish with everything white for ever.

Men, women and children, indeed all the whites who came into his hands, he massacred. And forbidding burial, he left stacks of corpses rotting in the sun to strike terror into the French detachments as they toiled behind his flying columns.

Leclerc now tried to get hold of Toussaint by using his own sons to decoy him. It had been a plot carefully laid by Bonaparte in Paris as far back as the previous October. Bonaparte would not send the boys back, and Toussaint's enemies did not scruple to try turning their minds against him.[8] But when the time came for the expedition,

[8] Toussaint's letter to them, 22 Prairial, An VII, *Les Archives Nationales*. F. III. 210.

Bonaparte sent for them and their tutor, the Abbé Coisnon. He spoke kindly to them, gave them presents, told them what a great man their father was, how well he had served France, assured them that the expedition was merely to strengthen San Domingo against its enemies, told them that he would send them on in advance to tell their father all this, and asked their tutor to undertake the journey with them: his priestly vocation would help. He had high officials entertain them to dinner. By some chance the boys were not sent on in advance, but they and their tutor sailed with Leclerc. Bonaparte had given Leclerc a long rigmarole of a letter (signed with his own hand at last) guaranteeing liberty to the blacks, and asking Toussaint to assist Leclerc in the government of the country (presumably for the week or so before he was shipped off to France), all with an undercurrent of threats against him if he resisted. This Leclerc now despatched to Toussaint by the boys and the priest, hoping that the defeats and defections would have cowed Toussaint and that fatherly affection would do the rest. All along the road the crowds, glad to see the General's children back from Paris, came out to welcome them, shouted greetings, embraced them while they told of their messages of goodwill. Unknown to themselves, they were breaking down the spirit of resistance of the people. Toussaint was away, but late on the evening of the next day he came hurrying in. The boys threw themselves into his arms while tears streamed down the cheeks of the stern old soldier. Coisnon had hitherto kept himself carefully in the background, but (it is his own account) judging the moment ripe, he stepped forward with a solemn reminder of duty to France and produced the letter.

The whole elaborate deception was a miserable failure. Toussaint—how well he knew these men—did not even bother to read the whole of the letter. He looked at half of it and was about to speak when Coisnon began a long eulogy of Bonaparte, his kindly reception of the boys, the peaceful nature of the expedition, etc. Dessalines would in all probability have shot Coisnon out of hand and taken his sons. But Toussaint was a different type. To Coisnon he made a dignified response. Bonaparte's words announced peace, Leclerc's actions declared war: "In the midst of so many disasters and acts of violence I must not forget that I wear a sword." If Leclerc desired peace, let him stop the march of his army.

They talked far into the night, and Toussaint could not contain his indignation as he understood that his sons were being offered to him as the price of his surrender. Yet that night, with the tears again flowing, he told the priest that while he was prepared to sacrifice his life for the freedom of the blacks, he would send the boys back lest Leclerc should think he was keeping them by coercion or undue influence. Two days later the letter for Leclerc was ready, and he sent it back with the boys, proposing a suspension of hostilities. Leclerc sent Isaac and Placide back again, promising that if Toussaint only came to discuss with him all would be well. He would appoint Toussaint his first lieutenant. If not, after four days he would declare Toussaint an outlaw. What he really wanted was to get Toussaint into his hands.

Isaac and Placide entreated Toussaint to see Leclerc. He refused. What were Rigaud, Pétion, Villate, Chanlatte, his personal enemies, doing in the French Army? If, now that the blacks had some power, the French treated them in that way, how would they treat them when they were powerless?

But moved by the entreaties of the boys and their obvious love for France, he told them he would not attempt to influence them. France or San Domingo. "My children, make your choice; whatever it is I shall always love you." His own son Isaac declared for France, but Placide threw himself on his father, sobbing that he feared the future, feared slavery, and would fight with him. At once Toussaint gave him command of a battalion of his guards, which he led into battle a few days later. Madame L'Ouverture, with a woman's instinctive sense of immediate reality, would not give up Isaac and made him stay.[9]

Luckily for this narrative, we have the complete series

[9] Lacroix, *Mémoires pour Servir* . . . Vol. II, pp. 119-126.

of letters written by Leclerc from San Domingo to Bonaparte, the First Consul, and the Minister of Marine. For
the student of any period of history, but particularly of
imperialism, they are documents of priceless value:

*"I have great need of the reinforcements. You
must see how difficult it is . . . I have already 600
sick, the majority of my troops having embarked five
months ago. Cultivation is in good condition.*

*"Above all count on my devotion. Many of those
who envied my command in Paris would be wiped
out here. I shall prove to France that you have made
a good choice."* [10]

*"Three months before our arrival . . . Moïse had
sought to supplant Toussaint and to do this, he had
begun the massacre of 600 to 700 whites. Toussaint
had him shot and has rid us of him. . . ."* [11]

*"Toussaint has sent to make me proposals for the
suspension of hostilities. I believe not a word of it. He
is the most false and deceitful man in the world. . . .*[12]

*"I have already more than 1,200 men in hospital.
Calculate on a considerable waste of life in this country. . . .*

*"I am here without food or money. The burning
of Le Cap and the districts through which the rebels
have retired deprives me of all resources of this kind.
It is necessary that the Government send me provisions, money, troops. That is the only means of en-
suring the preservation of San Domingo. I have here
no resources in commerce; the traders at Le Cap are*

[10] Leclerc to the First Consul. February 9th, 1802. The letters
are transcribed from the Archives of the Minister for War, by
General Nemours. See *Histoire Militaire de la Guerre d'Indé-
pendence . . .* , Vol. II, pp. 53-120.
[11] February 15th, 1802, to the Minister of Marine.
[12] "O Wad some power . . ."

*only the agents of the Americans and the Americans
are of all Jews the most Jewish . . ."* [13]

Leclerc had been merely playing with Toussaint.
When his reinforcements arrived he issued a proclamation
putting Toussaint and Christophe outside the law, and prepared to overwhelm them in the plain of Gonaïves. Desfourneaux would leave the River Salée and passing by way
of Limbé and Plaisance arrive at Gonaïves. Hardy would
leave Le Cap and by way of Marmelade and Ennery
descend on Gonaïves. Rochambeau would leave Fort
Dauphin and by way of St Raphael arrive at Gonaïves.
Humbert and Debelle would defeat Maurepas and drive
him back on Gonaïves, while Boudet coming up from Port-
Républicain would cut off the retreat and stab Toussaint's
forces in the back.

Toussaint, with half his 18,000 troops in the ranks of
the enemy, could only delay and harass the advance, devastate the country and deprive Leclerc of supplies, while
retiring slowly to the mountains. He was too good a soldier
to attempt to defend every possible point where Leclerc
might land, and had secreted his munitions and stores in
strategic places, whence they could feed as many lines of
retreat as possible. He would raid Leclerc's outposts, make
surprise attacks, lay ambushes, give the French no peace,
while avoiding major engagements. With the coming of
the rains, the French, worn out, would fall victims in thousands to the fever, and the blacks would descend and drive
them into the sea. But first he had to extricate himself from
the steel ring that Leclerc was drawing round him.

It is necessary to describe this campaign in some detail. The political manœuvres were based on the progress
of the war, and the war was the supreme test of the people
of San Domingo. Bonaparte's army did not fall from the
sky, nor were his soldiers entirely the product of his own
unparalleled genius for military command. They were in
the last analysis the result, one of the finest results, of the
revolutionary change in French society. Their irresistible

[13] February 15th, 1802. To the Minister of Marine.

élan, their intelligence, their endurance and morale, sprang from the new social freedom that followed the destruction of feudalism; their consciousness that they, the people, had done it, their faith in themselves as the bearers of liberty and equality all over Europe. None of the French rank-and-file in San Domingo guessed that they were fighting to restore slavery. The war was for them a revolutionary war.

But Toussaint's soldiers and generals, illiterates and ex-slaves, had been moulded by the same revolution. An army is a miniature of the society which produces it. If the black army had wobbled before the French, it was because San Domingo society as a whole did not know what to think of Leclerc's expedition, could not believe its vile purpose. But the few thousand who remained faithful to Toussaint were the advance-guard of the revolutionary army fighting a revolutionary war. They were for the moment outnumbered. If Toussaint had the help of some of the labourers, thousands of Mulattoes and the former free were joining Leclerc. But the liberty and equality which these blacks acclaimed as they went into battle meant far more to them than the same words in the mouths of the French. And in a revolutionary struggle these things are worth many regiments.

Hardy, coming from Le Cap, met Christophe at Bois-Pin on February 19th. Hardy drove Christophe from his position, but here the French received the first shock. Christophe, defeated, retired in good order and took up position at Ennery. On February 21st, Hardy attacked with the Napoleonic vigour that had swept and would sweep everything in Europe before it, until the army was mortally stricken in the Moscow campaign. Once again Christophe was dislodged. But still holding his men together, he took up position again at Bayonnais. The next day Hardy drove him back, but as signally failed to disrupt his forces. Still covering the town of Gonaïves, Christophe now took up position at La Coupe-à-Pintades, ready to meet the French the next day, the 23rd.

Toussaint was at Gonaïves. He did not approve of all this fighting. He preferred guerrilla warfare and the raising of the population, but those who remained faithful to him were eager to cross swords with Bonaparte's soldiers,[14] and Toussaint had to follow. Plaisance was treacherously surrendered to Rochambeau, and Toussaint, with 600 men and a few hundred auxiliaries, hastened to bar Rochambeau's way at Ravine-à-Couleuvres. It was a moment of great personal anxiety. His wife and family hiding in a retreat in the mountains had had to leave it, and Toussaint did not know where they were. But he prepared for battle with his usual disregard of his personal fate. Accompanied only by an aide and two labourers he reconnoitred with such daring that one of his guides who pushed on too far was captured by an outpost and immediately killed. Toussaint, going back, addressed his army: "You are going to fight against men who have neither faith, law nor religion. They promise you liberty, they intend your servitude. Why have so many ships traversed the ocean, if not to throw you again into chains? They disdain to recognise in you submissive children, and if you are not their slaves you are rebels. The mother-country, misled by the Consul, is no longer anything for you but a stepmother. . . . Uncover your breasts, you will see them branded by the iron of slavery. During ten years, what have you not undertaken for liberty? Your masters slain or put to flight; the English humiliated by defeat; discord extinguished, a land of slavery purified by fire and evolving more beautiful than ever under liberty; these are your labours and these the fruits of your labours. And the foe wishes to snatch both out of your hands. . . ."

He who had fought so hard to build spoke with fierce pride of the destruction which met the French on every side. The French would meet their fate. "Their bones will be scattered among these mountains and rocks and tossed

[14] Lacroix, *Mémoires pour Servir* . . . Vol. II, p. 228.

about by the waves of the sea. Never more will they be-
hold their native land . . . and liberty will reign over
their tomb." But never a word of independence.

Rochambeau, full of racial pride, thought it best to
recall to his men their victories on the Tiber, the Nile, and
the Rhine. They had not come thousands of miles to be
defeated by slaves.

At daybreak the battle began. It was the fiercest
battle of the war. Over and over again Toussaint charged
at the head of his men. During the day he learned that his
wife and family were hiding not far from the battle. "See
that they take the road to Esther," he told his informant.
"I have my duty to perform." Men threw away their arms
and grappled for life and death. At last, late in the afternoon, Toussaint put himself at the head of his grenadiers,
with a final attack drove Rochambeau over the river, and
then returned to his side of the stream. Both sides claimed
the victory, and have continued to do so to this day.[15]

Christophe had on the same day been driven back by
Hardy from La Coupe-à-Pintades and Hardy with Leclerc
marched into the town of Gonaïves. The other appointees
to the rendezvous were absent. Neither Humbert from
the North nor Boudet from the South had arrived to complete the encircling movement. Their failure was due to
events which are of the first importance, actual and symp-
tomatic.

Humbert with 1,500 men left Port-de-Paix and attacked Maurepas with 2,000 men and an auxiliary corps
of labourers, intending to roll him down into the plain of
Gonaïves. But Maurepas beat off his attack and pursued
him into the town so hotly that he would have had to em-

[15] General Nemours, a Haitian, a great admirer of Toussaint,
and one who has made a careful study of this campaign, con-
tradicts traditional Haitian history. He describes this battle as
a defeat for Toussaint. But he bases his conclusions on, among
other points, the supposed treachery of Maurepas. In Volume II
of his work, however, he disproves the treachery of Maurepas,
on evidence acquired after he had published Volume I. The result of the battle must for the time being remain undecided. See
Nemours, *Histoire Militaire* . . . , Vol. I, pp. 210-211 and Vol.
II, pp. 250-252.

bark but for a timely reinforcement sent from a warship in the harbour. On learning this, Leclerc ordered Debelle from Le Cap with another 1,500 men to join Hardy, dislodge Maurepas and drive him toward Gonaïves. Both of them now attacked. Maurepas beat the two of them and once more chased them into the town, which, but for the fleet, would again have fallen into his hands. Leclerc could no longer deal with Christophe and Toussaint. He had to send Hardy and Desfourneaux to the rescue of Humbert and Debelle. Equally disastrous to Leclerc's plans had been the work of Dessalines in the South. His bold conception of a return march on Port-Républicain and the speed with which he executed it were too much for the French. Luck, and astonishing luck, alone saved them, as Lacroix, in command at Port-Républicain, has himself admitted.[16] In the West Province were two bands of maroons, one of them led by Lamour Derance, a name destined to become famous in this war of independence. Black though they were, they had been partisans of Rigaud, and still more hated Dessalines, because as commander of the district he had half destroyed their forces for raiding and for practising Voodoo, strictly forbidden by Toussaint. They from their mountain fastnesses now saw Dessalines approaching, and guessed his aim. They hastened to warn the French at Port-Républicain and offer their submission and alliance. French and creoles were alike astonished. Lacroix accepted gladly, an ambush was laid, and Dessalines' advance guard of 1,000 men was destroyed at a stroke. Dessalines' plan of surprise was ruined but he nevertheless marched on the city. Feeling his way by a preliminary skirmish, he found it well prepared, and therefore decided to retire. Boudet had followed him from St Marc, but uncertain as to what this demoniacal black general would do next and utterly exhausted, he stayed at Port-Républicain, while Dessalines and Lamartinière set off northwards to make contact with Toussaint.

Leclerc's first attempt had failed completely. Tous-

[16] *Mémoires pour Servir . . .* , Vol. II, p. 143. "I was miraculously saved by good fortune."

saint, Christophe, and Dessalines had their forces intact, held the internal lines of communication, and were in touch with each other. It is this first phase of the campaign which revealed the strength and skill of the local army. Of Toussaint's generals only two carried out an immediate and uncompromising resistance to the French. They were Maurepas and Dessalines. Both their campaigns were brilliantly successful. Had he dismissed Agé, put Lamartinière in charge at Port-Républicain with orders to get rid of traitors, primed his brother Paul for resistance, placed Belair and others whom he could trust in key positions, and had Moïse to raise the labourers on the North plain as in the old days, the French would never have been able to capture all the coast towns, and would have been in immense difficulty to hold those they might take. Equally important is the fact that, as Leclerc himself early recognised, victories on one side or the other would draw the waverers. Under a strong impulse from the black army and the black labourers the defection of men like Laplume and Clairveaux was unlikely. Between the alien Leclerc on the one hand, and the masses and the bulk of the army united under Toussaint on the other, they would probably have remained. In every revolution there are many who hesitate and though decisive action may not be immediately effective, vacillation is certain to lose them all.

Yet, denuded as it was, the remains of the army had done its work in the first shock. The rainy season would soon be coming, Leclerc had to get the black generals in his power, and that seemed as far off as ever. But here another stroke of luck befell him. Maurepas, victorious over Debelle and Humbert, understood that Leclerc would now send more detachments to overwhelm him, and he prepared to evacuate his position and make contact with Toussaint and Christophe. In addition to Maurepas' known education and character, he had under him the crack regiment of San Domingo, the Ninth Brigade, of which all San Domingo boasted that it never surrendered.

But Desfourneaux had lived and fought under Toussaint in San Domingo, with the black soldiers. And while Leclerc's armies were attacking, Desfourneaux was writing letters like these: "You know me, Commandant André, and you know that no one has worked harder for your liberty than I. You were a captain under me five years ago, and you have always conducted yourself well. The Commander-in-Chief instructs me to tell you that you will be maintained in your command if you decide to come to me and join us in restoring order and tranquillity in your country. If you agree, send me someone to fix things at once. I have never broken my word. You can count on me." [17] Desfourneaux asked another of Toussaint's officers to denounce the abominable slanders that the rebels were spreading about the intentions of the Government. "You know me, I would not serve in this army if its operation had any other aim than to consolidate your liberty and safeguard your persons and your property." [18] Was Desfourneaux sincere? The question is irrelevant. It was Leclerc's decisions that mattered, and even if Desfourneaux were sincere, when Leclerc unmasked himself Desfourneaux was not going to join the men he had deceived. But such appeals were powerful. If the French had come merely to restore French authority, what was the use of this war? Toussaint even then had not declared independence, and had never made any clear governmental pronouncement about Leclerc's intention to restore slavery. Their correspondence proves that some of these officers revolted at the relentless command to burn and ravage the country yet once more. Guibert, holding the key position of Gros-Morne, surrendered, and then, one by one, as each realised the difficulties previous defections put him in, a line of commandants submitted to the French. They were welcomed and confirmed in their commands. Thus Maurepas found himself cut off. He cursed his treacherous subordinates, told them that they wanted to become slaves again. If they wanted to go, said Maurepas, they could at least have told him, so that he

could withdraw his own forces in time. Obviously these
officers did not want to be slaves again and the struggle
still seemed a question of taking which side you wanted.

Maurepas could now stay and be annihilated, or join
the French and retain his command. He surrendered. Leclerc welcomed him warmly, as well he might. The masses
in the North were moving, but the surrender of Maurepas
"stopped the growth and the development of the new
movement of insurrection that Boyer . . . and Rear-Ad-
miral Magon could scarcely restrain with the soldiers of
the artillery and of the fleet with which they were reinforced." [19] The vacillation of the leaders was killing the
revolutionary ardour of the people at every turn. "It was
to the moral effect produced by the surrender of Maurepas," continues Lacroix, "that the Captain-General Leclerc
owed the possibility of pursuing the revolt of Toussaint
L'Ouverture to its last hiding-place." Worse still, to prove
his loyalty, Maurepas was set to clear the country of "the
brigands," in other words the revolting masses. That was
now his duty; Leclerc carefully surrounded him with white
troops, and Maurepas had no choice. To weaken him, Leclerc distributed numbers of his men in other regiments.
So that the masses saw themselves hunted down and
rounded up by white troops aided by the men whom they
had hitherto looked upon as their staunchest defenders.

Morally and materially strengthened, Leclerc now
began another movement which should converge on Toussaint, Christophe and Dessalines at Verrettes, instead of
Gonaïves. Maurepas, instead of a victorious enemy, was
an ally, and Boudet, refreshed, was on the way from Port-
Républicain. Leclerc was becoming anxious.

> "I am master of the North but almost all of it has
> been burnt and I can expect no resources from it.
> There are labourers assembled and armed in twenty
> spots.

[19] Lacroix, *Mémoires pour Servir* . . . , Vol. II, p. 48.

*"The rebels are still masters of a part of the West
and they have burnt the positions they no longer hold:
for the present I can expect no supplies from
there . . .*

*"The Government must not think of the money
it is spending to ensure the finest colony in the world
and preserve those it possesses in the Antilles, for it
is here at this moment that is being decided the question of knowing whether Europe will preserve any
colonies in the Antilles."* [20]

Near to Petite-Rivière in the interior is the fortress of
Crête-à-Pierrot, commanding the entrance to the mountainous Cahos regions where Toussaint was reserving his forces
for the moment. It is not of great natural strength, being
on ground rising to no more than a height of 300 feet, but
it was strongly fortified. In the confusion which followed
the early successes of the French, the blacks had abandoned
it, and Dessalines with Lamartinière marching North from
Port-Républicain was about to raze it to the ground when
Toussaint stopped him. Toussaint had shaken off Rochambeau after the battle of Ravine-à-Couleuvres. He threw
out a light curtain of troops in front of Rochambeau, the
French general followed them, and they led him in a great
circle over the Grand Cahos mountains, to disappear altogether after days of pursuit. Toussaint meanwhile drew off
his main forces and arrived just in time to meet Dessalines
and place a new plan before his generals. Burning with
fever, outnumbered and surrounded, he was about to attempt the most audacious stroke of the war, a new offensive, and therefore wanted Crête-à-Pierrot held. He entrusted it to Dessalines. The men with him now could be
depended on never to submit to the French, and were following him partly out of political conviction, partly out of
personal loyalty. There were Mulattoes and blacks among
them, but he spoke to them all as his children. "Yes, you
are all my children—from Lamartinière who is white as

[20] February 27th, 1802. To the Minister of Marine.

white, but who knows that he has Negro blood in his veins, to Monpoint, whose skin is the same as mine. I entrust to you this post." They replied that he could rely on them living or dead, and at the head of a few hundred soldiers Toussaint set out for the North. He would get through Leclerc's advancing forces, raise and organise the labourers, and by threatening or cutting the long French line of communications with Le Cap, make Leclerc alter his plans or throw his forces into confusion. Twelve years later Napoleon, in the greatest of all his campaigns, the campaign of 1814, would attempt the identical manœuvre in face of the allies swarming on Paris.

Dessalines undertook the defence. He threw up a redoubt at some distance from Crête-à-Pierrot, left detachments to man them both, and went to meet Debelle who was coming south toward Verrettes to make contact with Boudet. Dessalines would not give battle but retired toward Crête-à-Pierrot, keeping his forces just ahead of the hotly pursuing Debelle. As he reached the ditch which surrounded the fortress Dessalines jumped into it and all his men followed, leaving the French exposed. A withering fire from the fortress mowed them down. Four hundred fell and two generals were wounded. Hastily retreating, they took up position outside the fortress and sent to Leclerc for reinforcements. Dessalines entered the fortress and completed the preparations for the defence. But already his untutored mind had leapt forward to the only solution, and, unlike Toussaint, he was taking his men into his confidence. As they prepared the defence he talked to them.

"Take courage, I tell you, take courage. The French will not be able to remain long in San Domingo. They will do well at first, but soon they will fall ill and die like flies. Listen! If Dessalines surrenders to them a hundred times he will deceive them a hundred times. I repeat, take courage, and you will see that when the French are few we shall harass them, we shall beat them, we shall burn the harvests and retire to the mountains. They will not be able

to guard the country and they will have to leave. Then I
shall make you *independent*. There will be no more whites
among us." [21] Independence. It was the first time that a
leader had put it before his men. Here was not only a programme, but tactics. The lying and treacherous Bonaparte
and Leclerc had met their match at last.

While Dessalines remained in Crête-à-Pierrot, Lamartinière took command of the redoubt. His wife, Marie-
Jeanne, had joined him and took her share in the defence.
Dessalines, naked to the waist, with dirty boots, a hole in
his hat where a bullet had passed through, patrolled the
ramparts, glasses in hand. He had thrown small detachments of scouts right round the fortress, awaiting the approach of the French reinforcements. Getting the news
from Debelle, Leclerc knew that Crête-à-Pierrot had to be
taken as quickly as possible, and ordered a concentration
there of all his forces. Boudet arrived first. Dessalines, on
the ramparts, placed a barrel of powder next to where he
stood, and with a lighted torch in his hand invited those
of the garrison who wished to become slaves of the French
to leave. "We are going to be attacked. If the French put
their feet in here, I shall blow everything up." With one
voice the garrison replied, "We shall die for liberty." Boudet
sent a herald to the fortress, but Dessalines wanted no lying messages and shot him down, whereupon Boudet engaged one of the outposts. The blacks retreated before him
until they reached the ditch; then they jumped in, and a
terrific fire of artillery and musketry cut the French to
pieces. The French broke, Boudet was wounded, and Lacroix gave the command to retreat, leaving the ground
covered with dead and wounded. As these retired, Dugua,
Chief of Staff, accompanied by Leclerc, arrived with his
division, and led his troops at the fortress. They reached
the ditches, and the relentless fire from Dessalines' artillery
was too much for them. They wavered, and seeing them
waver, the garrison, uttering loud hurrahs, threw planks
across the ditch and, drums beating the attack, pursued the
retreating Frenchmen. These turned back and charged

[21] Sannon, *Histoire de Toussaint-L'Ouverture*, Vol. III, p. 121.

with the bayonet. The blacks appeared to fly before them. But it was only to jump into the ditches again, when the fire from the fortress decimated the French ranks. Dugua fell wounded in two places, Leclerc was slightly wounded, and the French that day lost nearly 800 men. Some days after came Rochambeau. Having lost Toussaint, he arrived with his forces fresh and ready for battle. He was warned of the two previous disasters, but having silenced the fire of Lamartinière's redoubt by an intensive bombardment, he attacked it, leading his division in person. He was beaten back, was himself wounded, and his division lost 300 men.

The French had thus lost 1,500 men outside Crête-à-Pierrot. Twelve thousand of them under Leclerc now encircled the 1,200 men in the fortress. Dessalines had left to raise the labourers on the countryside, but the garrison gave him their word not to surrender. Fired by the determination and courage of their leader the besieged ran up the red flag at the four corners of the fortress, intimating that they were neither giving nor taking quarter.

The black garrison, beating off assaults and hurling defiance at ten times its number, Toussaint, travelling swiftly northward to cut Leclerc's communications: Bonaparte's periods were in a tangle, and Leclerc was getting very, very anxious. It was now half-way through March, and the rainy season was almost there. Feverishly Leclerc set his men to fortify their positions. Pétion was in the besieging army with a corps of Mulattoes and former free, and it was Pétion who devised ways and means of investing the fortress by the use of local material. But their hard fighting and labours in this strange and unaccustomed climate wore down the French soldiers. This was not the way they had conquered in Italy, in Egypt, in the Pyrenees, and on the Rhine. Dessalines, raiding their lines from the neighbouring hills, kept them constantly on the alert. By subjecting them to this unceasing strain, they would fall easy victims to the fever in the rainy season.

And these blacks were bewildering enemies. They had the organisation and discipline of a trained army, and at the same time all the tricks and dodges of guerrillas. A black appeared among Boudet's soldiers, claiming to be a deserter. As Doudet in the midst of his guard questioned him, he seemed overwhelmed with fear. But he was a scout, and having learned all he wanted to know he made a dash for safety. Boudet, who saw his movement first, tried to stop him, but the black nearly bit off his thumb. Then, dashing beneath the legs of a horse, he overthrew the soldiers who tried to stop him, plunged into the river, and escaped amid a shower of bullets. He was struck, for on the opposite bank he collapsed, but a party of his own people carried him off.

Dessalines' relentless murders of all whites were having their effect. The French soldiers were retaliating, and Leclerc and his generals were shooting their prisoners, hundreds of blacks at a time—600 at one shooting. The black labourers, though not leaping to the attack, were hostile to the invading whites. They watched their movements from a distance, and fired at their flanks. If the French despatched a body of men to disperse them, they fled. As soon as these rejoined the main body, the labourers reappeared again.

"It was evident that we no longer inspired moral terror, and it is the greatest misfortune that can befall an army." [22] Lacroix could see the effect on the population of this indomitable challenge to the famous army of the First Consul.

The dishonest political position of the French Army was now taking its toll. The soldiers still thought of themselves as a revolutionary army. Yet at nights they heard the blacks in the fortress singing the *Marseillaise*, the *Ça Ira*, and the other revolutionary songs. Lacroix records how these misguided wretches as they heard the songs started and looked at the officers as if to say, "Have our barbarous enemies justice on their side? Are we no longer the soldiers

[22] Lacroix, *Mémoires pour Servir* . . . , Vol. II, pp. 161-162.

of Republican France? And have we become the crude instruments of policy?" [23]

A regiment of Poles, remembering their own struggle
for nationalism, refused to join in the massacre of 600
blacks, ordered by Leclerc, and later, when Dessalines was
reorganising the local army, he would call one of his regiments the Polish regiment.

Toussaint had no mercy on the local whites, but he
treated the French prisoners with courtesy and care, spoke
frequently to them, explained his stand. Later, as the army
went to pieces, some soldiers deserted to the blacks. All
that was needed was a highly political detachment of white
Jacobins fighting in the black ranks, and calling on Leclerc's
soldiers to come over.

But the garrison had neither doubts nor scruples. Being without water, they kept in their mouths balls of lead
in order to quench an insupportable thirst. Nobody complained. The officers asked the chief of ambulance for doses
of poison to prevent them falling alive into the hands of the
French, and the wounded asked their companions in case
of evacuation to kill them before they left.

The French, well supplied with artillery, began a
three days' bombardment, intending to beat the fortress
and the redoubt to dust, and their black and Mulatto
allies were a mighty support. Pétion's skill in artillery threw
cannon-ball after cannon-ball into the fortress. When his
men complained of always being put in the front, he
rebuked them. "Wretches," he said in a low voice as if
ashamed that the French should hear, "are you not honoured to be placed first? Be quiet and follow me." Lacroix
asked Bodin, "that valorous Negro," to hold a pontoon. "Do
not worry, General," was the reply. "They will take it when
I am dead." Nervous for another in a difficult position, Lacroix told him to be of good cheer. "Do not be worried,
General," replied Henin. "Ten years now I have cheerfully
made war for the Republic. Why should I not do it for a
quarter of an hour for friendship?"

It would have been difficult enough in any circum-

[23] *Ibid.*, p. 164.

stances to tear the epaulettes from the shoulders of these niggers, both majors, but it would be trebly so after the services they were rendering with such gallant, even debonair loyalty. Every day of war was piling up mountains in the way of Bonaparte's clear and precise instructions.

Toussaint had started with little over a thousand men, but as he went along he raised the labourers, and at the sight of him and the sound of his great voice they came. He appeared before Ennery and the garrison fled. Leclerc sent Hardy to follow him. Toussaint threw out his curtain of troops which led Hardy in the wrong direction, made him describe a circle, and at the end remain like ,Rochambeau with no troops to fight against. He commanded Christophe, who was in the mountainous districts of Petite-Rivière, to go to Grande-Rivière in the North and keep the road to Le Cap and the Spanish part of the island open. In Marmelade, Grande-Rivière, Dondon, Sans-Souci, Port-Français, his own Northern districts whose spirit he had so ruthlessly broken, the labourers were massing now. One of his adherents held the mountains of Limbé, another the mountains around Plaisance. Desfourneaux held Plaisance itself, guarding Leclerc's communications with Le Cap. If Toussaint took Plaisance he would join hands with Christophe and Maurepas, raise the whole of the North plain, capture Le Cap and then with his authority restored in the North, take Leclerc in the rear. He launched the first attack on the fort Bedourete, as usual leading the charge with sword drawn. While the battle raged, Desfourneaux from Plaisance sent reinforcements, and Toussaint himself went to meet these. To his amazement he saw advancing against him soldiers wearing the uniform of the Ninth Brigade, the crack corps under the command of Maurepas. He recognised at once what had happened. Riding out alone to within five or six paces of the regiment, he spoke to them. "Soldiers of the Ninth, will you dare to fire on your general, your fathers and your brothers?" The black soldiers fell on their knees before him and he would have won them back.

But the Europeans with them fired on Toussaint. His own soldiers rushed up to protect him. As that moment a young officer handed to Toussaint a letter from Dessalines and was immediately shot, dying in Toussaint's arms. The captain of Toussaint's dragoons was grievously wounded at his side, and holding the wounded man on his horse Toussaint galloped away.

Dessalines' letter told him that Crête-à-Pierrot and the redoubt were completely invested with such large forces that he could not relieve them. He abandoned the project of marching on Le Cap, and sent to tell Dessalines that he was returning to relieve the fortress.

But Dessalines could not wait. On March 24th, the third day of the bombardment, the French captured a black man and a black woman. The man said he was blind, only the whites of his eyes could be seen and he could scarcely walk, while the old black woman with him said that she was deaf. Suspecting them to be spies the French beat them mercilessly, but they only sobbed and wailed, said nothing and lay as if unable to move. Lacroix, on his rounds, took pity on them, and asked that they should be allowed to go about their business; but not until the French threatened to shoot them did they get up and walk. As soon as they were out of reach, they began to dance, and ran to the fortress to give Dessalines' order to evacuate.

At nightfall Lamartinière left the redoubt and joined the main force. There were only 800 of them now, but they were going to make the attempt to cut their way through. Magny was Lamartinière's superior officer, but in moments of crisis it is merit that counts, and by common consent Lamartinière took command. Between eight and nine in the evening the men of the garrison threw themselves on Lacroix' division. Strong fortifications and a fierce gunfire stopped them. Suddenly reversing their tactics, they retreated and attacked the division of Rochambeau. They broke through, Rochambeau fled into a neighbouring wood to save his life, and Lamartinière and Magny, with 700 men, rejoined Dessalines, having accomplished one of the most remarkable feats of arms of the period.

Toussaint reached the fortress just too late, and did not know that the evacuation had taken place. Reconnoitring, he detected a weakness in the disposition of Leclerc's forces, and he planned to raid that general's headquarters and arrest him with the whole of his staff. He was as daring and as tireless as ever, but his politics still lagged behind events. If he had captured Leclerc and his staff, he was going to send them back to France with an account of Leclerc's conduct, and ask the First Consul to send someone worthy of confidence to whom he might hand over the government. He seemed still to be hoping that if he defeated Leclerc, Bonaparte would see reason and the valuable connection with France be maintained. But the days for that were over. Dessalines had pronounced the word independence. Magny and Lamartinière and the garrison of Crête-à-Pierrot had defied not Leclerc but France. Toussaint was still thinking in terms of the decree of February 4th, 1794. The black revolution had passed him by.

The capture of Crête-à-Pierrot was a great victory for Leclerc, but a victory that had cost too much. The garrison had escaped with the loss of less than half its men, Leclerc had lost 2,000 dead, several of his officers were severely wounded (Dugua was to die), and he entered the fortress to find only the wounded, the cannon spiked, the war material and stores destroyed. Leclerc begged his officers to moderate the casualties in their reports, but even as it was Bonaparte was profoundly moved by the disastrous losses before Crête-à-Pierrot, and sent to say so.

Leclerc sent Rochambeau and Hardy northwards to maintain and strengthen his communications with Le Cap. He asked Lacroix to enter Port-Républicain in such a way as to efface the bad impression which had been created in the population by the repeated checks all over the country and the losses in front of Crête-à-Pierrot. Lacroix placed his men in two ranks instead of three, the sections marched at great distances from each other, and all the officers were mounted. He had artillery harnessed to animals sent to

meet him. He distributed these among his columns, and by
this careful window-dressing made the moral effect which
he intended in Port-Républicain——or at any rate thought
he did.

With the fall of Crête-à-Pierrot, Leclerc believed that
he no longer needed to keep on good terms with the Mulattoes. Anxious to carry out some at least of Bonaparte's
instructions, he had Rigaud and his family arrested and
sent back to France. Some trifling excuse was given as the
pretext, but this deceived no one. When Rigaud went on
board and an officer announced to him that he was a prisoner and demanded his sword, with a movement of indignation he threw it into the sea——an involuntary acknowl-
edgement of the colossal fool he had made of himself in
deserting Toussaint for Hédouville. On arriving in France
he would be imprisoned. Rigaud gone, the leader of the
Mulattoes was now Pétion. He, it seems, had heard nothing of Rigaud's deportation until he read the notice affixed
to the door of Lacroix' house in Port-Républicain. Then, it
seems, for the first time, Pétion understood what old Toussaint had understood so many years before. Madagascar
(or its French equivalent) was still a possibility. Pétion
was, like Toussaint, a noticeably quiet man, but on reading
the notice he said, loud enough to be heard by French officers, "It was well worth the trouble to make him come
here, and give him as well as us this disappointment." It
was the beginning of Mulatto wisdom.

Toussaint had only regret for the misguided Rigaud.
"It was against me that they brought that general here. It
is not for me that they are deporting him. I regret his fate."
Why did he not seek contact with Pétion and propose to
him a pact of independence? The arrest of Rigaud, their
leader, had startled all the Mulattoes. But Toussaint, even
while he was harrying Leclerc, was secretly seeking means
of coming to a compromise with him, a compromise that
Leclerc would soon be glad to accept.

But Leclerc now once more had hopes of easy victory.
On April 5th reinforcements of 2,500 men arrived at Le
Cap, and he changed his tactics. He would attack the

black leaders singly in their mountain fastnesses with some of the fresh troops and well-sandwiched detachments of Toussaint's old soldiers: if he could not destroy them at a stroke he would do it piece-meal. Hardy therefore attempted to drive Christophe from Dondon. But Christophe chased him back into Le Cap, taking revenge for the earlier defeats at Hardy's hands. Boyer attacked Sans-Souci, holding the fortress of Ste Suzanne and the districts around. The blacks in Boyer's force deserted, and Sans-Souci made prisoners of all the whites who were not killed. Clauzet attacked Marmelade. The blacks drove him off, making numerous prisoners.

To read English and French accounts of their operations in San Domingo one would believe that but for yellow fever they would have been easily victorious. But up to April there had been no yellow fever. Toussaint had lost more than half his forces even before the campaign began. Leclerc had raised thousands of black troops, and some of Toussaint's troops had fought with him. Yet in the eight weeks of February and March 17,000 French veterans had landed, 5,000 were in hospital, 5,000 were dead, and the first period was not yet complete. The "war to the death" and the hunting down of the black generals who would not present themselves to be deported was a total failure.

"The rainy season has arrived. My troops are exhausted with fatigue and sickness. . . . The districts of Grande-Rivière, Dondon, Marmelade are unpracticable in this rainy season. I could hold them only with a corps of 4,000 to 5,000 men. It would not be possible to feed them." [24]

"I have tried several times to make Toussaint and all the generals surrender. . . . But even though, Citizen Minister, I should succeed in making these men submit, I would not be able to adopt those rigorous measures which are needed to assure to France

[24] April 19th, 1802. To the Minister of Marine.

*the undisputed possession of San Domingo, until I
have 25,000 Europeans present under arms.*

*"I have pointed out to you, Citizen Minister, the
difficulties of my present position. You can easily
judge what would happen if war broke out with the
English. They would infect our coasts. They would
lose no opportunity to cut my communications by sea
and by attacking and blockading the Mole. They
would furnish assistance to the insurgents, who in
their turn would acquire a new preponderance and
who, from their present defensive, would seek to take
the offensive."* [25]

Leclerc was in a situation even worse than his letter
revealed. It was already late April, the rainy season was
beginning, and Toussaint was powerfully placed. In the
North, fired by Toussaint's audacious march, the blacks
were now swarming out and reinforcing the regular army
by guerrilla methods. They were attacking the French columns on all sides, without respite, disappearing suddenly,
only to reappear a few miles further on. They hung enormous stones over the roads and dropped them on to the
French passing below, rolled rocks down the precipices and
mountain sides to spread confusion among them. They dug
precipices in the roads and covered them with branches,
and the French horsemen fell into them. They blockaded
the paths with thorny bushes and trees. And while the
French struggled through these obstacles, from neighbouring trees, shrubs, and carefully chosen eminences, they
picked them off at leisure. Macaya at Limbé, Sylla in the
mountains of Plaisance, Sans-Souci at Ste Suzanne and
Vaillière, Dessalines at Marchand in the Artibonite, Charles
Belair at Calvaire and Plassac, not far from Crête-à-Pierrot,
holding the entry to the Grand Cahos mountains, all these
generals and partisans were absolutely devoted to Toussaint, inexpugnable from their positions and ready to fight
the French to the death.

The indefatigable Toussaint was not waiting on the

[25] April 21st, 1802. To the Minister of Marine.

British, and was at that moment preparing the very offensive which Leclerc dreaded. He planned to swoop down on the French at four points: Dessalines to take Marmelade, Belair to join him and both to attack Crête-à-Pierrot, Vernet, a Mulatto who had remained faithful, to take Gonaïves, and Toussaint himself to take Plaisance and Limbé. But Toussaint from the start looked on this war as a disaster. He wanted to come to terms with Leclerc, and now Leclerc, sadly fallen from his high hopes of the arrest and deportation of the black generals, was anxious to come to terms himself.

Instead of repudiating the French, seeking contact with the Mulattoes, some of whom had remained with his army, and calling on all to fight for freedom, the property of the whites and independence, Toussaint now wrote a reply to Bonaparte's letter and sent it to Boudet. He assured Bonaparte of his devotion and submission to his orders, and affected to believe that Leclerc had acted in opposition to Bonaparte's instructions. If Bonaparte would send another general to take command of the colony all would be well. If not, by his continued resistance Toussaint would only be assisting Leclerc in doing all the evil possible. By this offer he gave Bonaparte the opportunity to withdraw from a hopeless expedition with dignity and send someone else to negotiate with Toussaint for the new relation with France which Toussaint wanted. At the same time Toussaint by his new offensive on all points would strike terror into the hearts of Leclerc and the French, and force them to a truce. It was magnificent diplomacy but ruinous as a revolutionary policy. The slopes to treachery from the dizzy heights of revolutionary leadership are always so steep and slippery that leaders, however well-intentioned, can never build their fences too high.

Toussaint gave Christophe permission to negotiate with Leclerc, and was reading Leclerc's letters to Christophe and supervising Christophe's replies. Leclerc proposed to Christophe to seize Toussaint. Christophe indignantly rejected the treachery. Leclerc understood that he had gone too far, and proposed an interview with Christophe. Toussaint told Christophe to go and hear what Le-clerc had to say. Christophe went. Leclerc assured him of his good faith, promised to maintain him and all his offi-cers in their commands, and Christophe submitted.

It was a terrific blow to the revolution. When Tous-saint and the others reproached him, Christophe, a man known to appreciate the comforts of life, replied that he was tired of living in the woods like a brigand. Christophe has been blamed—wrongly. The fault was entirely Tous-saint's. His combination of fierce offensives with secret negotiations was too tortuous a method for Christophe. It was a policy suited for war between two national States, not for a revolutionary war. True, the masses did not know of the negotiations, but it was the results that mattered. Christophe was an ex-slave, a man of the revolution, one of Toussaint's staunchest supporters. If he surrendered to the French, why should the black labourers go on fighting? Once more the masses had received a shattering blow—not from the bullets of the enemy, but from where the masses most often receive it, from their own trembling leaders.

With Christophe went 1,200 soldiers, 100 pieces of cannon, a quantity of ammunition and 2,000 white inhabit-ants. Limbé and Port-Français passed into the hands of the French without a shot fired, and Marmelade was left open. But Leclerc was now thoroughly afraid of Toussaint and preferred to negotiate rather than to fight. Toussaint was not in any way depressed. He told Leclerc in one letter that the mischief he had done was evidence of the mischief he could do, and that he would sell dearly a life that had been at some time useful to the mother-country. Leclerc was extremely conciliatory; he used Christophe as a go-between, and informed Toussaint that it would be a won-derful day when he submitted himself to the orders of the Republic. Toussaint sent him three of the aides-de-camp and his secretary and after a conference lasting several hours submission was arranged on three conditions: indis-putable liberty for all in San Domingo, maintenance in their grades and functions of all the native officers, Tous-saint to keep his staff and retire where he wished on the territory of the colony. Bonaparte had stringently enjoined Leclerc not to leave any officer above the rank of captain on the island. Toussaint would submit only on the condition that every officer was maintained not only in his grade, but in his functions. How carefully the imperialists maintain the fiction about native troops being no good except under white officers! It was the trained army that Bonaparte wished to behead, and it was that army that Toussaint wanted to maintain. Despite the submission, the victory was still with Toussaint. He had an interview with Dessalines and Charles Belair, his nephew, and persuaded them to submit also. There was nothing else for them to do and they agreed, Lamartinière, Magny, and all the army joining the French.

The whole French Army was as glad as it was astonished at this sudden peace. Lacroix and another officer, Lemmonier-Delafosse, have testified to the relief of the French at this unlooked for submission.[26] Toussaint's strength was so obvious that even though they were ashamed to negotiate on these terms they were glad to do so. Nor were their secret humiliations and fears reassured by the behaviour of Toussaint. He never at any time acted like a defeated commander. Leclerc wrote him flattering letters, and invited him to a meeting in Le Cap. Without warning Leclerc, Toussaint suddenly rode into the city on May 6th with his staff and a company of dragoons, accompanied by the French General Hardy. Some few hooted, and Toussaint said to Hardy, "So men are everywhere. I have seen them at my foot, these men who are cursing me; but they will regret me soon."

They will regret me soon. What would Hardy think of this? But the great body of people in Le Cap came out to cheer him: They hailed him as the liberator, mothers pointed him out to their children, and girls strewed flowers in his path. At Leclerc's headquarters he drew up his dragoons in formation and went in with his aides-de-camp, the

[26] General Nemours has listed a mass of evidence on French military opinion of the great strength of the blacks at the time of submission. *Histoire militaire . . . ,* Vol. III.

dragoons remaining in the courtyard with swords drawn. Toussaint had intended to enter Le Cap alone, but they refused to leave him. Leclerc's officers gave him a distinguished welcome, and sent to call Leclerc, who was dining on board ship. He hastened back at once, and after giving Toussaint a salute threw himself into his arms and asked him to come into his private office.

"General," he began. "We can only praise you and admire you for the way you have borne the burden of governing San Domingo. . . ."

Toussaint, stern and aloof, asked him why he had brought sword and fire to a peaceful country. Leclerc tried to make excuses—Toussaint did not accept them.

"I agree," said Leclerc, "but I was not master of myself. Let us forget the past and rejoice, General, at our reconciliation." [27]

Contrary to his usual diplomatic manner Toussaint, with the drawn swords of his guards outside, would not respond to Leclerc's overtures. He refused the post of lieutenant-general. Paul L'Ouverture came to greet him. Toussaint, who did not yet know of the confusion with the letters, repelled him before the whole company. Leclerc invited him to dinner, but although he accepted he would not eat. Afraid of being poisoned, he drank only a glass of water and near the end of the meal had a scrap of cheese, cut very carefully from the centre of the piece that was offered to him. Two days after, Leclerc asked him to dismiss his guard, and Toussaint bade them good-bye, asking them to submit to the new order. As they listened to him, Magny, the hero of Crête-à-Pierrot, in front, they wept at this sad ending to the great campaigns that had begun when, from a horde of half-naked slaves, they had organised themselves into a little band to study war and fight for liberty. Toussaint was visibly moved, but he controlled himself. After embracing his chief officers he took the road to his plantation at Ennery. As he drew near the crowds came out to meet him. "General," they asked, "have you abandoned us?" "No, my children," he answered, "all your

[27] Isaac L'Ouverture, *Mémoires*.

brothers are under arms, and the officers of all ranks retain their posts." That was the issue. Would the blacks retain their army or not?

A few days later Dessalines entered Le Cap to make his formal submission. He also came with morale unbroken. French general officers were walking about in the streets. Nobody took any notice of them, but at the cry of "Dessalines!" the whole population rushed to prostrate themselves before him. Lacroix saw this and understood what it meant, noted too the boldness and assurance with which Dessalines spoke to him and the other Frenchmen.

Dessalines and his division took service with Leclerc. Toussaint, glad that the destruction was over, and having confidence in the army still intact, began with his usual energy to cultivate his plantations. Although he had no confidence in Leclerc at all, he thought himself safe for the moment. He would watch developments. At any crisis he would be there. It was his ultimate confidence in the army and the people that led him to make his mistake. At the back of his mind he knew that they could never be beaten. But, his eyes fixed on the French, he did not know that he had lost the confidence of Dessalines, who was no longer looking to him for leadership, but was working out his own road to independence.

Full of chagrin at his failure to carry out Bonaparte's instructions, Leclerc committed the error of writing false despatches home.

". . . Two days later General Toussaint sent his adjutant-general with a letter signifying little, but in which I saw a very pronounced desire to surrender. I replied to this general that I would receive his submission, but that if he did not surrender promptly, I would march against him; that for the rest he should send me one of his confidential servants to tell me what he desired. He sent his private secretary with one of his aides-de-camp, letting me know that he desired to have the rank of lieutenant-general and a special command; that each of his generals should resume the

command he had enjoyed at the time of my entry, and that he should have under his orders only his own troops. I replied to him that he would not be employed, that he would have to withdraw to one of his estates which he would be unable to leave without my permission; that the generals as well as the troops would be employed, but only when I judged it suitable and it seemed to me advantageous. That as for him he had only to surrender to me at Le Cap, that I gave him my word of honour that he would be free to go where he wished after the conference. For the rest that his troops must be all assembled and ready to carry out my orders in four days' time. . . .

"If circumstances force me sometimes, Citizen Minister, to appear to deviate from the goal of my instructions, believe me I do not lose sight of them and I yield something to circumstances only to master them afterwards and to make them serve in the execution of my plan.

"As my reports which you order to be printed appear here in the newspapers, it is impolitic to insert anything in them which might destroy the ideas of liberty and equality which are on everybody's lips here." [28]

"General Toussaint has surrendered here. He left perfectly satisfied with me and ready to carry out all my orders. I believe that he will carry them out because he is persuaded that if he did not I would make him repent it." [29]

"Sickness is causing frightful havoc in the army under my command. . . .

"I have at this moment 3,600 men in hospital. For the last 15 days I have been losing from 30 to 50 men a day in the colony and no day passes without from 200 to 250 men entering the hospitals, while not more

[28] May 26th, 1802. To the Minister of Marine.
[29] May 5th, 1802. To the Minister of Marine.

than 50 come out. My hospitals are overcrowded.

"To be master of San Domingo I need 25,000 Europeans under arms. You see that I have only half that number. There is not a moment to lose in sending me reinforcements. . . ." [30]

"For the rest, Citizen Minister, assure the First Consul that I have not for a moment lost sight of the direct instructions he had given me, as much from the political point of view us from the commercial, and that I shall consider it a happy day for me when the national commerce by itself will be capable of provisioning San-Domingo and the French army; in this way must a colonial war result in the triumph of commerce." [31]

"Here is a list of the chief persons whom death has taken off since my last despatch. . . .

"At the moment of writing many generals or superior officers are sick. Of 16 persons who lived in General Hardy's house, 13 are dead.

"All General Ledogin's secretaries are dead, also. An association of traders in timber had been set up at Le Cap. This house comprised seven persons; all seven died within eight days. I ordered the chief officer of health to draw up a report for me on this sickness. According to this report it seems that this sickness is that which is called Yellow fever or Siamese disease; that this sickness reigns every year in the Antilles at the time of the passage of the sun in this hemisphere, but that it displays at Le Cap more intensity than is usual on account of the miasmas exhaled by the burnt houses. This sickness is heralded in some people by symptoms which are either slight pains or pains in the bowels or shivering. In others, the sickness affects them suddenly and kills within two days or three; but of those attacked not one fifth have escaped death.

[30] May 8th, 1802. To the Minister of Marine.
[31] May 8th, 1802. To the Minister of Marine.

The sickness attacks equally those who are in comfortable positions and who care for themselves well, and those whose means do not permit them to take precautions necessary to their health." [32]

"My position becomes worse every day. Sickness carries off the men. Toussaint is not to be trusted, as I had indeed expected, but I have drawn from his submission the object I had expected, which was to detach from him Dessalines and Christophe with their troops. I am going to order his arrest, and I think I can reckon sufficiently on Dessalines, of whose mind I have made myself master, to charge him to go and arrest Toussaint. I do not think I shall miss him. What makes me take this daring resolution, Citizen Consul, is that it is necessary for me to revive in the colony the idea of my strength by some act of rigour, but if I did not receive reinforcements, my position would become worse. Do not be surprised if I say that it is possible to miss him. For the last fortnight this man has been extremely mistrustful. It is not that I have given any handle to his mistrust, but he regrets the power. . . . As soon as I am assured of his person, I shall make him leave for Corsica and give orders that he should be imprisoned in one of the castles in that island. . . .

"I beg you to give orders that 10,000 men be sent to me immediately.

"My health has been very unsteady. It is a little better, but this climate is extremely unfavourable to me. All I desire is to be able to remain here until next Ventôse. I hope at that period to have sufficiently advanced my work in order that I might leave it to my successor without any anxiety.

"Despite the ravages made here by death there is no discouragement in the army." [33]

[32] June 6th, 1802. To the Minister of Marine.
[33] June 6th, 1802. To the Minister of Marine.

The yellow fever had the French Army in its grip. Toussaint and Dessalines had known that this was coming, had calculated on it, and but for Christophe and Toussaint it is unlikely that Dessalines would ever have submitted. Soon it would be time to strike, and Dessalines, who had formerly worshipped Toussaint, determined to get him out of the way, as well as Christophe, for their pro-French leanings. He pretended to be absolutely devoted to Leclerc, and suggested to him that the colony would never be at peace unless Toussaint was sent out of it. Christophe and Clairveaux told Leclerc the same: they were sincere. Dessalines was equally sincere that Haiti would only be at peace when Toussaint was removed, only the peace he planned was the destruction of Leclerc and the expulsion of everything French from the island. Faithful and loyal assistant to Toussaint, he knew his chief well enough to doubt his capacity to take the steps Dessalines saw would be necessary. He saw what had to be done and could trust no one except himself to do it. Since the days of Crête-à-Pierrot, Dessalines had his programme for national independence ready, and Rochambeau, who knew him well, ceaselessly warned his brother officers that Dessalines meditated treachery. Leclerc knew that it was Dessalines who mattered, and feeling himself master of Dessalines he took the step.

Toussaint was not plotting. Leclerc reproached him with suspicious actions. Toussaint proved that he was working on his plantations and nothing more. On June 7th General Brunet wrote to Toussaint asking for a meeting at his headquarters. The letter overflowed with assurances of good faith and the personal sincerity and honour of the writer. Toussaint was not well, and he had received warnings from friends that Leclerc intended to arrest him. Nevertheless, he decided to go. It may be that he had confidence in Brunet's assurances. But his whole career, all his policy, his whole attitude to Leclerc from the beginning to the last, deny this. If he did not go to this interview for fear of arrest, then he would have to fly and begin the war again, in a position infinitely worse than when he had come to terms. On the other hand, it was unlikely that Leclerc would dare to arrest him while Dessalines, Belair, and the others still had command of their troops. It was here that he was wrong. He met Brunet at eight in the evening accompanied by only two officers. The men talked for a few minutes, and then Brunet begged to be excused for a moment. As soon as Brunet left, some grenadiers with fixed bayonets, having Ferrari, Leclerc's aide-de-camp, at their head, entered the house. Toussaint rose and drew his sword. Ferrari with lowered point went up to him. "General, we have not come here to do you any harm. We merely have orders to secure your person." And Toussaint submitted. They bound him like a common criminal, arrested his aide-de-camp, arrested his wife, son and niece, treating them with every indignity; they broke into his house, stole his money, his jewels, and his family papers, destroyed his plantations. They rushed the family on board a frigate which was waiting in the harbour of Le Cap and embarked them for France.

As Toussaint stepped on board the boat he spoke to Savary the captain some words which he had doubtless carefully prepared, his last legacy to his people.

"In overthrowing me, you have cut down in San Domingo only the trunk of the tree of liberty. It will spring up again by the roots for they are numerous and deep."

The news of Toussaint's arrest came like a cold shock to the whole population. Whatever Toussaint had done, he stood for liberty. Round about Ennery and in the mountains the drums were beating and calling the people to revolt, and in the heights of Plaisance, Dondon, and around, the mass insurrection against Leclerc began. But the population as a whole gave little sign of interest. Leclerc was deceived, but not Lacroix and others of his officers. Dissimulation is the refuge of the slave, and the unnatural calm frightened some of the whites. The black masses did nothing because they did not know what to do. They saw Maurepas, Dessalines, Christophe and their officers maintaining their commands. Leclerc, as he had said from the time he came, swore that he had no designs against liberty. Toussaint had fought, then submitted, and now, as Leclerc said, he had been guilty of treason. Leclerc proclaimed that he had two letters proving Toussaint's treason, and published one. It was a forgery, for when the Home Government asked him for proofs in order to bring Toussaint to trial, he confessed that he had none. Let post mortem and retrospective arguments about morality be the happy hunting-ground of well-fed professors! Leclerc had been instructed to get rid of Toussaint, and had got rid of him.

But the arrest did not help Leclerc.

"If the First Consul wishes to have an army in San Domingo in the month of October, he must have it sent from France, for the ravages of sickness here are too great for words. Not a day passes without my being told of the death of someone whom I have cause to regret bitterly. . . . Man cannot work here much without risking his life. Since my arrival in this country I have often been in very poor health from having worked too hard. The Government must seriously think of sending me a successor.

"It is quite impossible for me to remain here more than six months. I reckon by that time to hand over the colony free from the state of war to the one who will be designated to replace me.

"My health is so wretched that I would consider myself very fortunate if I can last that long." [34]

"I have notified you, Citizen Minister, in one of my last dispatches, of the pardon which I had been pleased to grant General Toussaint. This ambitious man, from the moment I pardoned him, has not ceased his underhand conspiracies. The reports which have reached me even through General Dessalines of the way he has behaved since his submission leave me

[34] June 11th, 1802. To the Minister of Marine.

no doubt on that score. . . . I gave orders for his arrest. It was no easy matter. I am sending to France with all his family this man who is such a danger to San Domingo. The Government, Citizen Minister, must have him put in a very strong place situated in the centre of France, so that he may never have any means of escaping and returning to San Domingo, where he has all the influence of the leader of a sect. If in three years this man were to reappear in San Domingo, perhaps he would destroy all that France had done there. . . . I entreat you, send me some troops. Without them I cannot undertake the disarming of the population, and without the disarming I am not master of this colony." 35

"The mortality continues and makes frightful ravages. Consternation exists among the troops in the West and South. . . ." 36

"After Toussaint's embarcation some men tried to make a disturbance. I have had them shot or deported. Since then some colonial troops seemed to be getting rebellious: I have had their leaders shot.

"These troops are now concealing their discontent. The disbandment is being effective. The black generals are well aware at this moment that I am going to destroy their influence entirely in this country; but they dare not raise the standard of rebellion: (1) because they detest each other and know very well that I would destroy them, the one with the aid of the other; (2) because the blacks are not brave and this war has scared them; (3) because they are afraid to measure themselves against the man who destroyed their leaders. Under these circumstances I am marching steadily and rapidly towards my goal. The South and West are almost disarmed. In the North the disarming will begin in eight days.

"The police is being organised, and as soon as the

---

85 *Ibid.*
86 July 4th. 1802. To the Minister of Marine.

disarmament is over and the police in position, I shall
strike the last blows. If I succeed, as is probable, then
San Domingo will be really restored to the Repub-
lic. . . .

"*You cannot keep Toussaint at too great a distance*
from the sea and put him in a position that is too safe.
This man has raised the country to such a pitch of fa-
naticism that his presence would send it up again in
flames. . . .

"*Since our landing here, we have been constantly*
in the breach.

"*Since the day that we have no longer had cause to*
fear the weapons of the rebels, the sickness has been
making frightful havoc amongst us. I shall be very
fortunate if my health permits me to execute all that
I say, but I have no inclination to spend a second
year in San Domingo. It is too cruel to exist as I am
existing, maintaining my existence only by artifices. If
at the end of my operations the Government has not
sent me a successor, then I shall use the power given
me by the First Consul by word of mouth, of quitting
San Domingo when my operations are over." [37]

It was July, and Leclerc, months behind in his programme, his soldiers dying in thousands, now had to disarm the revolutionary North. It was now or never. Naturally
the best persons to use were the black generals. The insurrection was spreading daily in the North and at the call
for arms it doubled there and spread to South and West.
Derance, Samedi Smith, Jean Panier, and other nameless
petty chieftains, North, South and West, each in his own
district summoned the blacks to revolt. Give up their arms?
What for? Sonthonax had told them: "If you wish to keep
your liberty use your *arms* on the day that the white authorities ask you for them, because any such request is the
infallible sign and precursor of the return to slavery."

As they were driven from one place they reappeared

[37] July 6th, 1802. To the Minister of Marine.

in another—one region would be "pacified," but as soon as the soldiers moved to another, the first broke out again. The French, disheartened, began to blame Leclerc for not getting rid of all the black and Mulatto generals along with Toussaint. "But no one observed that in the new insurrection of San Domingo, as in all insurrections which attack constituted authority, it was not the avowed chiefs who gave the signal for revolt but obscure creatures for the greater part personal enemies of the coloured generals." [38] It is a recurrent tale, this.[39] It is the curse of the masses always, now as then, that those who have shouted most always quail when the time for action arrives, or worse still find some good reason for collaborating with the enemy. Christophe, Maurepas, and the rest hunted down these "brigands." The French feared Lamartinière, and ambushed him even while he was in their service—a pitiable

[38] Lacroix, *Mémoires pour Servir* . . . , Vol. II, p. 225.
[39] Michelet had shown that such was also his view of the French Revolution. But it is in Georges Lefebvre, the great contemporary historian of the French Revolution, who on occasion after occasion exhaustively examines all the available evidence and repeats that we do not know and will never know who were the real leaders of the French Revolution, nameless, obscure men, far removed from the legislators and the public orators.

G. Lefebvre, *La Fuite du Roi*, p. 187 (mimeographed lectures): "It is wrong to attach too much importance to any opinion that the Girondins or Robespierre might have on what needed to be done. That is not the way to approach the question. We must pay more attention to the obscure leaders and the people who listened to them in stores and the little workshops and dark streets of old Paris. It was on them that the business depended and for the moment, evidently, they followed the Girondins. . . . It is therefore in the popular mentality, in the profound and incurable distrust which was born in the soul of the people, in regard to the aristocracy, beginning in 1789, and in regard to the king, from the time of the flight to Varennes, it is there that we must seek the explanation of what took place. The people and their unknown leaders knew what they wanted. They followed the Girondins and afterwards Robespierre, only to the degree that their advice appeared acceptable.

"Who then are these leaders to whom the people listened? We know some. Nevertheless, as in all the decisive days of the revolution, what we most would like to know is forever out of our reach; we would like to have the diary of the most obscure of these popular leaders; we would then be able to grasp, in the act so to speak, how one of these great revolutionary days began; we do not have it."

death for that splendid officer. Dessalines hunted down "brigands" with the rest, biding his time.

But the insurrection grew always, and while it grew the fever took its toll. The French could bury their dead in formal fashion no longer, but threw them into huge holes at night, lest the blacks should see how the army was wasting away. As if that could hide it. Leclerc, his health broken, went to Tortuga to recuperate. Feeling better, he left the island to come back to Le Cap. As soon as he left an insurrection burst behind him. It was crushed there, only to break out among the blacks around Môle St Nicholas. In early July the rumours began to spread through the island that the French Government was restoring slavery.

Once more the masses had shown greater political understanding than their leaders. Bonaparte had indeed taken the step. Richepanse in Guadeloupe had carried out instructions similar to those of Leclerc. There the Mulattoes ruled. He had defeated them, had deported their leaders and others, some 3,000 people in all, and had the black population under his feet. And Leclerc's boastful letters, telling lies about the way he had beaten Toussaint, had done the rest.

The French officers had been ashamed to let Bonaparte know the true results of their battles with the black generals. After the defeat of Debelle by Maurepas, Desfourneaux wrote to Dugua: "He (Debelle) has attacked Maurepas . . . , he has been repulsed and grievously wounded. It is feared that he will die. Maurepas holds his position unshaken with 3,000 men and six pieces of artillery. . . . This information is very exact. . . ." [40] But when Dugua reported this to the Minister of War it was translated into: General Debelle, after divers engagements with Maurepas, general of brigade (a Negro), has received the submission of this chief who has judged it more prudent to become a servant of the Republic than to get him-

[40] Nemours, *Histoire Militaire* . . . , Vol. II, p. 261.

self piked by our gallant soldiers whose ardour it is impossible to resist." [41]

With these smoothly false reports Bonaparte must have thought that the job, if not quite finished, would not present much difficulty, and there was no more necessity to prevaricate.

He did not begin with San Domingo or Guadeloupe. He started with the French colonies that had been restored by Britain to France at the Treaty of Amiens. At a session of the Legislature in May, Bruix explained the new policy. "Free peoples are jealous of their noble prerogatives. They have their egoism; but the sentiment must not be carried too far"—not as far as the French West Indies at any rate. The blacks were referred to as "the guilty," and many proposed that they should be terrorised by decimation. The Abbé Grégoire, still a legislator of France, sat listening to them. Perhaps in his mind's eye the gallant old priest saw, not these heartless rapacious representatives of the new bourgeois France, but the Convention on that day of February 4th, eight years before, when slavery had been abolished without a debate. But the Paris masses were in the streets then. The Abbé Grégoire said nothing, and Bonaparte, noticing it, asked him for his opinion. "I think," replied Grégoire, "that listening to such speeches is sufficient to show that they are spoken by whites. If these gentlemen were this moment to change colour they would talk differently." Bonaparte swore at him, and the restoration of slavery for Martinique, Ile-de-Bourbon, and other islands was passed by 211 votes to 60.

But the maritime bourgeois were clamouring for more. In a few days the slave-trade was officially restored for all the colonies, and the incoming Africans were to be slaves as of old; followed step by step the prohibition of coloured people coming to France, the restoration of the prohibition of mixed marriages, and discrimination against Mulattoes. Bonaparte stopped short at actually declaring slavery restored in San Domingo and Guadeloupe. But even before the first decree in May he had written to Richepanse and

41 *Ibid.*, Vol. II, p. 266.

Leclerc telling them to restore slavery when they saw fit.
Rumours of all this were coming through to San Domingo,
while Leclerc, with Bonaparte's instructions still his secret,
continued to assure the blacks that he had no intention of
restoring slavery.

As soon as Richepanse received Bonaparte's final instructions, he restored slavery. Every ship was bringing
back émigré colonists to San Domingo, thirsting for revenge, eager for the old days. "No slavery, no colony."
They said it openly, while Leclerc denied it, and the black
and Mulatto population listened in alarm. Agents of the
maritime bourgeois were busy trying to place orders.

Then one day late in July a frigate, the *Cockarde,* entered the harbour of Le Cap having on board blacks deported from Guadeloupe. That night some of them jumped
overboard and swam ashore to give their brothers in San
Domingo the news that slavery had been restored in Guadeloupe. The insurrection became general.

This unexpected exposure of Bonaparte's secret intentions threw Leclerc into mortal terror.

"Do not think of establishing slavery here for some
time. I think I can do everything in order that my
successor should have only the Government's decision to put into effect. But after the innumerable
proclamations I have issued here to assure the blacks
of their liberty, I do not wish to contradict myself;
but assure the First Consul that my successor will find
everything ready." [42]

"The districts of Plaisance, Gros Morne, Port-de-
Paix, St Louise, Le Borgne, are in revolt . . . but
. . . I hope that this will be the last crisis.

"The malady is making such frightful progress that
I cannot calculate where it will end. The hospitals
alone at Le Cap have lost this month 100 men a day.

"To the maladies and insurrections must be added
the shortage of cash in which you leave us. If that continues ever so little, with the reinforcements I expect

[42] August 2nd, 1802. To the Minister of Marine.

*and the hospitals so costly, I shall see my troops in
revolt, because I shall not be able to administer to
their needs."* [43]

"My position is no better; the insurrection spreads,
the malady continues. . . .

"All the blacks are persuaded, by letters which
have come from France, by the law which re-established the slave-trade, by the decree of General Richepanse which re-established slavery in Guadeloupe,
that the intention is to make them slaves again, and
I can ensure their disarmament only by long and stub-
born conflicts. These men do not wish to surrender. It
must be admitted that on the eve of settling everything here, the political circumstances of which I have
spoken to you above have almost destroyed my work.
The unfortunate measures you have adopted have
destroyed everything and inflamed minds. We will no
longer be able to reduce the blacks except by force of
arms. For this we need an army and funds, without
which the prosperity of San Domingo is in grave
danger.

"I have asked you, Citizen Minister, for a successor.
That letter, like many others I have addressed to you,
has received no reply. The Government must think of
sending me a man who can replace me at need. It is
not that I am thinking of quitting my post at a difficult
moment, but my health is continually becoming worse,
and there is no one who might replace me to the advantage of the Republic.

"I shall do all I possibly can to prevent the insurrection from spreading between now and the first
Vendémiaire. By that time the 9,000 men you have
promised me will no doubt have arrived. I shall go
through the rebel districts with the same vigour I
adopted in my first campaign. Terror will precede me

[43] *Ibid.*

and woe to those who will not obey me blindly; but for that I need money and troops." [44]

"*Death has wrought such frightful havoc among my troops that when I tried to disarm the North a general insurrection broke out.*

"*. . . I fear nothing from Christophe, but I am not so sure of Dessalines. The first attacks have driven the rebels from the positions they occupied; but they fell back to other cantons and in the insurrection there is a veritable fanaticism. These men get themselves killed, but they refuse to surrender. . . .*

"*I entreated you, Citizen Consul, to do nothing which might make them anxious about their liberty until I was ready, and that moment was rapidly approaching. Suddenly the law arrived here which authorises the slave-trade in the colonies, with business letters from Nantes and Havre asking if blacks can be sold here. More than all that, General Richepanse has just taken a decision to re-establish slavery in Guadeloupe. In this state of affairs, Citizen Consul, the moral force I had obtained here is destroyed. I can do nothing by persuasion. I can depend only on force and I have no troops.*

"*. . . Now, Citizen Consul, that your plans for the colonies are perfectly known, if you wish to preserve San Domingo, send a new army, send above all money, and I assure you that if you abandon us to ourselves, as you have hitherto done, this colony is lost, and once lost, you will never regain it.*

"*My letter will surprise you, Citizen Consul, after those I have written to you. But what general could calculate on a mortality of four-fifths of his army and the uselessness of the remainder, who has been left without funds as I have, in a country where purchases are made only for their weight in gold and where with*

[44] August 6th, 1802. To the Minister of Marine.

*money I might have got rid of much discontent? Could
I have expected, in these circumstances, the law relating to the slave-trade and above all the decrees of
General Richepanse re-establishing slavery and forbidding the men of colour from signing themselves
as citizens?*

*"I have shown you my real position with the frank-
ness of a soldier. I am grieved to see all that I have done
here on the point of being destroyed. If you had been
a witness of the difficulties of all sorts which I have
overcome, and the results I had obtained, you would
grieve with me on seeing my position; but however
disagreeable it may be, I still have hopes of succeeding. I make terrible examples, and since terror
is the sole resource left me, I employ it. At Tortuga,
of 450 rebels I had 60 hanged. To-day everything is
in perfect order.*

*"All the proprietors or merchants who come from
France speak of slaves. It seems that there is a general conspiracy to prevent the restoration of San Domingo to the Republic.*

*". . . Send me immediately reinforcements, send
me money, for I am in a really wretched position.*

*"I have painted a pessimistic picture of my situa-
tion. Do not think that I am in any way cast down by
what is happening. I shall be always equal to circumstances whatever they may be, and I shall serve you
with the same zeal as long as my health permits me.
It is now worse, and I am no longer able to ride. Bear
in mind that you must send me a successor. I have no
one here who can replace me in the critical situation
in which the colony will be for some time. . . . Jérémie is in revolt. I have no other news from that quarter.*

*"Christophe and Dessalines have begged me not to
leave them here after my departure. That allows you
to judge of the confidence they have in me. I hope in
the first days of Brumaire to be able to send to France
or elsewhere all disruptive persons. . . . When I*

leave, the colony will be ready to receive the régime which you wish to give it, but it will be for my successor to take the final step. If you agree, I shall do nothing contrary to what I have proclaimed here.

"General Richepanse conducts himself in a manner which is very impolitic and very clumsy in so far as San Domingo is concerned; if I had not cut off many heads here, I should have been chased from the island long ago, and would not have been able to fulfil your plans." [45]

"The black generals lead the columns; they are well surrounded.[46] I have ordered them to make terrible examples and I use them always when I have something terrible to do. . . .[47]

"The decrees of General Richepanse have repercussions here and are the source of great evil. The one which restored slavery, from having been issued three months too early, will cost the army and the colony of San Domingo many men.

"P.S.—I have just heard of a bloody fight that General Boyer has experienced at Gros-Morne. The rebels have been exterminated; 50 prisoners have been hung; these men die with an incredible fanaticism; they laugh at death; it is the same with the women. . . . This frenzy is the result of the proclamations of Richepanse and the fire-eating proposals of the colonists." [48]

"It appears to me from the orders that you send me that you have not got a clear idea of my position here. You order me to send the black generals to Europe. It would be very simple to arrest them all the same day; but I use these generals to quell the revolts which never stop. . . .

[45] August 6th, 1802. To the First Consul.
[46-47] Leclerc's emphasis.
[48] August 9th, 1802. This letter is not among those collected by General Nemours. It is quoted from Poyen, *Histoire Militaire de la Révolution de Saint-Domingue*, Paris, 1899, p. 258. This is the official French history.

*"I have just discovered a great plot which aimed
at raising the whole colony in revolt by the end of
Thermidor. It was only partially executed for lack of
a leader. It is not enough to have taken away Toussaint, there are 2,000 leaders to be taken away."* [49]

The masses were fighting and dying as only revolutionary masses can, the French Army was wasting away,
despair was slowly choking Leclerc. But still these black
and Mulatto generals continued to fight for Leclerc against
the "brigands," and the Mulattoes and former free continued to stick to the French, hoping that the fate of
Guadeloupe and Martinique would not befall them. In
August Charles Belair, heart-broken since Toussaint had
been arrested—Toussaint used to call him his Labienus—
and stirred to resentment at the cruelty of the French,
joined the insurrection, and as if they were only waiting
for someone in authority to lead them the whole population
of the Artibonite revolted with him. This did not suit Dessalines. Belair was his rival, Toussaint's favourite, and
Belair had in the early days of the expedition saved the
lives of many whites. Dessalines invited him to an interview, hinting at a combination against the French. Belair
and Sanite came, for the women were now fighting side
by side with the men. Dessalines arrested them both and
sent them to Leclerc. It was a treacherous crime, but it
was not treachery to the revolution, for in the very month
of August Dessalines and Pétion, while they hunted down
"brigands," came to an understanding at last.[50] But Clairveaux the Mulatto, Christophe, Laplume, Paul L'Ouverture, Maurepas, stood waiting, God knows for what,
and without them neither Dessalines nor Pétion could
move.

With a skill and tenacity which astonished their sea-
soned opponents, the little local leaders not only beat off
attacks but maintained a ceaseless harrying of the French

---

[49] August 25th, 1802. To the Minister of Marine.
[50] Sannon: *Histoire de Toussaint-L'Ouverture*, Vol. III, p. 120.

posts, giving them no peace, so that the soldiers were worn out and nerve-wracked, and fell in thousands to the yellow fever. When the French sent large expeditions against them they disappeared in the mountains, leaving a trail of flames behind them, returning when the weary French retreated, to destroy still more plantations and carry their attacks into the French lines. Running short of ammunition, the labourers in the mountains around Port-de-Paix attacked this important town, drove out the garrison, killed the whites, burned the houses that had been rebuilt, and took possession of the fort with 25,000 pounds of powder. Who comes to recapture it? Maurepas, who had commanded in the district and had so valiantly driven off the attacks of Humbert, Debelle and Hardy. He and the French, with a vigorous counter-attack, recaptured the fort, but "the insurgents with incredible activity . . . men, women and children, all had got back to the mountains more or less heavily laden." The masses of the North plain ran to put themselves under the guidance of these new leaders.[51]

All that the old gang would do was to threaten Leclerc. Some of the blacks who had been slaves attempted to purchase their freedom from their former masters. These refused, and singled out as their private property high officials and officers, men who had shed their blood on the battlefield and served with distinction in the administration. Christophe told General Ramel that if he thought slavery was to be restored, he would burn the whole of San Domingo to the ground. A black general dining with Lacroix pointed to his two daughters and asked him, "Are these to go back to slavery?" It was as if they could not believe it. So your liberal or social-democrat hesitates and dithers until the sledge-hammer of Fascism falls on his head, or a Franco launches his carefully prepared counter-revolution.

---

[51] Lacroix, *Mémoires pour Servir* . . . , Vol. II, p. 223.

Leclerc was merely waiting for reinforcements to arrest and deport these leaders. It was only the strength of the insurrection which was preventing him. The masses were fighting by instinct. They knew that whatever party the old slave-owners belonged to aimed at the restoration of slavery. Yet these new ruling-class blacks and Mulattoes clung to the tails of Leclerc. One night Clairveaux and Christophe were dining with Boudet and Lacroix, and Lacroix asked the two coloured men why the insurrection was spreading. "You are a European," Christophe told him, "and you are young. . . . You have fought only in the armies of the mother-country and therefore you cannot have any prejudices regarding slavery. I will therefore speak to you without reserve. The revolt grows because distrust is at its height. If you had our skin, you would not perhaps be so confiding as myself who am entrusting my only son, Ferdinand, to General Boudet, that he may be educated in France. I am not concerned about the brigands who have given the signal for the insurrection. The danger does not lie there; the danger is in the general opinion of the blacks. Those of San Domingo are frightened because they know the decree of the 30 Floréal, which maintains slavery and the slave-trade in the colonies restored to France by the treaty of Amiens. They are alarmed at seeing the First Consul restore the old system in these colonies. They are afraid lest the indiscreet talk that is heard here on all sides should find its way to France and suggest to the Government the idea of depriving the blacks of San Domingo of their liberty."

Leclerc was now frantic.

"If the French Government wishes to preserve San Domingo, it must, Citizen Minister, on the receipt of my letter give orders for 10,000 men to leave at once. They will arrive in Nivôse and order will be entirely established before the hot season. But if this malady is to last three months more, the Government must renounce the colony. . . .

"Although I have painted such a horrible situation I

*ought to say that I am not without courage. . . . For
four months now I exist merely by adroitness, without
having any real force; judge if I can fulfil the intentions of the Government."* [52]

. ."*The mountain chain from Vaillières up to and including Marmelade is in insurrection . . . I will be
able to protect the plain only supposing that the malady stops in the first ten days of Vendémiaire. Since
the 8 Fructidor it has assumed a new force, and I lose
100 to 120 men a day. To hold these mountains when
I shall have taken them, I shall be* obliged to destroy
all the provisions there and a great part of the labourers. I shall have to wage a war of extermination
and it will cost me many men. A great part of my
colonial troops have deserted and passed over to the
rebels.[53] *Let the Government send me 10,000 men
independent of the reinforcements already promised
to me. Let it send them at once by ships of the state
and not by merchant vessels whose arrival is always
slow. . . . Let it send me two million francs in coin
and not in paper. . . . Or let it prepare for an in-
terminable cruel war in San Domingo and perhaps
the loss of the colony. It is my duty to tell you the
whole truth. I tell it to you. . . . The news of the
slavery re-established in Guadeloupe has made me
lose a great part of my influence on the blacks. . . .*

"*Bear in mind also the question of my successor for
I am thinking seriously of quitting this country. . . .*

". *. . I leave this to go back to my bed, where I
am hoping not to stay long. I wish you better health
and more pleasant thoughts than mine. Since I am in
this unfortunate country I have not had a moment's
peace."* [54]

"*My position becomes worse from day to day. I am
in such a miserable plight that I have no idea when*

52 September 13th, 1802. To the Minister of Marine.
53 Leclerc's emphasis.
54 September 17th, 1802. To the Minister of Marine.

*and how I will get out of it . . . I had believed up to
the present that the ravages of the malady would stop
in Vendémiaire. I was wrong; the malady has again
taken new strength and the month of Fructidor cost
me more than 4,000 dead. I had believed from what
the inhabitants told me that the malady would stop in
Vendémiaire. They tell me to-day that it may possibly
last to the end of Brumaire. If that happens and it
continues with the same intensity the colony will be
lost. Every day the party of the rebels grows larger
and mine diminishes by the loss of whites and the
desertion of blacks. . . . Dessalines, who up to now
had never thought of insurrection, thinks of it to-day.
But I have his secret; he will not escape me. This is
how I discovered his thoughts. Not being strong
enough to finish up with Dessalines, Maurepas and
the others, I use one against the other. All three are
ready to be party leaders, no one declares himself so
long as he will have the others to fear. In consequence
he has begun to make reports against Christophe and
Maurepas, insinuating to me that their presence was
harmful to the colony.*

*"I reiterate what I have told you. San Domingo is
lost to France if I have not received on the 16 Nivôse
10,000 men who must all come at the same time.*

*"I have told you my opinion on the measures taken
by General Richepanse at Guadeloupe. . . .*

*"I have painted my position in dark colours; this is
what it really is and that is the entire truth. Unfortunately the condition of the colonies is not known in
France. We have there a false idea of the Negro, and
that is why I send you an officer who knows the country and has fought in it. The colonists and the men
of business think that a decree of the French Government would be sufficient to restore slavery. I cannot
say what measures I shall take, I do not know what
I shall do. . . ."* [55]

[55] September 26th, 1802. To the First Consul.

"*I reply in detail to your letter of the 9th Thermidor.*

"General Toussaint. *I do not lack evidence to bring him to trial if you wish to have recourse to what he did before the amnesty which I accorded him; for what happened after that period I have nothing. In the present state of affairs, his judgment and execution will only embitter the blacks.*

"Deportees. *I shall continue to send to Corsica those whom I shall deport.*

"Present position. *All my army is destroyed. . . . Every day the blacks leave me. The unfortunate decree of General Richepanse. . . .*

"Generals of colour. *This is a very delicate question and if the 10,000 men had arrived, I would have no cause to speak to you about them any more.*" [56]

But the black generals clung to the French.

It was not that Christophe, for instance, trusted Leclerc. Christophe was so nervous that he maintained communication with some of the very insurgents he was hunting down. As the inevitable forced itself upon him, he took refuge in openly defying Leclerc. One night, invited to dinner, he would not go until he had his own soldiers placed so as to be able to come to his rescue. A white officer filled his glass over and over again. In a sudden rage Christophe turned to him. "You puny little white, if I had drunk the wine you poured out for me I would have wanted to drink your blood and the blood of your general, too." There was consternation at the table. Leclerc accused Christophe of treason and called the officers of his guard. "Useless to call them," said Christophe. "Mine are under arms and with a single word I can make you prisoner. I remain subject to you as I was to Toussaint; had he said

[56] September 26th, 1802. To the Minister of Marine.

to me, 'Hurl this island into the sea,' I would have done
my best. This is the way I obey or command." He condemned Leclerc for his treachery to Toussaint, "whose
genius led us from slavery to liberty . . . whose glory fills
the world," and who was now in chains. He called Leclerc
a parricide. "It is this crime, doubtless, that the Consul
wished to reward in giving you the government of San
Domingo." Leclerc, impotent, sat and took it. But that did
not help the masses.

In despair Leclerc called a meeting of the colonists
and generals to consider what was to be done to stop the
ever-spreading insurrection.[57] The colonists, deaf to all
except the memory of the good old days, were unanimous:
"No slavery, no colony." Christophe was at this meeting
and protested against this policy; the injustice of it; its
certain consequences: the destruction of the colony, its
loss to France. The colonists were adamant. Only then did
it seem that the black and Mulatto generals understood
that there was no hope. Yet as late as October 2nd a military tribunal consisting entirely of coloured men tried
Charles Belair and his wife and had them shot. They died
bravely, both of them, his wife facing the firing-squad and
refusing to have her eyes bound. Arrested by black leaders,
condemned and shot by black leaders. It was another slap
in the face of the black masses.

But Dessalines was now in danger. He had fooled
Leclerc, but he had not fooled Rochambeau, who never
ceased to warn the other French officers that Dessalines
was not to be trusted.[58] To maintain confidence Dessalines
had chased and shot "brigands" with the utmost ferocity.
It was now October, three months after he had come to
his understanding with Pétion. But afraid of Christophe,
Clairveaux, Maurepas and the rest, he could do nothing.
Neither he nor Pétion had the decisive authority that Toussaint or Rigaud would have been able to use in this crisis.

[57] Proclamation of Christophe, 1814. Reprinted in Beard, *Life
of Toussaint L'Ouverture*, p. 326.
[58] Rochambeau to Quantin. 2 Brumaire AN XI. (Oct 24th,
1802) *Les Archives du Ministère de la Guerre*. B[7]. 8.

Despite the shooting of Belair on the 2nd, when Dessalines came to see Leclerc a few days later he sensed that he was in danger. He affected to be discouraged, and asked Leclerc to send him to France. Leclerc, reassured, cheered him up, and told him that new troops were coming from France and that together they would strike a great blow. Leclerc saw Dessalines trembling in all his limbs at this good news. "There will be an earthquake!" he shouted, and left. Crude, coarse, and stained with crimes, he deserves his place among the heroes of human emancipation. He was a soldier, a magnificent soldier, and had no other pretensions. But hatred of those who deserved to be hated and destroyed had sharpened his wits, and he played a great part.

The sands were running out. Leclerc could hardly struggle out of his bed now to write. By the time he was writing the last letters he had an opinion of the blacks very different from that with which he had begun.

"*The state in which the colony of San Domingo finds itself by the fatal destruction of its army and by the insurrections excited by the decrees of General Richepanse in Guadeloupe appears to me so disturbing that I have decided to send you General Boudet. . . . Believe what he will tell you.* We have in Europe a false idea of the country in which we fight and the men whom we fight against. . . .*" [59] [60]

"*None of your letters announce to me what are the measures that the Government has taken to repair the loss of my army caused by the epidemic which continues its ravages. However, since the month of Floréal my despatches have continually informed you of the ravages which it has caused. To-day my army is destroyed. . . .*" [61]

[59] September 27th, 1802. To the First Consul.
[60] Leclerc's emphasis.
[61] October, 1802. To the Minister of Marine.

On the night of October 11th at a reception given by
Pauline Leclerc, Clairveaux, the Mulatto, said openly for
everyone to hear, "I have always been free; only new circumstances have enabled me to elevate my reviled colour.
But if I fancied that the restoration of slavery would ever
be thought of, that instant I would become a brigand."

The Mulattoes were for the most part hostile to the
return of slavery. But despite his threats, Clairveaux still
hesitated. It was Pétion who acted and forced his hand.
Pétion was holding positions near Le Cap, with Mulatto
troops. All these men were only waiting on their leaders.
At Pétion's command they spiked the guns, disarmed the
Europeans, and with a singular humanity which they would
soon regret allowed these to go back to Le Cap. Pétion
then went to Clairveaux, told him that the colonial troops
were in revolt, and that if he did not wish to pay with his
head for these defections, the only thing was to join. Then
only did Clairveaux join. Together Pétion and Clairveaux
had 3,000 coloured soldiers devoted to them. Leclerc had
but 300 white soldiers in Le Cap and had no suspicions of
Mulatto defection. But for the vacillation of Clairveaux, a
sudden movement would have put Le Cap and Leclerc
himself into their hands entirely.[62] As it was the French
had time to take the alarm, summon reinforcements, and
put themselves in a state of defence. Thus when Pétion and
Clairveaux did make the attack they were checked. But all
white Le Cap was badly frightened. Leclerc sent over a
thousand blacks on board ships in the harbour to get them
out of the way; and when the battle began and he felt himself in danger, he ordered that they should be drowned.
The sailors massacred them and threw them overboard.

Dessalines in the West was waiting. He had been preparing for weeks now, not giving in the arms that he was
taking as he had done at first. As soon as he learned that
Pétion and Clairveaux had started, he left Gonaïves and
set out for Petite-Rivière, giving the word to his supporters

62 Poyen, *Histoire Militaire de la Révolution* . . . , p. 271.

to be ready to raise the labourers at a given signal. The priest of Petite-Rivière invited him to breakfast and he went, not knowing that word had already come for his arrest and that he was to be taken at the presbytery. Madame Pageot, the curé's servant, a Mulatto, laid the table and then brought Dessalines a bowl of water in which to wash his hands. Looking hard into his eyes, she pressed her elbows to her sides and then moved them backwards, a sign that he was going to be bound. Already the soldiers were surrounding the house. Dessalines bolted for the door. The curé called to him. He replied that he had to perform some military duty. He sprang on his horse, and followed by his guard he rode off towards Artibonite, firing three pistol-shots in the air and crying out "To arms! To arms!" It had been a near thing.

Christophe still hesitated for a day or two, but on October 14th he joined Pétion and Clairveaux at last. The Mulattoes in the South still stuck to the French, but in the North and West the masses now had trained soldiers and leaders.

Leclerc, through illness or bitterness, never wrote this news to his brother-in-law or to the Minister. He sent to beg Christophe to come back, promising him honours and riches. Christophe replied that he was rich and honoured enough in possessing liberty himself and in securing the liberty of his colour. On the night of November 2nd Leclerc died. But before he died he knew that he had failed, and that San Domingo was lost to France. Of 34,000 French soldiers who had landed, 24,000 were dead, 8,000 were in hospital, and 2,000 exhausted men remained. Thousands of brave black soldiers were dead for no other crime than that of refusing to be slaves once more. The colony was devastated, and blacks and whites were murdering each other with a growing ferocity, in what was called a race war, but whose origin was not in their different colours but in the greed of the French bourgeoisie. Leclerc knew that, whatever reinforcements were sent, all was over. Before he died he confessed his grief over an enterprise undertaken on men and by men worthy of a better fate, on account of the services they had rendered and still would have been able to render to France. We owe him no thanks for the admission. It did not in any way mitigate the blood that would yet be shed and the suffering still to be borne before the people of San Domingo freed themselves from this abomination of murder, greed, cruelty, sadism, inhumanity, let loose upon them by Napoleon and his government, in the name of a superior civilisation.

"Unfortunately the condition of the colonies is not known in France. We have there a false idea of the Negro. . . .

"We have in Europe a false idea of the country in which we fight and the men whom we fight against."

There the ex-slaves of the San Domingo Revolution established their affinity with the population of revolutionary France. Between 1789 and Waterloo in 1815 the people of France staggered Europe and the world with the colossal scope of their achievements in war and in peace. No one had previously conceived that so much power was hidden in a people. Hilaire Belloc has perhaps expressed it best when he said that after August 1792 the reactionary classes of Europe armed against this new monster and set themselves two tasks, to reach Paris and to destroy democracy. The first task, he continues, took them twenty-two years; on the second they are still engaged.

We see the same in San Domingo. The population had been transformed. No one could have guessed the power that was born in them when Boukman gave the signal for revolt on that stormy August night in 1791. Rebellion, war, peace, economic organisation, international diplomacy, administration, they had shown their capacity. Now the new nation was to undergo its final test.

What happened in San Domingo after Leclerc's death is one of those pages in history which every schoolboy should learn, and most certainly will learn, some day. The national struggle against Bonaparte in Spain, the burning of Moscow by the Russians that fills the histories of the period, were anticipated and excelled by the blacks and Mulattoes of the island of San Domingo. The records are there. For self-sacrifice and heroism, the men, women and children who drove out the French stand second to no fighters for independence in any place or time. And the reason was simple. They had seen at last that without independence they could not maintain their liberty, and liberty was far more concrete for former slaves than the elusive forms of political democracy in France.

Rochambeau succeeded Leclerc, and he was confident of success. Although in the North and West the French held only Le Cap and a few towns, Spanish San Domingo was absolutely quiet; the great body of Mulattoes in the South, especially the rich proprietors, were still loyal. Rochambeau, setting out for Le Cap to take command, left the black Laplume holding command in the South, and Laplume remained faithful to the end. The French were in a critical position, but Rochambeau asked for 15,000 troops at one stroke to destroy the "brigands," then another 10,000, and finally another 10,000. "These three despatches are indispensable. . . . A point not less essential for the success of our army is the total destruction or deportation of the black and Mulatto generals, officers and soldiers." How that black army worried them! Rochambeau asked to send that rascal Toussaint to the galleys: "If he comes here I shall hang him without trial." [63]

Before long he received 10,000 men from Bonaparte. Also the fever was abating, and convalescents began to return to their regiments. Rochambeau captured Fort Dauphin and Port-de-Paix, and grew even more confident. What seemed to have confused him was the policy of Dessalines and Pétion. Christophe and Clairveaux were attacking, but blacks and Mulattoes had long recognised Dessalines as Commander-in-Chief, with Pétion as his

[63] Poyen, *Histoire Militaire de la Révolution* . . . , p. 326. Lacroix does not deal with this section. Writing as late as 1819 he dared not set down the truth. But he wrote a memorandum for Napoleon in which he sets down the full details of the course of events. *Les Archives Nationales*, AF. IV. 1212.

unofficial second-in-command. Dessalines travelled over the island reorganising the local troops. Many of the petty chiefs and rank-and-file viewed him, as was natural, with distrust. He and Pétion won them over or hunted them down and destroyed them. Dessalines drilled the raw levies daily, preparing for a campaign on a grand scale. In the middle of January Rochambeau asked for authorisation to restore slavery at once.[64] Leclerc had not even dared to confide Bonaparte's authorisation to him, so utterly opposed were the sentiments of even post-revolutionary France to the reactionary savagery of the maritime bourgeois.

While waiting for this authorisation Rochambeau began on his own account to exterminate the Mulattoes. They outnumbered the whites, and looking forward to the restoration of white supremacy he thought it as well to get rid of as many as possible: Rochambeau hated the Mulattoes more than the blacks. One night at Port-République he gave a great ball to which he invited several of the Mulatto women. It was a magnificent fête. At midnight Rochambeau stops the dancing and begs them to enter into a neighbouring apartment. This room, lit by a single lamp, is hung with black draperies in which white material figures as skulls; in the four corners are coffins. In the middle of their horrified silence the Mulatto women hear funeral chants sung by invisible singers. Dumb with terror they stood rooted to the spot, while Rochambeau told them: "You have just assisted at the funeral ceremonies of your husbands and your brothers." [65]

The French shot and drowned them, hundreds at a time, and not only shot the rich but confiscated their property.[66] By early March the Mulatto South was in full insurrection. But the Spaniards in the West and Laplume still

---

[64] To the Colonial Minister. 25 Nivôse. An XI. (January 14th 1803.) Les Archives du Ministère des Colonies.
[65] Sannon, Histoire de Toussaint-L'Ouverture, Vol. III, p. 150. This incident is found in two early historians, Ardouin and Delattre, who are referred to by Sannon.
[66] Lacroix. Memorandum to Napoleon. Les Archives Nationales; AF. IV. 1212. Poyen, Histoire Militaire de la Révolution . . . , pp. 371-372.

stuck to the French. Rochambeau received in all 20,000 men after Leclerc's death.[67] But by now Dessalines was ready.

We cannot describe that war in detail. It was a war not so much of armies as of the people. It was now a war with the racial divisions emphasizing the class struggle—blacks and Mulattoes against whites. Leclerc had proposed a war of extermination, and Rochambeau waged it. As late as November 4th Kerverseau, who had served a long time under Toussaint, was confident that the French could still count on the "free Negroes and proprietors as much as on the whites." [68] But he counted without Rochambeau's precipitancy. One week later his tone had changed. "This is no longer a war. It is a fight of tigers. One has to be in a transport of frenzy to keep it up, and I have to keep on telling the troops: 'It is no longer bravery I want from you. It is rage.' But one cannot always be in a rage, and humanity makes us weep sometimes." [69] He wept but he fought.

Rochambeau drowned so many people in the Bay of Le Cap that for many a long day the people of the district would not eat fish. Following the example of the Spaniards in Cuba and the English in Jamaica, he brought 1500 dogs to hunt down the blacks. The day they arrived there was a fête.[70] In the grounds of a former Jesuit convent an amphitheatre was constructed, and on a certain day a young black was led in and bound to a post, while the whites of Le Cap, the women in brilliant costumes, sat waiting—(and Toussaint had shot Moïse and the blacks of Limbé, Dondon and Plaisance for their hostility to these very people). To the sound of martial music arrived Rochambeau, surrounded by his staff. But when the dogs were let loose they did not attack the victim. Boyer, chief of

[67] Lacroix, *Mémoires pour Servir* . . . , Vol. 2. B.253.
[68] Kerverseau to Lacroix. November 4th, 1802. *Les Archives du Ministère de la Guerre*, B⁷. 8.
[69] *Ibid.*, November 11th, 1802.
[70] Beard, the English author, says that the white ladies of Le Cap went down to meet the dogs the day they were landed and greeted them with kisses.

staff in place of the dead Dugua, jumped into the arena and with a stroke of his sword cut open the belly of the black. At the sight and scent of the blood the dogs threw themselves on the black and devoured him in a twinkling, while the applause ran round the arena and the band played. To encourage them in a liking for blood blacks were daily delivered to them, until the dogs, though useless in battle, would throw themselves on blacks at sight.[71] The French burned alive, hanged, drowned, tortured, and started again their old habit of burying blacks up to the neck near nests of insects. It was not only hatred and fear, but policy. "If France wishes to regain San Domingo she must send hither 25,000 men in a body, declare the negroes slaves, and destroy at least 30,000 negroes and negresses—the latter being more cruel than the men. These measures are frightful, but necessary. We must take them or renounce the colony. Whoever says otherwise lies in his throat and deceives France."[72] This was the general opinion of the whites. Kill them all off and get new ones who know nothing about liberty and equality. They chained 16 of Toussaint's generals to a rock where they wasted away 17 days. They drowned old Pierre Baptiste. The wife and children of Maurepas were drowned before his eyes, while the sailors nailed a pair of epaulettes into his naked shoulders. Some of the French, it is fair to say, turned in horror from this barbarism. A few captains of boats refused to drown the blacks handed over to them, but sold them into slavery instead. Some others landed them on deserted beaches in San Domingo or on other islands. Allix, Commander of Port-Républicain, would not accept 10,000 shot sent him to tie to the feet of those to be drowned. Rochambeau banished him. Mazard, another sea-captain, worked as hard to save blacks as most of his colleagues to drown them. But these were drops in the ocean. It was the

[71] Lacroix Memorandum. *Les Archives Nationales*. Sannon, *Histoire de Toussaint-L'Ouverture*, Vol. III, pp. 152-153.
[72] Letter from Le Cap, October 6th (14 Vendémiaire An XI). *Les Archives Nationales*. Quoted in Lothrop Stoddard, *The French Revolution in San Domingo*, p. 347. Needless to say, Stoddard has no objection whatever to this policy.

policy of the Tories that the British followed in Ireland, in 1921, not the remonstrances of the *Manchester Guardian* or the Society of Friends. So it is, so it always has been.

Dessalines was a one-sided genius, but he was the man for this crisis, not Toussaint. He gave blow for blow. When Rochambeau put to death 500 at Le Cap and buried them in a large hole dug while they waited for execution, Dessalines raised gibbets of branches and hanged 500 for Rochambeau and the whites in Le Cap to see. But neither Dessalines' army nor his ferocity won the victory. It was the people. They burned San Domingo flat so that at the end of the war it was a charred desert. Why do you burn everything? asked a French officer of a prisoner. We have a right to burn what we cultivate because a man has a right to dispose of his own labour, was the reply of this unknown anarchist.[73] And far from being intimidated, the civil population met the terror with such courage and firmness as frightened the terrorists. Three blacks were condemned to be burnt alive. A huge crowd stood round while two of them were consumed, uttering horrible cries. But the third, a boy of 19, bound so that he could not see the other two, called to them in creole, "You do not know how to die. See how to die." By a great effort he twisted his body in his bonds, sat down and, placing his feet in the flames, let them burn without uttering a groan. "I was there," said Lemmonier-Delafosse, "spectator of the heroic death of this wretch, greater than Mucius Scaevola. . . . These were the men we had to fight against." [74] Another thrown to the dogs showed no anger, but stroked them and encouraged them while he presented his limbs to be destroyed.[75] With the women it was the same. When Chevalier, a black chief, hesitated at the sight of the scaffold, his wife shamed him. "You do not know how sweet it is to die for liberty!" And refusing to allow herself to be hanged by the executioner, she took the rope and hanged herself.

[73] Lacroix Memorandum. *Les Archives Nationales.*
[74] Lemmonier-Delafosse, *Seconde campagne de Saint-Domingue précédée de souvenirs historiques et succints de la première campagne*, Paris, 1846.
[75] Lacroix Memorandum.

To her daughters going to execution with her, another woman gave courage. "Be glad you will not be the mothers of slaves."

The French, powerless before this fortitude, saw in it not the strength of the revolution but some peculiarity special to blacks. The muscles of a Negro, they said, contracted with so much force as to make him insensible to pain. They enslaved the Negro, they said, because he was not a man, and when he behaved like a man they called him a monster.

In the spring of 1803 Bonaparte was preparing vast armaments to send to San Domingo during the coming autumn. With sublime impudence he blamed the blacks for what was happening in San Domingo. At a meeting of the Institute at which Grégoire was present he said that the friends of the blacks should hide their heads at the news from San Domingo. That the blacks would not docilely submit to be slaves again was an unpardonable crime and they wreaked their vengeance on the man whom they considered mainly responsible for their disappointment. It was Toussaint's resistance which had upset all calculations.

The balked greed of Bonaparte and the French bourgeoisie, their hatred of the "revolted slave" who had ruined their plans, can be judged from the brutality with which they persecuted him. He landed at Brest on July 9th, saw his family for the first time since they had left Le Cap, and never saw them again. Not only Leclerc but Bonaparte feared him, and Bonaparte feared too the French Revolution which he and his kind had stifled. In a closed carriage and under instructions devised and carried out with the greatest rigour and secrecy, they hurried him across France. Bonaparte, it seems, was afraid that attempts might be made to rescue him. There were no blacks in France to do this, and such an attempt could have been anticipated from scattered Jacobins stirred to anger at this final degradation of the revolution—the restoration of slavery. But such fears were far-fetched. At one town some French officers who had served under him heard that he was passing through and asked to be allowed to salute their old commander.[76] That was all.

On August 24th, with his faithful servant, Mars Plaisir,[77] Toussaint was imprisoned in the Fort-de-Joux, situated in the Jura mountains, at an altitude of over 3,000 feet. Leclerc was writing his frantic letters charged with fear of the black leader. He could send no evidence on which to accuse him. But Governments do not need evidence, and Bonaparte did not murder Toussaint judicially because he feared the repercussions in San Domingo of a trial and execution. But he was to be got rid of and Bonaparte decided to kill him by ill-treatment, cold and starvation. On Bonaparte's strict instructions his gaolers humiliated him, called him Toussaint, gave him convict's clothes to wear, cut down his food, and when the winter came reduced his allowance for wood; they took away his servant.[78] Bonaparte sent his aide-de-campe, Caffarelli, to interview him, to find out where he had hidden his treasure, and what secret arrangements he had made with the British. Caffarelli had seven interviews with him and could find out nothing: there was nothing to find out. Toussaint had no treasure. He had not sold himself to the British.

The régime tightened always. His gaolers, still on Bonaparte's advice, watched him eat his food, watched him perform his natural functions. They feared that he might escape, and wanted him to die as quickly as possible, thinking that once the great leader was gone their chances in San Domingo would be better. He had medical attendance at first, but his gaoler soon dispensed with it. "The construction of Negroes being totally different to that of Europeans, I have dispensed with his doctor and his surgeon who would be useless to him." [79]

[76] Isaac L'Ouverture. Mémoires.
[77] He was a Mulatto—typical of Toussaint.
[78] Nemours, *Histoire de la Captivité et de la Mort de Toussaint-L'Ouverture*. Paris, 1929. The definitive account of Toussaint's captivity with many of the most important documents printed in full.
[79] Poyen, *Histoire Militaire de la Révolution* . . . , p. 224. Poyen quotes the gaoler's official report.

He was 57 and quite early he broke down. He wrote long reports of his conduct, addressed letters to Bonaparte asking for trial, appealed to his greatness and magnanimity.

"I have had the misfortune to incur your anger; but as to fidelity and probity, I am strong in my conscience, and I dare to say with truth that among all the servants of the State none is more honest than I. I was one of your soldiers and the first servant of the Republic in San Domingo. I am to-day wretched, ruined, dishonoured, a victim of my own services. Let your sensibility be touched at my position, you are too great in feeling and too just not to pronounce on my destiny. . . ."

In the warning to the Directory, as in his proclamations to his soldiers and to his people, so now in his personal grief the limitations of his political conceptions stood revealed. The sombre cadences in which he begged for trial are evidence of his fatal sincerity. Despite the treachery of France he still saw himself as a part of the French Republic "one and indivisible." He could not think otherwise. The decree of the 16th Pluviôse had marked in his mind the beginning of a new era for all French blacks. His experiences of French Commissioners, his fears for his people, his hard sense of reality, had driven him along the road of independence. But there was a limit beyond which he could not go. He had a profound conviction that the French could never restore slavery in San Domingo and he falsely believed that, once the means of defending liberty for all were safeguarded, no sacrifice was too great to make the French see reason. That was why his chief concern in prison was the fate of his wife and children. About the future of San Domingo he maintained an unshakable silence. His words to the captain when stepping on the boat were the last he ever said on that subject. The maintenance of liberty for all had been his life's work and the words and the silence afterwards were certainly intentional.

Shivering with cold, he was spending his first winter in a cell inadequately warmed, where the walls ran with moisture. His iron frame, which had withstood the privations and fatigues of ten incredible years, now huddled before the logs measured out by the orders of Bonaparte. The hitherto unsleeping intellect collapsed periodically into long hours of coma. Before the spring he was dying. One April morning he was found dead in his chair.

There is no drama like the drama of history. Toussaint died on April 7th, 1803 and Bonaparte must have thought that half the battle against San Domingo was now won. But in Toussaint's last hours his comrades in arms, ignorant of his fate, were drafting the declaration of independence.

For some months after November 1802, the national army still carried the French flag, and in December a rumour had spread among the French that the blacks and Mulattoes were not fighting for independence because they still carried the French colours. To end this Dessalines summoned a conference at Arcahaye. From the red, white and blue of the tricolour, the white was removed, and instead of the initials R. F. (République Française), "Liberty or Death" was inscribed. The new flag was unfurled on May 18th. On that very day some officers from the South, hastening back to their commands, were in danger of being captured by a French cruiser. Rather than surrender, Laporte, the senior officer, ordered the boat to be sunk and drew a pistol on himself, while the crew disappeared below the waves shouting, "Long live independence!" A few weeks after the Arcahaye Conference San Domingo learned that the war between Britain and France had begun again: Rochambeau was cut off by the British fleet.

This was welcome news, but the San Domingo blacks now knew all that there was to be known about imperialism. The British policy was opportunist. They attempted no hostilities against the coast towns and they allowed American vessels to provision Rochambeau at Le Cap.[80]

80 Sannon, *Histoire de Toussaint-L'Ouverture*, Vol. III, p. 185.

They were probably waiting to see if Rochambeau could win a temporary victory, at least in a part of San Domingo, when they could step in and capture it from the French. But in time they threw their full weight on the side of Dessalines, supplying arms and ammunition. Dessalines, however, sought no co-operation of any kind, and paid both English and Americans spot cash for all they sold him.[81]

The war in Europe was the turning point. Spanish San Domingo still remained quiet, but North, West, and South the revolution for national independence drove the French out of the fortified positions they occupied and penned them in the coastal towns.

It was a people's war. They played the most audacious tricks on the French. One night Lacroix wished to make a reconnaissance. He heard at a musket's distance a low voice saying, "Platoon, halt! To the right, dress!" This was repeated twenty times along an extended line. Soon he heard commands in creole from several chiefs not to whisper nor to smoke. The French made their dispositions and waited all night for a sudden attack. When day came, they found that they had been the dupe of about a hundred labourers. "These ruses, if one paid too much attention to them, destroyed one's morale; if they were neglected, they could lead to surprises." [82]

Not only on land but on sea the blacks and Mulattoes took an irresistible offensive. Building light boats they skimmed over the rivers and around the coasts, attacking ships, massacring the prisoners, and carrying off plunder. The French were helpless against them. The blacks ran their boats on shore, hid them, and carried on guerilla warfare against the French soldiers, then disappeared to sail quickly down the rivers and appear unexpectedly at sea. They captured two vessels, one from Nantes and one from Havre, which had escaped the blockade, and slaughtered all on board. The French, facing annihilation, defended themselves with desperate valour. But under the pressure of the attack and the blockade, a division broke out between the army and the local whites. Rochambeau, without money, levied heavy subventions on them and the local whites rebelled. They had been willing to live under Toussaint. Though some of them wished Leclerc had not come, being white, they had joined Leclerc's army and grasped eagerly at the chance to reassert white domination. But now that they saw their plantations destroyed, San Domingo in ruins, their lives in danger, and their possessions confiscated, they turned on Rochambeau and reproached him, some being anxious now only for peace with the blacks. The struggle became hopeless for the French, hopeless in their own internal divisions, hopeless in the numbers against them and the spirit which moved in the black army. The accounts must be read in the histories of Haiti and the memoirs of the French officers who survived. On November 16th the blacks and Mulattoes concentrated for a last attack on Le Cap, and the strongly fortified posts surrounding it.

Clairveaux, the Mulatto, was in command, and with him was Capois Death, a Negro officer, so called on account of his bravery. From early morning the national army attacked. In the afternoon under a crossfire of musketry and artillery Capois led the assault on the blockhouses of Bréda and Champlin, shouting "Forward, forward!" The French were strongly entrenched and drove off the blacks again and again only to see them return to the attack with undiminished ardour. A bullet knocked over Capois' horse. Boiling with rage he scrambled up and, making a gesture of contempt with his sword, he continued to advance. "Forward, forward!"

The French, who had fought on so many fields, had never seen fighting like this. From all sides came a storm of shouts. "Bravo! Bravo!" There was a roll of drums. The French ceased fire. A French horseman rode out and advanced to the bridge. He brought a message from Rochambeau. "The Captain-General sends his admiring compliments to the officer who has just covered himself with so much glory." [83] Without a shot fired from the blacks, the horseman turned and rode back to the blockhouse and the battle began again. The struggle had been such a nightmare that by now all in San Domingo were a little mad, both white and black.

Half a century later Lemmonier-Delafosse (who believed in slavery) wrote his memoirs: "But what men these blacks are! How they fight and how they die! One has to make war against them to know their reckless courage in braving danger when they can no longer have recourse to stratagem. I have seen a solid column, torn by grape-shot from four pieces of cannon, advance without making a retrograde step. The more they fell, the greater seemed to be the courage of the rest. They advanced singing, for the Negro sings everywhere, makes songs on everything. Their song was a song of brave men and went as follows:

'To the attack, grenadier,
    Who gets killed, that's his affair.
    Forget your ma,
    Forget your pa,
To the attack, grenadier,
    Who gets killed, that's his affair.'

"This song was worth all our republican songs. Three times these brave men, arms in hand, advanced without firing a shot, and each time repulsed, only retired after leaving the ground strewed with three-quarters of their troop. One must have seen this bravery to have any conception of it. Those songs shouted into the sky in unison by 2,000 voices, to which the cannon formed the bass, produced a thrilling effect. French courage alone could resist it. Indeed large ditches, an excellent artillery, perfect soldiers gave us a great advantage. But for many a day that massed square which marched singing to its death, lighted by a magnificent sun, remained in my thoughts, and even to-day after more than 40 years, this majestic and glorious

[83] Sannon, *Histoire de Toussaint-L'Ouverture*, Vol. III, p. 195.

spectacle still lives as vividly in my imagination as in the moments when I saw it."

It had stirred even such a hater of colour as Rochambeau to a chivalrous gesture. Dessalines, the local leader, was stationed on a neighbouring hill. Himself known as the bravest of the brave, even he was overcome at the spirit of Capois and his men, and dumb with admiration he sat watching the attack, twiddling his legendary snuff-box in his hand. A sudden torrential rain stopped the fighting. But it was the end. That night Rochambeau held a council of war and decided to evacuate the island. Toussaint had been dead only seven months, but his work was done. Of men who had cowered trembling before the frown of any white ruffian, he had made in ten years an army which could hold its own with the finest soldiers Europe has yet seen.

"There is no longer any doubt, my dear General," wrote the triumphant Dessalines to one of his officers in the South, "the country is ours and the famous *who will have it* is decided."

On November 28th, the day before that fixed for his departure, Rochambeau tried to come to terms for his men and ships with the British waiting for him outside the harbour. The British made the harshest terms, and Rochambeau threatened to land at Caracol and retreat to Spanish San Domingo, which still remained in the hands of the French. Dessalines warned him that if he did not clear out at once his ships would be bombarded with red-hot shot. Since early morning the furnaces of Fort Picolet had been burning, and Rochambeau had no alternative but to surrender to the British. Of 60,000 soldiers and sailors who had sailed from France nearly all had perished, and the few who remained were to rot and waste for years in English prisons.

On November 29th Dessalines, Christophe, and Clairveaux (Pétion was ill) issued a preliminary proclamation of independence, moderate in tone, deploring the blood-shed of the previous years. On December 31st at a meeting of all the officers held at Gonaïves the final Declaration of Independence was read. To emphasise the break with the French the new State was renamed Haiti. Dessalines made an attempt to take Spanish San Domingo, but the French Revolution had never had any support there, and he failed. On October 1804 he had himself crowned Emperor. Private merchants of Philadelphia presented him with the crown, brought on the American boat the *Connecticut,* his coronation robes reached Haiti from Jamaica on an English frigate from London. He made his solemn entry into Le Cap in a six-horse carriage brought for him by the English agent, Ogden, on board the *Samson.*[84] Thus the Negro monarch entered into his inheritance, tailored and valeted by English and American capitalists, supported on the one side by the King of England and on the other by the President of the United States.

Early in the new year, 1805, the whites in Haiti were massacred by the orders of Dessalines. All histories are full of this. A representative of the British Government[85] once threw it in the face of the Haitian delegate at a meeting of the League of Nations. He would have been more cautious if he had known the part his own highly civilised country played in this supposedly typical example of black savagery.

The patience and forbearance of the poor are among the strongest bulwarks of the rich. The black labourers of San Domingo had had provocation enough from the whites to justify the massacre of three times their number. But up to October 1802, although they knew that slavery would be restored if they lost the war, they, poor wretches, still retained some traces of humanity, and even then some of the whites might have escaped massacre. All that the labourers wanted was to be left in peace with the assurance

[84] See note 87 on p. 371.
[85] Lord Cecil.

that the whites would not seek to make them slaves again. But Leclerc's letters tell us that he had resolved on a war of extermination. That in plain words was the massacre of as many blacks as possible. The drowning of over a thousand in Le Cap harbour at one stroke was no act of panic —it was deliberately done. This started the race war, and Rochambeau completed it by attempting to exterminate blacks and Mulattoes as well.

But the San Domingo whites, as they saw Rochambeau's policy and arms failing, turned once more to the blacks. Dessalines' moderate proclamation of November 29th reassured them. Dessalines even invited the white émigrés to return and enjoy their property. The blacks did not want their goods—"Far from our minds is such an unjust thought." The retiring French offered the whites places in their ships. They refused almost unanimously.[86] Abominable hypocrites as they were, now that their last bid for supremacy had failed, they were willing to accommodate themselves to an independent black State.

Why they were not allowed to do so was due not so much to the justified hate of the blacks but the calculated savagery of imperialism. Let us grant freely that Dessalines wanted to destroy all the whites. He had arranged with Rochambeau to protect the French wounded. As soon as Rochambeau left, he massacred them. But Christophe had certainly no such intention, and all Clairveaux' history shows him to have been a man who would not harbour any such ideas. But when the Congress met at Gonaïves in December, there were three Englishmen present, one of them Cathcart, an English agent. They swore that the English would trade with San Domingo and accord their protection for its independence only when the last of the whites had fallen under the axe.[87] These civilised cannibals in their greed for trade wanted to drive a wedge between

[86] Poyen, *Histoire Militaire de la Révolution* . . . , p. 436.
[87] Guy, *La Perte de Saint-Domingue. Du Traité d' Amiens au Couronnement de Dessalines. D'après les mémoires* . . . *conservés aux Archives des Colonies. Fonds Moreau*, f. 283. M. Camille Guy, *Bulletin de géographie historique et descriptive*, No. 3, 1898, pp. 17-18.

Haiti and France to break all possibilities of unity, and instead of using their influence in the right direction chose to make these propositions to a people exasperated by centuries of provocation and strained to breaking-point by Leclerc's invasion and Rochambeau's cruelties. This is one of the most infamous and unjustifiable crimes in all this wretched history. Though there is no evidence, the Americans were probably in it too. All through Leclerc's campaign they took the part of the blacks, accused Leclerc of "crime, treason, assassination and sacrilege," [88] wrote in their journals of his perfidious machinations toward the "unfortunate Toussaint," and generally were consumed with that virtuous indignation characteristic of the Anglo-Saxon capitalist whenever property or profits is in danger. That the great majority of the British people would have revolted in horror from such barbarism there is no doubt, as the vast majority of Frenchmen after 1794 disapproved of slavery. But to-day as then, the great propertied interests and their agents commit the most ferocious crimes in the name of the whole people, and bluff and browbeat them by lying propaganda.

The first draft of the proclamation handed to Dessalines at the Congress was rejected by him as being too moderate. The second, which met with his approval, struck the new note, "Peace to our neighbours. But anathema to the French name. Hatred eternal to France. This is our cry." Dessalines was crowned in October 1804. The white proprietors still remained untouched. The black population, despite incendiary proclamations by Dessalines, inciting them against the whites, did not molest them at all. In January the command was issued to massacre them all, but even then no holocaust took place.

In February and March Dessalines undertook a campaign against the French in San Domingo. He besieged Santo Domingo, and on the twenty-second day of the siege the town was about to fall into his hands when a French

---

[88] Extracts from American papers among Leclerc's Archives. *Les Archives du Ministère de la Guerre.* B⁷6.

squadron appeared in the harbour, commanded by Admiral Missiessy. At the same time the rumour ran that another French squadron was in the harbour of Gonaïves. Dessalines, feeling that Haiti was menaced, raised the siege and hurried back home. It was then that the complete massacre took place. The population, stirred to fear at the nearness of the counter-revolution, killed all with every possible brutality. After the first slaughter Dessalines issued a proclamation promising pardon to all who were in hiding. They came out, and were immediately killed. Yet Dessalines took great care to protect the British and the American whites, and spared also the priests, the skilled workmen, and the officers of health. Toussaint had written to Bonaparte asking for just such persons as these to help. And even the fierce and uncultured Dessalines, though with the marks of the whip on his skin, would have been willing to let bygones be bygones if there had been any semblance of good feeling or generosity on the other side. This is not idealism. We have Bonaparte's letter when he was about to direct his energies to the East. He was willing to let Toussaint govern then. And at St Helena he confessed that the expedition had been a mistake, and he should have ruled the island through Toussaint L'Ouverture. He had been convinced at last by the only argument that imperialists understand.

The massacre of the whites was a tragedy; not for the whites. For these old slave-owners, those who burnt a little powder in the arse of a Negro, who buried him alive for insects to eat, who were well treated by Toussaint, and who, as soon as they got the chance, began their old cruelties again; for these there is no need to waste one tear or one drop of ink. The tragedy was for the blacks and the Mulattoes. It was not policy but revenge, and revenge has no place in politics. The whites were no longer to be feared, and such purposeless massacres degrade and brutalise a population, especially one which was just beginning as a nation and had had so bitter a past. The people did not want it—all they wanted was freedom, and independence seemed to promise that. Christophe and other generals strongly disapproved.[89] Had the British and the Americans thrown their weight on the side of humanity, Dessalines might have been curbed. As it was Haiti suffered terribly from the resulting isolation. Whites were banished from Haiti for generations, and the unfortunate country, ruined economically, its population lacking in social culture, had its inevitable difficulties doubled by this massacre. That the new nation survived at all is forever to its credit for if the Haitians thought that imperialism was finished with them, they were mistaken.

Pitt, Dundas and the rest were very satisfied. The wonderful colony of San Domingo was no longer a rival. Having failed to get it for themselves, they turned their minds definitely away from the West Indies. But France wanted the colony back. Only the war with England and the destruction at Trafalgar of the French fleet (weakened by the loss of all the sailors in San Domingo) prevented another expedition. The French bourgeoisie bided its time. Always they planned to restore slavery. Mauviel, the Bishop who had been spared by Dessalines, acted as a spy, and informed Bonaparte of the various fortifications and plans for defence. The reverend gentleman, deprecating that "his sphere was not the military art," modestly submitted to Napoleon an actual plan of campaign. Most of the blacks, he was sure, wanted to be slaves. But above all in the colonies, "with the difference of colour, and with their warm climate, religion was necessary to restrain the effervescence of the passions. Without it the blacks would again abandon themselves to their brutal instincts and would indulge in new excesses. It is only by speaking to them in the name of God that one would henceforth be able to persuade them that the state of dependence in which they are placed is in the order of the Divine Providence." [90] Nevertheless,

---

[89] Poyen, *Histoire Militaire de la Révolution* . . . , p. 470.
[90] Mauviel. Memorandum to Napoleon. *Les Archives Nationales* A.F. IV. 1212.

after restoration there should be an armed police and gendarmerie, "mobile columns patrolling all points," light boats constantly cruising in the harbours. Religion, it seemed, was not enough.

How to make these future slaves accept slavery? Another gentleman proposed that they should be taught to read but not to write. Thus they could read their prayers and improving books, in which they would learn of the cruelties practised by the Spaniards and the English on the Red Indians. Particularly he wanted put in how the English invited the Red Indians to celebrate a treaty of alliance and poisoned them in rum.[91] Yet another proposal suggested that an expedition should "not only draw forth into activity the dormant and stagnant capital of individuals in France itself, but also attract monied men of other countries. . . ." This proposal came from England or America, for it was written in English. The rulers of Haiti were to be pensioned and pardoned.

Those who knew San Domingo, however, knew that there would never be any more slavery for the blacks there, and Lacroix' proposal was to exterminate those who remained and bring fresh ones from Africa.[92] This was the prevailing opinion. Lacroix was a brave soldier and a highly educated man. He knew the black leaders personally. Even after the defeat he wrote in high praise of them and their people, but there is nothing so fierce as an imperialist in the colonies.

Finally[93] those black Haitian labourers and the Mulattoes have given us an example to study. Despite the temporary reaction of Fascism, the prevailing standards of human liberty and equality are infinitely more advanced and more profound than those current in 1789. Judged relatively by these standards, the millions of blacks in Africa and the few of them who are educated are as much pariahs in that vast prison as the blacks and Mulattoes of San Do-

---

[91] Various Memoranda on America. *Les Archives du Ministère des Affaires Etrangères.*
[92] Lacroix. Memorandum to Napoleon.
[93] See Preface to the Vintage Edition, p. vii.

mingo in the eighteenth century. The imperialists envisage
an eternity of African exploitation: the African is backward, ignorant. . . . They dream dreams. If in 1788 anyone had told the Comte de Lauzerne, the Minister; the
Comte de Peynier, the Governor; General Rochambeau,
the soldier; Moreau de Saint-Mery, the historian; Barbé de
Marbois, the bureaucrat, that the thousands of dumb brutes
who were whipped to labour at dawn and whipped back
at midnight, who submitted to their mutilations, burnings,
and other savageries, some of whom would not even move
unless they were whipped, if these fine gentlemen had been
told that in three years the blacks would shake off their
chains and face extermination rather than put them on
again, they would have thought the speaker mad. While
if to-day one were to suggest to any white colonial poten-
tate that among those blacks whom they rule are men so
infinitely their superior in ability, energy, range of vision,
and tenacity of purpose that in a hundred years' time these
whites would be remembered only because of their contact
with the blacks, one would get some idea of what the
Counts, Marquises, and other colonial magnates of the day
thought of Jean-François, Toussaint, and Rigaud when the
revolt first began.

The blacks of Africa are more advanced, nearer ready
than were the slaves of San Domingo. This is the appeal
written by some obscure Rhodesian black in whom burns
the fire that burnt in Toussaint L'Ouverture:[94]

*"LISTEN to this all of you who live in the country,
think well how they treat us and to ask for a land. Do
we live in good treatment, no; therefore let us ask one
another and remember this treatment. Because we
wish on the day of 29th April, every person not to go
to work, he who will go to work, and if we see him it
will be a serious case. Know how they cause us to suffer, they cheat us for money, they arrest us for loafing,
they persecute us and put us in gaol for tax. What reason have we done? Secondly do you not wish to hear*

[94] Command 5009.

*these words, well listen, this year of 1935, if they will
not increase us more money stop paying tax, do you
think they can kill you, no. Let us encourage surely
you will see that God be with us. See how we suffer
with the work and how we are continually reviled and
beaten underground. Many brothers of us die for 22s.
6d. is this money that we should lose our lives for? He
who cannot read should tell his companion that on the
29th April not to go to work. Those words do not
come from here, they come from the wisers who are
far away and enable to encourage us.*

"*That all. Hear well if it is right let us do so.*

"*We are all of the Nkana.*

"*Africans—Men and Women.*

"*I am glad,*

"*G. Loveway.*"

Such men as Loveway are symbols of the future.
Others will arise, and others. From the people heaving in
action will come the leaders; not the isolated blacks at
Guys' Hospital or the Sorbonne, the dabblers in *surréalisme*
or the lawyers, but the quiet recruits in a black police
force, the sergeant in the French native army or British
police, familiarising himself with military tactics and strategy, reading a stray pamphlet of Lenin or Trotsky as Toussaint read the Abbé Raynal.

Nor will success result in the isolation of Africa. The
blacks will demand skilled workmen and teachers. International socialism will need the products of a free Africa
far more than the French bourgeoisie needed slavery and
the slave-trade. Imperialism vaunts its exploitation of the
wealth of Africa for the benefit of civilisation. In reality,
from the very nature of its system of production for profit
it strangles the real wealth of the continent—the creative
capacity of the African people. The African faces a long
and difficult road and he will need guidance. But he will
tread it fast because he will walk upright.

BIBLIOGRAPHY

PRIMARY SOURCES. (MSS.)

FRENCH ARCHIVES.

Les Archives Nationales contain many thousands of official reports and private letters dealing with the whole period from 1789 to 1804. This is the main field of research.

Les Archives du Ministère de la Guerre contain another huge collection of documents: the correspondence of Leclerc and the papers of his staff, with other miscellaneous collections such as parts of Toussaint's correspondence (captured during the war), the papers dealing with his journey through France, etc.

Les Archives du Ministère des Colonies contain not only letters from San Domingo, but copies of letters of the Minister to French officials in the colonies.

Les Archives du Ministère des Affaires Étrangères contain a small and miscellaneous collection of documents, some of great importance.

La Bibliothèque Nationale.

The MSS. department contains three volumes of the correspondence of Toussaint with Laveaux and two volumes of the correspondence of Sonthonax. These are of great value.

SAN DOMINGO ARCHIVES.

La Mission du Général Hédouville by A. Michel is based on the collection of Dr. Price Mars, and the book attests that this collection contains original manuscripts of the first importance. It is to be hoped that extracts from them will be published some day.

BRITISH ARCHIVES.

The Public Record Office contains the original correspondence of the Secretary of State with the British officials in Jamaica for the period (C.O. 137) and Foreign Office papers (France), both of which deal extensively with San Domingo.

The British Museum contains scattered MSS on the slave-trade and the West Indies.

The writer does not claim to have examined these archives exhaustively. Those at *Les Archives Nationales* alone would take many years. But much of the ground has been covered by other writers which makes independent research easier.

Unfortunately *suppressio veri* and *suggestio falsi* are not the only devils to be contended with. Hard experience has taught the lesson that it is unwise to take anything on trust and an examination of even apparently bona fide quotations (with reference duly attached) has unearthed some painful instances of unscrupulousness.

PRIMARY SOURCES. (Printed.)

The debates in the revolutionary Assemblies are found in *Le Moniteur* of the period. They are indispensable.

The Correspondence of Napoleon.

The great collection of documents dealing with the history of Paris during the French Revolution and published under the auspices of the Municipal Council of Paris. Not only are they the foundation of any modern study of the revolution, but scattered through them are important references to the colonial question, to San Domingo, to Toussaint L'Ouverture, etc. The most useful for the San Domingo revolution are *La Société des Jacobins* by Aulard (6 vols.), *Les Clubs Contre-Révolutionnaires* by Challamel (1 vol.), *Paris pendant la Réaction Thermidorienne et sous le Directoire* by Aulard (4 vols.), *Paris sous le Consulat* by Aulard (4 vols.).

With this must be included the *Receuil des Actes du Directoire Exécutif* edited by Debidour and published under the direction of the Ministry of Public Instruction.

The Club Massiac, The North Province, The West Province, The South Province, Chambers of Agriculture, Chambers of Commerce, Raymond, Vincent, Laveaux, deputies to the French Assemblies, public and private emissaries of officials, private individuals, every conceivable organisation or person participating in or remotely connected with these events, published pamphlets, many of which are semi-official or even official in character. The pamphlet literature is therefore enormous. La Bibliothèque Nationale has a terrifying collection; that in the British Museum, though very much smaller, is good.

SPECIAL BIBLIOGRAPHY

Despite the importance and interest of the subject, it was for long difficult to find in English or French a comprehensive and well-balanced treatment of the San Domingo revolution in short compass. Both in insight and objectivity the modern Haitian writers are easily the best. For a short survey the following books are recommended.

Michel, Antoine: *La Mission du Général Hédouville à Saint-Domingue*, Imprimerie "La Presse" 618. Rue Dantes Destouches. Port-au-Prince, Haiti 1929.

A projected work in five volumes of which only one has appeared. Based on original documents, analysed with skill and impartiality, this book gives much new information and destroys many legends.[1]

Fortescue, Sir John: *History of the British Army*. Vol. IV. Parts I and II. London 1906.

Fortescue gives a full account of the British expedition. His treatment of San Domingo history, based on research among British archives, is very useful but only for those who understand the Tory mentality. Thus Fortescue glowingly describes the attachment of slaves to their masters and believed that the British offer of freedom after five years of soldiering could be reasonably compared with the French slogan of immediate liberty for all; and when in 1798 Toussaint and Rigaud begin a co-operate effort to drive the British out of San Domingo, Fortescue simply cannot understand why.

Lacroix, Pamphile de: *Mémoires pour Servir à l'Histoire de la Révolution de Saint-Domingue*. 2 Vols. Paris 1819.

Lacroix took part in Leclerc's expedition and much of his work is based on first hand information and his personal experiences. Modern research has proved him wrong on many points. He is biased in favour of the French. Yet his book is indispensable and fully deserves its reputation.

[1] M. Michel died in 1938.

Nemours, General A.: *Histoire Militaire de la Guerre d'Indépendance de Saint-Domingue.* 2 Vols. Paris 1925 and 1928.

This treats of the war of independence down to the surrender of Toussaint. General Nemours is a Haitian who has worked over the terrain in person and has done extensive research among the archives in France. He is an enthusiastic admirer of Toussaint but exceptionally fair.

Poyen, Colonel A. de: *Histoire Militaire de la Révolution de Saint-Domingue.* Paris 1899.

This is the official French account. Poyen misunderstands the whole campaign, both the offensive plan of Leclerc and the defensive plan of Toussaint. (See Nemours' *Histoire Militaire,* Vol. I, Chapters XIV to XVI.) He quotes abundantly from Leclerc's letters, yet states explicitly (p. 331) that the French Government never intended to restore slavery: there is no limit to the brazenness of these imperialist historians. Poyen, however, is a careful, scholarly writer and is useful for the period following the death of Leclerc which is treated by neither Lacroix nor Nemours.

THE FRENCH COLONIAL TRADE.

Deschamps, L.: *Les Colonies pendant la Révolution.* Paris 1898.

Gaston-Martin: *L'Ère des Négriers, 1714-1774.* Paris 1931. This is an exhaustive and well-balanced study.

Gaston-Martin and others: *La Doctrine Coloniale de la France en 1789, etc.*

No. III of the modern series: *Cahiers de la Révolution Française.*

This is a useful but in parts misleading summary. Thus one of the writers speaks of the decree of February 4th, 1794, which abolished slavery as the decree "which was to cost the lives of so many men" (p. 57), and also as "a generator of disorders," a dishonest misrepresentation.

Saintoyant, J.: *La Colonisation Française pendant la Révolution* (1789-1799). 2 Vols. Paris 1930. M. Saintoyant has made an admirable study of the French colonies during the whole period. San Domingo, as the most important of them, has ample treatment. The author writes as a Frenchman who regrets the loss of a great French colony, but he does not manipulate his information or evade truths awkward for his case. He gravely underestimates the difficulties of the French Commissioners, particularly of Sonthonax and Roume. It seems almost impossible for bourgeois writers to understand that standards and methods of administration satisfactory in normal times are for that precise reason useless in trying to form a judgment of a revolutionary period.

Saintoyant, J.: *La Colonisation Française pendant la période Napoléonienne* (1799-1815). Paris 1931.

Sannon, P.: *Histoire de Toussaint-L'Ouverture.* Imprimerie Aug. A. Heraux. 3 Vols. Port-au-Prince, Haiti 1920-1933.

The best biography yet written of Toussaint.

Schœlcher, V.: *Vie de Toussaint-L'Ouverture.* Paris 1899.

Schœlcher is a French radical of the nineteenth century. He hates slavery, hates Bonaparte, and though his heart is in the right place, despite many shrewd comments, he is too uncritical to be trustworthy. But he has digested an enormous amount of original material of which he prints many extracts. All modern writers on the San Domingo revolution are indebted to him and his book should be read, although with extreme caution.

Vaissière, P. de: *Saint-Domingue, 1629-1789. La Société et la Vie Créoles sous l'Ancien Régime.* Paris 1909.

This book is a masterpiece of careful research and vivid presentation. No better introduction to the revolution could be found, though the reader must be on guard against de Vaissière's bias in favour of the local aristocracy.

THE FRENCH REVOLUTION.

It is impossible to understand the San Domingo revolution unless it is studied in close relationship with the revolution in France. Fortunately the French historical school of the French Revolution is one of the greatest historical schools of Western civilisation, combines scholarship with the national spirit and taste, and with that respect for the Revolution without which the history of revolution cannot be written.

The greatest of them all is Michelet, who wrote over a hundred years ago. His father was a man of '93; he was able to talk to many survivors of the Revolution; he examined the records of the Paris Municipality which were destroyed in the days of the Commune in 1871; he came to the French Revolution after a massive study of the French and European history which preceded it. He has very little to say of the colonial question, but I believe that many pages in Michelet are the best preparation for understanding what actually happened in San Domingo.

The inevitable advances in research, scholarship and approach are best found in the work of four deservedly famous historians.

Aulard, whose sympathies were Girondin and Dantonesque, concentrated on the political events of the Revolution.

Mathiez, who was inspired by the events of the Russian Revolution, gave a life-long service to the rehabilitation of Robespierre.

The modern study of the Revolution begins before these two masters, with Jaurès, who wrote the first volume of his history at the beginning of the century and completed the work before the Russian Revolution. He established once and for all the economic basis of the Revolution; showed the insight into the parliaments of the Revolution that would be expected from a great parliamentarian; one of the early labour leaders of Europe, he shows a sympathetic understanding of the great mass movements which Aulard had neglected and by which Mathiez, though recognising their importance, had been repelled.

The crown of this work of over a century has been attained by M. Georges Lefebvre, whose one-volume history of the Revolution, and his mimeographed series of lectures to students at the Sorbonne, are a fitting climax to a lifetime of indefatigable scholarship, sympathetic understanding, and balanced judgment of all parties, groups and individuals in the Revolution, which it would be difficult to parallel.

In the period after World War II, Daniel Guérin, strongly influenced by Marxism and the decline of the Russian Revolution from its Leninist standards, has produced a brilliant, original and well-documented iconoclastic study, which centres around the conflict between Robespierre and the various mass movements.

Unfortunately not all of these books are translated into English. The best general book in English is still Kropotkin's brief history of over fifty years ago. Kropotkin thought the Revolution was a wonderful event and was neither afraid nor embarrassed to say so. Many Americans have done meticulous studies of special periods and aspects, and both in England and the United States one-volume studies have appeared which seek to embody the latest researches. - But they are of little value, for the writers, particularly in England, usually try to be what is known as "fair to both sides." Thus the reader is led to see most of the explosive incidents of the Revolution, which was really a series of gigantic explosions, as unfortunate excesses. A reactionary historian might miss much of the creative actions and ideas of the revolutionary forces, but he would hardly fail to portray the clash of an irresistible conflict, of suddenly emergent forces pursuing unsuspected aims. In a revolution excesses are the normal, and the historian who does not accept that does not accept the revolution and therefore cannot write its history.

I have sought all through to show the direct influence of the Revolution on events and leading personalities in San Domingo. On page 338 I have given a quotation from M. Lefebvre, and elsewhere I have tried to show the close parallels, hitherto unsuspected, which can be found between events in two populations so widely separated and so diverse in origin and composition. Studies of events, in France and in San Domingo, will not fail to unearth more.

SAN DOMINGO BEFORE THE REVOLUTION.
(History and Geography.)

Boissonade, P.: *Saint-Domingue à la Veille de la Révolution et la Question de la Représentation aux États-Généraux*. Paris 1906. A scholarly piece of research.

Charlevoix, Père: *Histoire de l'Ile Espagnole ou de Saint-Domingue*. Amsterdam 1733. A standard work.

Edwards, Bryan: *A Historical Survey of the French Colony of San Domingo, etc*. London 1796. A good comprehensive study.

D'Auberteuil, Hilliard: *Considérations sur l'État Présent . . . de Saint-Domingue*. Paris 1776. A study by a man of independent judgment, notable for its sympathetic attitude towards the slaves.

De Wimpffen, Baron F.: *Voyage à Saint-Domingue pendant les années 1788, 1789 et 1790*. Paris 1790. This is a travel book that deserves reading, not only for its description of the colony, but for its own sake.

Labat, Père: *Nouveaux Voyages aux Iles de l'Amérique*. A very famous old travel book.

Moreau de Saint-Méry: *Description Topographique, Physique et Politique de Saint-Domingue*. 2 Vols. Philadelphia 1797. A standard work, learned and comprehensively written, but with all the white bias of the time, e.g. the natural inferiority of Mulattoes to whites, etc.

There are many contemporary memoirs and travel books, among others, by Ducœurjoly, Descourtilz, Girod-Chantraus, Colonel Malenfant and Malouet. Descourtilz (*Voyage d'un Naturaliste*, Paris 1809) was a prisoner in Crête-à-Pierrot during the siege, and has preserved some historically useful information.

ABOLITION OF THE BRITISH SLAVE TRADE.

Brougham, H.: *The Colonial Policy of the European Powers*. Edinburgh 1803.

Clarkson, T.: *Essay on the Impolicy of the African Slave Trade*. London 1788. The title best explains this book.

Clarkson, T.: *History of the Rise, Progress and Accomplishment of the Abolition of the African Slave Trade*. London 1839. Clarkson's two books show that he had no illusions as to the economic basis of his case.

Coupland, R.: *Wilberforce*. London 1923.

Coupland, R.: *The British Anti-Slavery Movement*. London 1933.

Both these books are typical for, among other vices, their smug sentimentality, characteristic of the official approach of Oxford scholarship to abolition. As the official view, they can be recommended for their thorough misunderstanding of the question.

Ragatz, L. F.: *The Fall of the Planter Class in the British Caribbean*. London 1928. This is yet another of those monumental pieces of research into European history which American scholarship is giving us in such profusion.

Wilberforce, R. I. and S.: *Life of Wilberforce*. London 1838.

Parliamentary History.
Parliamentary Debates.
Hansard.

THE MULATTOES.

Lebeau, A.: *De la condition des Gens de couleur Libres sous l'ancien Régime.* Poitiers 1903.

THE SLAVES.

Frossard, A.: *La Cause des Négres Esclaves.* 2 Vols. Lyons 1789.

Peytraud, L.: *L'Esclavage aux Antilles Françaises avant 1789.* Paris 1897.

SAN DOMINGO 1789-1804.

Three books are indispensable.

Ardouin, B.: *Études sur l'Histoire d'Haiti.* 6 Vols. Paris 1853. Ardouin has written a very curious book. He is a Mulatto and hates Toussaint, hates the French (Roume, Sonthonax and all), and twists his evidence to suit his purpose. A Haitian scholar has informed the writer that he has detected Ardouin suppressing portions of letters which would prejudice the particular point he was proving. There is no reason to doubt this. Yet Ardouin has covered a vast deal of ground. His hatred sharpens a remarkable acuteness and his book is one of the most valuable sources for any serious work on the San Domingo revolution.

Garran-Coulon, J.: *Débats entre les accusés et les accusateurs dans l'Affaire des Colonies.* 6 Vols. Paris 1798. This is the official report of the trial of Sonthonax and Polverel. It contains a mass of information, much of it contested on the spot by opponents and therefore all the more valuable.[1]

Garran-Coulon, J.: *Rapport sur les Troubles de Saint-Domingue* . . . 6 Vols. Paris 1799. This is the official report of the first three years of the revolution prepared for the Legislature on the basis of the mass of material at its disposal. It is a mine of information.

There are other useful general histories, notably:

Dalmas, M.: *Histoire de la Révolution de Saint-Domingue.* 2 Vols. Paris 1814.

Justine Placide: *Histoire de l'Ile d'Haiti.* Paris 1826.

[1] The book seems to be rare. The author could find only one copy in Paris, in the library of the Minister of Marine.

Madiou, T.: *Histoire d'Haiti.* 2 Vols. Port-au-Prince 1817.

Lemmonier-Delafosse. *Seconde Campagne de Saint-Domingue.* Havre 1846.

The writer took part in the campaign.

Stoddard, T. Lothrop: *The French Revolution in San Domingo.* Boston and New York 1914. With industry and ingenuity, Lothrop Stoddard pursued his vendetta against the Negro race. His thesis is that the white race destroyed itself in San Domingo through its determination to preserve its racial purity, and with the aid of extracts from the correspondence of irresponsible private persons and by ignoring whatever does not fit into his case, he builds up a mirage of proof. In various footnotes we give examples of his methods.

Métral, A.: *Histoire de l'Expédition des Français à Saint-Domingue, sous le Consulat de Napoléon Bonaparte.* Paris 1825. The book includes the Mémoires of Isaac L'Ouverture. Isaac writes from memory and makes obvious mistakes but his testimony is useful on many points.

BIOGRAPHIES OF TOUSSAINT L'OUVERTURE.

These are on the whole very poor. The best known and most useful are Gragnon-Lacoste: *Toussaint L'Ouverture.* Paris 1877. This is a panegyric which, however, preserves some useful information.

Waxman, P.: *The Black Napoleon.* New York 1931. A superficial book.

Saint-Remy: *La Vie de Toussaint L'Ouverture.* Paris 1850.

Saint-Remy, a Mulatto, hated L'Ouverture like poison, and his biography is a scornful attack. Three years later, however, he seems to have mellowed. He published Toussaint's "Mémoires," an apologia, written for Bonaparte, by Toussaint, in the Fort-de-Joux, dealing chiefly with his activities just before and during Leclerc's expedition. Saint-Remy's introduction is almost friendly.

Nemours, A.: *Histoire de la Captivité et de la Mort de Toussaint-L'Ouverture.* Paris 1929. A thorough and well-documented study.

During the Napoleonic war, Marcus Rainsford and James Stephen wrote panegyrics of Toussaint in English. These books are little more than propaganda pamphlets.

In 1855 the Rev. J. R. Beard published a life of Toussaint in which he makes him out to be an admirable example of a Protestant clergyman turned revolutionary. Beard, however, read industriously and his information is, on the whole, accurate.

In 1935, *The Black Consul,* a translation from the Russian, by Anatoli Vinogradov was published in London. The writer prints a long bibliography prefaced with a note stating that he has used "only those sources whose authenticity is beyond dispute." Singularly fortunate in this certainty of the authenticity of his sources, he makes a singularly unfortunate use of them. He confuses the Mulattoes with the blacks and makes Toussaint go to Paris with the Mulatto delegation; he gives Dessalines a quite gratuitous university education in Paris (p. 355), thereby ruining the greatest lesson of the revolution; he makes Biassou write a "remarkable" article printed as a pamphlet in Paris (p. 318); he makes Vincent a Negro (p. 331), mentions Rigaud once (p. 378), calling him "one Rigaud a Mulatto"; and perpetrates similar violences against French history. The book would not have been mentioned here but for the enthusiastic welcome it received in almost the whole British press.

Césaire, Aimé: *Toussaint L'Ouverture, Présence Africaine.* This is a recent biography by the celebrated poet, dramatist and politician of the French West Indian island of Martinique. The book, as could have been expected, is extremely competent and gives a good picture of Toussaint and the San Domingo Revolution. I find, however, that it lacks the fire and constant illumination which distinguish most of the other work of Césaire.

APPENDIX

From Toussaint L'Ouverture to Fidel Castro

Toussaint L'Ouverture is not here linked to Fidel Castro because both led revolutions in the West Indies. Nor is the link a convenient or journalistic demarcation of historical time. What took place in French San Domingo in 1792-1804 reappeared in Cuba in 1958. The slave revolution of French San Domingo managed to emerge from

> . . . The pass and fell incensed points
> Of mighty opposites.

Five years later the people of Cuba are still struggling in the same toils.

Castro's revolution is of the twentieth century as much as Toussaint's was of the eighteenth. But despite the distance of over a century and a half, both are West Indian. The people who made them, the problems and the attempts to solve them, are peculiarly West Indian, the product of a peculiar origin and a peculiar history. West Indians first became aware of themselves as a people in the Haitian Revolution. Whatever its ultimate fate, the Cuban Revolution marks the ultimate stage of a Caribbean quest for national identity. In a scattered series of disparate islands the process consists of a series of unco-ordinated periods of drift, punctuated by spurts, leaps and catastrophes. But the inherent movement is clear and strong.

The history of the West Indies is governed by two factors, the sugar plantation and Negro slavery. That the majority of the population in Cuba was never slave does not affect the underlying social identity. Wherever the sugar plantation and slavery existed, they imposed a pattern. It is an original pattern, not European, not African, not a part of the American main, not native in any conceivable sense of that word, but West Indian, *sui generis,* with no parallel anywhere else.

The sugar plantation has been the most civilising as well as the most demoralising influence in West Indian development. When three centuries ago the slaves came to the West Indies, they entered directly into the large-scale agriculture of the sugar plantation, which was a modern system. It further required that the slaves live together in a social relation far closer than any proletariat of the time. The cane when reaped had to be rapidly transported to what was factory production. The product was shipped abroad for sale. Even the cloth the slaves wore and the food they ate was imported. The Negroes, therefore, from the very start lived a life that was in its essence a modern life. That is their history—as far as I have been able to discover, a unique history.

In the first part of the seventeenth century, early settlers from Europe had made quite a success of individual production. The sugar plantation drove them out. The slaves saw around them a social life of a certain material culture and ease, the life of the sugar-plantation owners. The clever, the lucky and the illegitimate became domestics or artisans attached to the plantation or the factory. Long before the bus and the taxi, the small size of the islands made communication between the rural areas and the urban quick and easy. The plantation owners and the merchants lived an intense political life in which the ups and downs of sugar and in time the treatment and destiny of the slaves played a crucial and continuous role. The sugar plantation dominated the lives of the islands to such a degree that the white skin alone saved those who were not plantation owners or bureaucrats from the humiliations and hopelessness of the life of the slave. That was and is the pattern of West Indian life.

The West Indies between Toussaint L'Ouverture and Fidel Castro falls naturally into three periods: I. The Nineteenth Century; II. Between the Wars; III. After World War II.

I. THE NINETEENTH CENTURY

The nineteenth century in the Caribbean is the century of the abolition of slavery. But the passing of the years shows that the decisive patterns of Caribbean development took form in Haiti.

Tousaint could see no road for the Haitian economy but the sugar plantation. Dessalines was a barbarian. After Dessalines came Christophe, a man of conspicuous ability and within his circumstances an enlightened ruler. He also did his best (a cruel best) with the plantation. But with the abolition of slavery and the achievement of independence the plantation, indelibly associated with slavery, became unbearable. Pétion acquiesced in substituting subsistence production for the sugar plantation.

For the first century and a half of Haiti's existence there was no international opinion jealous of the independence of small nations; no body of similar states, ready to raise a hue and cry at any threat to one of their number; no theory of aid from the wealthy countries to the poorer ones. Subsistence production resulted in economic decay and every variety of political disorder. Yet it has preserved the national independence, and out of this has come something new which has captured a continent and holds its place in the institutions of the world.

This is what has happened. For over a century after independence the Haitians attempted to form a replica of European, i.e., French civilisation in the West Indies. Listen to the Haitian Ambassador, M. Constantin Mayard, in Paris in 1938:

French our institutions, French our public and civil legislation, French our literature, French our university, French the curriculum of our schools . . .

Today when one of us [a Haitian] appears in a circle of Frenchmen, "welcome smiles at him in every eye." The reason is without doubt that your nation, ladies and gentlemen, knows that within the scope of its colonial expansion it has given to the Antilles and above all to San Domingo all that it could give of itself and its substance . . . It has founded there, in the mould of its own national type, with its blood, with its language, its institutions, its spirit and its soil, a local type, an historic race, in which its sap still runs and where it is remade complete.

Generation after generation the best sons of the Haitian élite were educated in Paris. They won distinctions

in the intellectual life of France. The burning race hatred
of pre-independence days had vanished. But a line of investigators and travellers had held up to international
ridicule the hollow pretensions of Haitian civilisation. In
1913 the ceaseless battering from foreign pens was re-
enforced by the bayonets of American Marines. Haiti had
to find a national rallying-point. They looked for it where
it can only be found, at home, more precisely, in their own
backyard. They discovered what is known today as Negritude. It is the prevailing social ideology among politicians
and intellectuals in every part of Africa. It is the subject
of heated elaboration and disputation wherever Africa
and Africans are discussed. But in its origin and development it is West Indian, and could not have been anything
else but West Indian, the peculiar product of their peculiar history.

The Haitians did not know it as Negritude. To them
it seemed purely Haitian. Two-thirds of the population
of French San Domingo in Toussaint's time had made the
Middle Passage. The whites had emigrated or been exterminated. The Mulattoes who were masters had their
eyes fixed on Paris. Left to themselves, the Haitian peasantry resuscitated to a remarkable degree the lives they had
lived in Africa. Their method of cultivation, their family relations and social practices, their drums, songs and music.
such art as they practised and above all their religion
which became famous, Vodun—all this was Africa in the
West Indies. But it was Haitian, and the Haitian élite
leapt at it. In 1926 Dr. Price Mars in his famous book,
Ainsi Parla L'Oncle (This is What Uncle Said), described
with loving care the way of life of the Haitian peasant.
Rapidly, learned and scientific societies were formed. The
African way of life of the Haitian peasant became the axis
of Haitian literary creation. No plantation labourer, with
free land to defend, rallied to the cause.

The Caribbean territories drifted along. At the end
of the nineteenth century, Cuba produced a great revolution which bears the name "The Ten Years' War." It produced prodigies—no West Indian pantheon but will have
among its most resplendent stars the names of José Martí
the political leader and Maceo the soldier. They were men
in the full tradition of Jefferson, Washington and Bolivar.
That was their strength and that was their weakness. They

were leaders of a national revolutionary party and a national revolutionary army. Toussaint L'Ouverture and Fidel Castro led a revolutionary people. The war for independence began again and ended in the Platt Amendment of 1904.

It was just one year after the Platt Amendment that there first appeared what has turned out to be a particular feature of West Indian life—the non-political writer devoted to the analysis and expression of West Indian society. The first was the greatest of them all, Fernando Ortiz. For over half a century, at home or in exile, he has been the tireless exponent of Cuban life and *Cubanidad*, the spirit of Cuba. The history of Spanish imperialism, sociology, anthropology, ethnology, all the related sciences are his medium of investigation into Cuban life, folklore, literature, music, art, education, criminality, everything Cuban. A most distinctive feature of his work is the number of solid volumes he has devoted to Negro and Mulatto life in Cuba. A quarter of a century before the Writers' Project of the New Deal began the discovery of the United States, Ortiz set out to discover his native land, a West Indian island. In essence it is the first and only comprehensive study of the West Indian people. Ortiz ushered the Caribbean into the thought of the twentieth century and kept it there.

II. BETWEEN THE WARS

Before World War I Haiti began to write another chapter in the record of the West Indian struggle for national independence. Claiming the need to recover debts and restore order, the Marines, as we have seen, invaded Haiti in 1913. The whole nation resisted. A general strike was organized and led by the literary intellectuals who had discovered the Africanism of their peasants as a means of national identity. The Marines left, and Negroes and Mulattoes resumed their fratricidal conflicts. But Haiti's image of itself had changed. "Goodbye to the Marseillaise," a famous phrase by one of the best-known of Haitian writers, signifies the substitution of Africa for France in the first independent West Indian state. Africa in the West Indies would seem to have been evoked by an empirical need and accidental circumstance. It was not so. Long before the Marines left Haiti, the role of Africa in the consciousness of the West Indies people had proved itself to be a stage in the development of the West Indian quest for a national identity.

The story is one of the strangest stories in any period of history. The individual facts are known. But no one has ever put them together and drawn to them the attention they deserve. Today the emancipation of Africa is one of the outstanding events of contemporary history. Between the wars when this emancipation was being prepared, the unquestioned leaders of the movement in every public sphere, in Africa itself, in Europe and in the United States, were not Africans but West Indians. First the unquestioned facts.

Two black West Indians using the ink of Negritude wrote their names imperishably on the front pages of the history of our time. Standing at the head is Marcus Garvey. Garvey, an immigrant from Jamaica, is the only Negro who has succeeded in building a mass movement among American Negroes. Arguments about the number of his followers dispute the number of millions. Garvey advocated the return of Africa to the Africans and people of African descent. He organised, very rashly and incompetently, the Black Star Line, a steamship company for transporting people of African descent from the New World back to Africa. Garvey did not last long. His movement took really effective form in about 1921, and by 1926 he was in a United States prison (some charge about misusing the mails); from prison he was deported home to Jamaica. But all this is only the frame and scaffolding. Garvey never set foot in Africa. He spoke no African language. His conceptions of Africa seemed to be a West Indian island and West Indian people multiplied a thousand times over. But Garvey managed to convey to Negroes everywhere (and to the rest of the world) his passionate belief that Africa was the home of a civilisation which had once been great and would be great again. When you bear in mind the slenderness of his resources, the vast material forces and the pervading social conceptions which automatically sought to destroy him, his achievement remains one of the propagandistic miracles of this century.

Garvey's voice reverberated inside Africa itself. The King of Swaziland told Mrs. Marcus Garvey that he knew the name of only two black men in the Western world:

Jack Johnson, the boxer who defeated the white man Jim
Jeffries, and Marcus Garvey. Jomo Kenyatta has related
to this wirter how in 1921 Kenya nationalists, unable to
read, would gather round a reader of Garvey's newspaper,
the *Negro World*, and listen to an article two or three
times. Then they would run various ways through the forest, carefully to repeat the whole, which they had mem-
orised, to Africans hungry for some doctrine which lifted
them from the servile consciousness in which Africans lived.
Dr. Nkrumah, a graduate student of history and philosophy at two American universities, has placed it on record
that of all the writers who educated and influenced him,
Marcus Garvey stands first. Garvey found the cause of
Africans and of people of African descent not so much
neglected as unworthy of consideration. In little more than
half of ten years he had made it a part of the political
consciousness of the world. He did not know the word
Negritude but he knew the thing. With enthusiasm he
would have welcomed the nomenclature, with justice
claimed paternity.

The other British West Indian was from Trinidad,
George Padmore. Padmore shook the dust of the cramping
West Indies from his feet in the early 1920's and went to
the United States. When he died in 1959, eight countries
sent representatives to his funeral, which was held in
London. His ashes were interred in Ghana; and all assert
that in that country of political demonstrations, there never
has been a political demonstration such as was evoked by
these obsequies of Padmore. Peasants from remote areas
who, it could have been thought, had never heard his
name, found their way to Accra to pay the last tribute to
this West Indian who had spent his life in their service.

Once in America he became an active Communist. He
was moved to Moscow to head their Negro department of
propaganda and organisation. In that post he became the
best known and most trusted of agitators for African independence. In 1935, seeking alliances, the Kremlin separated Britain and France as "democratic imperialisms"
from Germany and Japan, making the "Fascist imperialisms" the main target of Russian and Communist propaganda. This reduced activity for African emancipation to
a farce: Germany and Japan had no colonies in Africa.
Padmore broke instantly with the Kremlin. He went to

London where, in a single room, he earned a meagre living by journalism, to be able to continue the work he had done in the Kremlin. He wrote books and pamphlets, attended all anti-imperialist meetings and spoke and moved resolutions wherever possible. He made and maintained an ever-increasing range of nationalist contacts in all sections of African society and the colonial world. He preached and taught Pan-Africanism and organised an African Bureau. He published a journal devoted to African emancipation (the present writer was its editor).

This is no place to attempt even a summary of the work and influence of the most striking West Indian creation between the wars, Padmore's African Bureau. Between the wars it was the only African organisation of its kind in existence. Of the seven members of the committee, five were West Indians, and they ran the organisation. Of them, only Padmore had ever visited Africa. It could not have been accidental that this West Indian attracted two of the most remarkable Africans of this or any other time. A founder-member and a simmering volcano of African nationalism was Jomo Kenyatta. But even better fortune was in store for us.

The present writer met Nkrumah, then a student at the University of Pennsylvania, and wrote to Padmore about him. Nkrumah came to England to study law and there formed an association with Padmore; they worked at the doctrines and premises of Pan-Africanism and elaborated the plans which culminated in Nkrumah's leading the people of the Gold Coast to the independence of Ghana. This revolution by the Gold Coast was the blow which made so many cracks in the piece of African colonialism that it proved impossible ever to stick them together again. With Nkrumah's victory the association did not cease. After independence was signed and sealed, Nkrumah sent for Padmore, installed him once more in an office devoted to African emancipation and, under the auspices of an African government, this West Indian, as he had done in 1931 under the auspices of the Kremlin, organised in Accra the first conference of independent African states, followed, twenty-five years after the first, by the second world conference of fighters for African freedom. Dr. Banda, Patrice Lumumba, Nyerere, Tom Mboya, were some of those who attended the conference.

Jomo Kenyatta was not there only because he was in jail.
NBC made a national telecast of the interment of his ashes
in Christiansborg Castle, at which Padmore was designated
the Father of African Emancipation, a distinction challenged by no one. To the degree that they had to deal with
us in the period between the wars, many learned and important persons and institutions looked upon us and our
plans and hopes for Africa as the fantasies of some po-
litically illiterate West Indians. It was they who completely
misconceived a continent, not we. They should have
learned from that experience. They have not. The same
myopic vision which failed to focus Africa is now peering
at the West Indies.

The place of Africa in the West Indian development
is documented as few historical visions are documented.

In 1939 a black West Indian from the French colony
of Martinique published in Paris the finest and most famous poem ever written about Africa, *Cahier d'un retour
au pays natal* (Statement of a Return to the Country
Where I was Born). Aimé Césaire first describes Martinique, the poverty, misery and vices of the masses of the
people, the lickspittle subservience of the coloured middle
classes. But the poet's education has been consummated
in Paris. As a West Indian he has nothing national to be
aware of. He is overwhelmed by the gulf that separates
him from the people where he was born. He feels that he
must go there. He does so and discovers a new version
of what the Haitians, as had Garvey and Padmore, had
discovered: that salvation for the West Indies lies in Africa,
the original home and ancestry of the West Indian people.

The poet gives us a view of Africans as he sees them.

> . . . my Negritude is not a stone, its
>   deafness a sounding board for
>   the noises of the day
> my Negritude is not a mere spot of
>   dead water on the dead eye of
>   the earth
> my Negritude is no tower, no cathedral
>
> it cleaves into the red flesh of the
>   teeming earth
> it cleaves into the glowing flesh of
>   the heavens

> it penetrates the seamless bondage of
>   my unbending patience
>
> Hoorah for those who never invented
>   anything
> for those who never explored anything
> for those who never mastered anything
>
> but who, possessed, give themselves up
>   to the essence of each thing
> ignorant of the coverings but possessed
>   by the pulse of things
> indifferent to mastering but taking the
>   chances of the world . . .

In contrast to this vision of the African unseparated from the world, from Nature, a living part of all that lives, Césaire immediately places the civilisation that has scorned and persecuted Africa and Africans.

> Listen to the white world
> its horrible exhaustion from its
>   immense labours
> its rebellious joints cracking under
>   the pitiless stars
> its blue steel rigidities, cutting
>   through the mysteries of the
>   flesh
> listen to their vainglorious conquests
>   trumpeting their defeats
> listen to the grandiose alibis of their
>   pitiful floundering

The poet wants to be an architect of this unique civilisation, a commissioner of its blood, a guardian of its refusal to accept.

> But in so doing, my heart, preserve
>   me from all hate
> do not turn me into a man of hate of
>   whom I think only with hate
> for in order to project myself into
>   this unique race
> you know the extent of my boundless
>   love

> you know that it is not from hatred
>   of other races
> that I seek to be cultivator of this
>   unique race . . .

He returns once more to the pitiful spectre of West Indian life, but now with hope.

> for it is not true that the work of man
>   is finished
> that man has nothing more to do in the
>   world but be a parasite in the world
> that all we now need is to keep in step
>   with the world
> but the work of man is only just beginning
>   and it remains to man to conquer all
>   the violence entrenched in the recesses
>   of his passion
> and no race possesses the monopoly of beauty,
>   of intelligence, of force, and there
>   is a place for all at the rendezvous
>   of victory . . .

Here is the centre of Césaire's poem. By neglecting it, Africans and the sympathetic of other races utter loud hurrahs that drown out common sense and reason. The work of man is not finished. Therefore the future of the African is not to continue not discovering anything. The monopoly of beauty, of intelligence, of force, is possessed by no race, certainly not by those who possess Negritude. Negritude is what one race brings to the common rendez-vous where all will strive for the new world of the poet's vision. The vision of the poet is not economics or politics, it is poetic, *sui generis*, true unto itself and needing no other truth. But it would be the most vulgar racism not to see here a poetic incarnation of Marx's famous sentence, "The real history of humanity will begin."

From Césaire's strictly poetic affinities* we have to turn our faces if even with distinct loss to our larger general purpose. But *Cahier* has united elements in modern

---

* Baudelaire and Rimbaud, Rilke and D. H. Lawrence. Jean-Paul Sartre has done the finest of critical appreciations of *Cahier* as poetry, but his explanation of what he conceives Negritude to mean is a disaster.

thought which seemed destined to remain asunder. These had better be enumerated.

1. He has made a union of the African sphere of existence with existence in the Western world.

2. The past of mankind and the future of mankind are historically and logically linked.

3. No longer from external stimulus but from their own self-generated and indpendent being and motion will Africa and Africans move towards an integrated humanity.

It is the Anglo-Saxon poet who has seen for the world in general what the West Indian has seen concretely for Africa.

> Here the impossible union
> Of spheres of existence is actual,
> Here the past and future
> Are conquered, and reconciled,
> Where action were otherwise movement
> Of that which is only moved
> And has in it no source of movement—

Mr. Eliot's conclusion is "Incarnation"; Césaire's, Negritude.

Cahier appeared in 1938 in Paris. A year before that *The Black Jacobins* had appeared in London. The writer had made the forward step of resurrecting not the decadence but the grandeur of the West Indian people. But as is obvious all through the book and particularly in the last pages, it is Africa and African emancipation that he has in mind.

Today (but only today) we can define what motivated this West Indian preoccupation with Africa between the wars. The West Indians were and had always been Western-educated. West Indian society confined black men to a very narrow strip of social territory. The first step to freedom was to go abroad. *Before they could begin to see themselves as a free and independent people they had to clear from minds the stigma that anything African was inherently inferior and degraded.* The road to West Indian national identity lay through Africa.

The West Indian national community constantly evades racial categorisation. After Ortiz, it was another white West Indian who in the same period proved himself to be the greatest politician in the democratic tradition whom the West Indies has ever known.

Arthur Andrew Cipriani was a French Creole in the island of Trinidad who came into public life as an officer in a West Indian contingent in World War I. It was in the army that many of the soldiers, a medley from all the British West Indian islands, for the first time wore shoes consistently. But they were the product of their peculiar history. The speed with which they adjusted themselves to the spiritual and material requirements of a modern war amazed all observers, from General Allenby down. Cipriani made a reputation for himself by his militant defence of the regiment against all prejudice, official and unofficial. To the end of his days he spoke constantly of the recognition they had won. By profession a trainer of horses, it was only after much persuasion that, on his return home after the war, already a man over forty, he entered politics. He at once put himself forward as the champion of the common people, in his own phrase, "the barefooted man." Before very long this white man was acknowledged as leader by hundreds of thousands of black people and East Indians. An utterly fearless man, he never left the colonial government in any doubt as to what it was up against. All who ever heard him speak remember his raising of his right hand and his slow enunciation of the phrase, "If I raise my little finger . . ." Against tremendous odds he forced the government to capitulate on workmen's compensation, the eight-hour day, trade union legislation and other elementary constituents of democracy. Year after year he was elected mayor of the capital city. He made the mayoralty a centre of opposition to the British Colonial Office and all its works.

Cipriani always treated West Indians as a modern contemporary people. He declared himself to be a socialist and day in and day out, inside and outside of the legislature, he attacked capitalists and capitalism. He attached his party to the British Labour Party and scrupulously kept his followers aware of their privileges and responsibilities as members of the international labour movement. Cipriani was that rare type of politician to whom words expressed realities. Long before any of the other territories of the colonial empires, he not only raised the slogans of national independence and federation of the British West Indian territories, he went tirelessly from island to island mobilising public opinion in general and the labour movement in particular in support of these slogans. He died in 1945. The islands had never seen before and have not seen since anything or anybody like him.

The West Indian masses jumped ahead even of Cipriani. In 1937, among the oil field workers in Trinidad, the largest proletarian grouping in the West Indies, a strike began. Like a fire along a tinder track, it spread to the entire island, then from island to island, ending in an upheaval at the other end of the curve, in Jamaica, thousands of miles away. The colonial government in Jamaica collapsed completely and two local popular leaders had to take over the responsibility of restoring some sort of social order. The heads of the government in Trinidad and Tobago saved their administrations (but earned the wrath of the imperial government) by expressing sympathy with the revolt. The British Government sent a Royal Commission, which took much evidence, discovered long-standing evils, and made proposals by no means unintelligent or reactionary. As usual they were late, they were slow. Had Cipriani been the man he was ten years earlier, self-government, federation and economic regeneration, which he had advocated so strenuously and so long, could have been initiated then. But the old warrior was nearly seventy. He flinched at the mass upheavals which he more than anyone else had prepared, and the opportunity was lost. But he had destroyed a legend and established once and for all that the West Indian people were ready to follow the most advanced theories of an uncomprising leadership.

III. AFTER WORLD WAR II

Cipriani had built soundly and he left behind a Caribbean Labour Congress devoted to federation, independence and the creation of an enlightened peasantry. But what has happened to Castro's Cuba is inherent in these unfortunate islands. In 1945 the Congress, genuinely West Indian, joined the World Federation of Trade Unions. But in 1948 that body split into the World Federation of Trade Unions of the East and the International Confederation of Free Trade Unions of the West. The split in the international split the Caribbean Labour Congress and it lost its place as the leader and inspirer of a genuinely West Indian movement. The British Colonial Office took the coloured middle class under its wing. These gradually filled the Civil Service and related organisations; they took over the political parties, and with the parties, the old colonial system.

What is this old colonial system? It is the oldest Western relic of the seventeenth century still alive in the world today, surrounded on all sides by a modern population.

The West Indies has never been a traditional colonial territory with clearly distinguished economic and political relations between two different cultures. Native culture there was none. The aboriginal Amerindian civilisation had been destroyed. Every succeeding year, therefore, saw the labouring population, slave or free, incorporating into itself more and more of the language, customs, aims and outlook of its masters. It steadily grew in numbers until it became a terrifying majority of the total population. The ruling minority therefore was in the position of the father who produced children and had to guard against being supplanted by them. There was only one way out, to seek strength abroad. This beginning has lasted unchanged to this very day.

The dominant industrial structure has been the sugar plantation. For over two hundred years the sugar industry has tottered on the brink of disaster, remaining alive by an unending succession of last-minute rescues by gifts, concessions, quotas from the metropolitan power or powers.

SUGAR MANUFACTURERS' "GRIM FUTURE"
From our Correspondent
Georgetown, Sept. 3

The British West Indies Sugar Association's chairman, Sir Robert Kirkwood, has stated here that cane sugar manufacturers were facing a grim future and the position was reaching a stage where beet sugar production should be restricted to provide cane manufacturers with an enlarged market. Sir Robert pointed out that Britain's participation in the European Common Market should be no threat to sugar manufacturers in the region provided preferences under the Commonwealth sugar agreement were preserved.

You would be able to read the same in any European newspaper at regular intervals during the last two hundred years. Recent official reports on the life and labour of the plantation labourer are moved to language remarkably similar to that of the non-conformist agitators against plantation slavery. There are economists and scientists to-day in the West Indies who believe that the most fortunate economic occurrence would be a blight that would destroy the sugar cane completely and thus compel some new type of economic development.*

As they have been from the first days of slavery, financial power and its mechanism are today entirely in the hands of metropolitan organisations and their agents.

Such a Westernized population needs quantities of pots, pans, plates, spoons, knives, forks, paper, pencils, pens, cloth, bicycles, buses for public transport, automobiles, all the elementary appurtenances of civilisation which the islands do not manufacture, not forgetting Mercedes-Benzes, Bentleys, Jaguars and Lincolns. In this type of commerce the dominating elements are the foreign manufacturers and the foreign banks. The most revealing feature of this trade and the oldest is the still massive importation of food, including fresh vegetables.

The few industries of importance, such as oil and bauxite, are completely in the hands of foreign firms, and the local politicians run a ferocious competition with each other in offering inducements to similar firms to establish new industries here and not there.

As with material, so with intellectual necessities. In island after island the daily newspaper is entirely in the hands of foreign firms. Radio and television cannot evade the fate of newspapers.

In 1963 the old colonial system is not what it was in 1863; in 1863 it was not what it had been in 1763 or 1663. The fundamentals outlined above, however, have not changed. But for the first time the system is now threatened, not from without but from within, not by communism, not by socialism, but by plain, simple parliamentary democracy. The old colonial system in the West Indies was not a democratic system, was not born as such. It cannot live with democracy. Within a West Indian island the old colonial system and democracy are incompatible. One has to go. That is the logic of development of every West Indian territory, Cuba, the Dominican Republic, Haiti, the

* None will dare to say so publicly. He or she would be driven out of the territory.

former British colonies, the former French colonies, and even Puerto Rico, the poor relation of the wealthy United States.

The supreme wrong of West Indian politics is that the old colonial system has so isolated the ruling classes from the national community that plain, ordinary parliamentary democracy, *suffused with a sense of nationa. identity*, can remake the islands.

Statistics of production and the calculations of votes together form the surest road towards misunderstanding the West Indies. To which for good measure add the antagonism of races. The people of the West Indies were born in the seventeenth century, in a Westernized productive and social system. Members of different African tribes were carefully split up to lessen conspiracy, and they were therefore compelled to master the European languages, highly complex products of centuries of civilisation. From the start there had been the gap, constantly growing, between the rudimentary conditions of the life of the slave and the language he used. There was therefore in West Indian society an inherent antagonism between the consciousness of the black masses and the reality of their lives, inherent in that it was constantly produced and reproduced not by agitators but by the very conditions of the society itself. It is the modern media of mass communication which have made essence into existence. For an insignificant sum per month, the black masses can hear on the radio news of Dr. Nkrumah, Jomo Kenyatta, Dr. Julius Banda, Prime Minister Nehru, events and personalities of the United Nations and all the capitals of the world. They can wrestle with what the West thinks of the East and what the East thinks of the West. The cinema presents actualities and not infrequently stirs the imagination with the cinematic masterpieces of the world. Every hour on the hour all variations of food, clothing, household necessities and luxuries are presented as absolutely essential to a civilised existence. All this to a population which over large areas still lives in conditions little removed from slavery.

The high material civilisation of the white minority is now fortified by the concentration of the coloured middle classes on making salaries and fees do the work of incomes.

Sometimes a quarter of the population is crowded into the capital city, the masses irresistibly attracted by the contrast between what they see and hear and the lives they live. This was the tinder to which Castro placed a match. Historical tradition, education in the sense of grappling with the national past, there is none. History as taught is what it always has been, propaganda for those, whoever they may be, who administer the old colonial system. Power here is more naked than in any other part of the world. Hence the brutality, savagery, even personal cruelties of the régimes of Trujillo and Duvalier, and the power of the Cuban Revolution.

This is the instrument on which perform all West Indian soloists, foreign or native. Take the French West Indian islands of Martinique and Guadeloupe. The colonial administration declared and acted for Vichy, the mass of the population for the Resistance. Vichy defeated, the islands whole-heartedly became departments of France, anxious to be assimilated into French civilisation. But the hand of the Paris administration, notoriously heavy in the provincial administrations of France itself, is a crushing weight on any attempt to change the old colonial system. To-day the mass of the population, disillusioned, is demanding independence. Their students in Paris are leading the struggle with blood, with boldness and with brilliance available to all who use the French language.

The British system, unlike the French, does not crush the quest for a national identity. Instead, it stifles it. It formed a federation of its Caribbean colonies. But the old colonial system consisted of insular economies, each with its financial and economic capital in London. A federation meant that the economic line of direction should no longer be from island to London, but from island to island. But that involved the break-up of the old colonial system. The West Indian politicians preferred the break-up of the Federation. Two of the islands have actually been granted independence. The Queen of England is their queen. They receive royal visits; their legislatures begin with prayers; their legislative bills are read three times; a mace has been presented to each of these distant infants by the Mother of Parliaments; their prominent citizens can receive an assortment of letters after their names, and in time the prefix "Sir." This no longer lessens but intensifies the battle between the old colonial system and democracy. Long before the actual independence was granted, large numbers of the middle classes, including their politicians, wanted it put off as far into the distance as possible. For the cruiser in the offing and the prospect of financial gifts and loans, they turn longing eyes and itching feet towards the United States.

The Caribbean is now an American sea. Puerto Rico is its show piece. Puerto Rican society has the near-celestial privilege of free entry into the United States for their unemployed and their ambitious. The United States returns to the Puerto Rican Government all duty collected on such staple imports as rum and cigars. American money for investment and American loans and gifts should create the Caribbean paradise. But if the United States had the Puerto Rican density of population, it would contain all the people in the world. Puerto Rico is just another West Indian island.

In the Dominican Republic there is no need to go beyond saying that Trujillo had gained power by the help of the United States Marines and all through the more than quarter-century of his infamous dictatorship he was understood to enjoy the friendship of Washington. Before the recent election of his successor, Sr. Juan Bosch, the French newspapers stated as an item of news that members of the left in the Dominican Republic (names were given) were deported to Paris by the local police, who were assisted in this operation by members of the FBI. Trujillo gone, Duvalier of Haiti is the uncrowned king of Latin American barbarism. It is widely believed that despite the corruption and impertinence of his régime, it is American support which keeps him in power: better Duvalier than another Castro.

Such a mass of ignorance and falsehood has surrounded these islands for so many centuries that obvious truths sound like revelations. Contrary to the general belief, the Caribbean territories taken as a whole are not sunk in irremediable poverty. When he was Principal of the University of the West Indies in Jamaica, Professor Arthur Lewis, former head of the faculty of economics at Manchester University and at the time of writing due to head the same faculty at Princeton, tried to remove some cobwebs from the eyes of his fellow West Indians:

This opinion that the West Indies can raise all the capital it needs from its own resources is bound to shock many people, because West Indians like to feel that ours is a poor community. But the fact of the matter is that at least half of the people in the world are poorer than we are. The standard of living in the West Indies is higher than the standard of living in India, or China, in most of the countries of Asia, and in most of the countries of Africa. The West Indies is not a poor community; it is in the upper bracket of world income. It is capable of producing the extra 5 or 6 per cent of resources which is required for this job, just as Ceylon and Ghana are finding the money they need for development by taxing themselves. It is not necessary for us to send our statesmen around the world begging for help. If help is given to us let us accept it, but let us not sit down and say nothing can be done until the rest of the world out of its goodness of heart is willing to grant us charity.*

The economic road they have to travel is a broad highway on which the sign posts have long been erected. Sr. Juan Bosch began his campaign by promising to distribute the land confiscated from the baronial plunder of the Trujillo family. His supporters rapidly transformed this into: "A house and land for every Dominican." Not only popular demand and modern economists, but British Royal Commissions during the last sixty years, have indicated (cautiously but clearly enough) that the way out of the West Indian morass is the abolition of the plantation labourer and the substitution, instead, of individual landowning peasants. Scientists and economists have indicated that an effective industry is possible, based on the scientific and planned use of raw material produced on the islands. I have written in vain if I have not made it clear that of all formerly colonial coloured peoples, the West Indian masses are the most highly experienced in the ways of Western civilisation and most receptive to its requirements in the twentieth century. To realise themselves they will have to break out of the shackles of the old colonial system.

* Study Conference of Economic Development in Underdeveloped Countries, August 5-15, 1957, University of the West Indies, Jamaica.

I do not propose to plunge this appendix into the turbulent waters of controversy about Cuba. I have written about the West Indies in general and Cuba is the most West Indian island in the West Indies. That suffices.

One more question remains—the most realistic and most pregnant question of all. Toussaint L'Ouverture and the Haitian slaves brought into the world more than the abolition of slavery. When Latin Americans saw that small and insignificant Haiti could win and keep independence they began to think that they ought to be able to do the same. Pétion, the ruler of Haiti, nursed back to health the sick and defeated Bolivar, gave him money, arms and a printing press to help in the campaign which ended in the freedom of the Five States. What will happen to what Fidel Castro has brought new to the world no one can say. But what is waiting in the West Indies to be born, what emerged from the womb in July 1958, is to be seen elsewhere in the West Indies, not so confused with the pass and fell incensed points of mighty opposites. I speak now of a section of the West Indies of which I have had during the past five years intimate and personal experience of the writers and the people. But this time the people first, for if the ideologists have moved closer towards the people, the people have caught up with the ideologists and the national identity is a national fact.

In Trinidad in 1957, before there was any hint of a revolution in Cuba, the ruling political party suddenly declared, contrary to the declaration of policy with which it had won the election, that during the war the British Government of Sir Winston Churchill had given away Trinidad property and it should be returned. What happened is one of the greatest events in the history of the West Indies. The people rose to the call. Mass meetings and mass demonstrations, political passion such as the island had never known, swept through the population. Inside the chains of the old colonial system, the people of the West Indies are a national community. The middle classes looked on with some uncertainty but with a growing approval. The local whites are not like whites in a foreign civilisation. They are West Indians and, under a strong impulse, think of themselves as such. Many of them quietly made known their sympathy with the cause. The political leader was uncompromising in his demand for the return. "I shall

break Chaguaramas or it will break me," he declared, and
the words sprouted wings. He publicly asserted to mass
meetings of many thousands that if the State Department,
backed by the Colonial Office, continued to refuse to discuss the return of the base, he would take Trinidad not
only out of the West Indian Federation but out of the
British association altogether: he would establish the independence of the island, all previous treaties entered into
under the colonial régime would automatically become
null and void, and thus he would deal with the Americans.
He forbade them to use the Trinidad airport for their military planes. In a magnificent address, "From Slavery to
Chaguaramas," he said that for centuries the West Indies
had been bases, military footballs of warring imperialist
powers, and the time had come to finish with it. It is the
present writer's opinion (he was for the crucial period
editor of the party journal) that it was the response of the
population which sent the political leader so far upon a
perilous road. They showed simply that they thought the
Americans should quit the base and return it to the people.
This was all the more remarkable in that the Trinidad
people freely admitted that Trinidad had never enjoyed
such financial opulence as when the Americans were there
during the war. America was undoubtedly the potential
source of economic and financial aid. But they were ready
for any sacrifices needed for the return of the base. They
were indeed ready for anything, and the political leadership had to take great care to do or say nothing which
would precipitate any untoward mass intervention.

What was perhaps the most striking feature of this
powerful national upheaval was its concentration on the
national issue and its disregard for all others. There was
not the slightest trace of anti-American feeling; though the
British Colonial Office was portrayed as the ally of the
State Department and the demand for political independence was well on the way, there was equally no trace of
anti-British feeling. There was no inclination towards non-
alignment, not even, despite the pressure for independence,
anti-imperialism. The masses of the people of Trinidad
and Tobago looked upon the return of the base as the first
and primary stage in their quest for national identity. That
they were prepared to suffer for, if need be (of this I am
as certain as one can be of such things) to fight and die for.

But in the usual accompaniments of a struggle against a foreign base, they were not in any way concerned. Not that they did not know. They most certainly knew. But they had had a long experience of international relations and they knew precisely what they wanted. Right up the islands, the population responded in the same way to what they felt was a West Indian matter. The press conference of the political leader was the most popular radio programme in the West Indian islands. It was 1937-38 all over again. "Free is how you is from the start, an' when it look different you got to move, just move, an' when you movin' say that is a natural freedom make you move." * Though the British flag still blew above them, in their demands and demonstrations for Chaguaramas they were free, freer than they might be for a long time.

The West Indian national identity is more easily to be glimpsed in the published writings of West Indian authors.

Vic Reid of Jamaica is the only West Indian novelist who lives in the West Indies. That presumably is why he sets his scene in Africa. An African who knows the West Indies well assures me that there is nothing African about Reid's story. It is the West Indies in African dress. Whatever it is, the novel is a *tour-de-force*. African or West Indian, it reduces the human problems of under-developed countries to a common denominator. The distinctive tone of the new West Indian orchestra is not loud but it is clear. Reid is not unconcerned about the fate of his characters. The political passions are sharp and locked in murderous conflict. But Reid is detached as no European or African writer is or can be detached, as Garvey, Padmore, Césaire were not and could not be detached. The origin of his detachment appears very clearly in the most powerful and far-ranging of the West Indian school, George Lamming of Barbados.

Confining ourselves strictly to our purpose, we shall limit ourselves to citing only one episode from the latest of his four powerful novels.

Powell, a character in *Season of Adventure*, is a murderer, rapist and altogether criminal member of West Indian society. Suddenly, after nine-tenths of the book, the author injects three pages headed "Author's Note." Writing in the first person he accounts for Powell.

* *Season of Adventure*, by George Lamming.

Until the age of ten Powell and I had lived together, equal in the affection of two mothers. Powell had made my dreams; and I had lived his passions. Identical in years, and stage by stage, Powell and I were taught in the same primary school.

And then the division came. I got a public scholarship which started my migration into another world, a world whose roots were the same, but whose style of living was entirely different from what my childhood knew. It had earned me a privilege which now shut Powell and the whole *tonelle* right out of my future. I had lived as near to Powell as my skin to the hand it darkens. And yet! Yet I forgot the *tonelle* as men forget a war, and attached myself to that new world which was so recent and so slight beside the weight of what had gone before. Instinctively I attached myself to that new privilege; and in spite of all my effort, I am not free of its embrace to this day.

I believe deep in my bones that the mad impulse which drove Powell to his criminal defeat was largely my doing. I will not have this explained away by talk about environment; nor can I allow my own moral infirmity to be transferred to a foreign conscience, labelled imperalist. I shall go beyond my grave in the knowledge that I am responsible for what happened to my brother.

Powell still resides somewhere in my heart, with a dubious love, some strange, nameless shadow of regret; and yet with the deepest, deepest nostalgia. For I have never felt myself to be an honest part of anything since the world of his childhood deserted me.

This is something new in the voluminous literature of anti-colonialism. The West Indian of this generation accepts complete responsibility for the West Indies.

Vidia Naipaul of Trinidad does the same. His Mr. Biswas writes his first article for a newspaper.

DADDY COMES HOME IN A COFFIN

U.S. Explorer's Last Journey

On Ice by M. Biswas

. . . Less than a year ago Daddy—George Elmer
Edman, the celebrated traveller and explorer—
left home to explore the Amazon.
Well, I have news for you, kiddies.
Daddy is on his way home.
Yesterday he passed through Trinidad.
In a coffin.

This earns Mr. Biswas, former agricultural labourer
and keeper of a small shop, a job on the staff of this paper.
Mr. Biswas wrote a letter of protest. It took him two
weeks. It was eight typewritten pages long. After many re-
writings the letter developed into a broad philosophical
essay on the nature of man; his son goes to a secondary
school and together they hunt through Shakespeare for
quotations and find a rich harvest in *Measure for Measure*.
The foreigner may miss this bland reproduction of the
modus operandi of the well-greased West Indian journalist,
politician, prime minister.
Mr. Biswas is now a man of letters. He is invited to a
session of local literati. Mr. Biswas, whose poetic peak is
Ella Wheeler Wilcox, is bewildered by whisky and talk
about Lorca, Eliot, Auden. Every member of the group
must submit a poem. One night after looking at the sky
through the window Mr. Biswas finds his theme.

He addressed his mother. He did not think of rhythm;
he used no cheating abstract words. He wrote of coming up to the brow of the hill, seeing the black, forked
earth, the marks of the spade, the indentations of the
fork prongs. He wrote of the journey he had made a
long time before. He was tired; she made him rest.
He was hungry; she gave him food. He had nowhere
to go; she welcomed him . . .
"It is a poem," Mr. Biswas announced. "In prose."

. . . "There is no title," he said. And, as he had expected, this was received with satisfaction.
Then he disgraced himself. Thinking himself free
of what he had written, he ventured on his poem
boldly, and even with a touch of self-mockery. But
as he read, his hands began to shake, the paper rus-
tled; and when he spoke of the journey his voice
failed. It cracked and kept on cracking; his eyes tic-

kled. But he went on, and his emotion was such that at the end no one said a word . . .

The West Indian had made a fool of himself imitating American journalism, Shakespeare, T. S. Eliot, Lorca. He had arrived at truth when he wrote about his own West Indian childhood, his West Indian mother and the West Indian landscape. Naipaul is an East Indian. Mr. Biswas is an East Indian. But the East Indian problem in the West Indies is a creation of politicians of both races, seeking means to avoid attacking the old colonial system. The East Indian has become as West Indian as all the other expatriates.

The latest West Indian novelist is one of the strangest of living novelists. Beginning in 1958 he has just concluded a quartet of novels.* He is from British Guiana, which is a part of the South American continent. There are nearly 40,000 square miles of mountains, plateaux, forest, jungle, savannah, the highest waterfalls in the world, native Amerindians, settled communities of escaped African slaves—all largely unexplored. For fifteen years, over this new territory, Wilson Harris worked as a land surveyor. He is a member of a typical West Indian society of 600,000 people which inhabits a thin strip of coastline. Harris sets the final seal on the West Indian conception of itself as a national identity. On the run from the police a young Guianese, half-Chinese, half-Negro, discovers that all previous generations, Dutch, English, French, capitalists, slaves, freed slaves, white and black, were expatriates.

". . . All the restless wayward spirits of all the aeons (who it was thought had been embalmed for good) are returning to roost in our blood. And we have to start all over again where they began to explore. We've got to pick up the seeds again where they left off. It's no use worshipping the rottenest tacouba and tree-trunk in the historic topsoil. There's a whole world of branches and sensations we've missed, and we've got to start again from the roots up even if they look like nothing. Blood, sap, flesh, veins, arteries,

---

* *Palace of the Peacock, The Far Journey of Oudin, The Whole Armour, The Secret Ladder*. London: Faber & Faber.

lungs, heart, the heartland, Sharon. *We're the first potential parents who can contain the ancestral house.* Too young? I don't know. Too much responsibility? Time will tell. We've got to face it. Or else it will be too late to stop everything and everyone from running away and tumbling down. And then All the King's Horses and all the King's Men won't be able to put us together again. Like all the bananas and the plantains and the coffee trees near Charity. Not far from here, you know. A small wind comes and everything comes out of the ground. Because the soil is unstable. Just pegasse. Looks rich on top but that's about all. What do you think they say when it happens, when the crops run away? They shrug and say they're expendable crops. They can't begin to see that it's *us,* our blood, running away all the time, in the river and in the sea, everywhere, staining the bush. *Now* is the time to make a newborn stand, Sharon; you and me; it's up to us, even if we fall on our knees and *creep* to anchor ourselves before we get up."

There is no space here to deal with the poet in the literary tradition, or the ballad singer. In dance, in the innovation in musical instruments, in popular ballad singing unrivalled anywhere in the world, the mass of the people are not seeking a national identity, they are expressing one. The West Indian writers have discovered the West Indies and West Indians, a people of the middle of our disturbed century, concerned with the discovery of themselves, determined to discover themselves, but without hatred or malice against the foreigner, even the bitter imperialist past. To be welcomed into the comity of nations a new nation must bring something new. Otherwise it is a mere administrative convenience or necessity. The West Indians have brought something new.

> Albion too was once
a colony like ours . . .

> . . . deranged
By foaming channels, and the vain
> expanse
Of bitter faction.

All in compassion ends.
So differently from what the heart
    arranged.

Passion not spent but turned inward. Toussaint tried and paid for it with his life. Torn, twisted, stretched to the limits of agony, injected with poisonous patent medicines, it lives in the state which Fidel started. It is of the West Indies West Indian. For it, Toussaint, the first and greatest of West Indians, paid with his life.

INDEX

CITIZENS

A Chronicle of the French Revolution

By Simon Schama

In this *New York Times* bestseller, award-winning author Simon Schama presents an ebullient country, vital and inventive, infatuated with novelty and technology—a strikingly fresh view of Louis XVI's France. One of the great landmarks of modern history publishing, *Citizens: A Chronicle of the French Revolution* is the most authoritative social, cultural, and narrative history of the French Revolution ever produced.

History

ISLAND PEOPLE

The Caribbean and the World

By Joshua Jelly-Schapiro

This masterwork of travel literature and history provides a kaleidoscopic portrait of the Caribbean and illuminates its fierce grip on the world's imagination. From the moment Columbus gazed out from the deck of the Santa María in 1492 at what he mistook for an island off Asia, the Caribbean has been subjected to the misunderstandings and fantasies of outsiders. Forged by more than three centuries of mass migration and slave labor, the region and its diverse peoples have helped shape the modern world—through politics, religion, economics, music, and culture. Joshua Jelly-Schapiro takes us from Cuba to Jamaica, Puerto Rico to Trinidad, Haiti to Barbados, chronicling with wit and keen insight this "place where globalization began."

Travel/History

AFTER THE DANCE
A Walk Through Carnival in Jacmel, Haiti
By Edwidge Danticat

As a child, acclaimed author Edwidge Danticat was terrified by Carnival festivities—until 2002, when she returned home to Haiti determined to understand the lure of this famed event. Here she chronicles her journey to the coastal town of Jacmel, where she met with the performers, artists, and organizers who re-create the myths and legends that bring the festival to life. In the process, Danticat traces the heroic and tragic history of the island, from French colonists and Haitian revolutionaries to American invaders and home-grown dictators. Part travelogue, part memoir, part historical analysis, this is the deeply personal story of a writer rediscovering her country along with a part of herself—and a wonderful introduction to Haiti's southern coast and to the beauty and passions of Carnival.

Travel/Memoir